Praise for *The Women's Fight*

"After many years of scholars writing a new social history of the Civil War's home front, here is a magisterial work on women—all women, white and black, North and South. Glymph captures the complexity, the conflicting allegiances, the profound experience of loss and sorrow, the political behavior of ordinary and unusual women who fought in their own ways for their 'domestic sanctuaries,' for freedom itself, to save lives and protect homes, and for the fate of two nations. Rooted in a lifetime of ⟨…⟩ search, Glymph writes with passion about real wom⟨…⟩ ⟨…⟩sformation."
—DAVID W. BLIGH⟨…⟩ ⟨…⟩ing
Frederick⟨…⟩

"In the burgeoning literatu⟨…⟩ ⟨…⟩ war, *The Women's Fight* is unique both because o⟨…⟩ ⟨…⟩s argument and the depth of its research. Glymph not only describes how the war affected women of all kinds but also examines their interactions with one another across boundaries of race, region, and class. The result is a fascinating and illuminating account that sheds important new light on America's greatest crisis."
—ERIC FONER, author of *The Second Founding: How the Civil War and Reconstruction Remade the Constitution*

"Thavolia Glymph has written the first history of the Civil War that brings to light the full panoply of women's thoughts and experiences. With eloquence, brilliance, and an unrelenting commitment to rendering the complexity of her gendered framework, she presents the war's meaning to slave and free, black and white, Unionist and Confederate, elite and poor, combatant and noncombatant, and citizen and stateless refugee— all women in the 'house divided against itself' and in the fight that tore the nation asunder."
—EVELYN BROOKS HIGGINBOTHAM, Harvard University

"Remarkably expansive and deeply penetrating, *The Women's Fight* reorients our understanding of the Civil War. From battlefield to home front, from household to refugee encampment, Glymph shows us, with deftness and originality, the complex and contradictory social experiences that only the revolution of emancipation could produce and that only the gendered perspective she offers can provide. Black and white, rich and poor, Southerners and Northerners together compose this kaleidoscopically stunning account. A brilliant and beautifully rendered work of history."
—STEVEN HAHN, New York University

THE WOMEN'S FIGHT

THE LITTLEFIELD HISTORY OF THE CIVIL WAR ERA

Gary W. Gallagher and T. Michael Parrish, editors

This book was supported by the Littlefield Fund for
Southern History, University of Texas Libraries

This landmark sixteen-volume series, featuring
books by some of today's most respected Civil War
historians, surveys the conflict from the earliest rumblings
of disunion through the Reconstruction era. A joint project
of UNC Press and the Littlefield Fund for Southern History,
University of Texas Libraries, the series offers an
unparalleled comprehensive narrative of this
defining era in U.S. history.

THE WOMEN'S FIGHT

The Civil War's Battles for Home, Freedom, and Nation

Thavolia Glymph

The University of North Carolina Press

Chapel Hill

Designed by April Leidig
Set in Arnhem by Copperline Book Services, Inc.
Manufactured in the United States of America

The University of North Carolina Press has been a member
of the Green Press Initiative since 2003.

Cover illustration: *Sherman's March to the Sea*,
drawn by F. O. C. Darley (1883); Library of Congress
Prints and Photographs Division.

Library of Congress Cataloging-in-Publication Data
Names: Glymph, Thavolia, 1951– author.
Title: The women's fight : the Civil War's battles for home,
freedom, and nation / Thavolia Glymph.
Other titles: Civil War's battles for home, freedom, and nation
Description: Chapel Hill : The University of North Carolina Press, [2019] |
Series: Littlefield history of the Civil War era | Includes bibliographical
references and index.
Identifiers: LCCN 2019035106 | ISBN 9781469653631 (cloth) |
ISBN 9781469672502 (paperback) | ISBN 9781469653648 (ebook)
Subjects: LCSH: United States—History—Civil War, 1861–1865—Women. |
United States—History—Civil War, 1861–1865—Social aspects. | United States—
History—Civil War, 1861–1865—Participation, Female | Women and war—
United States—History—19th century. | BISAC: HISTORY / Women
Classification: LCC E628 .G58 2019 | DDC 973.7082—dc23
LC record available at https://lccn.loc.gov/2019035106

To
Sebastian,
Kristal, and
Morgan

CONTENTS

Part III. The Hard Hand of War

FIGURES

INTRODUCTION

O N JULY 4, 1861, a group of Maryland women addressed an appeal to General-in-Chief Winfield Scott calling for peace. Casting themselves as "the pure element of the nation's greatness," and wrapping their appeal tightly in the armature of patriotism and patriarchy, they called on white men to remember women's "natural rights" and hear their "agonizing cries" for the "protection GOD has entrusted to man in our behalf." Though claiming to "know no distinction in party broils," they offered a muscular defense of the South and the wars of conquest that had given slavery room to grow and expand across the continent. They reminded Scott of the proud military history, forged in the war with Mexico, on which he had built his career. They called on him to remember that the men he had fought alongside in Mexico who now stood on the opposing field were his offspring, "the sons of your training!" They called out the names of his former "comrades"—from the "good and noble [Robert E.] Lee upon the plains of Mexico," and "the great Johnston [who] gave the victorious Cerro Gordo to the glorious galaxy of your battles," to P. G. T. Beauregard and the "loved" Jefferson Davis, "whose name is a talisman of virtue, to whom a suffering people cling." Their politics, they stated, placed them alongside the men of their state, who protested that the soil of Maryland should be "profaned by the tread of martial feet." As great a profanity, they declared, was the danger the war presented to the "domestic sanctuaries of the 'Old Dominion.'" On behalf of home, they asked Scott to "restore our fettered nation to its primal greatness." In putting their protest in the form of a broadside, the petitioners placed it deliberately in the public record, "upon the register of our archives." Most at stake, they reminded Scott and all who read their appeal, were the "domestic sanctuaries" that they understood as precious, private, and state-sponsored political spaces. They signed their petition, the "Women of Maryland."[1]

A few months earlier, a different assessment of slavery and the nation's "domestic sanctuaries" was cast about the streets of Maryland. In a conversation overheard on the streets of Baltimore between "two negresses," one was said to have remarked: "Wait till the fourth of March and then won't I slap my missus' face!" March 4 was not a randomly chosen day. It was the day President Abraham Lincoln was to be inaugurated.[2] Unlike the appeal of the "Women of Maryland," this conversation did not find its way into a published statement of the principles of the other women of Maryland. It was not typeset as a broadside. It was not formally addressed to anyone in a high office. Yet it was no less a formal declaration of principle and a rebuke of the notions of "domestic sanctuaries" and "primal greatness" championed by the "Women of Maryland." It was no less a rights claim. The "two negresses" would certainly have welcomed the "tread of martial feet" in their state. The Civil War highlighted the different rights claims of black and Southern white women who identified with the "Women of Maryland" and the collision course they had long been traveling. It also put the politics of black women on a collision course with Northern women who believed "that in order to crush this rebellion entirely, and secure union and peace to the country hereafter, the loyal free-labor element of the South must be affiliated with the free laborers of the North, and that they should occupy together the lands heretofore held by a landed slaveholding aristocracy."[3]

The Civil War brought American women into unprecedented contact across the divides of race, gender, class, and region. It revived old, largely unanswered and even unformulated questions about the meaning of home, freedom, citizenship, national belonging, and women's relationship to these ideas and each other. How do state-sanctioned gendered and racially gendered policies make and sustain dominant notions of home? What happens when war destroys the home and turns women into refugees, displaced persons, and targets of military law and military fire?[4] How does a society respond when women are put in unaccustomed places and take on unaccustomed roles? How did the long history of women in America and their immediate experiences prepare women to defend their homes or fight for the right to build new, free homes? The Civil War forced Americans to reassess and grapple with dominant notions and assumptions about what makes a structure a home, a domestic sanctuary, a site of care and refuge for women and children. In the process, it illuminated the role women had played in supporting or protesting these notions. It forced a reckoning with long-standing laws and customs that had worked to prevent the creation of any semblance of home for enslaved people and left the majority of white homes economically and politically fragile.

When the Civil War began, despite their experience in, or knowledge of, America's previous wars, the vast majority of American women would have had little reason to believe it would disturb their homes or their place within them to any significant extent. Lincoln's initial call for 75,000 men contained no suggestion of a long, drawn-out war. That calculation changed as the conflict inched closer to women's homes and communities, then entered them, and resulted in over a million military casualties. Devastation on the home front—in crops unplanted or destroyed, homes burned, families separated, and civilian lives lost—brought hard reckonings. These moments came at different points in the war for women depending on their class and race, and where they lived, and they felt its impact differently. Wealthy slaveholding women, forced to flee their homes and witness some of the first stirrings of the slaves' wartime rebellion in 1861, saw their domestic sanctuaries begin to disintegrate. The vast majority of Northern white women faced no direct military threat to their homes and, with the exception of the destruction occasioned by Gen. Robert E. Lee's ill-fated invasion of Pennsylvania in 1863, only Northern black women would also see their homes destroyed.

In the North and South women responded enthusiastically as calls came for their husbands, fathers, and sons to enlist and demands on the material resources of their households increased. Some from the start, like the two black women on the Baltimore corner, understood that the idea of home as a place of safety and protection was not designed to include their homes. They were women who believed that the patriarchal home stood in the way of full citizenship and saw the war as an opportunity to enact revolutionary transformations in society, including greater rights for women and an end to slavery and racial discrimination against free black people. Poor white women, whose homes had never offered them exemption from household or wage labor or a sanctuary from public intrusions of any kind, from the first challenged a call to war couched in the protection of home.

Over the past thirty years, a new body of scholarship has transformed our understanding of the home front, the impact of the Civil War on American women, and the active roles women played in the war. Renewed attention to slaveholding and nonslaveholding white women in the South, abolitionist women and Northern working-class women, free black and enslaved women, has substantially revised the long-standing historiography of women in the war pioneered by scholars like Mary Elizabeth Massey.[5] Building on this impressive body of scholarship and revisionist Civil War military history, this book seeks to unravel a different story—a story of ordinary women and extraordinary women less well-known, who stood not outside war but directly in its path in one way or another, whether at their designated post— home—or far away from it. The sometimes-gendered duties associated with this post should not confuse us.

War exposes in fine detail the politics of the most powerful and the smoldering demands of the most vulnerable and exploited. Civil wars do so with particular force. In the American case, already embattled fault lines of race, gender, and class became more visible and brittle. Poor, working-class, and enslaved women could see more clearly where American life had provided room for some women to maneuver and enjoy rights and privileges denied to them, and the payoff. Slaveholding women did not enjoy the same full array of freedoms and rights as their fathers, husbands, and sons. Nor did they stand equal before the law. But the capacity to see themselves and be seen as both inside the law—with a right to shelter and food—and outside the law—untouchable by virtue of their gender—gave them the confidence to act in ways that poor, working-class, and black women could not and perhaps would not have desired. Though limited, the rights they enjoyed were sufficient to garner support for the dominant political and social order by the most-privileged American white women. Access to smaller rights generally quieted discontent at the denial of full citizenship rights and purchased consent to race and class discrimination. Not all white women had access to the same racial privileges. Smaller rights empowered elite women, in collaboration with men of their class, to deny even small rights to less privileged women.[6] Their confidence in their place in the world would not in the end save them from the destruction that war brought to their homes and, for Southern white women, the crushing defeat of their proslavery national ambitions.

Historians speak of the Civil War as four wars—the fight on the formal battlefield between the armies of the United States and the Confederacy, the war that brought armies to the home front, the slaves' war, and the war in the West. This book explores the world of women at war in the first three of these spaces and their intersections. It is concerned with the ideas and ideologies that drove women's allegiance in support of the United States—for Union and slavery, Union and emancipation, or simply, Union—or in support of the proslavery Confederacy and maps the different forms these allegiances took. It tells the story of women who fought for radical transformations in American society, women who fought against them, and women for whom the daily struggle for bread left little room to master the politics of war, women who just wanted their husbands, fathers, and sons home. It is a story about high politics and the rupturing of high politics by politics from below, and how ideas about the meaning of home and belonging shaped those politics and women's everyday encounters and response to the war and to each other.

This is a book, then, about women's fight across the divides of space, race, and class as they moved into each other's worlds as slaveholders, black and

white refugees, missionaries, agents of freedmen's aid societies, abolitionists, Unionists, and freedom seekers. Union general William Tecumseh
Sherman once remarked that the history of women in the Civil War could
be summarized as a story of "the mourning and wailing of widows and
orphans."[7] Sorrow is an inescapable part of war and so too are mourning
women and orphans. The history of women in war is unavoidably a story
of death and suffering, scarcities of food and clothing, homelessness and
displaced persons, and often statelessness. But women's history in and with
war has always been more than that. Women have always been more than
the passive participants Sherman's characterization suggested, as Sherman
surely well knew. Women were more than the ones left to mourn or, as some
believed, the ones designed by nature to mourn.

War has historically been considered a space of men not by any inher-
ent nature of war but by the nature of patriarchy and the power men have
held. Men historically give the orders for war and fight its battles. With rare
exceptions women historically did not command armies or hold elective or
other offices empowered to declare war. Historically, they have had no official role in recording what took place on the fields of battle or in the halls of
congresses. The history of war, written largely from the perspective of statesmen, generals, and soldiers, concerned itself preeminently with battles and
battlefield plans, casualty rates, and the politics and diplomacy of war, all
critically important subjects to be sure. But the spaces in which women live
during times of war are no more inviolate than the spaces in which men
fight, and the two are never completely cordoned off from each other. War
is not a set piece; its borders in real time are not beholden to the maps car-
tographers or military engineers draw. During the Civil War, mapmaking
was still a craft and a labor-intensive process designed to produce a legible
landscape for armies on the march and in battle.[8] Whether military maps
designed to meet the needs of a particular war or maps repurposed from
other purposes for war, in war, maps set the stage for where armies will
gather and where battles will be fought. They have literal and symbolic importance. But the most carefully rendered lines on maps only symbolically
contain soldiers and guns. They can easily collapse under the stress of battle
and erase in the process the idea of a fixed barrier between the battlefront
and the home front.

Just as Civil War maps that staked out the geographical coordinates for
making war could not always hold soldiers to a defined field of battle, neither could they always legibly mark the coordinates of where women stood.
Women appeared on the battlefront and warring men on the home front,
and the home front could become a battlefield. Traditional lines of affiliation

and allegiance among women often broke down and disintegrated. Indeed, they sometimes proved as fanciful as presumptions about the relationship of battlefield to home front. The barriers that separated poor and working-class women from elite women, and enslaved women from slaveholding and wealthy Northern women, did not completely fail during the Civil War, but they lost some of their potency and capacity to bear the weight of white supremacy. Sometimes they broke apart completely and spectacularly.

In the South, a shifting landscape of the relations of power began to emerge with the outbreak of war, the flight of slaveholding women at the approach of U.S. military forces, and slave resistance. At that moment, the old terms by which slaveholding women had fashioned their lives came up against a new terrain marked by increased contestation. That fight appeared in many forms, as when, for example, enslaved women fought the reformation of white homes in exile and led efforts to occupy or destroy the homes planters left behind. Previously denied the right to move about freely or to have a free home, enslaved women reconfigured the spaces of power on plantations, and a sizeable number left them altogether. As refugees, black women trespassed the space of men on the battlefront and protested the idea of a Union war against the Confederacy that was not also a war for emancipation.

The shifting landscape of power also appeared in upcountry districts in the South where poor and nonslaveholding white women voiced their opposition to the war in protests against slaveholding women refugees whose presence added to the burdens and stressors the war placed on their communities and vulnerable family economies. Turning the tables, they denied resources to the elite women refugees. Their voices rang out in old and new registers of discontent as they struggled to take care of families harmed by the added burdens of Confederate conscription laws that taxed their meager crops and carried their husbands and sons to war.

In the North, women abolitionists prepared to support the Union war effort and turn it into an opportunity to push harder for emancipation and prepare the enslaved for freedom while advancing their own dreams of freedom. Other Northern women were prepared to work for Union only. Racism and class divisions marred the efforts of both groups in important ways. Northern middle-class women who went south to aid the Union cause and the cause of emancipation sometimes expressed more sympathy for slaveholding women than the desperately poor white and black women they encountered. In their work as nurses, missionaries, teachers in the South or as wives of military officers and the men who led Federal refugee relief programs, they carried ideas about race and class that made it hard to see enslaved women's fight as a fight for the Union and freedom. These ideas could also accommodate the notion that they too could be mistresses. Some took advantage of opportunities that gave them access to the domestic labor of black women and took to life in planter homes that simulated the life they imagined the departed mistresses had lived. Even the abolitionists among them who championed emancipation had learned to see the black home as an aberration. They approached their work with former slaves in the wartime South from this ideological foundation.

The abolitionist argument, as Thomas Holt argues, was mired in notions inimical to black freedom. "Portraying slavery as an inhuman travesty," he writes, "left slaves themselves looking like something less than human, which might ultimately prove counterproductive. Slaves might be objects of pity, surely, but not candidates for admission to the body politic. Unmanned men and deflowered women could command sympathy but not empathy, which implies imagining oneself in the other's place."[9] Northern women's continued ties to slavery through stock holdings in sugar manufacturing concerns, Southern railroads, Cuban plantations, and marriage to men who financed and transported the cotton crops to Liverpool and Manchester, England, and Lyon, France, and insured the bodies of enslaved people sometimes undermined their commitment to emancipation. In neither their reminiscences nor their wartime letters did they directly address the ties to slavery that made possible their privileged status and the leisure that allowed them to give their time in support of the Union cause or abolition. Their actions broke the silence.

The majority of Northern women faced more mundane considerations—the loss of sons, brothers, husbands, and fathers; exploitative industrial labor; and diminishing returns from their household economies. The war was fought mainly on Southern soil, but their homes and communities did not escape unscathed.[10] Like Southern women, Northern women sent pleas for help to soldier husbands when there was no money for food, to clothe their children, or pay the mortgage on the farm or rent on a flat. Like Southern women, they scoured casualty lists and went to the front in search of loved ones in battlefield hospitals. They were demographically diverse—rich and poor, black and white, newly arrived immigrants, and people who traced their ancestry to the first European immigrants—and diverse in their politics. The Civil War laid bare the economic foundation of these differences, prominently displaying the borders that marked class and race in the North. It magnified the distance between elite women and the rural farmwomen deemed too "rustic" or "unrefined," and the black and largely Irish domestic servants who cleaned their homes. These lines did not always run

in clear-cut ways. Northern middle-class and elite white women who supported emancipation and better working conditions for poor white women
and organized to support white soldiers' wives were largely silent when
Northern almshouses turned away the wives of black soldiers. Poor white
women who waged factory strikes in the North showed no inclination to
join their struggle to that of free black women laborers nor with enslaved
women's strike against the plantation system.

North and South, "thousands and thousands of broken-hearted women
at home, who quietly acquiesced in this great sacrifice out of love and loyalty to their country's flag" believed their efforts consecrated the soldiers'
sacrifices. Some, like the Women of Maryland, believed they experienced "a
grief more sore than any enlightened woman has ever borne," but as they
stepped forth to support the Confederacy or the United States, there were
those—black and white—who remembered that women had been "heroic"
before.[11] But they did not speak with one voice, in the South or the North. Before the nation could have any peace, Northerner Dorothy Stevens believed,
"*slavery* must be completely crushed out." Among Northern women, this was
a minority view. Proslavery Northern women protested that the war should
not have anything to do with slavery or emancipation. For Clara Barton, the
field of work was "the open field between the bullet and the hospital," where
she made "gruel—not political speeches."[12] There was also a degree of general apathy.[13]

In exploring the story of the divisions between Confederate women and
Northern Union women, between wealthy and poor women in the North
and South, between Southern Unionist and Confederate women, between
Democratic and Republican women, between enslaved women and slaveholding women, and between enslaved and Northern white women, this
book revisits familiar questions in new ways. Despite the revisionist work
of recent decades that has moved the historiography of women in the war in
important new directions, the story of women in the Civil War continues to
be written largely along the lines of the regional divide imposed by slavery's
geographical borders, lines that are assumed to correspond legibly to the
political divides over the question of slavery. This approach favors the study
of Northern and Southern women separately rather than in juxtaposition. It
disfavors class analysis.[14]

American women took their stand first and foremost on the basis of sectional political ties, but the politics of race and class were not far behind.
How Northern and Southern women—black and white—understood the
meaning of "women in the war" was also highly correlated to their race,
class, and citizenship status. These factors determined how they understood

what they were fighting for and how they fought. They influenced perceptions in the larger society about which women had a right to claim the protection of the state, citizenship rights, and the right to freedom and free homes. The resulting rifts and alliances become clearer when we study women in war across sectional, race, and class lines. To be sure, regional distinctions were crucial, and sectionally based studies of women in the Civil War have unquestionably advanced the historiography. They also reflect the historical development of the archive and the decisions historians make about which lives deserve study and what constitutes political thought and political action. Thus, poor and working-class Southern white women have garnered much less attention comparatively in histories of the Civil War than Northern elite and slaveholding women. And even when they enter the scholarship, it is mainly as soldiers' wives who took to the street in violent protest of the sorry state of affairs in which the Southern rebellion placed them. The larger story of their politics suffers.

The labels scholars use or employ to mark women's political identities tend to obscure not only the politics of the poor but also the places where women across political and racial divides had common political concerns and where they had none. Just as not all Southern white women were Confederate women, neither were all Southern Unionist women poor or white, nor all Yankee women white. The population of Southern white women included Unionists and the population of Southern Unionists included enslaved and free black women. The labels *civilian, combatant, noncombatant, slave, white,* and *black* also carried legal, political, and social meaning. They marked one's proximity to humane consideration by military commanders, soldiers, abolitionists, and agents of freedmen's aid societies, and Northern white women more broadly. This made a difference in how women experienced the war and fought. These labels have also influenced how historians interpret the archival record and thus how women's fight has been understood historically. African American women worked in support of the Union's war as nurses, cooks, spies, and laundresses, and at least one disguised as a soldier served in the 8th New York Cavalry. They were all abolitionists. They sheltered escaped and injured Northern soldiers who had lost their way or were sick or injured in their cabins. They were Union women but unmarked as such; no one at the time called them that, and few have since. To white Northerners, Southern "Unionist women" were by definition white, which made them eligible for human consideration and, concretely, for support systems and privileges denied black women Unionists.[15] This book seeks to uncover the places where these distinctions were made and collapsed.

Unraveling the ways Union commanders and Northern aid societies saw and classified women's identities is important to understanding their different treatment. It explains why Union commanders could sympathize with and court Southern white women Unionists but not enslaved or emancipated women. Why they could provide white women who came into Union lines with food, lodging, and travel free of charge and not consider placing them in refugee camps. Why they did not tell them they had to work on abandoned plantations and government farms to take care of themselves, their children, and the elderly among them or require them to reimburse the Federal government for rations. By contrast, the Federal government funneled black women from refugee camps to work growing and picking cotton on abandoned plantations, sometimes taxing their skimpy wages, ostensibly to pay for the care of orphans, the disabled, and the elderly. In this way, black women experienced what Wendy Brown describes as the conferring of "rights" that "in the very same gesture with which they draw a circle around the individual, in the very same act with which they grant her sovereign selfhood, they turn back upon the individual all responsibility for her failures, her condition, her poverty, her madness—they privatize her situation and mystify the powers that construct, position, and buffet her."[16]

Mystification and erasure surround the story of enslaved women who pinned the U.S. flag to their chests and fought for the nation and their freedom and organized soldiers societies, women like Mary who was sold with her daughter in 1864 for $4,000 and remained enslaved for the duration of the war, and women like Lismene, manumitted by a free woman of color in 1863, who claimed freedom by various routes during the war.[17] No other group of American women had to wage war on as many fronts while endowed with so few rights as African American women. Because they were not white, the rights and privileges accorded white women did not accrue to them. The story of black women's fight, the war they waged for Union and freedom and to be accorded even the small rights white women claimed, continues to exist on the margins of the Civil War historiography. Their politics and their wartime struggles remain largely invisible.

Men knew that maintaining morale on the battlefield and the home front would require women to shoulder multiple responsibilities. They did not expect women to go to the front as soldiers (or even nurses) or become treasury department clerks. They did expect women to provide vital support as part of the machinery of making war. Their parlors were potential spaces for the manufacture of war matériel; their gardens were seen as sources of supplementary foodstuffs for hungry soldiers. The protection of white planter homes and recognition of the importance of the cash and food crops grown by enslaved people had prompted Confederate leaders to adopt a policy to ensure that at least one adult male remained on every plantation. Short-ages of men for military service and protests by poor white people of the measure's class bias forced a policy change, but the dependence on women to support the war effort remained. And if necessary, some believed, women could be called upon to pick up arms to protect the home front. When war came, slaveholding women immediately began forming sewing groups and committees to send packages to the front. They and the Confederate govern-ment expected poor and working-class women to do their part. Efforts to make them do so fueled existing class divisions.[18] The effort "to make class interest synonymous with national interest," Drew Faust notes, "placed new demands on people requiring renegotiations of power within the South." This made "the creation of Confederate nationalism" a "political and social act but one that reopened unfinished antebellum debates and conflicts."[19]

The world of the Civil War was at once new and deeply familiar. The war did not place American women in every respect at a Rubicon they had never before crossed or that was exceptional in American history. Women faced new and often unprecedented demands and challenges to be sure but also ones that were deeply familiar. The often unstated but powerful assumption that the Civil War represented a whole new experience for American women holds a powerful interpretative sway in the historiography. As a result, such matters as women's treatment by Civil War armies, beliefs about who had a right to a home, and notions about the sanctity of home stand as aberrations in the history of American women and the conduct of war, indeed outside of history and the world of the Civil War.

A conceptual framework that does not take the ideology of separate spheres as the jumping off point but rather thinks about the history of women in the Civil War in the context of previous wars, gender and class struggles, and slave resistance offers a different path. To challenge the no-tion of discontinuity is not to dismiss or minimize the ways the Civil War was profoundly novel.[20] At the same time, there was much that was not. The American Civil War did not usher in a completely unknown world. American women had experienced elements of what is called "hard war" before—in the Revolutionary War, the War of 1812, and the slaves' wars where battle-fronts had collapsed into the home front. In some ways, the Civil War merely elaborated long-standing ruptures with old struggles "fought under radi-cally different conditions and with different resources" that "responded to both the continuities and discontinuities, each of which is constitutive of any given moment."[21]

No one in 1861 would have predicted the magnitude of the destruction to come. Certainly, few—least of all the men and women who had championed secession and the establishment of a proudly proslavery nation—believed that secession and the formation of the Confederate States of America would lead to the destruction of American slavery. They believed, rather, that taking these steps would strengthen the institution of slavery. The future seemed bright. Cotton production had doubled in the decade between 1850 and 1860, reaching an all-time high. There was every expectation that this trend would continue, ensuring an economic ballast for the new nation. And, if they succeeded, no longer would slaveholders have to endure news of slaves being rescued by abolitionists or legislative compromises that to their minds failed to go far enough to protect their constitutional right to hold human beings as chattel property. No longer would they have to watch as their once unrivaled political power in the nation's capital diminished in spite of the wealth they continued to produce with enslaved labor. The citizens of the republic they hoped to build would include none who would blush at the fact that slavery stood at its core.

The call by white women of Lowndes, Alabama, in 1860 for a boycott of Northern goods was one of the early expressions of the confidence white women too placed in a nation where "slavery constituted 'an essential element.'"[22] That faith was shared by white Northern women who saw slavery as key to their prosperity and future happiness. When Harriett and George W. Palmer of Syracuse, New York, cast their future with the South in 1859, they gave up the life of a grocer's family for a new home in Saltville, Virginia. George Palmer quickly became a town leader and a key player in the salt manufacturing business. Within three years, at the age of thirty-one, he owned extensive saltworks, including part of the 6,904-acre Preston Salt Works, worked by over 100 enslaved people. He owned $25,000 in real and personal property. Harriet Palmer, accustomed to having domestic servants in her Syracuse household, carried at least one white woman servant, born in Germany, with her to Virginia.[23]

Just as the Civil War exposed to wider public view Northern and Southern white women's support of slavery, it exposed the inner workings of their home life, including domestic abuse. White women spoke more openly of rape and other forms of sexual assault against enslaved girls and women and of the abuse they themselves suffered at the hands of white men. They gossiped about romantic entanglements between their husbands and the governesses they employed to teach their children. They broadcast their husbands' failure to protect them and their homes as they experienced forms of violence and statelessness black women had long endured. War forced thousands of white women to take to the roads in search of safety and freedom, putting them on the road not as leisure travelers but as refugees and displaced persons. Like slaves, they were forced to carry badges of identification and faced, in addition to the humiliation this entailed, public ridicule by black and poor white women they considered their inferiors.

Only a minority of women took their struggles to the public streets, riverways, and the battlefield. Only a minority became refugees. The majority of American women stood and fought (or not) on the ground where the war first found them. All would learn, however, "what it costs a republic to have nursed rebellion tenderly at its breast."[24] The Civil War left difficult and painful legacies for black and white women, their families, and homes. It changed and challenged the lives of all women in the nation, though it did so with different force and to different ends. It made demands of all women and presented opportunities to all. It empowered some in real and important ways and disempowered others. The precise ways this unfolded varied immensely by region, proximity to the battlefield, the impact of Federal and Confederate military policy, race and class, women's particular histories and struggles prior to 1861, and the contingencies of war.

How women made, processed, and responded to the challenges of war is my subject. If, in the first days and months of the war, most kept to their usual routines, even then they knew that nothing was normal. By the end of the war none could. The vast majority would never see a battlefield, but all would experience the impact and effects of war. What follows is an attempt to tell a small part of the story of women in the Civil War as wives and mothers, citizens and noncitizens, partisans and noncombatants, and political actors. When war came on April 12, 1861, with the attack on Fort Sumter, it changed the calculations for everyone.[25] For young Fannie Green of Michigan, the realization that the nation was really at war may have come with a letter from her brother penned on April 22. "Everybody is full of war," he wrote from school in Ann Arbor. "The ministers pray war, the professors make war speeches . . . the boys in the streets shriek war. Young men enlist to go to war and everything is war."[26] Had Fannie Green lived in New York, she might have attended or witnessed the mass meeting in Union Square that month that brought out residents adorned with the symbols of patriotism. "Almost every individual, man, woman and child, carried the sacred colors in some shape or other," and "the ladies at the windows had knots of ribbon, tri-colored bouquets, and flags without number," wrote one resident.[27] Similar scenes erupted in the South. "Charleston, being 'the cradle of the war,'" a white woman from the city wrote, "we were among the first to organize soldiers' relief societies, and the services of every woman were needed, and only too gladly rendered."[28] By the end of the war, the work of sewing and mending for the soldiers continued though less robustly, but mass meetings and streets filled with citizens adorned in patriotic attire had virtually disappeared. And cotton and black people had proved unreliable partners for a proslavery nation-building project, a Union with a slavery project, or a Union without slavery but which tied black people's freedom to cotton. Central to all of this was the fight for home.

The domestic space—home—arose historically in Western culture as a space of production, kinship, reproduction, and shelter to shield, protect, and nurture the family. The notion of home as a protective shield has operated differently in different times and societies. In the United States, race (and class) determined who could claim home as a sanctuary and who could not. It determined which children deserved to have the benefit of vulnerability.[29] The institution of slavery made these distinctions all the more profound and pronounced and made the homes of slaveholders contested sanctuaries. Slavery meant that black people who lived and worked in white homes in the South were particularly vulnerable to injury and violation. It had required, perforce, white homes equipped for war, with warlike shields. The Civil War fueled an unprecedented militarization of the Southern home front. "The militaristic nature of plantation production" that had always extended to the production of the plantation household was now on public view as never before.[30] Northern homes were not without class or race conflict. The use of domestic servants in the homes of wealthy Northerners ensured that much, even if class conflict there was less visible to the world and less critiqued then and now.

This book tells the story of women in the North and South who made sacrifices of the kind men throughout time have called upon women to make in times of war but rarely acknowledge as political. It takes a measure of what was worked out and not worked out between 1861 and 1865 as women fought to build free homes or maintain unfree ones as they supported the armies of one side or the other. The Civil War radically transformed the United States and had enormous consequences for the view that homes were meant to be domestic sanctuaries for some and not others. Americans understood that slavery was the principal cause of the Civil War, and they understood slavery's role in the production of white homes and Northern and Southern white women. This understanding figured large in the justifications for war and the calls for men to sign up to fight. They also figured prominently in the calls for new kinds of free homes. Finally, there are women more famous in Civil War literature who get barely a mention in this book, or no mention at all, but not because they are not important to the story of women in the war. In some cases, their lives have already been wonderfully documented and chronicled by other scholars. But more germane to this project was an interest in exploring the ways women's fight in the Civil War was a fight among and between women and with the men who sought to control how they could fight.

PART I

SOUTHERN WOMEN

Chapter One

HOME AND WAR

"Domestic Sanctuaries" on the Run

In Civil Society people are at their home—the center of social life
hallowed by many of the most delightful recollections & associations
that render life desirable. They are in the enjoyment of the family
institution, which, of all others, is the most influential to form aright
the character, stability, & glory of the Nation. . . . Wherever war sweeps
along . . . residences, gardens, orchards, and fields are thrown open
to the indiscriminate use of strangers, families are scattered,—
go wandering as refugees in unaccustomed regions & beg for their
subsistence at the door of public commiseration & charity.
—REV. FRANCIS SPRINGER

I have never before felt so dispirited about the war. It seems to stretch
interminably before us, carrying off all the youth and worth of the
Country. I can see nothing but desolate homes and broken hopes.
—HARRIOTT MIDDLETON

WANTED
A WHITE WOMAN, who CAN cook AND wash for a small family.
A good recommendation required. Apply corner of Senate and Bull streets.
—*Daily Phoenix* (Columbia, South Carolina), September 9, 1865

"IT SEEMS STRANGE that we should be in the midst of a revolution so
quiet, and plentiful and comfortable does it seem up here," Margaret
Ann Meta Morris Grimball wrote in her diary in early December 1860.
"Every thing [*sic*] goes on as usual, the planting, the negroes, all just the
same, and a great Empire tumbling to pieces about us, and a great pressure
in the money market in all parts of the country, we strange to say, were never
so easy, and I hope thankful."[1] By the following December, Grimball's world
had changed dramatically. "We are on the Frontier," she wrote in December

1861, invoking the colonial settler language of a world bereft of civilization. She soon faced "a great calamity" when eighty-four of her family's slaves left "all together" for Edisto Island in the Union-occupied lowcountry.[2] From the start of the war to the end, enslaved people resisted efforts to force them to help build a slaveholding nation-state, and by March 1862 the resistance had come to Grimball's home. Her life was no longer "so easy." Enslaved women and men, supported unwittingly by the arrival of U.S. military forces, staked their claim to freedom on the destruction of the foundation of her claim. As a refugee, she also faced the hostility of poor white women. The language in which Grimball voiced her anguish betrayed her familiarity with violence against one's personhood, family, dignity, humanity, and home, the kinds of violence directed at enslaved and poor white people and their homes. Her anguish and the words in which she voiced it became a familiar refrain in the letters and stories of slaveholding women as the war bore down on them and their homes.

The Civil War set women across the South in flight. The flight of low-country slaveholding women and their lives as refugees at the heart of this chapter was unique in many ways, particularly in its timing, the manner of its initial presentation, and to some extent, the particular nature of the conflict it generated with nonslaveholding women. The increasingly common experience of white women on the run and homeless challenged proslavery ideology. As their numbers grew, the "claims of home and country, wife and children" that had supported Southerners' call to war succumbed to this reality. By the end of the war, enough "terror-stricken" white women and children had been forced into the streets and were "wander[ing] aimlessly from place to place" to embarrass the battle cry that called men to die for home but sent them to fight and die for slavery, as if the two things everywhere meant the same thing. The embarrassment was visible in the sight of white men clinging "to the tops of the coaches as they pulled out" of railroad stations in the final days as Union forces closed in. In the cars below, the women they had gone to war to protect mingled indiscriminately with cows and baggage.[3] In such scenes, slaveholding ideology and the slaveholders' revolution lay among the ruins. All around the departing women and men were strewn the remnants of the institution of slavery that had made a special place for white women no less than for white men. In the coming years, the war that arrived in South Carolina slaveholding country in 1861 spread everywhere that the U.S. army placed its flag, as well as far beyond the areas of contact. In war, "the very foundation of the classic Southern household—a household resting on slave labor—would crumble."[4]

The Civil War witnessed the first major sustained assault on planter homes. At once physical, psychological, and political, it forced reckonings in the meaning of home that white Southerners had not anticipated, bringing wrenching transformations to white and black homes. Southern homes—whether those of poor white people; white nonslaveholders more broadly; small, middling or rich planters; or black homes—had never been inviolate spaces. Few white women knew or experienced life on a "pedestal," and the homes of enslaved people were routinely violated. War, however, made it harder to hide the injuries that took place within and against white and black homes or to shelter the plantation home's pretensions to domesticity wrapped in the claims of proslavery ideology.[5] Northern resistance to the expansion of slavery, James Henry Hammond had charged in 1858, was tantamount to "making war upon us to our very hearthstones."[6] War exposed the fragility of those hearthstones as never before. By 1865, the Civil War had in one way or another touched virtually every household in the South. Ideas about the meaning of home were vital to the ideological framing of the Southern call to arms. The "homes of a people," the Alabama Supreme Court wrote in 1877, constitute "the true officinæ gentium—the nurseries of States."[7] Although the ruling came after the Civil War, it spoke strikingly to slaveholders' understanding of home as a purpose-built institution with an intimately political relationship to the state. "Nothing is more easily demonstrable than the fact that slavery owes its continuance in the United States chiefly to the women," abolitionist George Bourne wrote in 1835.[8]

The making of a proslavery nation required keeping "home" intact. That in turn required keeping elite slaveholding women and enslaved people at home in their designated places. "Tranquility in the nation could not be achieved unless there was serenity in the home," Catherine Hall writes in reference to nineteenth-century Britain.[9] This was no less true for the United States and the South, especially where slavery challenged "tranquility in the nation" and "serenity in the home." War exacerbated the challenge. Americans who remembered the devastation of the home front during the Revolutionary War and the War of 1812—the torching of homes by loyalists and rebel forces, the loss of slaves, and refugees on the road—perhaps best understood that things might not turn out well for slaveholders. The descendants of Eliza Lucas Pinckney, matriarch of one of South Carolina's most powerful aristocratic families, recalled taking refuge at Hampton Plantation in McClellanville during the Revolutionary War. It was one of many stories from the past of how poorly home traveled in war.

The need to protect white women and white homes became the battle cry of Confederate mobilization and helped keep men in the field for four years. The question of states' rights and disputes over tariffs were disputes over whether slavery should be allowed to exist everywhere in the United States. Code words like *racial amalgamation, submission, degradation, subjugation,* and *annihilation* were used to stoke fears in the "dawning of an abominable new world in the South, a world created by the Republican destruction of the institution of slavery." In this world the white Southern home and white woman would be degraded and subjugated. And, as a result, so would the white man.[10] The protection of home and women—the protection of slavery—carried powerful ideological weight and the capacity to mobilize the white South for war. But could the idea of the white home as an inviolable space sustain the fight? And what did it mean that it was offered in the first place as a justification for war? The answers had consequences for morale on the home front, the prosecution of the war by both armies, and for how women fought and fared.

From 1861 to 1865, white women in the South fought a war for which they were ill prepared. They bore losses they were not prepared to shoulder. Even those who had championed secession alongside or independently of their husbands, fathers, and brothers and remained steadfast supporters of slavery and the Confederate cause to the end were often shocked by how much they were called to bear.[11] They knew men would die in battle. They did not anticipate that some of them would also lose their lives in the war to protect slavery. They knew defeat would mean financial ruin. They did not foresee that financial ruin would encompass the loss or destruction of their hearths. They anticipated that they might have to bear shortages but not that some would face starvation and become refugees and vagabonds. They knew from experience that enslaved people could not be fully trusted to have their backs in the event of war, but proslavery ideology had taught them that the enslaved would save not destroy white homes. Having long championed the fiction of slave loyalty, they seemed dumbfounded by slaves who viewed the destruction of the plantation household as integral to the destruction of slavery and a necessary part of claiming their freedom. They were stunned that their slaves would decline to join them in exile.

The Confederate project from its inception endangered the Southern project of the white home and the white family. By the end of the war, the danger had been realized at the intimate and sovereign levels. As a proslavery project, the white home was indispensable to the work of white supremacy and its entitlements or, in the words of Saidiya Hartman, "the selective recognition of humanity that undergirded the relations of chattel slavery."[12]

That selective recognition was designed to make some homes "delightful," beautiful spaces for the "enjoyment of the family institution" to "the glory of the nation." It subsumed the enslaved to work and pay for that delight. But war, as Rev. Francis Springer recognized, threw white homes "open to the indiscriminate use of strangers," forcing families to scatter and wander "as refugees," to beg for food and shelter.[13]

The slaveholders who had called for war to protect white homes and white women seemed not to recognize how open those homes already were to the eyes of strangers and the impact this would have on their effort to build a proslavery nation. The institution of slavery had brought strangers—the people they enslaved—into their homes, notwithstanding the speeches, sermons, loose talk, and everyday actions that proclaimed the enslaved to be members of the slaveholding family. The actions of slaves during the Civil War confirmed their stranger status and contributed to the destruction of the white home as it had been.[14] Southern homes crumbled, literally and symbolically, under the weight of battlefield losses, shortages of food and other basic necessities, growing disaffection among the population at large, and slave resistance.

When the war put white women on the road involuntarily, it tested the Confederacy's ability to defend white homes and slavery and prevent the degradation of white women. White women refugees embodied a large ideological problem. Spectacles on the road and in the communities in which they settled, they reminded those who stayed put what could happen to them. If going to war was to prevent the "dawning of an abominable new world," what did it mean when elite white women were subjected to poverty and the marks of bondage, and poor white women were trampled upon?

Numerically, white women refugees represented a small percentage of Southern white women and the South Carolina refugees at the center of this chapter an even smaller proportion still. Yet while their wartime experience was in many ways unique, by the end of the war white women refugees in other parts of the Confederacy could tell similar stories. That the vast majority of Southern white women did not become refugees is unsurprising given that over two-thirds of all the counties in the Confederacy never saw Union forces.[15] But the existence of even one white woman refugee was a problem for the Confederate government and for all white Southerners irrespective of class.[16] "Dislocations and deprivations plagued white and black, rich and poor," as Catherine Clinton writes.[17] They also spoke to the very meaning of the war. The presence of white women refugees was symbolically and politically important and mattered in a material sense.

The exodus of slaveholders, Mary Elizabeth Massey wrote, would "create a new social class of refugees," but refugees were not a new phenomenon in American life, nor were Americans unfamiliar with warfare that destroyed homes and family life. However, in its duration and strength, the destruction that took place during the Civil War was different from anything Americans had previously experienced, and so was the problem of refugees. We can trace this destruction as it spread across the South from, for white women, its traumatic beginnings in the South Carolina lowcountry to the Mississippi River valley. The particular nature of the slave economy in the lowcountry, home to the nation's wealthiest and most powerful slaveholders, and Union occupation in November 1861 made the flight of lowcountry slaveholders significant for the entire Confederate project.[18]

The white refugee problem was at first limited geographically to the most militarily contested areas. Virginia plantations near Washington, D.C., witnessed "the first mass exodus" of slaveholding families, epitomized by the flight of women like Mary Custis Lee and Judith McGuire. McGuire and her husband would spend most of the war shuttling from place to place and room to room.[19] But it was the mass exodus of lowcountry South Carolina slaveholders in 1861 that foretold the larger-scale white refugee problem to come, its import for the Confederate project, and the transformation of the relationship between home and state in the Confederate South. With Union forces breaking Confederate control of the Mississippi valley in 1863, slaveholding women fled Louisiana, Mississippi, and Tennessee. Some headed to Texas, among them Kate Stone, her mother, and sister, whose sojourn would last two and a half years, some east to the hills of North Carolina.[20]

Even though women could not vote or participate in the political process in any formal sense, men went to war knowing that they had the support of the vast majority and that women were politically engaged and "knowledgeable about political affairs."[21] Some two decades before the Civil War, Harriet Warren of Mississippi noted, "Dress and Politicks are all the fashion. The ladies make banners and speeches and go to all the Political meetings." A native South Carolinian, Warren compared the Civil War moment to the excitement surrounding the nullification crisis of the 1830s.[22] Before the war Southern white women "filled the galleries of state legislatures and Congress" and sparred with Northern and British abolitionist women in defense of slavery and their way of life. New York–born Julia Gardiner Tyler, the second wife of President John Tyler, boldly defended slavery and the slaveholding women with whom she identified. While claiming, on the one hand, that slaveholding women knew "nothing of political conventions, or conventions of any sort than such as are held under suitable pastors of the Church," she championed, on the other hand, their vested interest in the national and international politics surrounding the question of slavery.[23]

Tyler took umbrage at the widely circulated antislavery letter addressed to American women abolitionists by the Duchess of Sutherland. Slaveholding women not only supported the institution of slavery but did so knowledgeably, Tyler asserted. "Politics is almost universally the theme of conversation among the men, in all their coteries and social gatherings," she wrote, "and the women would be stupid, indeed, if they did not gather such information from this abundant source. Hence they are not ignorant of the rapid growth of their beloved country." Tyler also took up the old proslavery canard that placed the blame for slavery and the Atlantic slave trade on the British. Britain, "in spite of all remonstrances on the part of the colonies" had encouraged slavery for 150 years "as a means of swelling her coffers." The duchess, she suggested, would do well "not to interfere in the South's 'domestic institutions'" and instead tend to problems in her own land. "Go, my good Duchess of Sutherland, on an embassy of mercy to the poor, the stricken, the hungry and the naked of your own land," Tyler wrote. "Leave it to the women of the South to alleviate the sufferings of their dependents [sic], while you take care of your own" and not worry about the slave, who "lives sumptuously in comparison with the 100,000 of the white population of London . . . is clothed warmly in winter, and has his meat twice daily, without stint of bread." The "well-clothed and happy domestics" who worked within the plantation household were well off, she opined, and invited the duchess to come see for herself.[24] The "happy domestics" were also not stupid.

On the Run

As she made her way from Baton Rouge to Greenwell Springs, Louisiana, in the late spring of 1862, Sarah Morgan recorded what was for her an extraordinary experience.

> Three miles from town we began to overtake the fugitives. Hundreds of women and children were walking along, some bareheaded, and in all costumes. Little girls of twelve and fourteen were wandering on alone. I called to one I knew, and asked where her mother was; she didn't know; she would walk on until she found out. It seems her mother lost a nursing baby too, which was not found until ten that night. . . . It was a heartrending scene. Women searching for their babies along the road where they had been lost, others sitting in the dust crying and wringing their hands.[25]

About a mile and a half from their home, a stranger offered Morgan's mother a ride. Morgan and her sister would eventually hitch a ride on a cart—not a lady's carriage—driven by two enslaved men. Their choice of seating was on top of a load of luggage or between a flour barrel and a mattress.[26] In this way, Morgan and her sister caught up with a group who had fled ahead of them. "White and black were all mixed together," along the road. Morgan praised the slaves who carried white babies and what bundles could be quickly gathered up and who, she said, told her they were "glad to get away with mistress things," even if that meant they could carry none of their own valuables.[27]

What made these scenes so extraordinary was that the "fugitives" were white women and children. The reality of elite white women birthing babies in the woods in flight and on the road, traveling on foot "alone on the road," catching rides with strangers while fleeing the army of the nation to which they had belonged and called their own just the year before, and white children in flight drowning in rivers and swamps was more than remarkable. It represented a stunning reversal of fortune. In her journal entry of May 30, 1862, Morgan captured a tiny but significant rupture in the fabric of the slave South and the race and class distinctions that governed it. White women like herself were clearly out of place. They were accustomed to having black people around them, but being "all mixed together" suggested a loss of the power to discipline the spaces of contact. A line had been crossed that would have seemed unimaginable when South Carolina fired the first shot of the war. Everything about their presence on the roads seemed unprecedented. Elite women customarily traveled in their best clothing. Now here they were "bareheaded" and improperly clothed. Mere girls were on the road alone and babies had become separated from their mothers.

Hundreds of miles away in Virginia, in a letter to his daughter Mary, Robert E. Lee also took note of the extraordinary sight of women, girls, and children "abandoning their homes, night and day" and "trudging through the mud and bivouacking in open fields." The women Lee observed were fleeing as U.S. military forces converged on Fredericksburg in late November 1862. In this instance, Confederate forces were able to assist with their transportation with wagons and ambulances.[28] Still, like Morgan, Lee recognized that a pillar of the South's domestic sanctuary had been shaken. The idea had indeed occurred to Morgan before she left home and ended up on the road. As she waited anxiously in Baton Rouge in fear that Union forces would burn the town, she anticipated the vagabondage to come: "O my home! I cannot live without you! Think of wandering around houseless and homeless, with not even the chance of making one for myself, for nothing is to be done! Beggared!"[29]

The election of President Lincoln, wrote Arthur Middleton Manigault of South Carolina, "satisfied the people of the Southern States that the time . . . had at last arrived when the South must withdraw from the Union." To the surprise of few, South Carolina became the first of the slave states to leave, passing an ordinance of secession on December 20, 1860.[30] The state's leaders prepared for war. Calls went out for men to form volunteer companies. Some units were short-lived or never got up to strength as men left for home before the first shot of the war was fired, "giving the potent reason that tho ready to fight when they left home they left wives & children dependant [sic] for daily support."[31] Those who initially enthusiastically volunteered their slaves to help build fortifications and roadways were soon eager to reclaim them.[32] In the end, lowcountry leaders were ill-prepared then for the arrival of a U.S. amphibious force on November 7, 1861, which one slaveholder wrote, delivered a "smashing blow upon our Sea Island plantations," triggering the flight of the area's slaveholders.[33]

The day after Federal troops landed at Port Royal Sound, a party of local scouts encountered "negroes all along the road with all imaginable articles of plunder from private residences & stores all of which are open." The town of Beaufort presented "a melancholy sight like a city of the dead. Not a living soul to be seen. Houses & stores open, furniture half moved out & every appearance of destitution."[34] Yet, for the scouts who had been mobilized to defend the state, far more troubling evidence of "the realities & horrors of war" appeared on the road between Pocotaligo and Port Royal. Here they encountered white refugees, "men, women & children . . . in all conceivable vehicles with their all & (some very little) saved from their deserted home." A "sadness marked every face." At Tombee Plantation, they found Thomas Chaplin's wife and daughters without money to leave and took up a collection of about forty dollars to assist them.[35]

Margaret Ann Meta Morris Grimball heaped disdain on the people of Beaufort who fled the approaching Union forces, "leaving the town to be sacked by the negroes." She thought the response of white women had been disgraceful. "The women were seized with a perfect panic and many fled into the interior, such terror-stricken creatures disgrace their Revolutionary heritage," she wrote.[36] But Grimball spoke from a still-safe space. The war had not yet reached her home at Grove Plantation in Colleton District. Within a few months, she had joined the migration, fleeing to Spartanburg in the South Carolina upcountry.[37] That caravan had begun to form less than a month after the war began. By mid-May 1861, Charleston had "the appearance of a military garrison" and "every cart & dray was loaded with furniture &c of families going off in Rail Road & cars engaged for weeks. One meets many sad faces & some parts of the city looked deserted at night, so many houses closed; every train of cars go filled with families & old men refugees to the up-country," noted Thomas Ravenel.[38] In the chaos of the early months of war, some slaveholding women became unintentional refugees when a routine trip to visit relatives placed them in territory claimed by the Confederacy but effectively controlled by the Federal government, turning a vacation into unplanned exile.[39]

The hurried evacuations in the wake of Federal reoccupation of lowcountry South Carolina, just seven months into the war, called into question the pronouncements of the Confederacy and the United States on the meaning of the Civil War, how it would be fought, and who would do the fighting and the mourning. U.S. congressional resolutions of July 1861 reiterated a policy of noninterference with "the rights or established institutions" of the South. U.S. commanders arrived with pledges of continued cooperation with slaveholders.[40] Having acted with full confidence in their right to secede and to own slaves without constitutional encumbrances or state interpositions of any kind, secessionists were not interested. The presence of white women on the road as refugees thus undermined one of the most fundamental tenets of proslavery thought and a rationale for mobilizing Southern white men.

As refugees, a generation of slaveholding women experienced dislocations of the kind their ancestors had known during previous wars but that were reserved largely for poor and enslaved women. Through forced migrations and dislocations that scattered their families and separated them from loved ones, war-fueled food and housing shortages, and gendered violence, they came to know something of the trauma suffered by enslaved women and poor white women, if not in anything like its full measure. In exile, sometimes "thousands of miles in search of a home," they came to know what it felt like not to know the whereabouts of a spouse, parent, or child. As they lost the ability to fully direct and control their own movement, they came to know how it felt to not have the freedom to move about in the world as they pleased, without fear and without needing permission. For the first time, slaveholding children experienced the pain and trauma of not knowing how to contact family members or if they would ever see them again. "I do not know where you are," a distressed Robert Sams wrote his mother, "or *any* of my *Family*."[41] Robert E. Lee's daughter knew where her father was, but at one point in the war, Lee barred her from sending him written communications. Lee told her that should she be caught with letters from him she would compromise both her own safety and that of the scouts who carried their correspondence.[42]

By the late spring of 1862, South Carolina planter Thomas Ravenel had joined other lowcountry slaveholders in decrying the occupation of the South Carolina lowcountry "by the enemy, agriculture arrested, negroes stolen & families in exile." For extra measure, he added, "Our citizens have been murdered, our females insulted, our churches desecrated & closed."[43] Slaveholders also worried about the impact the war was having on the marriage prospects of their children. The death of thousands of young men on the battlefield severely reduced the number of men eligible for marriage. The disintegration of slavery also meant that parents found it harder to provide sufficient money, land, slaves, or dowries for their children to establish independent households, further dampening prospects. Margaret Ann Meta Morris Grimball's worries about her children's marriage prospects were widely shared.[44]

Passes and Other Indignities

The Civil War inflicted chaos and humiliation. Many slaveholding women, often impoverished and vulnerable, even felt like slaves themselves. The diminution, and sometimes complete loss, of the power to command black people with near unbridled authority made this experience that much more salient. White women spoke the death of their children in ways enslaved people would have understood. "Children dying now I rather think a blessing when I think of how much sorrow they miss," Kate Foster wrote upon hearing that an uncle had lost two children.[45] Slaveholding women chafed at having to produce papers to prove their right to be on the road and to show ownership of the human property they claimed. Before the war, only slaves were required to show a pass documenting why they were out of place and to whom they belonged. Before the war, papers documented the purchase, sale, manumission, or inheritance of enslaved people, but slaveholders did not have to produce papers documenting their ownership of them in the daily routine of life.[46] In order to travel from the North to the South, from the South to the North, within territory reoccupied by the United States, or within the Confederate states they now had to produce a pass "just such as we give our negroes," an indignant Sarah Morgan wrote.[47]

Morgan's analogy was far from perfect, but it suggested how radically the lives of slaveholding women had changed. The passes now required of women like her seemed close enough in nature to the kind Keziah Goodwyn Hopkins Brevard gave or denied to her slaves: "Mary & Harry asked for papers to go to James H. Adams' this morning," Brevard wrote in 1860, and "I refused them."[48] Morgan was all the more offended that the power to limit her mobility rested with a man she considered beneath her in status. "Think of being obliged to ask permission from some low ploughman, to go in or out of our homes!" she exclaimed.[49] The "low ploughman" who held the power to manage and limit Morgan's ability to move about in the world was a Union officer charged with approving or denying passes in Baton Rouge. The irony was inescapable.

When the war began, some Southerners found themselves away from home in the North and abroad. Getting home, they discovered, meant subjection to humiliating searches and restrictions on their accustomed right to unimpeded mobility. Southern white women seeking to leave the nation's capital to go into the Confederacy were required to state under oath their name, age, address, the date they came into the lines of the United States and for what purpose, where they had resided while in the North, and their destination and purpose. The humiliations did not stop there. Once granted permission to depart, they were to be escorted out of the city and allowed to take no more than one trunk or package, which was subject to inspection. If caught smuggling contraband, they risked imprisonment.[50]

Southerners seeking to return to the country from abroad transiting through Northern soil prepared for extra and unaccustomed scrutiny. William Ravenel of Charleston advised his son, who was in Paris when the war began, to "erase every trace of your being a citizen of So. Ca. and have nothing in your trunk or about your person to indicate where you are from. You will be most rigidly searched at almost every point so be careful in the extreme."[51] It might have occurred to Ravenel that he was asking his son to take on the behavior of fugitive slaves.

Southerners also had to contend with internal passport systems adopted by cities, states, and the Confederate War Department. Thomas Ravenel complained in May 1861 of the "great difficulty" he encountered "in getting a passport which had to be presented to a soldier guard at the Depot & to an officer on the cars, the effect of martial law. Could scarce recognize that I was in a free country & city." He was just trying to get home.[52] A bigger problem than passes required under local martial law was the pass system adopted by the Confederate War Department. To William S. Oldham, who represented Texas in the Confederate Senate, it was exemplary of overreach by the Confederate government, evidence of "military despotism" and "gross usurpation and tyrannical arrogance to the traveling community." He protested the stationing of soldiers at railroad stations "to prevent people from entering the cars who had not the requisite pass." In the summer of 1862, as he made several trips from Raleigh and Thomasville, North Carolina, where he visited family, to Richmond, he had witnessed "hundreds" of women and children "excluded from the cars and forced to go to the Provost Marshall's office for passes."[53]

Some women took measures restricting their mobility as a point of pride, boasting of their agility in evading and outwitting Union blockades. Fleeing Columbia, South Carolina, at the approach of Sherman's army, Georgia DeFontaine described herself as "a perambulating conveyance of assorted goods." In the "war pockets" sewed into her skirt that reached to the hem and were anchored by a heavy cord hung about her waist, she claimed to have carried "one piece of flannel, twelve yards of dress goods, twelve yards of muslin, two pounds of tea, five pounds of coffee, two pounds of sugar, a silver cup, two dozen silver forks, the same of spoons, spools of cotton, silk, needles, thread, pins &c., &c" as well as a "watch, money, and private papers."[54] Susan Leigh Blackford boasted of similar exploits: "I took my silver sugar-dish, cream pot, bowl, forks and spoon and put them in the legs of a pair of your drawers I had in my trunk, tying up each leg at the ankle and buckling the band around my waist. They hung under, and were concealed by, my hoops. It did well while I sat still, but as I walked and when I sat down the clanking destroyed all hope of concealment." Blackford acknowledged "the ridiculous side of the situation."[55] For her part, Lucy Lindsay boasted of getting past a Union blockade with twenty-two pairs of socks for Confederate soldiers hidden in her homemade skirt while balancing a large supply of quinine and morphine in a wrap tied around her head.[56]

What these women did not acknowledge in their letters and diaries was how much they had come to resemble enslaved women smuggling food from the big house to feed their families, or the fugitive slaves described in newspaper advertisements as having bags slung over their shoulders containing all their worldly possessions. Their movement on the roads bore unsettling resemblance to slave coffles. The marks of displacement and violence that attached to them made them look more like black women and children refugees, and fugitive slaves. Slaveholding women did not acknowledge these ironies in writing, but they could not have been lost on them as they trafficked in contraband or carried food, clothing, jewelry, money, and other goods under their skirts, no more than the irony of having to produce a pass was lost on Sarah Morgan. As Drew Faust writes, "The relations of life were more than just out of joint; they seemed incomprehensible."[57] Whatever success white women refugees had secreting valuables on their bodies, it availed them little in holding on to the most valuable property they owned. The Civil War had no sooner begun than slaveholding women began to face the problems of refugee life with too few slaves to plant the crops and do the cooking, washing, and cleaning needed to support their households.

Reconstituting and Managing
Plantation Households in Exile

Anna B. Oswald belonged to one of the wealthiest slaveholding clans in the South Carolina lowcountry. Less than two weeks after Federal forces landed at Hilton Head, she joined the first wave of slaveholding women who fled the region. Her husband had joined the Army of South Carolina organized to defend the state's secession and could not be there to help. Like other women refugees, Oswald sought to bring order to her new life by restoring some semblance of the old. She carried into exile a skeleton crew of household slaves—Paul, Katy, Sophy, and a cook on loan from her father—but she wanted her own cook, Sarah, who remained on the plantation and without whom Oswald could not go forward in any way that made sense to her.

The problem was that she was no longer in a position to command Sarah's presence. More accurately, she no longer had the power to make good on the command. She considered an offer from her father to send someone to get Sarah but seemed to recognize immediately that the plan would probably fail. Instead she placed her hopes in a more personal appeal grounded in notions of paternalism and reciprocity. She would negotiate with Sarah.[58] Oswald recruited a female relative to deliver a message to Sarah in person outlining the terms of employment she thought would prove persuasive. She wanted Sarah to know first "that I am going to get Pa to make some arrangement about her husband, that I want him to swap Will for Ben" and that she "must bring all of her children and things." Thus, should Sarah consent to join Oswald in exile, she could be assured of having her children and husband with her. In addition, she would be reunited with her brother Josey, Josey's wife (Jane), and another enslaved woman she knew, perhaps a friend. Oswald sent word that Jane "picks cotton with the rest of the hand," suggesting that Jane, like Sarah, had labored in Oswald's household. Oswald's message of sweet enticement included the promise of "a nice house here in the yard all sealed & papered with a chimney that Pa says she can have to live in."[59] In effect, by Anna Oswald's sights, Sarah too could reconstitute her home and a semblance of her larger community of kin and friends. Oswald's effort to secure Sarah's labor seems extraordinary only if we neglect to consider their preexisting relationship. It might be best understood as an elaboration of that relationship.

In their efforts to reconstitute their homes in exile, slaveholding women like Anna Oswald clarified the process by which the plantation household existed as a material reality and an ideological apparatus and the importance of the imprint of the past on the new realities. Anna's efforts to persuade Sarah to join her spoke to the way things had been and how, under the pressure of war, they were changing. Before the war, supported by the income generated by the labor of enslaved people, Anna was at liberty to furnish and refurbish her home in any way she desired. She could determine how many and which slaves served her personally and the needs of her family, and the particular work each would do. She could command their presence and labor and she could dismiss, exchange, hire, or sell them at will. She could do these things as easily as she changed her wardrobe from morning to evening attire. This power slave-owning women took for granted. When a woman she owned gave birth in 1862, Catherine Edmondston declared straightforwardly: "If the child lives I intend to bring him up as a table servant, have him in by the time he can talk & never let him be rusty." Vineyard, the child's mother who delivered him without a nurse or midwife, would have no say in the matter.[60] The Civil War bolstered the ability of enslaved women to refuse the commands of slaveholding women, and the latter's power to do as they wished with black women and their children. Some white women saw that power stripped from them completely.

The negotiations Anna entered into with Sarah reveal a great deal about the disintegration of the material and ideological foundation of the plantation household and the resulting impact on the lives of slaveholding and enslaved women. They speak to the constraints that had corralled the breadth of slaveholding women's prewar power. What Sarah thought or said about Anna's plans cannot be ascertained directly from the available record. Anna's carefully crafted appeal nonetheless offers insight into the silence imposed by the archival record and the history of the struggle between enslaved and slaveholding women that they carried to the wartime struggle. The challenges and promises of the war shifted the scales toward enslaved women like Sarah and made possible radical renegotiations of power.

Anna Oswald came to the table in November 1861 ready to negotiate, based on what her prewar relationship with Sarah had taught her about what Sarah valued and what was negotiable. Her offer makes clear that she understood how much Sarah valued her family and the right to live with them and among other black people she cared about, and even to have "a nice house." But it is unlikely that Anna ever before had to couch her negotiations with Sarah so baldly, to acknowledge so openly Sarah's claims to a "home" of her own, to her own family, to her identity as a wife, mother, sister, and friend. In its adorned yet unadorned 1861 formulation, Anna's strategy signaled that this was not the first time the two women had negotiated the terms of Sarah's enslavement, and thus the extent of Anna's power. That past experience led Anna to believe she knew just what to do in the situation, what buttons to push. It had taught her what "indulgence"—a favored euphemism of slaveholders that reframed the problem of slave resistance—would most likely get her the result she wanted. Their prewar interactions would have familiarized Sarah and Anna with the psychological and ideological tools of the business of slaveholding. To Oswald's mind, Sarah's home in exile would feature the full tableau of a family—a slave family—as Sarah would have understood. As appealing to Sarah as the offer to have her family intact and by her side must have been, she would have understood that her own home would remain the home of an enslaved family, not the free home she must have envisioned.[61] It is unclear whether Sarah ultimately joined Anna, but one can easily imagine that she chose to take her freedom where she stood, in the company of others who became practically if not legally free after slaveholders fled the lowcountry and Union forces arrived.

Anna's gambit reflected the long history of the struggle between slaveholders and enslaved people over control of the black family and the compromises reached by 1861. Slaveholding men and women had long experience in assessing "what emotional pressures might break the slave of the particular behavior." In 1788, when John Peck sought to strike a deal to purchase a slave woman to serve his wife, he offered to purchase the woman's husband, Tom, and their children to seal the bargain.[62] As Joyce E. Chaplin writes, slaveholders became adept in applying psychological manipulation that aimed at "a deeper, more invasive type of control over slaves" and "to twist affection into tractability."[63] This manipulation played out in punitive sales of family members who resisted authority, the transfer of black people from the plantation household to field labor and vice versa, and other measures designed to ensure that the family and larger slave community would pay for individual acts of resistance. Oswald's offer was similarly structured. It made Sarah's happiness and that of her family dependent on Sarah's tractability. The vast majority of slaveholders did not truck in such open power exchanges, but they understood that they courted discontent and resistance when they trafficked in slaves and separated families through sale or other means.

The war was only months old when Anna Oswald rehearsed the use of antebellum rules on the new terrain of war. Over the course of the war, other white women would follow her example because it was what they knew how to do. They did so even as the power behind those rules evaporated, as white women's capacity to tear the homes of enslaved people apart, to order black people about at will, to determine solely at their discretion where, how, and with whom black people would live diminished. In their effort to rebuild the plantation home in exile, we see how the Civil War exposed to wider view the spaces in which women had struggled, the kinds of things that had been up for negotiation, and the terms of agreement reached. But the lesson of the war was that the past was a poor guide to the present. Black and white women occupied new terrain, unprecedented in their personal experiences, even as they held on to remnants of the past.

The changed terrain of war also forced Caroline Sams to calculate differently her power as a slaveholder. She went into exile in December 1861 and like Oswald carried only a few enslaved people with her—Jane and her two children, Julius and Hagar—too few to meet her needs. Unlike Oswald, she had her husband at her side. In the weeks that followed, Caroline and Miles Sams worked diligently to retrieve the slaves left behind at their now poorly named plantation, Retreat. Though he "risked his life by going over to the retreat to get them," Miles Sams succeeded in removing only thirty-one of the sixty-five people at Retreat to Lawtonville in the northern part of Beaufort Parish, where the family had taken refuge. The enslaved people taken from Retreat included Big Ben, Anna, Lavinia, Nancy, Gabriel, Moses, Ben, William, Chloe and two of her children, Cretia, Richard, Jonas, Hogan, Billy, and Hagar and her children. Pompey and March were brought from Charleston and Thomas from Savannah. Caroline Sams's stepfather, Rev. H. D. Duncan, congratulated the couple on their success in retrieving so many and prayed they would "get them all so that *we see the Lord is taller than all our fears.*"[64]

Caroline and Miles Sams mounted one more attempt to capture the thirty-four people who remained at Retreat. It failed miserably. "I sent the wagon & cart down last week & your Pa sent to tell them to come over & come up but not one of them came," Caroline Sams wrote her daughter, Emma. Finally, out of concern for the risk to his personal safety, she urged her husband to give up, "even if he lost them all." There was little they could do, she acknowledged, "unless the Negroes will come of their own free will." She had no faith that they would. "Very few of which will do so, particularly as our enemies are now hiring them to get out our cotton & getting it out $10 per bale."[65] She found it "very provoking" to "be so shamefully treated & impoverished" by their preference for freedom. Emma Sams applauded her parents' success "in getting so many of [the] people up" but supported her mother's efforts to dissuade her father from "going over for the rest" for fear that he would "be taken captive by those miserable demons," a fate "worst [*sic*] almost than death" or be betrayed by the slaves. "From what I hear," she wrote, "it must be very dangerous to go on any of the plantations even if the Yankees do not know when you reach there. . . . In some cases, the negroes may turn against you and make your hiding place known."[66] While slaveholding men typically focused on removing enslaved men, slaveholding women, tasked with reconstituting planter homes, kept enslaved women squarely in their sights even when they also had to take charge of relocated field hands.[67]

Lowcountry South Carolina slaveholders learned early on that the war they waged to protect the institution of slavery placed it in unparalleled jeopardy. In 1860, Miles Brewton Sams and Caroline M. Sams owned $60,000 in real and personal property. By 1862, they had lost the bulk of it. Inventorying their losses "on account of the invasion of the Enemy" that year, Miles Sams tallied 127 bales of cotton, 11 slave cabins, and the 34 slaves still at Port Royal. On secret excursions back to their plantation, he had personally pleaded with the slaves, but they had not budged.[68] The efforts he and his wife mounted chronicled the wartime erosion of mastery that had become apparent in the first year of the war, as in Anna Oswald's efforts to persuade Sarah to join her. Slaveholders who smuggled themselves back to their plantations hoping to retrieve slaves and other property, sometimes asking the enslaved to hide them, placed before enslaved people new evidence of slaveholders' vulnerabilities and loss of mastery that constitutes a powerful archive of slavery's disintegration.

Slaveholders stood to lose all they owned and all they were as enslaved people calculated a future without them. At the Oaks Plantation, Rachel, a revered woman in the community, allowed Daniel Pope to hide in her cabin, but she did not follow him into exile. Rina, laundress and ironer on the Pope place, and her daughter Elizabeth (Bella), the family nurse, and other slaves hid when Pope returned for them, frustrating his attempt to carry them into exile. Rina's instincts paid off. By the time she died in 1866, she and her daughter through their labor had purchased ten acres of land that she left to her daughter, along with a significant amount of cash and household goods.[69] Thomas Elliott was no more successful on a secret trip to one of his plantations to persuade black people to join his family in exile. They were "not inclined to come off," he wrote. Elliott's effort followed an attempt by his father to regain control over the slaves. Shortly after the arrival of Union forces, William Elliott tried to get a local military command to assist him in maintaining his mastery. "Finding my negroes insubordinate refusing to work and communicating with the Enemy, I applied to Genl Ripley—then in command—for a military force to [save property] and restrain the negroes," he wrote. He offered to personally command or accompany the expedition but Gen. Roswell S. Ripley, commanding the Second Military District of South Carolina, declined, stating that he had no authority to act in the matter. Elliott had some success with Robert E. Lee. "On the arrival of Genl Lee," he wrote, "I renewed my application, and his answer was that he had no adequate force to hold the island—but that he would send an expedition which might serve to burn the cotton, drive off the cattle."[70] But Lee offered no help in managing the enslaved people on Elliott's plantations.

Some slaveholders, failing in their efforts to retrieve enslaved people left behind, submitted claims for compensation to the Confederate War and Treasury departments for property they had abandoned. They couched these claims, as the law permitted, as losses occasioned by or "consequent upon the abandonment of the District, to the Enemy" or "slaves in the possession of the 'public enemy.'" The erasure of agency in this passive legal language accomplished two political goals. It gave cover to slaveholders' *active abandonment* of their property and covered over enslaved people's *active possession of themselves.*

Anna B. Oswald of St. Helena Parish took the proffered cover in recording her loss of mastery in the language of war. In her oath of March 1862, the fifty-two-year-old Oswald tallied her losses to the "public enemy" as follows: Lucy, cook and washer, age forty-four; Catherine, a full field hand, age thirty-nine; Matilda, age twenty-eight; Ann, age twenty-six; five young children (Lucy, Rachel, Emily, Samuel, and John) ranging in age from two to seven.[71] In making their claim for compensation, Mary and Andrew Johnstone also applied for reimbursement "consequent upon the abandonment of the District to the enemy on May 21, 1862." As a result, they lost an accomplished enslaved carpenter, eleven "prime" young men, and a woman collectively valued at $16,000 along with 800 acres of growing rice estimated at 32,000 bushels and valued at $32,000 to the "public enemy." They asked in addition in separate claims to be compensated for seventy bushels of rice already harvested and valued at $670 and for the services of eighteen enslaved men on the public works of Charleston. Slaveholders in such cases took no responsibility for their part in the abandonment. When he filed his family's claim before the magistrate of the Court of Pleas in Henderson County in January 1863, Andrew Johnstone had abandoned Annandale Plantation for Flat Rock, North Carolina.[72] Slaveholders expected, however, that the enslaved would not abandon them.

South Carolina slaveholders also sought reimbursement for slaves who died while working on military fortifications under resolutions passed by the South Carolina General Assembly in 1863. The 1864 report of the state auditor included the names of at least twenty-two slaveholding women among the claimants for compensation.[73] On the other end were slaveholders like the King family who succeeded in getting all of their slaves out and regrouped in middle Georgia.[74] Others succeeded in selling out early. The Grimballs congratulated themselves on being able to place some of their slaves with another slaveholder. The merchant firm of J. Fraser & Company brought relief to Frank Lowndes when it purchased his plantation on South Island, Georgetown District, for $130,000 in 1863 and the slaves for $200,000, the cost to be paid in stock or bonds at 7 percent. Thus, his son wrote, "If the Yankees burn the premises (which there is nothing to prevent) or the negroes abscond tomorrow it will be the loss of J. Frasure [sic] Co and not ours." Some slaveholders sold some people to pay for the upkeep of others. Charles Cotesworth Pinckney II sold thirty people to feed the rest and support his family, who were refugees in Cotesbury, South Carolina.[75] For a lucky few South Carolinians, Northern planters came to the rescue by purchasing plantations from slaveholders and taking charge of the enslaved people on them.[76]

If they managed to carry enslaved people with them into exile or to get them out later, slaveholding women had to figure out how they would manage and feed them, a problem that spread across the South. By the winter of 1862–63, Confederate women in Louisiana were in a panic as Grant moved into the northwestern part of the state in preparation for the Vicksburg campaign and established his headquarters at Winters Quarter Plantation on Lake St. Joseph in Tensas Parish. Like many of her peers, Amanda Stone made preparations to abandon her home at Brokenburn. She had one of her sons, William, home on furlough from the army in Virginia, take "the best and strongest" of the slaves—she owned seventy-seven in 1860—to look for a place to keep them while she looked for a place of safety for herself and her daughters. "Only the old and sickly with the house servants" remained behind. While driving the slaves to Texas, William Stone left some at Delhi to wait for an available train to move them on. Delhi and nearby Monroe were crowded with refugees from the eastern part of the state. Some he hired out to work at the salt works in Winfield, Louisiana, a distance of nearly 100 miles; his mother sent an overseer to take charge of them.[77]

Moving some of the people to the saltworks proved to be a bad decision. Several became sick, at least one died, and three men believed to be trying to get to their wives (who had already run away) fled but were captured. Amanda Stone acted immediately, going to the saltworks herself with her son and the overseer to put the slaves remaining at the salt works on the road to Texas. She sent two women from the works, Amy and Peggy, back to her temporary home in exile to wait on her family. They were "glad to have somebody to wait on us again," Kate Stone wrote. With her slaves running away and becoming gravely ill, Amanda Stone stood to lose the foundation of her immense wealth and of her identity as a "planteress." In 1860, that wealth was valued at $130,000 in real estate and $85,000 in personal estate. Slave flight was nothing new to Stone. In the 1860 census, she listed three people as fugitives: a sixty-year-old female, an eleven-year-old mulatto female, and a two-month-old male.[78]

The problem of finding work for refugee slaves was exacerbated by the diminishing quantity and quality of working farms and plantations available for rent or purchase. As early as 1861, many of the available places were dilapidated and barely inhabitable. The growing competition for decent places to rent or purchase forced some lowcountry families to look deeper and deeper into the interior, often in areas dominated by small and nonslaveholding farmers. They were often disappointed as the upcountry too "filled with refugees."[79] In September 1863, Thomas Ravenel traveled to the northeastern edge of the state looking for a farm to buy or rent in the event he had to relocate his family only to find "all places full of refugees from the low country."[80] Margaret Ann Meta Morris Grimball's husband tried Pickens, Darlington, Anderson, and Aiken in his search for a place for his family. Nothing suitable appeared in Pickens and Anderson and Aiken seemed too close to the enemy. In the sand hills of Darlington, the only options that came close to filling their need were a 150-acre farm located fifteen miles from the nearest railroad and a house in the town of Darlington Court House. In the end, they joined other lowcountry refugees who turned to Spartanburg.[81]

Some lowcountry families had to go as far as Cokesbury, in the northwestern part of the state, to find a place to rent or buy. Charles Coatesworth Pinckney II paid $9,000 for a place to relocate his family and slaves. For that, he got "worn lands and dilapidated dwellings."[82] Even having a vacation home to which one could retreat did not always mean livable conditions. Only two of the bedrooms in Harriott Middleton's home at Flat Rock were plastered, "the others merely boarded and papered."[83] By 1865, lowcountry slaveholding women talked about taking shelter in places they had never heard of before and under circumstances they never before would have tolerated. "There is a place called 'Marion' somewhere in the swamps," Harriett Rutledge Elliott wrote her sister, "where we may get shelter but you have no idea of the difficulty in finding any place. The up country is crammed & no place can be said to be safe."[84] Scenes of this sort epitomized the distance the South had traveled in time and in reckonings of home.

Finding a refuge away from Union armies and gunboats was but one problem solved, if poorly. The closely correlated problem of how slaveholders in exile would feed themselves, and the enslaved people they carried into exile plagued slaveholders from the beginning to the end of the war. Finding "some prospect for living" remained a challenge amid rising costs for goods and supplies.[85] One of the many problems Caroline Sams faced was how she would feed and work the thirty-one people she managed to remove. She had a few options, her stepfather advised. She could hire them out in a regular manner or "on shares" to local Lawtonville farmers, rent land for them to cultivate, or work them herself on her brother Robert's place. As a last resort, he would consider renting additional land himself and working them under the supervision of his overseer. Ultimately, he wrote, the decision was hers to make.[86] In the end, she decided to hire her brother's place and employ her own overseer.[87]

Mary Ann Meta Morris Grimball and her husband received an offer from their factor to house their slaves at the factor's plantation for a steep fee, the accommodations at the place being a barn and the overseer's house. They found a better deal but still struggled to find a place for themselves in the spring of 1862. "The upper districts are crowded with this unusual population and food is not abundant or cheap," wrote Grimball. By "unusual," she meant the large number of refugees from the lowcountry. Adding to their problems, the local people, she complained "take advantage" by charging extortionate rents or offering to sell property but refusing to rent.[88] Caroline Sams also found "money is a scarce article & every thing very high," requiring that they "exercise the most rigid economy to get along at all."[89] Writing from her home in exile in June 1863, Harriott Middleton could report that they were "not starving but living on bacon, rice and hominy."[90] Food shortages combined with fewer available doctors compromised the health of slaves and slaveholders alike. One refugee family from Hilton Head experienced all of these problems on the "dilapidated Plantation" in the interior they moved to in 1862. Pneumonia among the slaves led to the death of "Old Affy's daughter Doll." The local country doctor, "nearly run to death by his large & scattered practice only comes every other day, unless specially sent for, & leaves written directions for the intervening time," Mary Elliott wrote. Her father had "not the smallest genius for attending the sick, & the cure makes Mama dreadfully nervous & anxious, the labor falls sharply on me, which is very right & proper, only I am so ignorant of the pulse and things generally," she added.[91] In Louisiana, Kate Stone complained, "the people of Monroe seem determined to fleece the refugees."[92]

Slaveholding women who turned to the hire market for relief found little. Caroline Sams rejected the option of hiring out her refugee slaves "for what they will bring," reasoning that it would bring little income "as cotton cannot sell."[93] The larger problem was finding someone to take slaves on hire. As early as the end of 1861, planters trying to relocate their enterprises encountered an increasingly saturated market for hired slaves in the interior, and on the mainland broadly, triggered by the influx of enslaved people removed from the lowcountry. On the mainland farmers could get "as many as they wanted from the low-country" by offering only food and "no other compensation for their hire."[94] The interior market for enslaved labor contracted further as those who hired slaves found themselves unable to feed, clothe, and house them due to financial constraints. Some gave up and returned the slaves to their owners before their contracts were up or failed in other ways to fulfill their end of the bargain. Finding a place to put slaves to work became ever more daunting as the war continued.[95] James Miller hired Lottie and her family from Elizabeth A. Richardson of Front Royal, Virginia, but returned them in December 1863 before the end of the year, saying that he no longer had room for them. The move took the widow Richardson by surprise, adding to the stresses on her household. "It seems very hard for poor Ma to provide for them," her daughter noted.[96]

The situation on Elizabeth Richardson's farm was no less precarious for the enslaved people James Miller sent back. The farm Lottie and her family returned to in December 1863 had significantly fewer resources than the year before. By October 1863, only seven enslaved people remained on the Richardson farm. Two, a man and a boy, worked the fields, alongside three women who had previously worked in the Richardson home and now cut corn and seeded the fields. The number of slaves left to cook and clean for the large Richardson family was down to one woman and a child. The majority of the twenty-nine enslaved people the Richardson family reported in the 1860 census were thus missing. Most presumably had run away since the war began. With only seven slaves left to work a large farm and perform the household labor, and four of her six children still at home, Elizabeth Richardson had few options available to her. She turned back to the hire market for a source of income. At the end of 1863, she hired out three of the seven remaining slaves—Icy, Mary, and Simon—who left on January 2, 1864. By the spring of 1864, only one enslaved woman, Eve, remained in the Richardson household, and she was hauling manure with Jimmie.[97] When the war began, Elizabeth Richardson was a large slaveholder. Left a substantial inheritance, including slaves, at the death of her husband in 1859, she reported $25,375 in real estate, $30,500 in personal property, and twenty-nine slaves in 1860.[98]

Some slaveholders who fled in 1861 managed to return in 1863 or 1864 to plant crops under the cover of Confederate forces, while on plantations just beyond Federal lines, some continued to grow cotton, prosper, and live well.[99] Just 150 miles up the road from Port Royal at Plantersville, in Prince George, Winyah Parish, slaveholders lived in style throughout the war, "like fighting cocks—even in these hard times," confided one Carolinian. At Chicora Wood plantation, former governor Robert F. W. Allston maintained a reputation for hospitality. There a good dinner with brandy and wine could still be had in 1864.[100]

In the end, lowcountry slaveholders were among the first of the Southern planter class to experience most profoundly the ways secession and war made slavery—the institution they went to war to protect and with it their claims to mastery—less secure. The argument that the institution of slavery remained safe has long noted that during the war the vast majority of enslaved people did not flee or become free and no major slave uprisings took place. This did not mean, however, that slaveholders' mastery remained intact. Each time an enslaved person made it to Union lines, each time the Union armies recorded a military victory, each time a slaveholding woman became a refugee, each time a slave refused to join her in exile, and each time a poor white person raised her voice against the white refugees who poured into her community with their slaves, the control over enslaved people slipped a bit and slavery became less safe and secure.

Crushed and Subjugated

The majority of Southern white women would escape the war with their homes unscathed. Their homes were not burned, nor did they experience Union soldiers on their doorsteps or in their parlors. They did not become exiles from their homes. But the stories of those who lost their homes, who saw them invaded by enemy soldiers and became refugees fundamentally shaped how Confederate women understood their wartime experience at the time and long after the war had ended. Despite all they endured, most Confederate women put up a brave front. They not only had to but wanted to. "A belief that somehow independence could yet be won persisted much more on abstract assertions than faith in any tangible means of deliverance," George Rable writes. Facts on the ground suggested "strained logic, delusive hopes," and "a blindness to reality that turned into sheer fantasy."[101] Confederate women had learned, as people in war have done throughout time, to adapt to the unbearable such that they could describe a horrific battle or artillery duel as if recounting a normal event. Mary Waring and her friends watched the shelling of Spanish Fort in Mobile harbor from a third-story window, following which they went downstairs for a "pleasant lunch." Their brave front notwithstanding, Confederate women were not immune to the "deep emotional scars" the war left. For Emma LeConte, "apathy" combined with "a dull heart pain" at the prospect of defeat as she prepared to abandon her beloved Columbia, South Carolina, in January 1865.[102]

As a larger and vastly more powerful Union army than the one that landed in 1861 made its way to South Carolina in 1864, Confederate general P. G. T. Beauregard called on Southern white men to redouble the effort to protect their homes. "The claims of home and country, wife and children," he wrote, "uniting with the demands of honor and patriotism, summon us to the field." Gen. William T. Sherman described the call as "full of alarm and desperation."[103] It was already too late. Their wives and children now lived in a different world, and the spaces in which they could take refuge had shrunk considerably. Near Petersburg in early October 1864, two women who had walked about a mile appeared in Confederate lines hoping to see the commanding officer to "get some wagons to haul their goods and chattels from their home . . . between the opposing lines." They had also lost their slaves. A soldier made arrangements to help them haul what remained of their goods but told them there was nothing he could do about the loss of their human property. They "doubtless never had to work before," Henry Butler wrote, "but now all the servants are gone and all their brothers are in our army, while their parents are helpless, even to themselves."[104]

In December 1864, trains filled with white refugees from Atlanta stood stationary on tracks going nowhere. Women of the slaveholding class accustomed to lives of luxury were "living temporarily in the cars" alongside "their cows."[105] The fate of the Atlanta exiles was soon shared by slaveholders in Columbia, who fled as Sherman's army approached the South Carolina Piedmont. One of the last trains out of the city carried Confederate women fortunate to have influential contacts like the president of the Charlotte and South Carolina Railroad to call on to get a seat. With them rode the governor of the state, other politicians, and women treasury workers. "We were all refugees, going forward to an untried future," wrote Georgia DeFontaine of Charleston, now uprooted again.[106] As the train left Columbia, the treasury department workers began singing "Home, Sweet, Home," and the other passengers joined in. Arriving at Chester, some sixty miles north of Columbia, they got a glimpse of their fate: refugees who had preceded them lodged in "old, discarded cars which had been switched off on one side, fitted up as dwellings" and in which they "had placed their 'little all' that was left of the general wreck." From inside the cars came the sound of music from a harp and piano, "and the inmates seemed as happy and contented as if residing in their own beautiful homes," DeFontaine wrote. But she was not convinced by this stalwart display as she took shelter in a pitched roof attic over a drug-store that had once been the home of a shoemaker.[107]

By this point in the war, involuntary exile ordered by enemy soldiers was becoming more common than "voluntary" flight designed to get ahead of the enemy. Refugees from Florida landed in Mobile and Montgomery, Ala-bama, and Columbus, Georgia. More and more formerly wealthy Confeder-ate women were living "refugee-style."[108] Anderson Courthouse in the far northwestern corner of South Carolina experienced an "in-flux of the low-country refugees." Approximately seventy families, mostly from the Charles-ton area, included members of the some of the most prominent lowcountry families: the McPhersons, Lowndeses, and Manningtons.[109] Wealthy refu-gees continued to arouse deep resentment among local people, and not only from the poor.

Emmala Reed, the daughter of a wealthy lawyer and politician at Ander-son Courthouse sympathized with the refugees with "homes & property & money all gone" and forced to "buy things from the extorted farmers." She found their situation "degrading" but not enough to stir her or her fa-ther to go to their aid.[110] The door of the Reed household was also closed to the Confederate Treasury workers who made their way to Anderson Court-house. They were "strangers," Reed wrote. Again, she sympathized, but that was it. "Some applications to board ladies of the Treasury Dep't, but don't feel inclined." Her father was equally unmoved when "a refugee lady came to try & get board" at their home. "Mrs. Pensifoy of Charleston. Niece of Dr. Barnie belonging to the Treasury Dp't—all forced here, but can find no lodging I fear. Our hearts have not suffered enough yet to make us—merciful! Pa refuses to take any—'though we may yet be compelled."[111] Among wealthy white women, Reed was not alone in her resistance to help-ing white refugees. Sometimes, it was a matter of not having enough food themselves—though this was not the case for the Reed family. In Missis-sippi, a Confederate woman acknowledged the need and the difficulty of filling it: "I don't know what will become of all this people that is come to this poor part of the country, there was nothing to eat for them that was al-ready here, and these that came bring nothing with them they will be sure to starve." One newspaper editor offered a typology of need, grouping refugees into the deserving (people fleeing destroyed homes or occupied areas) and the undeserving (speculators and men seeking to avoid service).[112]

During and after the war, Confederate women debated what was worse: the "insults and outrages of a brutal foe," the assaults on the white home by former slaves, the insulting decrees from their own government, or outrages from Confederate soldiers. Although Union "outrages" and slave resistance

ranked at the top of that list, Confederate women also expressed disappointment with Confederate men's handling of the war and men who skipped out
of serving altogether. As Anne Sarah Rubin argues, "Very few Confederate
women wanted the war to end with a return to the Union. Many expressed
war-weariness, in both word and deed, but that was not the same thing as
rejecting the Confederacy itself. Women's experiences of the war, and their
commitment to the war effort, varied considerably with class, with region,
and with personality."[113]Confederate women's wavering commitment was
nevertheless significant. The war's impact on their place in the world, their
homes and families, mattered a great deal.

The war took hundreds of thousands of fathers, sons, and husbands,
but as George Rable writes, there remained this inescapable conundrum:
"Southern soldiers, who were supposed to epitomize the highest ideals
of Southern manhood, failed miserably to protect their homes."[114] Catherine Edmondston agreed, confessing in early May 1865 in her diary, "We
are *crushed*! Subjugated! And I fear, O how I fear, *conquered*." Edmondston
was not bashful in placing some of the blame for defeat on white men and
the seeming nonchalance she saw all around her, among people she knew,
and men particularly. The "saddest part, our people do not feel it as they
ought—like men who have lost their Liberty. The cup to them has not the
full bitterness which a once free people ought to find in the draught held to
them by a Victor's hand. They accept the situation tacitly, fold their hands,
& say 'resistance is vain,' 'we have done all that men could do,' we are out-
numbered, over-run, & have not the where withal to set an army in the
field."[115]

Susan Leigh Blackford recorded another humiliating spectacle. As Union
forces under Generals Philip Sheridan and George Custer approached Charlottesville, Virginia, near the end of the war, the women remained strong,
she wrote. They "all wanted to fight," though "how I do not know." The men
disappointed, however. "The professors were not so bold, and in accordance
to a plan they had already devised, met on the lawn and then marched, with
Mr. Minor at the head of the procession, with a white handkerchief fastened
to a walking-cane as an emblem of peace, to meet the general and ask for
protection for the college and its inmates. The women were very indignant
and scolded what they were pleased to call very dastardly conduct." For her
part, Blackford disagreed. The men, she thought, had no choice. Their response "was the wisest and the only thing which could have been done."[116]

At the same time, Blackford, having fled Lynchburg for Charlottesville,
cursed her husband in March 1865 for sending her to a place that proved un-
safe and crowded. "You are right in thinking that I have blessed you out for

sending me away. . . . This house is very much crowded. There are five persons in every room and we sleep three in a bed." She wrote about other women in similar and worse circumstances, like Ann Maury, wife of former U.S. Navy commander Matthew Fontaine Maury, who cast his lot with the Confederacy when war broke out, and their seven children. Maury and the children, including a one-year-old and three others under the age of eight, occupied the University of Virginia campus infirmary while the family of a relative took shelter in one of the student dormitories on Dawson's Row. Before the war, when the Maurys lived in Washington, D.C., Ann Maury could call on three women servants, all Irish immigrants. None of the Irish women seemed to have accompanied her to Charlottesville but she had access to some of the sixty-two slaves belonging to her husband's relative Reuben Maury.[117]

Delphine Taveau doubtless also cursed her husband for the plight in which she found herself. She and her children had become homeless while her husband was doing everything in his power to avoid deployment to the killing fields of Virginia. Augustin Taveau was not stationed far from his family, but he did little to relieve them from want. The sale of several of the family's slaves, including a mother and her child, had helped to cover the cost of the family's board temporarily.[118] The landlord served notice of intent to raise the rent from $65 to $80 per month and possibly $100. "So you see," Augustin Taveau wrote his wife, "we have fallen into the hands of the Philistines." He refused to pay "extortionate prices," but the landlord apparently refused to budge. Having placed his wife in an untenable situation, Taveau counseled her to turn to their acquaintances for "temporary refuge."[119] He did not offer to find refuge for her. She was essentially on her own. When Elias Ball offered the use of his Charleston home rent-free, Delphine Taveau accepted. But despite her much-straitened circumstances, she still believed she should have an enslaved woman as her own personal cook. Ball objected when she attempted to use his wife's personal slave as her cook. Dolly was not a cook but his wife's "own personal, and confidential servant," he informed Taveau. He offered to supply a house servant and chambermaid, but told Delphine Taveau she would have to find her own cook.[120]

By the end of the war, thousands of "REFUGEES FROM HAPPY HOMES" had been "reduced to knitting socks, plaiting straw, making flowers of chicken feathers to eke out a living in humble lodgings." Thousands of white women for the first time in their lives "moulded candles, dyed old clothing and made new garments from the 'ragbag'" and sold everything of value they had left to buy food or shelter. "Frequently during these days," one Confederate woman recalled, "I had commissions from friends at a distance, sending a rich dress pattern, a Brussels carpet, or a piece of silver, or some

expensive apparel laid aside for mourning with such requests as this: 'With
_____ in the army, our fences down, orchards destroyed, fowl yards sacked
and granary emptied I must have food for my children can you dispose of
this for me?' I have walked miles, going into every little shop, to dispose of
trifles for friends under such circumstances."[121]

Harriett Elliott admitted to feeling "broken spirited" but not "subjugated"
as she held out hope for foreign intervention in late February 1865. Otherwise, she wrote, "we are gone!"[122] That help was not coming and fewer and
fewer Southern white women believed the world they had known before the
war could be saved.[123] "We are in Yankee lines and cannot tell how long it
is to last," Georgiana Porcher wrote in early April.[124] Indeed, Yankee lines
now fully enveloped her world and were there to stay.[125] News of the end
"fell on the women of the South like a thunderbolt on a clear day," Mary
Rhodes confessed. "We had refused utterly to see or believe it possible; had
shut eyes and ears alike; it was too awful to think of, and we turned from it
with a shudder."[126] Mollie Houser, the daughter of a well-to-do carpenter in
Augusta County, Virginia, had already concluded by February 1864 that the
"Confederacy is almost gone up the spout."[127] The recognition came earlier
for Mary Elliott. "I was at Church today," she wrote in 1862, "a full congregation of women and children."[128] By the end, there were many such con-
gregations. "Never will I forget the Sunday the news came," Mary Rhodes
recalled of the day she learned of the defeat of the Confederacy. "There were
no men in church, and every woman's head was buried in silent anguish
and the faces of the children were white and scared; there was something
dreadful—they knew not what. The voice of the minister trembled as he
prayed; it was like the funeral of SOME BELOVED DEAR ONE. There was no
sermon; the pastor raised his hand and prayed for comfort and blessings
on his afflicted people, and we silently passed out. . . . We were a conquered
people."[129]

In the decades after the war, former slaveholding women increasingly
deflected some of the criticism of white men they had voiced during the
war when their homes were most vulnerable. A cult of disremembering positioned white women partisans as victims of Yankee "beasts."[130] With the
passage of time, the class conflict that had raged within the Confederacy
receded into the fog of the propaganda of reunion and what came to be
called the "Lost Cause."[131] Former Confederate women and their descendants joined their menfolk in attacking emancipation. "With one stroke of a
miscreant's pen 7 million people are reduced to Poverty," Caroline Pinckney
Seabrook wrote.[132] Just as they chose to disremember slaves as loyal, so they
disremembered the politics of poor and nonslaveholding white Southerners.

"There is not a Charleston family," wrote Elizabeth O'Neill Verner, "that does not have in its heart an especial love for some town in upper Carolina" for the "valiant band of women, mothers, aunts, and perhaps a grandmother" who had gone "forth into a strange new world armed with nothing but their fearless spirits and standards of life held high above material things."[133]

The declarations of independence and works of disremembering penned by planter women reinforced just how important the claims to home had been in the war. "In proportion as we have been a race of haughty, indolent, and waited-on people, so now we are ready to do away with all forms and work and wait upon ourselves," averred Kate Stone.[134] What she really revealed was not victory but defeat. In the end, the ideology and the political and military calculations that had anchored the South's bid for independence had failed in important ways to protect either white women or white homes, as many women testified. In October 1865, Mary Johnstone's cousin Capt. Thomas Pinckney along with her brother, Ralph Emms Elliott, returned to the mountains to find Piedmont, the Pinckney home at Flat Rock, "stripped of everything by the deserters and country people." Caroline Pinckney Seabrook, the daughter of Charles Cotesworth Pinkney II, also hoped to recover the family's furniture at Flat Rock, "which had been *stolen* by the *country people*," she wrote.[135] Beaumont, the Johnstone home, had also been stripped.[136]

Some planters were able to recover some of their personal property, aided sometimes by former slaves who knew who had taken it. At Beaumont, Jackson, the Johnstone's coachman, who remained behind when Mary Johnstone fled to Greenville, South Carolina, pointed a finger at the "country people." When Thomas Pinckney returned to check on the Pinckney family property, former slaves Sam and Eliza went around and collected furniture that had been taken from Piedmont, enough to furnish two rooms, and identified the poor white people who had taken it. "They told me where much of the furniture was to be found, which the country people had appropriated," Pinckney wrote.[137] Pinckney decided to use a soft approach to get them to return the property. "So thinking it was best to 'take things by the smooth handle,' we rode around to these homes and told the inmates we had heard that they had been good enough to take care of some of our things for us in our absence. We were returning again and would send our wagon round for them. The usual reply was, 'Yes, everything was just tore up and people were taking your things off so we just tried to save some of them for you.' We accepted their explanation and professed good offices with thanks and recovered all we could." According to Pinckney, the country people went a step further. He woke up one day to find his porch "piled with furniture and bedding" returned "under cover of night" by the country people.[138]

By the end of the war, slaveholding women had suffered a mighty fall from grace as Margaret Ann Meta Morris Grimball, perhaps the most avid chronicler of their defeat, recognized. "The end of the war found the old aristocracy reduced to many straits to get on and applying for and gladly taking very inferior places," she wrote. Anne Manigault was earning her bread as a matron at the Alms House in Charleston and her husband as steward. The wife and daughter of James Heyward and W. H. Heyward were taking in sewing. Adele Allston, the widow of one of the largest slaveholders, ran a boarding school, and "the Miss Manigaults teach in Yorktown."[139] It would take decades for some planter families to recover, if they did at all. The plantation belonging to Sophy and Thomas Chaplin had been confiscated by the Federal government. They would not regain title to the house and 300 acres of the land they had owned until 1890, just months before Thomas Chaplin's death. In the interim, they lived in overseers' cabins.[140] One woman was so embarrassed for her host when she found her living in an unfinished house with an uncovered porch "& evidence of poverty everywhere with untidiness betrayed in every department" that she cut short the visit.

The fall from grace had come much earlier for many white women. At Harpers Ferry, by the summer of 1862, the parlors of white homes had been transformed into horse stables: "many a horse has slept in once cozy parlours," a Union soldier wrote. The owner of one home, with four horses occupying her front parlor and the rest of the house practically gutted, applied to a Union provost marshal for permission to refit her home using materials from the deserted homes of her neighbors.[141] For others, change had come gradually. Near the Blue Ridge Mountains of Virginia, all remained "quiet & calm" in widow Sarah Branham's home in December 1861. She and her daughters Harriette and Ellen went about their normal routines. They ordered the hogs killed for winter meat, the lard dried, and sausage made; they attended church and kept up with news of the war.[142] A small slave labor force put in a wheat crop.[143] Ellen and Harriette managed the farm, sold the crops, paid and collected debts, and even loaned a local farmer sixty dollars.[144] This all-female household—Sarah's only son was in the Confederate army and neither daughter had married—unlike many such households, was wealthy enough bear the inflationary prices that were beginning to threaten the viability of many white homes.[145] As fighting closed in around their home in Louisa County, Virginia, in 1862, white refugees began making their appearance but initially they were few in number. When

Sarah Branham died in October 1862 the contending armies were beginning to make more incessant appearances in the region, and Confederate soldiers and officers began appearing at her door seeking food, a bed for the night, and even "a negro boy" to hire.[146]

By 1865, the appearance of U.S. military forces, slave resistance, and emancipation had profoundly changed the dynamic between black and white lives in the South, gender dynamics across race and class lines, and the meaning of home. Thousands of slaveholding women had become fugitives and refugees and lost both home and slaves. The homes of women who did not run were also ruined in one way or another. The war touched the lives of all women, even in areas not subjected to occupation. Nonslaveholding white women had experienced debilitating assaults on their already fragile household economies. U.S. military incursions and the demands of the Confederate government accelerated the stresses on black homes as well. In the end, the war transformed the homes of all Southerners and, in the process, Southerners themselves.

Slaveholding women constituted over half a million members of the Confederacy's slaveholding families, and, like slaveholding men, they acknowledged slavery as the cause of the war.[147] They had spoken proudly of their willingness to protect slavery and sacrifice all for independence, even should it mean, wrote Cordelia Scales, that "many of us find a *bloody grave*."[148] Enslaved people and Northern abolitionists understood this well enough.

February 1865 found Catherine Edmondston still hoping for victory in response to the latest optimistic proclamation from North Carolina governor Zebulon B. Vance calling for unity and "good cheer." "We will succeed," she wrote. But by April 11, 1865, she seemed resigned to defeat: "We have given & freely given all we could spare & were we asked to give more and live on vegetables, would do it cheerfully & willingly for the sake of *the Cause*." She was unwilling, however, to abide any pastel coloring of the Southern bid for independence or "forced patriotism." It "is not the thing, is not the way to treat a free & generous people, & ere long hearts will be alienated from the Government & system that thus tramples on our rights, our feelings, & our sacred honor," she wrote.[149] Robert E. Lee had surrendered the Army of Northern Virginia two days earlier.

In an 1858 speech before the U.S. Senate, James Henry Hammond boasted defiantly of "the harmony" of the South's "political and social institutions." They constituted the very "frame" of Southern society, he argued. And besides, the South already had "territory enough to make an empire that shall rule the world."[150] The Confederate States of America was established to make good on that claim, indeed to build a stronger, more robust empire of slavery than the one from which slaveholders seceded.[151] The end result proved Hammond wrong on both accounts. Neither the "frame" nor the territory held. Slavery was destroyed and, with it, the ability of slaveholders to reproduce themselves as a class.[152]

The Civil War highlighted the political and gendered claims that anchored the plantation house. Slaveholding women lost their accustomed power to control what happened in and to their homes. To the end of the war, slaveholding women continued to experience stinging insults to their place in the world. But one of many such cases was the slaveholding woman who found herself on the road walking to avoid Sherman's army headed to Savannah, "camping out in the woods at night with no shelter, crossing burnt trestles and swollen streams on logs."[153] Lee's surrender promised an end to the trampling on their place in the world and the literal trampling that had placed too many of them not only on the public road but in unprecedented and unwanted proximity to the worlds of poor white and enslaved people. It did not end their suffering. The barely disguised code words used to fuel support and stoke fears in 1861—*racial amalgamation, submission, degradation, subjugation,* and *annihilation*—returned at the end in pleas for continued resistance. For a man to do otherwise, a Richmond editor concluded, would be to "send his mother to the kitchen, his wife to the slops of the bed chamber, his daughters to the washtub, and his sisters to the scrubbing brush."[154] It was the "abominable new world" that slaveholders in 1860 and 1861 predicted would come if the institution of slavery was abolished.[155]

In November 1861, Mary Chesnut sat comfortably in her husband's third-floor library. From here she had a grand view of the beautiful lawn and oak trees, a comfortable perch from which to sew shirts for the soldiers, knit, read, and write in her journal. "Under my own vine and fig tree," she wrote, "with none to make me afraid."[156] By 1865, Chesnut was very much afraid, but she, like other Confederate women, fervently hoped and prayed the Confederacy would prevail. Their support remained steadfast, if shaken. Ultimately, we cannot know how common or deeply held this sentiment was held. As Gary W. Gallagher notes, it is impossible to determine with any precision what percentage of white Southerners in the seceded states either supported or opposed the Confederacy. He argues that a great many more supported than opposed it, that "undeniable evidence of substantial internal opposition to Jefferson Davis's administration and the war" notwithstanding, "one fact stands out: only a citizenry determined to achieve independence would have waged a conflict lasting four years, killing one in four of their white-military age males, and inflicting widespread economic and social dislocation."[157]

The internal opposition was still a significant impediment, and some observers found the spirit of the people worrisome. Col. William Dudley Gale, son-in-law of Confederate general Leonidas Polk, thought the Confederate people were too "buoyant & free of the spirit of resistance," except when their own personal safety was involved. "It seems that it requires a 'raid' to squeeze rebellion out of them," he wrote.[158] We do know that the diaries and letters upon which we depend for an assessment were written by women who, no matter their fervor, increasingly lacked the means to help support an army in the field or even provide for themselves. In 1865, Kate Cumming spoke to a refugee in Columbus, Georgia, who remained "an enthusiastic southerner." She "seems to glory in living as she does," Cumming wrote. She cautioned, though, that the woman was "much better off than many others, who would be thankful to have her place," including "many of the richest people in the country . . . living in tents or old sheds."[159]

In Georgia, Governor Joseph E. Brown appointed Ira R. Foster, the quartermaster general of Georgia, to take charge of locating a site and building a village to house white refugees that would be financed from the state's military fund. Some 75 to 100 families moved to the log cabin village in Terrell County called Fosterville Camp within a month of its construction. "To assist the residents in earning a living, 'implements of industry . . . and cotton cards' were distributed." Each cabin measured sixteen by eighteen feet, with a garden plot attached. The camp also had a church, doctors, and Sabbath schools.[160] Still, the mass displacement of Confederate citizens from places including Atlanta, and Fredericksburg earlier in the war, called into question the entire Confederate project. Even those who remembered the horrors of the Revolutionary War or were familiar with that history were shocked at the sight of Confederate women and children trudging the roads and living in shanties and refugee encampments.[161]

As slaveholding women worked to reconstitute home away from home, formerly enslaved women seized the openings the war presented to build free lives and free homes. Sarah no doubt understood Anna Oswald's offer of a nice cabin and a promise to keep her family intact as a sign of the changed political terrain. Her ability to negotiate and even refuse the offer posited the radical new opening in their relationship that promised a free life. In the antebellum South, Anna's power as a slaveholder gave her the prerogative to keep Sarah's family apart, a prerogative that proved much less substantial in war. All around Sarah in the lowcountry, black people were claiming their freedom on the ground abandoned by slaveholders and reoccupied by the United States. By 1862, their numbers had grown, as slaves from the mainland and adjacent islands made their way to the Federally occupied islands.

They included the slaves of Margaret Ann Meta Morris Grimball and her husband.

Grimball had long ceased feeling safe and secure as war raged around her. She went into exile dependent on the labor of enslaved people, but most of them ran away, determined as much to secure their freedom as she was to prevent this outcome. Her husband jailed those who did not get away in a workhouse before moving them to a plantation owned by a family friend while he shopped the upcountry for a more permanent place.[162] She hated that they had to sell forty-eight black people, some "old & some inferior & some very small children," for such a low price of "eight hundred & twenty round." She resented the man who purchased them, George A. Trenholm, because he profited from the war as a blockade runner when so many of her class suffered.[163]

In the glare of war, with their homes exposed to public view as never before, slaveholding women also worried about other dangers to their homes—Northern governesses, each other, and the "gossiping frivolous" women among them. Slaveholding women, Mary Chesnut wrote, lived "surrounded by prostitutes," in "a *monstrous* system" where the "Mulattos one sees in every family exactly resemble the white children—& every lady tells you who is the father of all the Mulatto children in everybody's household, but those in her own, she seems to think drop from the clouds or pretends so to think—. Good women we have, *but* they talk of *nastiness tho* they never do wrong; they talk day & night of."[164] Some of the "nastiness" in Southern households arose from relations between slaveholding men and governesses who flirted with them, "greatly to the disgust" of their wives, who themselves flirted "most violently" with other women's husbands. Meta Grimball called them all "rather trying additions to ones [sic] family." There was much to encourage slaveholding women to cling to a world in which they had power and poor white women—to whom they preferred to deny even membership in the white race—did not.

Many lowcountry slaveholding women and their families would never return from the journeys of exile begun in 1861. Others returned, broken financially and in spirit, to homes no longer secured by the labor of slaves and unrecognizable in other ways.

Chapter Two

POOR WHITE WOMEN
IN THE CONFEDERACY

"Enemies to Their Country"

> They neglected to plant crops, as it was far more easy to
> beg all the corn they wanted than to work it. Women whose
> husbands were at home, who never had been in the army, young
> girls and old women came in droves—every railroad car and
> steamboat were filled with "CORN WOMEN."
> —MRS. MARY RHODES

> I am a pore woman with a pasel of little children and I will
> starve or go naked me and my little children ef my husband
> is kept away from home much longer.
> —LYDIA A. BOLTON

> We are made as the filth of the world, and are the
> offscouring of all things unto this day.
> —1 CORINTHIANS 4:11–12

I T WAS THE END OF July 1863 when "an old rickety wagon loaded with three femines [*sic*] of the Anglo-American variety & several baskets of pies, drawn by two oxen, the driver, another woman on foot with one hand holding a heifer cord attached to the lead ox horn & with the other hand a lusty stick to goad the slow animals along," passed through the streets of the "half-ruined village" of Caswell, Missouri. From another direction came a rudely constructed two-wheel cart "also containing several feminines of the genus homo, & loaded with cakes & pies for sale among the soldiers," and "drawn by a yoke of oxen, the driver a woman." Union army chaplain Francis Springer recorded these scenes in language that made clear his dismay and disappointment at the display of unconventional gender roles before him: "Unwashed, half-clad, & school-less boys & girls," women "who chop the wood, bring the water from the spring, take care of the calves, milk the cows, go without shoes, & in general, are the factocum [*sic*] of the family." He was not without sympathy for these "Refugees from Secessia" who arrived almost daily in the summer of 1863, "loaded with bedclothes, wearing apparel, provisions, a few cooking utensils, & such other articles of family convenience as they could pack on or tie to the wagon bed." On their behalf and that of black women in Arkansas, Chaplain Springer appealed to the Ladies' Aid Society in his hometown of Springfield, Illinois, for help. As the chaplain at Fort Smith, he devoted much of his time to ending what he called "the miseries of the innocent whom the war drags within its destroying clench" and the resulting "sum of horrors too revolting for contemplation."[1] Springer viewed poor women with sympathy. "Suffering is here," he wrote. The "question was not whether it ought, but whether it can be relieved." He appealed for relief. "It is humanity that, with clattering teeth & trembling form stands out in the driving blast & the pinching cold: & to intensify the appeal for a relief of the suffering, it is *female* humanity that is exposed to the wintry storm,— aye more, it is *childhood's* tender form & helpless age pleading to be clothed & saved from brutalization or premature death."[2]

Poor white women and children hawking goods and driving carts were not an uncommon sight in antebellum America. Their presence on the roads during the Civil War, however, struck a different chord. There were more of them on the road, and they seemed poorer and more ragged. Those not on the road also drew concern. Edward Moren expressed shock at seeing women plowing fields in Alabama in 1862 and living "on the principle of 'root hog or die.'"[3] Poor and many yeoman women had always been on the roads of the South and commonly worked in the fields alongside their husbands, fathers, and sons. The sight of white women plowing and doing other farm chores looked differently in a war in which white men had loudly proclaimed the protection of white women and home as a reason to fight.

How poor white women fit or were to be incorporated into a war for slavery that was also a war for women and home garnered little attention at the beginning of the war. As the war wore on, they were increasingly visible as not only poor people but dissenters from the Confederate project. This made them a problem and gained them the attention of slaveholders, government officials, and military commanders. Their dissension took many forms—from conflict with white women refugees who moved into their communities (putting a strain on scarce resources and endangering their lives by bringing larger numbers of slaves into their midst) to supporting poor and working-class white men who refused to fight for the Confederacy and engaging in outright resistance to the Confederate project. Slaveholders

Refugees Leaving the Old Homestead.
(Courtesy of the Library of Congress)

viewed the resistance of the poor as tantamount to treason. Their loyalty questioned, even when their protests had nothing to do with support for the Confederate project, poor white women found themselves called out by wealthy white Southerners as belonging to an altogether different, and cowardly, race. As the Civil War brought rich and poor women into contact on new political and social ground, the result was rarely sympathy for each other's condition and more often resentment and animosity. As poor women themselves took to the roads in search of shelter, they became even more of a problem for slaveholders.

Before the war, poor and nonslaveholding white women in the South had lived largely apart from slaveholding women but could not escape their orbit. Even where physical distance separated them, they remained within the ambit of slaveholders' power and a cotton regime that pushed them and their family economies to the margins. Here many stood defiantly independent in their own economic enclaves but enthralled enough with the South's cotton economy and racial ideology to lay to the side the economic and political disabilities they faced. The Civil War challenged both the independent lives they had carved out and their quiescence. The "cries of the poor" posed a problem for the Confederate project and its ideological underpinnings.[4]

At first, calls for white Southerners to unite as white people across class lines in support of the war—calls premised on defending the sanctity of the white homes and the honor of white women—seemed to resonate almost as well among the poor as the rich. It was a project that poor white women could get behind. It gave poor white Southern women reason to believe they had a place in the Confederacy as white women. It smoothed a path for them to support the Confederacy, notwithstanding long-held and suppressed grievances against the planter class. It allowed them to couch their support as a fight for the white home as an inviolate sanctuary. There was every reason for poor and nonslaveholding women to believe they had a stake in the war from the toasts raised at an 1861 July 4 celebration in South Carolina. The revelers mourned the "death by Northern fanaticism and misrule" of the "Late United States" and toasted "the Cause of Constitutional Liberty" and "The Institution of Slavery,—just, humane, wise, and Christian; one of Earth's greatest blessings to the benighted African and a cause of the prosperity and welfare of the South." They also toasted "woman—her sanctuary the home" and "her mission, love, peace, and happiness," and the "free men who have gone to battle for their rights and the protection and sanctity of their homes," toasts more likely to resonate with poor white women. Poor white women could dismiss or ignore the toast to "King Cotton—its Empire is the World." Some in the audience perhaps hoped that one day they would have a stake in that empire.[5] To the end, more poor and working-class men stayed in the army than deserted, and some women too remained steadfast in their support of the Confederacy. Yet, the disproportionate demands the war placed on them made that support increasingly untenable for many.

Soldiers' wives, Stephanie McCurry argues, "emerged as a critical constituency in Confederate politics," and their identity as soldiers' wives "emerged as the self-definition for the great majority of poor white Southern women." But the resistance of the poor never sparked a revolution of the poor, nor did diversion of critical resources to address their plight and concerns ever seriously weaken or threaten the Confederate project that had paid them little mind. Neither did their protests necessarily make them allies of the Union cause. Indeed, some blamed the Union for their troubles. "I have but *little news* of interest," William Hooke wrote to his son in 1861, "except the lamentations of the women whose husbands & sons have gone and about starting to the war. If they women could get at *Lincoln* whom they blame *with* all this condition of things they would dispatch him before he could [say] Jack Robinson."[6]

If slaveholders' opening gambit gave poor white women a reason to feel that the Confederate project embraced them and their households, most, it seems, held onto to this belief as far and long as they could. Eliza Fulgham's appeal to Confederate president Jefferson Davis on behalf of "poor women" who were being "tromp[ed]" on and "turn[ed out] of doors" rested precisely on the idea that poor white women were equally citizens of the Confederacy.[7] Like rich white women, they sent their sons to war, sewed for the soldiers, sacrificed, and suffered for the war effort. Like rich white women, they were turned out of doors. But Fulgham's appeal specifically on behalf not of all white women but of "poor women" marked the difference between them. Poor women never had the same stake in the war as slaveholding women. The war allowed them to access Southern white womanhood in ways previously closed to them. It also revealed how starkly different their lives and stakes were.

The call to protect the South's "domestic sanctuaries" engaged white men and women across class lines in the fight to defend the South and slavery.[8] It encouraged white men to demonstrate their support by enlisting in the Confederate army and white women to spearhead the fight on the home front. Recruiting handbills called on white men to defend slavery and promised that in doing so, they fought for their hearths and the honor of their wives and white daughters. Only this kind of multipronged appeal could convince so many poor and nonslaveholding men to enlist and poor white women to endure the sacrifices that the absence of their husbands and sons entailed. It made the bid to establish a proslavery nation more manageable and likely to succeed. As Barbara J. Fields argues, a Confederate call for white Southerners to fight for slavery would have been poor propaganda and make it harder to create a sense of Confederate nationalism. "'We will never be slaves' was good secessionist propaganda. 'We must never let them take our slaves' would have been poor propaganda and the secessionists knew it." Or, in the words of Harold D. Woodman, "Proslavery writers could hardly be expected to defend the peculiar institution on the ground that it made the planters rich. In the face of obvious Southern economic backwardness and poverty, such a position would be tantamount to an argument for abolition in the eyes of anyone other than the favored planters."[9] In places like Augusta and Staunton, Virginia, where more than half of the young men who enlisted in the early months of the war were farmers and laborers, such arguments would have been fatal to the cause.[10] By the end of the war, however, too many such men were "hiding out in the hills," sometimes for years, "not daring to stay about their homes on account of the murderous threats & crimes of the brigand secesh" to avoid conscription agents and Confederate guerrilla units.[11] And too many of their wives were helping them hide.

Many poor women questioned the Confederate project from the first.

Those questions became more insistent as the demands of war dragged their household economies into deeper impoverishment. From the start their support of the Confederacy was less robust than slaveholders desired or believed it should be. In cities and rural areas, they joined their husbands and fathers in calling for more equitable conscription and tax policies and protested the forcible impressment of foodstuffs. Increasingly they asked why their families should be forced to starve as a result of a war in which "they had not been consulted."[12] The class divide that separated them from wealthy slaveholding women and the wives and daughters of the professional class became more glaring.

The politics of poor and nonslaveholding white Southern women was grounded in the particularities of their political economy and social worlds. Their relationship to the Confederate project took its cue from that history, ensuring that their experience would differ dramatically from that of small and large slaveholding women and the wives and daughters of lawyers, doctors, and businessmen.[13] In the towns and villages where elite women took up residence as refugees, these differences were prominently exposed. Their worlds had met before in these spaces but under quite different and less difficult circumstances.

A "Cowardly Race"

War changed the nature of previously routine encounters between slaveholding and nonslaveholding white women. Slaveholders had long migrated in the summer to the mountains and interior villages where they owned vacation homes or lodged in hotels. Each summer, enslaved people who labored in planter households made the journey with them. Before the war, nonslaveholders' relations with upcountry white Southerners were generally limited and peaceful. In the context of the Civil War, the gulf separating their social, economic, and political lives became more visible, the arenas of contact more hurtful and deadly. When planter women fled their homes and took refuge in communities where they had previously lived but part-time, grievances and resentments of long standing sometimes erupted into violent verbal and physical exchanges. Poor women became more vocal in calling out the "arrogance" of slaveholding women. Elite women became less cautious in verbalizing privately held notions that poor women existed on a different and inferior plane of white womanhood and constituted a separate race.

Slaveholders fleeing the Union army began arriving in the upcountry and western mountains of North and South Carolina in 1861. As their numbers increased, so did the tensions between them and local people with the most tenuous connection to slavery—the driving force of the Confederate project. The draft, which allowed exemptions for planter-class men and their overseers, made the tenuousness of that connection more visible. Class conflict became less manageable and more volatile. As Drew Faust writes, the arrival of lowcountry elites "in the more egalitarian Piedmont aroused much resentment, for upcountry Carolinians deplored their flight as cowardice, feared the increased numbers of potentially rebellious slaves in their midst, and worried about providing food and shelter for so many new residents."[14] Upcountry white people who owned no slaves, who lived on small farms and in small towns, came to view this migration as beneficial to slaveholders but not necessarily good for them. They protested the growing presence of lowcountry refugees and the slaves they brought with them, often on the same grounds that they and nonslaveholders throughout the South protested the Confederate Conscription Act of April 1862. Immediately after the act was passed, an editorial in the *Daily Journal* of Wilmington, North Carolina, criticized it "as not . . . reconcilable with our ideas of civil freedom." While conceding that the people of the South were rightly called to "submit for a time to many things, from a sense of duty and conviction of their necessity," the editorial argued that this was not one of those times.[15] For poor upcountry white Southerners, the wealthy refugees coming into their communities—even those who owned vacation homes in the area—were an added insult. The battles that played out in the North Carolina mountain communities like Flat Rock and Asheville epitomized the stakes involved.

Known as the "Little Charleston of the Mountains," the village of Flat Rock in western North Carolina was the largest and, arguably, most prestigious of the summer resorts founded by slaveholders from the South Carolina lowcountry. It counted among its founders some of the wealthiest and most powerful Charleston-based clans, families interlocked through marriage such as the Draytons, Izards, Memmingers, Rutledges, Rhetts, Cheveses, Middletons, Lowndeses, Porchers, and Johnstones. It was where Mary Barnwell Elliott Johnstone and her husband, Andrew, owners of Annandale, a rice plantation near Georgetown, South Carolina, built their summer home, Beaumont, an 800-acre estate. It attracted members of the powerful Baring family of Britain, who built "Mountain Lodge" near Mud Creek, on the model of an English country estate. Sixty enslaved people worked its more than 2,000 acres, and Susan Baring eventually lived there year-round. Those who summered in the mountains like the family of Charles Cotesworth Pinckney II routinely brought a full retinue of household slaves with them.[16]

Flat Rock's few other year-round residents included the wife and children of the French consul to Charleston and Savannah, Count Marie Joseph Marie Gabriel St. Xavier de Choiseul.[17]

Summer homes, whether in the mountain villages of North Carolina or in inland villages closer to the South Carolina coast and plantations on the barrier islands, provided a refuge from the lowcountry's sweltering heat and malaria, the mosquito-borne disease. The places where slaves toiled, "where rice & cotton are made," Mary Chesnut wrote, were no place for white people between May and December. Instead they made their way to Newport, Saratoga, and Europe and, increasingly, "Flat Rock, Buncombe, White Sulphur, &c, &c," she wrote.[18] Some lowcountry slaveholders also saw the village retreats as refuges from the distracting problem of class. For Thomas Gaillard, this was an important virtue of the planter resort at Pineville, South Carolina. Here, he wrote, "the most perfect unity of sentiment and thought prevailed" among residents "all connected with each other, and related by blood." Intermarriage erased the problem of "social inequalities."[19] Gaillard's assessment, however, was remarkable for what it left out. Pineville, in fact, seethed with "social inequalities," class resentment, and discontent, as Rose's war and other acts of the resistance by the enslaved demonstrated.[20]

In 1862, the Blue Ridge Mountains of western North Carolina became the site of protracted and sometimes violent class conflict. In that year, "the citizens of crab creek, mud creek, willow Little River, and other parts of the county" sent a "written warning" to Frank Lowndes demanding that he "remove from the state within a week all of his negroes until the war is over." Lowndes had just returned from his plantation in the lowcountry and found that many of the men had run off. He returned after ten days with "the wives of the absconding men and some others and has had in consequence an amusing piece of impertinence offered him from the citizens." The local people feared that the wives were also infected with rebellion or that their husbands would attempt to rescue them. Should Lowndes fail to take their warning seriously, they promised to do the job themselves and remove him and "his negroes—not choosing to leave their [own] wives and children among so many negroes."[21]

While they might not be able to avoid conscription, the local residents made clear that they would not risk the safety of their families by leaving them exposed to a potential slave rebellion. For the welfare of slaveholders' homes and families, they would not sacrifice their own. The arrival of slaveholders and their slaves made poor white women and children more vulnerable to the dangers slavery posed at the very moment they confronted the exemptions that allowed the husbands and sons of wealthy women to avoid military service. Their fathers, husbands, and brothers did not qualify for these exemptions, nor could they pay for substitutes.

In the former Cherokee Indian basin tributaries of Crab Creek, Mud Creek, and Little Willow Creek, "the citizens" were day laborers, subsistence farmers, and household producers who made their living spinning and weaving, cultivating fruit trees, corn, wheat, rye, potatoes, and cabbage. Wealthy planters hired them to build their houses and barns, make furniture, tend their gardens and livestock, and serve in their households. The local people were accustomed to the annual summer migration of slaveholders from the lowcountry accompanied by enslaved people. They had watched this migration grow with the construction of a plank road in 1851 linking Greenville, South Carolina, and Asheville, North Carolina, that made the area more accessible.[22]

In 1862, the "bitter feeling" between the wealthy refugees and local people turned violent. A "great deal of animosity is felt against the low country gentlemen it seems, ('this being a rich mans [sic] war')," Mary Elliott Johnstone wrote from her upcountry home, Beaumont.[23] Johnstone, one of the wealthiest and most avid chroniclers of refugee life in the mountains, knew of what she spoke. In 1860, she and her husband, Andrew, collectively owned 263 slaves (50 of whom were in her name), real estate valued at $125,000, and a personal estate valued at $150,000. Their Annandale Plantation in Prince George, Winyah Parish was one of the largest rice plantations in the lowcountry, producing nearly a million pounds of rice annually.[24] The "animosity" to which Johnstone referred was on display at a meeting where planter Frank Lowndes was attacked. The locals, whom Johnstone had derisively referred to as "the citizens" and now labeled "outlaws," "sneaked behind" Lowndes "and gave him a violent blow on his head with a rock." The attack came on the heels of another "friendly warning" from the "citizens," this one "a gentle hint" for Lowndes that he was to be hung unless he left the area. Johnstone claimed to be unfazed. The "ignorant natives" were "too cowardly a race" to induce anxiety on her part. She made fun of their demands, writing it off as bad manners, that refugee slaveholders leave the mountains and take their slaves with them, calling it "an amusing piece of impertinence."[25] She would soon have reason to rue that judgment.

Despite the growing tensions and the "bitter feeling" the "country people" held toward the lowcountry slaveholders, the mountains continued to attract wealthy refugees like Catherine "Kate" Boykin Miller Williams. Williams "seems delightfully situated at flat rock," wrote her sister Mary Boykin Chesnut in mid-November 1861. Williams and her husband, David R. Williams, owned a large plantation in Alachua County, Florida, and began spending summers at Farmer's Hotel in Flat Rock before the war. "Dunroy," the summer house they built at Little Mud Creek, was completed in 1862, and Williams and the children spent the war years there while her husband served in the Confederate army.[26] Slaveholders who did not own homes but had long-standing ties to Flat Rock, like Isabella Cheves, also sought shelter in the mountains during the war.[27] Cheves arrived in 1862 with her four children, her mother Harriott Kinloch Middleton, and some of her slaves. Others, like Isabella Cheves and Mary Chesnut, who had kin with homes at Flat Rock, came for short and long periods.[28]

As Union military victories in Tennessee and farther west squeezed the territory held by the Confederate armies, refugees came increasingly from far away. Refugees "with their negroes and household goods have actually passed here on their way to a safer place," Harriott Middleton wrote in the early fall of 1863.[29] Some were slaveholders who had migrated to Mississippi, Alabama, and Georgia before the war.[30] After their Mississippi plantation was plundered, Frances Devereux Polk, the wife of Confederate general Leonidas Polk, rented a house in Asheville, North Carolina, where her daughter Katherine Polk Gale joined her. In the spring of 1863, as she traveled through the countryside to her new home via the French Broad River, it seemed to Katherine Gale that "peace & plenty ruled everywhere; the country was so shut in from the world, it seemed almost impossible for the desolation of war to reach the happy homes along the route." She found Asheville delightful, nothing there to suggest the nation was at war. Compared to war-torn Mississippi, the mountains of North Carolina no doubt appeared calm. In addition, Gale's trip had also taken her through war-torn Atlanta, where the sight of "wounded, dead, & dying soldiers" at the train station undoubtedly affected her perspective. There, she wrote, she caught her "only glimpse of what actual war meant." Gale would soon catch another glimpse when a fire broke out at the house her mother had rented in Asheville. The family suspected the slaves, and their investigation into the "diabolical deed" led them to Jack, the cook, one of the dozens of enslaved people the Polks had removed from Mississippi to Asheville. Jack apparently had an argument with Gale's sister and was heard to say he would "burn her up." He was removed from Asheville but escaped on the way to his new destination. Even with Jack out of the way, the family was still afraid and hired a "mountaineer" to stand guard over them every night.[31] To local people, it would have been further evidence that the enslaved people who accompanied the refugees presented a danger to their lives as well. The added stress refugees placed on the mountain communities would soon explode.

In June 1864, "the natives" of Flat Rock took their "impertinence" directly to Mary Johnstone's door. On the excuse of needing a meal and feed for their horses, several men (the numbers range from four to six in various sources) appeared at the Johnstone home, apparently intending to take Andrew Johnstone prisoner. In the fight that ensued Johnstone was murdered "at his own dinner table." His fifteen-year-old son, Elliott, killed one of the attackers and wounded two others defending his family, making him a wanted man in the community. A company of Confederate soldiers that arrived the next day and found one of the attackers wounded on the lawn "gave him no quarter, but killed and buried him on the spot." The soldiers captured and court-martialed another attacker who had been wounded in the fight.[32] A relative of Mary Johnstone described the men as "Tories," a word slaveholders often applied to deserters and Southern white Unionists and that harked back to the civil war within the Revolutionary War.[33]

Whether the men who killed Johnstone had intended to only take him prisoner or whether it was a case of premeditated murder, the Johnstone household apparently had been a target for two years. In a letter to her cousin Susan Middleton in August 1862, Harriott Middleton, a refugee who owned homes on the South Battery in Charleston and at Flat Rock and Mary Johnstone's sister, wrote "that the country people here are planning to attack Mr. Johnstone's house." The locals had apparently gone to Johnstone to voice the same complaints they had conveyed to other slaveholders in the area, including their objection to his "bringing up his negroes from the plantation saying it would raise the price of provisions. A hundred men swore to put him and his people beyond the state line." In response, the "gentlemen in the neighborhood assembled at the house on the appointed day and so prevented any demonstration."[34]

Following Johnstone's murder, his family sent for his son from his first marriage, William Clarkson Elliott Johnstone, a Confederate scout stationed on Johns Island, to come to Flat Rock and "remove his fathers [sic] wife & children." The family feared for the safety of Johnstone's widow and six children among the dissident "citizens," especially for fifteen-year-old Elliott, who had killed one of the men and wounded two others. "Mary can't remain without Elliott," her brother wrote, "& his life will be forfeited if he is not brought away."[35] Accounts of the "shocking murder," and the son's defense of his family, appeared in the *Daily South Carolinian*, published in Columbia and circulated in the letters of planters.[36] "Mr. Andrew Johnstone was murdered at his own table at Flat Rock a few days ago, by So. Car. Tories," Augustin Taveau informed his wife from Charleston.[37]

Harriott Middleton, thirty-seven years old and never married, spent the first part of the war as a refugee at Flat Rock. In 1862 her mother, Harriott Kinloch Middleton, and sister, Isabella Cheves, along with Cheves's four children, joined her. Cheves also brought some of her slaves from Florida. The women worried constantly about "the food question," Union raids, and their vulnerability to deserters and local people who broke into homes. The "danger of a raid" lessened when two Confederate regiments were stationed at Flat Rock but did not disappear. There remained "much open talk of the discontent of the people around here who openly express their desire that the Yankees should come and threaten to break open our houses and carry off our corn," Harriott Middleton wrote as she prepared to leave for Columbia.[38]

Into the fall of 1864, the situation at Flat Rock remained dangerous for slaveholders. Following the departure of the Confederate soldiers, lowcountry planter Archibald Hamilton Seabrook worried that "deserters and tories" had "become so insolent and dangerous that in the language of one of our citizens we seem standing on a land mine here." The homes of the Barnwell, Pringle, and Singleton families had been pillaged, and another lowcountry slaveholder, Dr. Thomas Means, was told that if he did not vacate his house he would be put "in a coffin." Means and his family left their home and made plans to take refuge in Spartanburg, South Carolina. The shooting death of a woman in an incident at Crab Creek in which her two daughters were "badly wounded" further increased tensions.[39] The violence, her husband's death, and the opposition of the "natives" convinced Mary Johnstone to join the exodus from the area. She moved to Greenville, joining a large community of refugee slaveholders.[40] However, some slaveholders with summer homes at Flat Rock, like the Seabrooks and the family of Confederate treasury secretary Christopher Memminger, decided to stay.[41]

The deserters who plagued the North Carolina mountain region were part of a growing population of men who for various reasons took leave without permission from the Confederate state but with the encouragement of the women in their lives. North Carolina governor Zebulon B. Vance was convinced that wives, mothers, and daughters hid men from conscription agents and encouraged them to desert and wreak havoc in their communities. In a proclamation of May 1863, Vance addressed these women directly: "Certainly no crime could be greater, no cowardice more abject, no treason more base, than for a citizen of the State, enjoying its privileges and protection without sharing its dangers, to persuade those who have had the courage to go forth in defence of their country, vilely to desert the colors which they have sworn to uphold." He condemned the deserters as "miserable depredators" and the women who harbored them as "enemies—dangerous enemies to their country." He told them that their fathers, husbands, and sons were "marked" men and would be punished, if not now, in the postwar settlement.

Vance painted a stark picture of life after the war for women who failed to support the Confederacy. Soldiers abandoned on the battlefield by the cowardly husbands encouraged to desert would come home victorious and remember those who had stood against them and against their wives and children.

And when the overjoyed wife welcomes once more her brave and honored husband to his home, and tells him how in the long years of his absence, in the lonly [sic] hours of the night, ye who had been his comrades rudely entered her house, robbed her and her children of their bread, and heaped insults and indignities upon her defenceless head, the wrath of that heroic husband will make you regret in the bitterness of your cowardly terror that you were ever born. Instead of a few scattered militias, the land will be full of veteran soldiers, before whose honest faces you will not have courage to raise your eyes from the earth. If permitted to live in the State at all you will be infamous. You will be hustled from the polls, insulted in the streets, a jury of your countrymen will not believe you on oath, and honest men everywhere will shun you as a pestilence; for he who lacks courage and patriotism can have no other good quality or redeeming virtue.

Governor Vance offered the deserters one last chance to turn themselves in, to redeem themselves "from the disgrace and ignominy which you are incurring," assuring them "that no man will be shot who shall voluntarily return to duty."[42] According to one Flat Rock resident, some deserters accepted Vance's offer. But the troubles only worsened with rumors of a Christmas Eve attack involving enslaved people and deserters. The Boykin Reserves were ordered from Greenville to Hendersonville, two miles from Flat Rock, to put down the purported rebellion.[43]

The resistance of nonslaveholding white women trying to protect their meager granaries from confiscation by the state exacerbated the problem of feeding Confederate soldiers. A commissary officer in Virginia responded by making a list of all the owners of threshing machines, "showing who had threshed wheat and how many bushels" and ordered the confiscation of "concealed" supplies. At the same time, he promised to "take and pay for in Confederate money only so much as could be said to be the surplus." The threat apparently had the desired effect. It "stopped the habit of hiding everything by the Union people and gave us a safe supply," the officer wrote.[44] Much of this concealment was the work of women.

Upcountry nonslaveholders dependent on the labor of husbands and sons along with wives and daughters faced circumstances made direr by the growing presence of refugees. Overcrowding in upcountry towns added to growing scarcities in basic provisions, inflation, and labor shortages faced by poor white women and their families when men left to join the Confederate army. These conditions sparked more frequent confrontations with wealthy white refugees. Refugees complained that even when local people had surplus food to sell, they bargained hard: "Many of them refused to take currency in exchange for their produce at any price, and untold were the sufferings of the refugees for the actual necessities of life—flour, bacon, wood, and other things," a refugee from Charleston noted, adding that poor people had not forgotten "the story of Continental money." They were willing to barter "household goods, clothing in fact, almost anything except money was of marketable value."[45] On "a foraging expedition into the country," the Charleston refugee ended up bargaining with an upcountry woman for food, trading her a Garibaldi waist (a woman's shirt) for two turkeys. Upcountry citizens, she concluded, looked upon the Civil War "as A WAR OF THE ARISTOCRACY."[46] It was a novel moment: a slaveholding woman reduced not only to "foraging" but also to bargaining with a woman she considered beneath her in social status. Accustomed to bartering, a central feature of their subsistence economy, poor and nonslaveholding white women had an advantage in such negotiations.[47]

Poor white women proved that they were more than "ragged Mountain people," as Susan Leigh Blackford called the women who "came in with eggs and other things to sell." Like Mary Johnstone, she neither liked nor trusted them. When they brought news of the war, she made fun of them: they had "'hearn,'" she wrote, "that the Yankees were this side of Staunton." The words of these people were "so ignorant and stupid we put little confidence in their statements."[48] Slaveholding women commonly responded to the concerns of "native" white women with disgust and derision. Kate Stone, who took refuge in Texas with her mother and siblings, hundreds of miles from their home in Louisiana, seemed surprised by the negative reaction of poor women to refugees like herself. In the end, she wrote off their politics as "envy, just pure envy."[49] Some of the antipathy poor white people expressed for slaveholders in their midst no doubt could be attributed to envy, but it grew more organically from their concern that the slaveholders' gamble presented an existential threat to their homes, livelihoods, and families. Poor and nonslaveholding white Southerners increasingly rejected the notion that they should help bear the costs of a war to protect slavery. And the nature of the backlash they received was not unfamiliar to them.

The view of poor white people as an altogether different and "cowardly" "race" of people that women like Mary Johnstone, Susan Blackford, and Kate Stone shared evoked the proslavery ideology espoused by men like Daniel Hundley who declared that poor whites constituted a biologically distinct race. For Hundley, they were "about the laziest, two-legged animals that walk erect on the face of the Earth" and possessed of "a natural stupidity or dumbness of intellect that almost surpasses belief." He located these traits in their "blood."[50] They were the sort of people Johnstone had claimed she would have no trouble "shooting," though she might "much regret the necessity."[51]

"A Striking Level of Untraditional Disorderliness"

The female face of the Southern rebellion that Sherman and other Union commanders saw most often and wrote about the most was the face of the slaveholding woman. Poor women did not have property in human beings in Union lines to beg for. But the march of Confederate and Union armies increasingly drew them into the conflict and placed their homes, lives, and livelihoods in jeopardy. Some were Confederate soldiers' wives; some were Southern Unionists. They were women who could least afford to flee and, if they could, had far fewer viable options as places of refuge. Even if they had sufficient resources to run, they could not afford to rent or buy a farm or plantation in the interior, or even to rent a room. Food shortages, speculation, inflationary prices, and Confederate conscription of men and crops took an increasingly heavy toll on poor and yeoman household economies.[52] The family of Mary Hooke of Gloucester, Virginia, lost a significant part of its labor force when one son left to serve in the Confederate army, though Hooke still had the labor of her husband, who was too old for the 1862 draft. A neighbor's family was not so fortunate. Bob Wilson left with the militia with part of his wheat crop still in the field.[53] On the roads in flight from their Confederate neighbors, poor white refugees registered their growing disaffection with the Confederate nation-building project and the inability of the Confederate state to embrace and protect them. The sense of being deserted by the Confederate state was present in Lydia A. Bolton's plea to North Carolina governor Vance to "hear the crys of the poor."[54]

Poor and nonelite white women were judged harshly, whether or not they took to the roads. Thousands made destitute by the war were derided as burdens on the state and undeserving. The plight of poor white women, as we see in the writings of Chaplain Springer, unsettled Southern notions of class, patriarchy, and race. The *Richmond Daily Examiner* berated the women who rioted for bread in 1863 as no more than a "handful of prostitutes, professional thieves, Irish, and Yankee hags, gallow birds from all lands but our own," led by an "Amazonian-looking" huckster "who buys veal at the market gate for a hundred and sells the same for two hundred and fifty in the morning market." Mary Jackson, the leader of the Richmond riot, was thus labeled a cheat and gouger herself. The editor of the *Examiner* thought all the rioters should have been shot on the spot.[55] A poor soldier's wife responded to an offer by Gertrude Thomas's father to sell meal to families of volunteers for one dollar a bushel rather than the going rate of two dollars by noting that women like her had no way to get the meal as "they had no horses and could not be expected to turn themselves into beasts of burden," and that even at ten cents a bushel it would not be affordable unless delivered. Thomas called them "ungrateful wretches."[56] Such characterizations, and resentment of what aid they did receive, would follow poor and needy white women throughout the war. The editor of the *Southern Banner* spoke unabashedly on behalf of the formerly rich. While the "families of soldiers are wisely and amply provided for by the State Legislature," he wrote, "no legislation nor concerted action of committees had been had for men who have been deprived of their homes and stript [sic] of their whole fortunes."[57]

In 1861, North Carolina farmer Elizabeth Catron began a campaign to get her husband to come home and pay greater attention to his family. She reminded him of the promise he had made when volunteering that he would come home every month or two. She had looked for him in vain "several times" and could only conclude that he did not "even try to come." It was just like a man to appear accommodating and say what he thought a woman wanted to hear. As she put it, "Men are very fair when getting off."[58] Catron pleaded with her husband to send instructions on what she should do and "how to do it." The family was out of meat, and the hogs were eating all the corn. Should she butcher the hogs before they fattened, which would not be until Christmas, meaning they would have no meat for a month? Anyway, the hog she thought would make the best candidate for slaughter got the best of her. It "refused to be kild [sic] and died her self," she wrote, or else it had been poisoned. Catron assured her husband that it was not her intention to "disharten" him, but she needed him to know that his family suffered in his absence. Their sons were too young to take his place managing the farm. She needed her husband's help, even "if it is only by letter." Catron, however, was clearly not a novice at farming. In the 1860 census, she listed her occupation as farmer.[59] This would not have made her husband's contributions any less essential to the family economy.

The calls of poor women for their husbands to come home did not necessarily signal a lack of support for the Confederacy. As much as Lydia Bolton needed her husband's help, she made clear, in a letter to Governor Vance, that she did not expect that he would come home "and do nothen for the confederacy." Rather, she thought that he might find work that would qualify for an exemption. He could come and "burn cole," she wrote. As evidence of her support for the Confederate war effort, she noted that she had knit forty pairs of socks for the soldiers. Still, it took all she could earn to put bread on the table. The "crys of my little children," she told Vance, should not go unanswered.[60] Poor and nonslaveholding women did not have to work hard to convince their husbands and sons that enlistment in the Confederate army might not be in their best interest. From the start Confederate men from nonslaveholding families showed less enthusiasm than wealthy slaveholders accused of "conjuring up women's needs to serve their own wartime interests."[61]

Poor white women in the South began taking to the streets in 1861. In New Orleans on July 31, 1861, "several hundred women, many carrying babies or dragging along older children, marched to Mayor [John] Monroe's office, announced themselves to be families of soldiers and demanded food and rent money." Within the week, the city council appropriated $10,000 for relief and announced plans to open a food distribution center. The New Orleans Free Market opened soon thereafter, supported by donations of money and produce from wealthy planters, businesses, and small individual donations from visitors to the city and residents. By November 1861, over 2,000 families had enrolled, and an average of 1,700 families received provisions on market days, Tuesdays and Fridays. When Union forces occupied the city, over 1,800 families were receiving provisions.[62]

Whether or not they were soldiers' wives, many white women in New Orleans were poor. The city was full of German and Irish emigrants who arrived in the antebellum years. Large numbers were descendants of earlier waves of migrants dating back to the early eighteenth century, when Germans fled poverty in their homeland, with so many dying during the passage that the boats became known as "German Pest Ships." Thousands more, fleeing famine and economic dislocation, came as redemptioners and indentured servants in the wake of the Napoleonic Wars. By 1850, 25,000 Germans lived in Louisiana. In 1853 alone, some 53,000 German immigrants arrived in New Orleans, the nation's second-leading antebellum port of entry. By the mid-1850s, some 25 percent of the city's population was Irish.[63]

Despite a dramatic shift in the class composition of the German migrants in the late antebellum era to a professional class fleeing civil war in Germany, most of the Irish and Germans in New Orleans remained poor or on the edge of poverty. Women from Germany and Ireland labored as domestics and washerwomen. Twenty-one-year-old Barbara Warner was one of many who worked as a domestic, as was twenty-nine-year-old Barber Deusenbach; both were emigrants from Bavaria. Ellen Tierney, a twenty-six-year-old immigrant from Ireland, was a washerwoman. In 1860, Tierney had two children, ages four and one, and appears to have been a widow or never married.[64]

The occupation of New Orleans by Union forces made feeding the city's poor, including Confederate soldiers' wives, a Union problem. In the summer of 1862, George Dennison, special agent of the Treasury Department and acting collector of customs at New Orleans, reported that "men & women apply to the [Union] soldiers for bread for themselves & children."[65] Dennison dismissed the New Orleans supplicants as "poor white trash" but saw political opportunity in feeding them. He believed that Union welfare and the confiscation of the property of the rich to feed the needy could be used to foster Unionism among not just the poor but also "the middle & lower classes who are our friends, or will readily become so. The aristocratic scoundrels who have brought the middle and poorer classes to this condition take care of themselves & take no interest in the suffering of these deluded followers."[66] He was wrong, though, in seeing the poor as deluded. They were never deceived.

By the time bread riots erupted in cities across the South in 1863, the South's ability to feed itself had worsened considerably, with food shortages crippling large sections of the Confederacy. In North Carolina, poor women trained their sights on grain mills, government grain depots, government freight trains, and merchants.[67] In Richmond, Mobile, Atlanta, and Salisbury, North Carolina, protesting the "insupportable demands of the wartime state" on their lives, they demanded bread and an end to exorbitant prices. Armed with "six-barreled pistols, bowie knives, and hatchets" and calling for "Bread or blood" and "Bread or Peace," they targeted merchants accused of charging exorbitant prices and seized food and sometimes cash.[68] The protests, Stephanie McCurry writes, "had the approbation and perhaps prior permission of leading men in the community", who saw soldiers' wives "as best suited to do the dirty work the government had failed to do."[69] The riots were "not just social phenomena, rising organically out of the immiseration of war; nor were they just cultural phenomena that spoke to deep residual female moral values," she argues, "but manifestly political events—highly public expressions of soldiers' wives' mass politics of subsistence."[70] The riots forced the Confederate government "to divert food supplies from the army to the starving soldiers' families on the home front, and the state governors to undertake such a profound overhaul of the way they provided relief that it amounted to a complete rewriting of Confederate welfare policy."[71] In 1864, the Confederate Congress responded to the burden on poor families of the tax-in-kind adopted in April 1863 by exempting families with less than $500 in property.

Poor and nonslaveholding white women understood the disadvantages under which their households operated in comparison to slaveholding households. An early demonstration of the disparity occurred in late November 1861, when merchants in Savannah tried to raise prices. In response, a party of "gentlemen" paid them a visit and "gave them two days to lower their prices, or leave the place, or they would *mob* them." As a result, the store was "crowded with nice goods, good calicoe for 12 cts, and *nice thick* gentlemen's pants already made for $3.50 . . . plenty of nice Linsey Woolsey [*sic*], and delaines, and almost everything in the dry goods line . . . a gallon of kerosene oil for $1.50, soap 20cts per pound, Tea $1 . . . beautiful cotton diapers *very wide* for 15cts per yd." Anna Oswald applauded the action of men of her class as an example to others: "If every other neighborhood would do the same, it would be better for them."[72] It was the kind of leverage poor and other women less well-situated politically generally could not access.

Poor white soldiers' wives had garnered some support from the first year of the war that increased in the aftermath of the riots, but the idea that they too were undeserving also gained traction. Their wealthier neighbors often bitterly opposed the welfare programs established to help them and considered them inconsiderate beggars. In New Orleans, wealthy women accused them of selling donated provisions and demonized them as greedy, selfish, and cheats. They came from afar to receive handouts, elite women alleged, then took "the cars to *ride* to their homes." If they could afford to pay to ride the cars, surely they could afford to buy their own food. Other critics accused the women of being "fastidious" about what goods they would accept, when they should be grateful to get anything at all. Julia LeGrand claimed to have heard that "they curse their benefactors heartily when disappointed." LeGrand did not believe poor women had the right to be discerning about what they ate or wore.[73]

Mary Rhodes devoted a considerable part of her reminiscences to the problem of poor women for whom she had little sympathy. "The wife of the soldier whose family had been supported by his labor had to be cared for, now that their means of support were cut off," she acknowledged, and supported efforts to furnish them with corn, salt, and meat. But while some recipients of welfare might be deserving poor, she believed that too many were simply welfare cheats and traitors to the Confederate cause.[74] She disparaged them as "corn women," a "feature of the times." The women Rhodes criticized were in fact the wives and daughters of mostly small nonslaveholding farmers who lived in the Alabama counties north of her home whose household economies relied more on grain crops than cotton. While she allowed that their husbands made "good soldiers many of them," and that some were "really needy, and they were supplied abundantly," too many "soon became perfect nuisances." When "for various reasons, many of the wives of these soldiers failed in making a crop," they "were sent with papers from the probate judges to the counties south to get corn," she wrote. She accused them of looking only to take advantage of the goodness of the state, "thinking it an easy way to make a living." They neglected "to plant crops, as it was far more easy to beg all the corn they wanted than to work it." Some, she said, were not even soldiers' wives. But young and old, they "came in droves—every railroad car and steamboat were filled with 'CORN WOMEN.'" Twenty and thirty at a time, carrying sacks that could hold up to ten bushels of corn, they "got off at the stations and landings and scoured the country for miles, visiting every plantation and never failing to get their sacks filled and sent to the depot or river for them."[75]

After a while, Rhodes alleged, they stopped bringing papers at all but still came demanding corn. "When you objected to giving they abused you."[76] Overseers, she continued, were "in a constant fight with these poor women" because "they hated to give them the corn they were compelled to give." "The very sight of a corn woman made the overseers angry. They regarded them as they did the army worm," a view Rhodes clearly shared. When there was no corn to spare, Rhodes claimed that she and other women of her class gave the corn women money, which the poor women preferred because it saved them "the trouble of toting the corn, and they could buy it at home for the money." She claimed to have given one woman twenty-five dollars and received ingratitude in return. "Well, this wont go to buy much corn, but as far as it go we's obliged to you," the recipient replied by way of thanks. With her own eyes, Rhodes wrote, she saw "a party of them on a steamboat—on which they got free passage—counting their money," hundreds of dollars. A railroad official told her the money and corn went into the pockets of their husbands and fathers, who "met them at the depot and either sold the corn or took it to the stills and made it into whiskey."[77]

Rhodes's disparagement of poor white women also touched on other class issues such as hygiene. The women she seemed to hate were also in her view unclean. Yet she seemed equally peeved that some had valuable and marketable skills as spinners and weavers and were paid "at the highest prices." Indeed, in the antebellum era, many poor, nonslaveholding, and small slaveholding women earned cash as weavers and seamstresses to supplement their subsistence-based household economies. The war made those skills even dearer. In the community of Summerville, South Carolina, north of Charleston, it was the nonslaveholding women who "as a rule" owned the spinning wheels and hand looms. Sarah Hopton Russell, her daughter recalled, "befriended many of these women and besides extending sympathy to them assisted them materially in the way of needful articles and employment." "Mother would supply them with wool which they would spin and weave into cloth . . . which helped to supply a want greatly felt." Russell also arranged for the women to knit socks for the soldiers by furnishing them with yarn from a Charleston dry-goods store, for which they were paid. Small slaveholders like the Richardson family of Front Royal, Virginia, also depended on local weavers for cloth and to cut out clothing for the enslaved people on their farm, services they continued to hire during the war. In the fall of 1863 Elizabeth Richardson attempted to hire a local weaver she had used before. After several failed attempts, she gave up and turned to a different woman whose loom she was able to engage. In 1864, Sue Richardson had local weavers cut out linsey for their slaves and purchased four spools of black cotton from another local woman, paying one dollar in greenbacks.[78]

Poor women also bore the brunt of public criticism that Southern white women were not doing enough to support the Confederacy.[79] Elite women like Rhodes judged them negatively, in part because of their often less than enthusiastic support for the war. While some "were true and staunch to the cause," too many "grumbled and 'wished the thing over anyway,' as they had to work so hard and the war would not benefit them. Already it had deprived them of many things; they had nothing to gain, nothing to lose, and as to love of country, they had none of that. . . . 'they hated all rich people' 'the Yankee was fighting for money, and the Southern man for his niggers, or fear of the conscript officer,'" Rhodes offered.[80] She clearly understood that class standing affected support for the Confederacy, but she was unwilling to see the struggles of the poor as more difficult than her own. Unlike the poor women she castigated, she had an overseer to manage her crops and slaves. The tax and the impressment officers who carried away horses, mules, and cattle were constant irritations when they affected her. The tax-in-kind that left poor families further impoverished left her less wealthy but not poverty-stricken. From her perspective the corn allotments poor women received made the job of overseers, and hers, harder. She "had to persuade and argue, and try to keep the peace" and listen to all the grumbling. "All of these things *the Southern woman* had to contend with," she wrote, with "no one" to stand "between her and all that was conflicting and disagreeable" and settle conflicts, "at what cost of health and strength none knew, and she never complained."[81]

Not all elite women were unsympathetic to the needs and concerns of poor women. There were other women like Sarah Hopton Russell who saw the matter differently. The Greenville Ladies Association, formed on July 19, 1861, at Greenville Baptist Female College to support Confederate soldiers and a local hospital, used part of its funds to help support soldiers' wives and children. On at least one occasion, they paid the traveling expenses of a needy soldier.[82] Its location in upcountry South Carolina, where there were fewer large planters, may have played a role in this organization's greater sympathy toward poor and nonslaveholding white women. The mission of Greenville Baptist Female College was specifically to educate the children of villagers and small farmers, a mission quite different from most colleges for women in the South. The priority of its curriculum was to prepare students for careers as teachers, rather than for marriage. Unlike most other ladies associations, whose members typically sent enslaved women to work as washerwomen and perform other domestic tasks in military hospitals, the Greenville Ladies Association paid a washerwoman and hired a nurse along with a hospital superintendent. When the director of the organization learned that the washerwoman had not been paid, they asked for and "received authority from the Society to pay her at once."[83]

It is unclear how many elite women in the South attempted to support poor women by helping them find employment or sharing meager resources with them. The archives do not suggest that this was seen as an important project in the way that it was in the North. But there was also no equivalent to the U.S. Sanitary Commission in the South whose local branches farmed out sewing and knitting work to poor and working-class women. Wealthy women in the North also seemed to have played a larger role in this work on an individual basis. More prominent in the records elite women in the South left behind are complaints that meeting the needs of poor women was a drain on the Confederacy. They also often blamed poor women for low morale among Confederate soldiers and for urging men to abandon the fight. On one side stood "the Southern woman" who sent "bright and cheerful" letters to the soldiers; on the other, "the class [that] sent the letters which made men deserters," Rhodes wrote.[84] These criticisms emphatically placed poor women outside of Southern womanhood and cast them as enemies to the state. Deserters came from all classes of society and those from wealthier families did not escape criticism. "I am in favor of taking up and ejecting

from the country the first and every man who croaks, who expresses himself in a manner desponding or otherwise—which shall tend to discourage
our people," Henry Graves wrote his mother. "These people who go about
and do not say openly 'I hate the Confederacy,' but ominously and dolefully
shake their heads and predict every thing [sic] bad; these people are our
enemies—not open, but equally as hurtful as any."[85]

The pressure to desert felt by nonslaveholding men, however, rested on
different political and material circumstances. On principle, they could support a war waged as a defense of the Southern home or join in protest of
tariffs that favored the North, but to fully commit themselves to a war whose
principal aim was the protection of slavery was a different matter. When the
war brought untold suffering to their families, their opposition expressed
itself as desertion. Stationed far from home in North Carolina, 200 men from
Arkansas deserted over a two-month period in the spring of 1863.[86] A party
of 100 men sent to arrest them succeeded some months later in capturing
and returning several of them to their regiment. "I would not be surprised,"
George Butler wrote, "if some of them should be shot," though he did think
such punishment would be too severe. By the late summer of 1864, the regiment had been called to Virginia, but some of the deserters remained absent
without leave and two regimental officers were sent to Arkansas "to bring all
absent without proper leave of absence."[87]

Even after Arkansas, Tennessee, and Virginia joined the Union, the moun-
tainous enclaves "remained sources of festering disaffection." In a July 1861
editorial, John M. Daniel and Edward Pollard, editors of the *Richmond Examiner*, stated openly what many Southerners knew, that there was "lurking
in the Southern Community a deep-seated feeling of aversion to slavery . . .
among persons not to the manor born."[88] A striking element of the editorial, as Armstead Robinson noted, was the use of language so "similar to the
vocabulary often used to describe insurrectionary slaves."[89] So too were the
forms of resistance white Southern dissenters to the Confederacy adopted
and the forms of punishment they received.

Poor white and small slaveholding women and their families were more
likely than wealthy slaveholding women to experience state violence. Confederate soldiers murdered Nancy Franklin's three sons before her eyes following a raid in January 1863 by local people looking for salt. In the North
Carolina Piedmont, Phoebe Crook notified Governor Vance that "militia
soldiers preyed on women who were 'in no fix to leav [their] homes and [on]
others [who] have little suckling infants not More than two months old.'"
Local officials "were gathering up women suspected of harboring deserters
and 'Boxing their jaws and nocking [sic] them about as if they were Bruts.'"

Militia soldiers tortured the wife of the leader of one group of deserters. They "'tied her thumbs together behind her back & suspended her with a cord tied to her two thumbs thus fastened behind her to a limb so that her toes could just touch the ground.'"[90] When a North Carolina home guard arrested Chloe Yokely's son and two of her neighbors for draft resistance, they bound the men "with ropes and hustled them down the public road" as if they were slaves. Confederate officials had arrested her husband, Samuel, three times previously. On one of these occasions, they threatened to send him to Castle Thunder prison in Richmond if he did not produce his sons, "who were then lying out in the 'bushes,'" for service.[91] Chloe and Samuel Yokely were not poor whites. They were slaveholders but not rich ones and also staunch Unionists. In 1860, they held real estate wealth valued at $1,000 and personal wealth valued at $1,025.[92]

Unionist women and the wives of deserters from the Confederate army endured forms of punishment and torture that previously had been reserved for slaves. Correspondingly, the forms of resistance they and their menfolk adopted mirrored forms of slave resistance. They feigned illness and disease. One "soldier with dark skin" even claimed to be part black. Some "assumed the garb of women and worked in the fields."[93] White women secretly fed and clothed deserters and used warning signals to spread the alarm at the approach of Confederate militia, using their gender to camouflage their aid to men in the bush.[94] Poor white men hid out in the woods to avoid arrest by conscription officers. When poor white men and women took to the bush, they adopted a form of guerrilla warfare slaves knew well. "We have had a conscript commotion in this county and several others, the ignorant natives, asserting that there was no law to compell [sic] men to enlist, and many of them threatened to take to the Balsam and there resist to the death. When it came to the test however most of those liable formed into Volunteer companies," Mary Johnstone wrote.[95]

Just as the swamps had served as a place of refuge for the enslaved and a place from which they sometimes could take the fight back to plantations, white draft resisters took to the Balsam Mountains of western North Carolina. By the end of the war, North Carolina had the highest number of deserters of any state in the Confederacy.[96] Efforts to force men from these communities to serve taxed the resources of the Confederacy at the local level and in Richmond. W. H. Younce struggled unsuccessfully for most of the war to avoid conscription and deserted at least twice. A self-declared Unionist, he had also become an antislavery man. From "living in the midst of slavery, and daily observing the evils of the whole system, I had become thoroughly imbued with the anti-slavery doctrine, and every day was more and more convinced in my own mind that it was wrong." By the summer of 1861, he knew he was "marked and spotted as a 'Lincolnite,' "a Yankee sympathizer,' and a 'traitor.'" Still, he declared he would "not fight for a Government that seeks to enslave me, and whose cornerstone is slavery."[97]

James Bell of Alabama, pained by his son's choice to fight for the Confederacy, explained to him why it was a bad decision. All the slaveholders wanted, he told his son, was to have them "go fight for there infurnal [sic] negroes and after you do there fighting, you may kiss there [sic] hine parts."[98] Nonslaveholders by the hundreds of thousands enlisted, and many fought proudly for the South, but their patriotism had its limits.[99] Yeoman and nonslaveholding families resented the class basis of Confederate conscription laws and were further incensed by slaveholders' ability to remove their own families and slaves to safety while shirking other responsibilities. John Park, the mayor of Memphis, accused the city's elite of having "tried to inveigle poorer men 'into the service of standing guard'" in order to avoid assuming their share of guard duty.[100] In North Carolina, yeoman farmers accused their wealthy neighbors of using service in the local guard to avoid going to the front and of committing atrocities against Unionist women.[101] Younce wrote of the transformation of "men and neighbors, who had always passed for good men, and who had turned . . . into demons, murderers and savages. Conscripts were hunted like wild animals, and often shot and murdered. Their homes were often destroyed by the torch, and if spared were robbed of everything they had, and their families left without a crust of bread."[101] In Alabama, wealthy men had been in the front ranks of secessionists, then run "panic-stricken" before the Yankees, leaving the "poor and moderate men to do the fighting."[103] The politics of poor men was the politics of poor women. Even as they labored under severe proscriptions inimical to a democratic society, poor women forced slaveholders who had written them off as immaterial to the work of waging war and keeping up morale on the home front to reconsider that judgment.[104]

The much-maligned "corn women" were part of the "plain people" of the South whose allegiance both Abraham Lincoln and Jefferson Davis courted. They were the mountain yeomanry who "had done nothing whatever to help put down John Brown's raid." They were the yeomen of the Upper South states of Arkansas, North Carolina, Tennessee, and Virginia who saw the creation of a slaveholders' republic as a threat to their political liberties.[105] They were the people Catherine Edmondston called the "offscouring of the people and foreigners, people who can neither read or write." In an egregious corruption of either the words of the apostle Paul or a poet of the Lamentations (which reference she intended is unclear), she called them scum and rubbish. The annoyance that particularly set off her rant was news that white men from two counties in eastern North Carolina had joined the Yankees in raids in the Albemarle Sound. The "poor ignorant wretches," she wrote, had deserted the Confederate cause simply because they could not "resist a fine uniform and the choice of the horses in the country & liberty to help themselves without check to their rich neighbor's belongings." And what should be done with such people? The answer that appeared most readily to her was violent reprisal: "Justice to ourselves demands that we shoot them down like wolves on sight."[106]

Edmondston's description of Unionist men as more concerned with the trappings of elite life than the politics of their lives echoed the criticisms their wives and mothers endured. And she set her sights on them as well. Poor white women, she wrote, had "altered the balance of power between Confederate and Union men" in North Carolina. They had applauded and signed on to the looting of plantations by Federal soldiers, even joining black people in looting plantations. After the war, "as they scoured the countryside looking for scattered household items, once wealthy women sometimes found what the Federals had left behind in the hands of 'common whites.'"[107]

Militia officers sent to the North Carolina Piedmont to arrest deserters faced women prepared to defend their communities by force if necessary. A Moore County woman "delivered a 'very hearty blow'" to a militia officer who shot and wounded her son.[108] As Victoria Bynum writes, "With anti-Confederate men forced to hide in surrounding woods, women were often the first to face the threats and demands of Confederate authorities. Their deep loyalties to husbands and sons, as well as their determination to prevent damage to and confiscation of property prompted many women to ignore the boundaries of prescribed female behavior." At the same time, poor women also understood that the presence of deserters in their communities made them suspect and more vulnerable to violent reprisals from Confederate officials.[109]

Long before the end of the war, the complaints of poor white women that the Confederate government had left them to starve were echoed in the complaints of slaveholding women. Letters from elite women begging their husbands to desert increasingly showed up in army camps, as did mounting criticism of the Confederate government and army. A few days before the end came in April 1865 with the surrender of Lee's army, Catherine Edmondston, a staunch supporter of the Confederate cause as well as a staunch critic of poor whites, had had enough. In 1861, before the declaration of war, as other family members wavered, some supporting secession and some declaring themselves "Unionist," Catherine Edmondston was certain about where she stood. The formerly "Glorious Union" was no more: "when it ceases to be voluntary, it "degenerates into hideous oppression. Regret it heartily, mourn over it as for a lost friend, but do not seek to enforce it; it is like galvanizing a dead body," she wrote then. She may have still believed that in 1865, but she had also lost faith in the ability of the Confederacy to protect her home. It, too, it seemed to her, had degenerated into "hideous oppression." On April 10, 1865, it appeared in the form of "Impressing agents with orders from Gen [sic] Johnston to *take all the best our team*" of mules, with the rationale that this was to prevent the animals from being "of service to the enemy." Edmondston was furious. "We think," she wrote, "that as the Government confessedly is too weak to protect us, that at least it ought not thus to deprive us of the means of making a support—say to us, '*take care of yourselves*' & let us do the best we can." She had no use for what she called "forced patriotism."[110] When elite women were forced to beg and steal to feed themselves and their children, to trust that the people they had once claimed as slaves would voluntarily continue to put bread on their tables, they reached their limits. In the years after the war they would tell a different story of steadfast patriotism, but even before then, as Drew Faust writes, their "dedication to the cause proved to be conditional."[111] The conditional had proved unsustainable.

The moment when dedication to the cause of the Confederacy seemed unsustainable arrived earlier and with greater force for poor women. On farms small and large, corn shortages exacerbated overall food shortages for all. The loss of husbands, fathers, and sons to military service, impressment of black labor by both armies, the enlistment of black soldiers in the U.S. Army, and wartime emancipation meant crop reductions not only of cotton but of corn. This, together with the loss of local markets for whatever surplus poor people were able to produce, added to the distress on the home front broadly and for the poor especially. In Randolph County, Alabama, where a third of the population of slaves had been impressed, 8,000 white people were on relief.[112] As demand increasingly outstripped supply, state and county governments struggled to provide relief to soldiers' families and feed troops in the field. Soldiers from poor families had always suffered disproportionately because their mothers and wives had little or nothing to spare to supplement army rations, a problem that worsened as military losses removed large areas from Confederate control. The grain that was produced in central Kentucky, Middle Tennessee, and the larger Mississippi valley could no longer be easily accessed, especially after the fall of Vicksburg. Along the Eastern Seaboard, Union occupation, blockades, and naval incursions further diminished the ability of the Confederacy to grow food crops and to get what was produced to soldiers and civilians in need.

Military losses likewise affected the ability of steamboat captains and railroad officials to get produce and other supplies to civilians and soldiers, even when the railroads donated their services and planters donated the grain. As the territory of the Confederacy shrank, Southern railroads controlled fewer lines amid growing demand as the superintendent of the Memphis & New Orleans Steam Packet Company explained to Confederate general Albert Sidney Johnston's quartermaster. The demand for passenger travel and transport for troops strained capacity and at every stop "a large accumulation of freight consisting of hogs, corn—flour etc." piled up. The superintendent informed the quartermaster that "in a word the entire road is *crowded* with business to an extent unprecedented in the history of any branch of it." To further complicate matters, railroads faced severe deficits in the number of engines and cars.[113]

These problems also curtailed the ability of aid groups to support troops in the field. When the Greenville Ladies Association of South Carolina attempted to send goods to the front, they learned that the president of the railroad refused any longer "to take vegetables on passenger trains, owing to the pressure of business, but offered to do by freight train." With delays notorious and disabled tracks common, produce shipped on freight trains would likely spoil before reaching its destination.[114]

As the battlefield expanded and war touched more and more areas, with plantations consequently producing less corn and other foodstuffs, the competition for food increased tensions between slaveholding and nonslaveholding white families. In some places, formerly independent subsistence-farm families were forced to rely on neighboring plantations, which themselves had less. In Talladega County, nearly 4,000 people were "wholly dependent 'for subsistence upon the labor in the valley.'" The situation was made worse by the addition of white refugees fleeing other parts of the state and from other states. "There is a great deal of discomfort here about corn," Harriott Middleton, a refugee in North Carolina, wrote in early 1864. "The soldiers passing by have eaten up every thing, and I don't know what we are to do. Farmer says he will do what he can, but he is nearly 'cleaned out.' The country is full of rumours." Divisions of Georgia and Alabama cavalry not only "cleared the country of provisions" but also impressed horses and carried away other supplies.[115] The dire situation often led to desperate means. "Only think of Mr. [Richard Henry] Lowndes locking up his gate and putting all his corn in his daughter Caroline's room, at the risk of breaking through

the ceiling," Middleton wrote. In March 1864, her family paid "fifty gold dollars for fifty bushels of corn" and hoped it would last two months. By April
corn was selling for 125 gold dollars a bushel.[116]

Many places increasingly suffered serious food shortages, but not all. Stationed near the mountains "in one of Alabama's richest valleys," Lt. Col.
Daniel F. Griffin and the men of the Thirty-Eighth Indiana Veteran Volunteer
Infantry, "much to the disgust of the inhabitants," lived better than they
had for some time "on the fat of the land," with "plentiful hogs, chickens,
geese, ducks and sweet potatoes." Griffin was unsympathetic to the plight of
the enemy women and men to whom that fat belonged. "I guess it but right
that these people should feel some of the hardships of war; they will better
appreciate peace when it does come, and be not so ready to rush widely [sic]
into the vortex again."[117] By this point, many Southerners would have agreed
with Griffin that the rush to war had been a mistake. However, few places
like the rich valley in Alabama existed anymore in the South, and suffering
was felt broadly throughout the Confederacy. Crops had not been made, and
foraging by both armies left many areas stripped of food and draft animals
amid reports of families living "on animal feed mixed with hominy."[118] Cin-
ematic portrayals notwithstanding, not only were plantations stripped; the
homes of poor white people were as well.

For planter-class women, the war played out much differently from what
they had imagined in 1861. For their poor white neighbors, it was many
times more than they bargained for. They were unprepared for the arrival
of wealthy refugees and saw slaveholding women's efforts to reconstitute
their homes in exile as threats to their world and their homes. With their
fathers, husbands, sons, and brothers, they fought the intrusions and burdens slaveholders asked them to bear. Poor women, with fewer means and
outlets to announce their suffering, were just as devastated by the "gaping
holes that the dead left behind in the lives of the living." And so were their
menfolk. In front of Petersburg in 1864, just before meeting his own death,
a Confederate officer "begged his yeoman troops to follow him on a last
suicidal charge but few leapt over the parapet with him. . . . They had given
up dying for his dreams. By 1864, the war was lost, and with it, any chance
of making reality from planters' dreams of a heroic ruling class that tri-
umphed over all opponents and subordinates."[119] The mothers and wives
of these men had helped them see just how suicidal their position was. The
women, Bynum writes, "altered the balance of power between Confederate
and Union men and their behavior sharply contradicted traditional notions
about the 'natural' timidity and deference of their sex." Throughout the

South, and not just in North Carolina, many "displayed a striking level of untraditional disorderliness."[120]

In the summer of 1861, when she was still enchanted by the idea of a pro-slavery Confederate state, Catherine Edmondston was struck by what she perceived as "the universality & the eagerness with which women entered into the struggle!" She marveled at the young ladies who "took their knitting in their carriages as they rode out & knit in the intervals and indeed *during* their visit." The "hearts of the whole population was fired," she wrote. But that was not true. Edmondston ignored the slaves and the large population of Southern white women who had neither visiting carriages nor leisure time to visit, and who were not fired with "unanimity & self abnegation" for the slaveholders' cause.[121] The women she did not think to consider as part of the "whole population" or had simply ignored had taken pleasure in seeing women of her class on the road, disheveled and distressed. And they would have their say in the new order to come.

Near the end of the war, Alisha Hopton Middleton made her way back to Charleston from Summerville, where her family had taken refuge with many other prominent Charleston families. When she first saw the flag of the United States flying over the Citadel, she later wrote, "I remember well the intense feeling of aversion with which I regarded it after the four years of loyalty, devotion, and love for the Confederate flag, which feeling was only increased by the knowledge that it was triumphant while ours was in full retreat, that it was waving over Charleston, the last place on earth over which it had any right to float." For those white women whose hearts had never been fired to support the Confederacy or who had become Unionists during the war, the U.S. flag would mean protection and help. When the Federal government decided to mount a major effort to help manage the transition of the South to a democracy, the "Refugees from Secessia" would not be ne-glected. They were the refugees referred to in the title of the new bureau, the Bureau of Refugees, Freedmen and Abandoned Lands. They were the focus of the efforts of the U.S. Sanitary Commission in North Carolina. And in the Mississippi valley, they were one of "the two classes of sufferers" the Freed-men and Union Refugees Department of the Mississippi Valley Sanitary Fair had already placed in its sight in 1864. The formerly enslaved was the other. The organization took special pains to ensure that the "Union refugees," the "thousands of homeless whites, made so by the rebellion," would not be forgotten. A committee of fourteen men and twenty-two women represent-ing the Freedmen and Union Refugees Department printed and distributed a circular calling for funds and supplies. "For the 'Union refugees,'" it stated, "it would seem that no other plea can be needed, than the simple statement that they have been deprived of all their property, and have been driven from their homes, simply because they *would not be rebels*. We have all had to make sacrifices in this war for the Union, but what possible sacrifices can we have made, whose *homes* remain to us, which deserve to be mentioned in comparison with those which have fallen to the lot of these *impoverished and homeless Union refugees.*"[122]

Chapter Three

ENSLAVED WOMEN

Making War on Antislavery Ground

Old Master and Mistress had three boys, Eli, Billy and Dock.
They had to go to war and Old Mistress sho did cry. She say they
might get killed and she might not see em any more. I wonder why
all dem white folks didn't think of that when they sold mothers away
from they chillun. I had to be sold away from my mother. Two
of her boys was badly wounded but they all come back.
—MARTHA KING, former slave

They tell me some do[,] you will take back the Proclamation, don't do
it. When you are dead and in Heaven, in a thousand years that action
of yours will make the Angels sing your praises I know it.
—HANNAH JOHNSON, mother of a black soldier

God used me as a bearer of good news to my people.
—ELIZABETH RUSSELL, former slave

Skiffs bearing them away from their masters are
constantly met with floating down the river.
—GEN. THOMAS WILLIAMS

O N JANUARY 18, 1865, another soldiers' bazaar was held in Columbia, South Carolina. Among the "cakes, jellies, cream, candies—items brought through blockade or made by ladies" offered for sale were "beautiful imported wax dolls, not more than twelve inches high, raffled for five hundred dollars, and one very large doll I heard was to raffle for two thousand," Emma LeConte, wrote. LeConte had helped organize the event and was pleased to have so many wonderful items for sale but dismayed by the prices, especially for the dolls. "'Why,' as Uncle John says," she wrote, "'one could buy a live negro baby for that.'" LeConte's comment captured a large aspect of slavery—the commodification of black people of every age.[1]

Within three months of the grand bazaar held in the South Carolina State House, the Civil War would be over, and there would be no more selling of black babies by law. That result was owed in no small measure to the part enslaved women played in the destruction of slavery and the building and consolidation of the antislavery ground on which they stood. Caddie, enslaved in Mississippi, placed her response to freedom's arrival on this ground. When she heard that Lee had surrendered, she "threw down her hoe, she marched herself up to the big house, then she looked around and found the mistress. She went over to the mistress, she flipped up her dress and told the white woman to do something. She said it mean and ugly. This is what she said: 'Kiss my ass.'"[2] Caddie's actions mark the new ground on which black women stood and the eroded ground on which white women stood, despite their claims. "The women were never conquered. We told the Yankees things the men could not, and more than one Yankee left his office 'because of the women,'" Mary Rhodes wrote.[3] She was wrong. Kate Stone, exiled in Texas, experienced conquest at the hands of black women on more than one occasion as slavery disintegrated before her face. Among the many incidents that taught Stone that Confederate women were conquered was one between her mother and an enslaved woman named Jane. Called to account for a fight with another enslaved woman, Jane arrived with a carving knife in hand and "a very surly, aggressive temper." That night, she gathered her two children and headed for the Union camp at DeSoto, Mississippi. Two weeks later, Stone and her mother received word that Jane and her children had drowned. Stone recorded this cryptic reaction: "A short space of freedom for them."[4] Stone could not have helped contemplating, however, that even the short time Jane and her children enjoyed as free people represented a revolutionary moment for them and a signal loss for her and her place in the world. The world she fought to preserve, black women fought to destroy.

Black women sympathized with the Union, fought, prayed, sacrificed, and died for it and fought for their freedom. They were soldiers' wives and refugees who labored on plantations run or leased by the Federal government; they were cooks and field hands, mothers and daughters. The vast majority remained enslaved for the duration of the war, but they made Confederate-occupied plantations, farms, towns, cities, factories, and hospitals sites of resistance. The idea that they were, or could be, forceful and influential radical abolitionists or Union women, however, did not cross the minds of most white Northerners. It formed no part of the latter's everyday vocabulary and found no place in their political ideology or notions of gender and domesticity. It was unimaginable. Nor has it found much of a place in the historiography of the Civil War or the history of women's politics.[5]

Historians have written compellingly about how our understanding of women's political history suffers when we cannot imagine that politics and political identities can take shape across kitchen tables or that "farm tables" serve as sites for political gatherings or, as Judith Giesberg writes, "the everyday sites of politics in which northern women emerged during the war" as women "challenged the ways in which the war marked gender in both time and space." Lori Ginzberg imagines women in Jefferson County, New York, sitting around their farm tables thinking about their status as women and citizens and how best to protest their political subjection and how this informed the petition they drew up in 1846 calling for equal rights. Elsa Barkley Brown has documented the presence and participation of black women at political caucuses during Reconstruction that drew on a history of antislavery politics born in slave cabins and cotton fields. Our understanding of women's politics thus suffers too when we cannot imagine political identities taking shape in slave cabins and cotton fields.[6]

Slowly but surely, the Civil War enlarged the space for the slaves' war and transformed the terms of the bargains they had been called to make. By 1865, hundreds of thousands of enslaved women had fled slavery or otherwise thrown off its yoke, and the Federal government had substantially revised its original position on slavery, black men in uniform, and the place of black women in the war. In the process, the meaning of "women in the Civil War" was transformed. As understood by most Americans in 1861, the phrase encompassed only white women. White Northerners and Southerners took for granted that white women would form the home front phalanx. They would be called on to sacrifice loved ones and everyday material comforts, keep up morale on the home front, and contribute to morale on the battlefield. In return, there would be the consolation, Virginian Judith McGuire wrote, of knowing that "our children have gone forth in a just and righteous cause."[7] The enslaved woman in Green County, Kentucky, who had been made an invalid "through the task of bearing children each year and being deprived of medical care and surgical attention," who woke her four children up in the middle of the night so that they could say goodbye to their uncles—her brothers Jacob, John, Bill, and Isaac—who were leaving to join the Union army, proclaimed her understanding of a war for a different cause and a different sort of justice and righteousness. Leaving Greensburg, the brothers made their way to Camp Nelson at Nicholasville, Kentucky, eighty-two miles to the northeast, joining the more than 1,300 African American men who enlisted there in July 1864. Jacob was deemed too old to enlist and Isaac too

young. John served in the 6th Regiment, USCC, and Bill (William) served in
the 12th Regiment, USCHA, both units organized at Camp Nelson. And one
of children who had been aroused from their pallets to send their uncles off
would become a medical doctor.[8]

Antislavery Ground

The experience of slavery formed the philosophical ground—the "pure antislavery gospel"—for the war enslaved women waged against slavery and the
nation's gender ideals.[9] It was on this ground that Louisa, enslaved in the
newly built home of a Georgia state legislator, stood. Her master's house,
she told Sherman's soldiers, "*ought* to be burned" because it had been the
scene of "so much devilment . . . whipping niggers 'most to death to make
em work to pay for it."[10] The wartime destruction of slaveholding women's
clothing, portraits, homes, china, and furniture was but a new phase in the
slaves' war.

The Civil War not only enlarged but opened to wider view existing crevices
in Southern slave society that had allowed enslaved people to gain knowledge of the larger world. Rumors of sectional conflict and the threat of war
had long seeped beyond white homes and legislative bodies to the slave
quarters. Former slave George Washington Albright, who became a member of the Mississippi senate in 1874, recalled the unsuccessful efforts of
slaveholders in Holly Springs, Mississippi, to prevent news of John Brown's
attack at Harpers Ferry from spreading among the slaves.[11] Henry C. Bruce
and other slaves in Brunswick, Missouri, followed the rise of the Republican
Party and election campaigns in the 1850s. Despite slaveholders' efforts to
refrain from discussing politics in their presence, slaves "would listen carefully to what they had heard their owners say while talking to each other on
political matters . . . and as soon as the opportunity would admit, go to the
quarters . . . and tell what they had heard the master say about the politics
of the country." They "kept posted as to what was going on, and expected
to be set free if Fremont was elected." They traveled for miles at night or on
Sundays to listen to literate slaves read stolen papers and "from mouth to
ear the news was carried from farm to farm, without the knowledge of the
masters."[12]

In the months leading up to secession, slaveholders acknowledged the failure of their campaign of vigilance to fully secure their borders and prevent
the further politicization of the enslaved. They linked rumors of slave rebellion to slaves' knowledge of the sectional crisis and tried to plug the leaks.
They moved swiftly to squash real and perceived revolts and conspiracies.

Emma and Jess Ruben were hanged for murdering their master in Fannin County, Texas. Two months before the Battle of the First Bull Run, thirty-six slaves and a white preacher were hanged in White County, Arkansas, for attempted insurrection.[13]

In New Bern, North Carolina, occupied by Federal forces from March 1862 until the end of the war and subsequently home to many people who had escaped bondage, antislavery politics surely led black women to organize the Colored Women's Union Relief Association of New Bern, officered by Mrs. Mary Ann Starkey, president; Mrs. Hannah Snell, vice president; Mrs. Sarah Ann White, secretary; Mrs. G. Richardson, assistant secretary; Mrs. Phillis Henderson, treasurer; and Mrs. L. Newton, president of the committee. They were motivated, they wrote, by a "desire to give to the world our object, plans, constitution, and our officers, for the purpose of ameliorating the miseries of our colored soldiers in their struggle for freedom, whatever may be the occasion against oppression."[14] We can imagine these women sitting around the kitchen table in the home of Mary Ann Starkey and strategizing as they considered their status as former slaves and their future as free women, mothers, and potential citizens. Adopting the language of rights, they declared their determination to play a role in the struggle for freedom and "against oppression." In ways large and small, black women joined their antislavery politics to the nation's larger political goals and their own emancipatory ones using familiar democratic discourse.

The closer war came, the closer slaves listened and read. Liza Strickland recalled first hearing the question of emancipation connected to the sectional conflict in the winter before the war began. It was then, she said, that black people in her community began predicting war.[15] The literacy of a few enslaved people played a critical role in keeping those who had not been taught to read informed about the war. Susie King Taylor "had been reading so much about the 'Yankees'" it made her "very anxious to see them."[16] Chana Littlejohn and the other enslaved people on Peter Mitchell's plantation relied on one of their own, Isabella, to keep them informed about the progress of the war. Minnie Davis's mother stole "newspapers and read up about the war, and she kept the other slaves posted as to how the war was progressing."[17] Like enslaved men, enslaved women adopted illicit and ingenious means to learn to read and write. Mary Anne Patterson listened to the men who counted and weighed the cotton she carried to the wagon. "Pretty soon," she stated, "I could of [have] counted my own cotton."[18] Hanna Fambro testified that on the plantation near Macon, Georgia, where she was enslaved, enslaved people knew all about the war because one of them regularly stole the overseer's paper and read the war news to the rest.

They believed the war would set them free. She was just a child at the time, but her memories were vivid. So too were the memories of an ex-slave from central Georgia who followed Sherman's army to Savannah. "We colored chaps knew when the war commence, though we didn't clearly understand what it was all about, but occasionally we got a hint from the older slaves, who had better opportunities for getting news, that somehow, we were the cause of the misunderstanding—the 'unpleasantness.'"[19]

Black religious and fraternal institutions were also important sources of knowledge and support during the war as they had been in the antebellum era. As one former slave recalled, "The negro preachers preached freedom into our ears and our old men and women prophesied about it." Cindy Mitchell was one of the prophesying preachers. She had her own church, and years after the war a hundred families followed her ministry to a new location.[20] In some areas, in the Upper South border states especially but also in parts of the Deep South, fraternal organizations continued to support fugitive slaves during the war. The black Masonic lodge at Portland, Kentucky, an important institutional resource on the Underground Railroad, continued to help black people escape slavery and get to freedom. Union soldiers also sometimes helped. Mattie Jackson recalled that she and her mother, enslaved in Missouri, kept up with news of the war through newspapers, some of which came by way of Union soldiers who "took much delight in tossing a paper over the fence to us."[21]

Knowledge about the war sometimes came from the highest authorities in the Confederate government. When away from home, Confederate vice president Alexander Stephens left his enslaved body servant, Henry Stephens, in charge of his Crawfordsville, Georgia, house. Henry Stephens passed on news he gleaned from Alexander Stephens's correspondence and conversations. The Confederate vice president also sometimes spoke directly to the enslaved people, telling them what was going on militarily and politically.[22] Perhaps Stephens's faith that slavery was black people's "natural and normal condition," his faith that the "cornerstone" of the Confederacy, its founding principle, rested on "the great truth that the negro is not equal to the white man," as he stated in his famous speech at Savannah in March 1861, encouraged his recklessness. It was a common mistake, one that slaveholding women also made.

Although slavery had allowed enslaved women but cramped room to breathe, in that narrow space they created and nurtured family and community and an antislavery politics that prepared them to move forcefully in their own defense when war came. The young girl tried and sold for burning down the home of a woman who held her in bondage and the mother who had "four babies killed within her by whipping, one of which had its eye cut out, another its leg broken," had developed an antislavery politics through their lived experiences.[23] So had Susanna, who stood her ground when her master threatened to shoot her pigs. She reminded him that it was only because of the pigs that she had salt and winter shoes for her children.[24] With each act of resistance (and obedience) before the war, with each step they took to get to freedom in the North, black people gave lie to the proslavery argument.[25] In running away, working extra hours to supplement the meager rations and clothing slaveholders supplied, nurturing their children and teaching them about the character of slaveholders, fighting for their homes and families even when they knew could be casually torn apart, pleading from the auction block to keep their families intact, or turning a handkerchief into an elaborate turban, enslaved people turned the policed and cramped quarters of the slave community into spaces of resistance and life. Sometimes this required making the most repulsive of bargains.

On the auction block, Jeffrey, Chattel No. 319 in the auction catalog, sought to make a bargain only a person enslaved could in any way see in a favorable light. The woman he loved, Dorcas, Chattel No. 278, was also on the auction block, and Jeffrey beseeched the man who had just purchased him to buy Dorcas as well. "I loves Dorcas," and she loved him, he proclaimed. Jeffrey knew, however, that the love the couple shared would not be enough to persuade the buyer to keep them together, so he offered a slave's bargain, vowing that if allowed to stay together, they would be "good" slaves and produce "healthy and strong" children. But understanding that the promise of Dorcas's tractability and reproductive capacity, as important as it was, might not be enough, Jeffrey spoke also to her productive capacity, a key factor in the market's evaluation of her value. Dorcas was a "prime woman," indeed, an "A1 woman," tall and long-limbed, strong and healthy. Hoping to convince his new master to keep his family together, Jeffrey in effect sought to help auction his family with the promise of a profitable return to the would-be buyer. In the end, his pleas went unanswered. Jeffrey and Dorcas were sold separately.

Elisha, Chattel No. 5, similarly proffered a slave's bargain in the hope of keeping his family together. As he and his wife, Molly, Chattel No. 6, and their children, Israel and Vardy, Chattels No. 7 and No. 8, waited their turn to be sold, Elisha made his plea in market terms. He was a prime rice hand and experienced carpenter, a "good" slave, he stated, and Molly, a first-rate rice hand. Like Jeffrey, he called on his wife and children to step forward to help facilitate their sale as a family unit. His wife came forward "with her hands crossed on her bosom" perhaps hoping that this would provide some protection against the assault on her body and humanity that was about to take place, made a "quick, short curtsy," and stood "mute." Elisha talked "all the faster," a reporter for the *New York Tribune* wrote, as he performed the unspeakable, calling on his wife and children to help him keep their family together. He asked Molly to show her "good arm," still capable of doing a "heap of work." He asked her to show her teeth, how regular and sound they were, to prove that she was still a "young gal yet." He called on his son, Israel, to "'walk aroun' an' let the gen'lm'n see how spry you be.' Then, pointing to the three-year-old girl who stood with her chubby hand to her mouth, holding on to her Mother's dress and uncertain what to make of the strange scene," he promised that while Vardy was only a small child, she would make a "prima gal by and by." There they stood, an enslaved family, marketed as a "'fus rate bargain.'" Like Jeffrey, Elisha too failed to convince a buyer that keeping his family together was a good bargain.[26]

Jeffrey and Elisha made their appeals at the widely publicized 1859 auction of 436 of Pierce Butler's slaves.[27] In his coverage of the event, Mortimer Thomson of the *New York Tribune* wrote that Elisha "made no appeal to the feelings of the buyer; he rested no hope on his charity and kindness, but strove only to show how well worth his dollars were the bone and blood he was entreating him to buy."[28] Like thousands before them, Jeffrey and Elisha played the part of "information broker" in an effort to intervene in the sale and the value of their own bodies and those of their families. Such bargains were part and parcel of the "obscenity of the slave market" that forced people "to perform their own commodification."[29] By 1859, such scenes were a staple of the American landscape. Many decades before, John Randolph of Roanoke, Virginia, wrote that the greatest orator he had ever heard was a slave mother, "and her rostrum was the auction block."[30]

The auction block underwrote the purchase of pianos, wedding dresses, the education of slaveholding women and men, tours of Europe, northern vacations, the purchase of vacation homes, gifts to white children, marriage presents, and the maintenance of the slave society of the South generally. As one former slave testified, slaveholders had "all our labor for their own use and get rich on it and they say we are lazy and can't take care of ourselves," which he saw as patently "not just."[31] As important, the auction block symbolized and articulated the politicization and militarization of black and white homes in the South. The more numerous sales that took place on a smaller scale in the yards and parlors of big houses, in small-town courthouse yards, and on the byways of Southern roads were but small-scale manifestations of the same phenomenon, in which women no less than men were buyers and sellers.[32]

As enslaved women built upon and extended the prewar struggles, they carved out new arenas of struggle and spaces for themselves on the side of Union and freedom. This work rested in no small measure on the memory of past struggles and the physical and psychological violence they had endured. In North Carolina, the memory of Lissa Lawson's pain and her death endured into the twentieth century. On the auction block Lawson pleaded with the man who bought her and her husband, Cleve Lawson, to also buy their baby daughter. He refused. There was no profit to be gained in buying a baby, he said. Lissa Lawson's grandson—the child of the baby she was forced to leave behind—was raised by his aunt and carried his grandmother's story into freedom. In the 1930s, Dave Lawson told an interviewer how "Lissa cut up powerful" when forced to leave her baby behind and how Drew Norwood, her new master, laughed and said "he would give her a puppy" from among the plentiful hounds on the plantation to replace the child she would be forced to leave. The story she was about to hear, Dave Lawson told the interviewer, was "no nice tale." It was not "nice," he repeated, but it was true. The first time he heard it, he "didn't sleep none for a week," he said. The story ended with the death of his grandparents and their master. One day Lissa's husband saw Norwood watching her "slender swayin' body" in the field, her "smooth warm brown skin, with a 'lustful look in his eyes.'" The concupiscence Cleve Lawson thought he saw, however, was not sexual desire but lust for the profit his wife could fetch on the auction block. When Norwood told Lissa to get ready to go to South Boston to be sold, her husband begged him to change his mind, but Norwood would not be moved. Determined not to lose his wife, Cleve hatched a plan to kill Norwood. He tied him up and he and Lissa, according to the story, poured boiling hot water down his throat until he died. They did not run but waited for the punishment sure to come. They were hanged side by side under the oak tree in the yard of their cabin.[33]

Victoria Perry's antislavery politics were shaped by the memory of the beatings her mother, Rosanna Kelly, endured at the hands of Bert Mabin. Perry's mother, who often wept and prayed at night, never lost faith that she and her children would be free one day, for "the Good Lord won't let this thing go on all the time." Those prayers seemed to be answered when Union soldiers finally arrived in Newberry, South Carolina, near the close of the war.[34] Another woman, Chloe Ann, had fought slaveholders and beaten back slave-catching dogs. She had seen all but two of her children sold, all of them while she was away in the fields. Each time her master sold one of the children, her daughter recalled, she would "raise a ruckus." At other times, she would just cry, knowing how powerless she was against "the slavery law."

Like Rosanna Kelly, Chloe Ann believed the slavery law would end—the "time was comin." She prayed that slavery would be destroyed before she died, but she did not wait quietly. In the meantime, she continued "cussin and fightin and rarin."[35] Fannie Moore's mother had also long prayed for the deliverance of her children from a world where they were recognized no "more than effen dey was a dog" and believed her prayers had been answered when freedom came. Moore's mother was whipped more for fighting the overseer when he beat her children than for anything else. Celia Robinson's mother, given a fifteen-minute break to leave the cotton field and return to the quarters to nurse her infant, knew she could not meet the deadline and would just go somewhere to wait out the time and pray that her baby would die.[36]

Wartime

On the new ground of war, the memory of past struggles and the sometimes-damnable bargains took concrete shape in slaves' wartime rebellion. It sat with Chloe "playing away like the very Devil" on the piano in a slaveholder's home and moved through the bodies of the "two damsels upstairs dancing away famously." This was the scene that confronted Henry Ravenel when he returned on a secret trip to his plantation to bring out more of his slaves.[37] He was clearly riveted by the performance, which must have triggered memories for him as well. Perhaps Chloe and dancing damsels did have the devil in them. We can well imagine them as silent observers to the occasions when the piano had entertained slaveholders, understanding how their labor had paid for it and other luxuries. The performance Henry Ravenel came upon, like others of its kind, was its own fire bell in the night. When enslaved people destroyed the furnishings in planter homes or repurposed them, they also did so in recognition of how their labor had made possible the luxuries slaveholders enjoyed. On Daniel Pope's plantation, Rina and the other Pope slaves had redistribution in mind when they seized boards from the plantation house to improve their living conditions. They used the boards as flooring for their cabins—floors previously consisting of sand and lime—and to build lofts for sleeping and storage.[38]

Enslaved women put their antislavery politics to work in many ways. In South Carolina, they stood guard at night over a supply of cotton to prevent their master from burning it to keep it from falling into the hands of the Federal government. The United States labeled the cotton abandoned property, but the women and men who had labored to produce it saw it as *their* property, the hard-won return of their labor whose proceeds would enable them to buy clothes, shoes, and salt.[39] That their stand undermined the Confederate effort was an added benefit. At St. Andrews Bay, Florida, enslaved women joined in helping the Union army destroy the extensive saltworks that lined the bay, including 27 buildings, 22 large steamers, and 200 kettles in the West Bay alone.[40] In the Mississippi valley, they stood with their husbands and fathers, who, with muskets aimed "at their breasts," resisted Confederate orders to cut down trees to block creeks and rivers and thereby impede the Union effort. They fled to Union lines despite death threats, fighting slaveholders' efforts to carry them into the interior while sending their husbands and sons to work on Confederate fortifications.[41]

Enslaved women's antislavery politics greeted Union military forces at every turn. Wherever Union navy vessels and armies appeared, women and children, increasingly without the company of husbands and fathers, greeted them praying for refuge. Initially, they were more often turned away or ignored than not, but the unrelenting exodus from plantations eventually forced military commanders to assist in transporting them to freedom and establishing refugee camps. During the siege of Fort Hudson, for example, the navy sent a steamer to rescue an estimated 1,200 men, women, and children stranded on the banks of the Mississippi River.[42] Enslaved women like Julie rejected the plea of the woman who held her as a slave to stay when Union gunboats appeared at their plantation on the Mississippi River, leaving with other slaves and taking her bed and other belongings with her. Once safely on a Union gunboat, they gave three cheers, "loud and long and strong," one for the men who had rescued them, one for Yankee soldiers, and one for the U.S. government.[43] As Union forces moved deeper into the Confederate interior, into areas where enslaved people had been hemmed in by the presence of Confederate guerrillas (or overly eager black drivers like the one who demanded the return of four slaves who had taken refuge on a Union gunboat), and news spread of the Emancipation Proclamation, more and more slaves moved to claim their freedom.[44]

When President Lincoln finally approved the enlistment of black soldiers, he secured in the bargain an undrafted, unwanted army of black women and children who shored up the antislavery ground that would transform the war for union that the United States set out to fight into a war for emancipation as well. On the battlefield and in Union lines, the former slaves proved their loyalty to the flag in the face of opposition from Union soldiers and officers. "Displays of loyalty by blacks were frowned upon," one sympathetic officer testified. "The whole economy of the post commanders," which he believed was approved from the top by the commanding officer, "was to discourage freedom and nationality," including flying the U.S. flag on the Fourth of

July.[45] Black people resisted at every turn. "You can easily understand that we watched the progress of the war with deepest concern, for we understood, in a vague way, that our friends at the North were doing battle for us, or, at least, were on our side—and all our sympathies were with them," a former slave who followed Sherman to freedom testified.[46]

Decades after the war, Elizabeth Russell recalled with pride her role in carrying information to other slaves. "I was very small at the time of the Civil War," she stated, "yet I served my people as a secret service agent." Russell used her position as a nurse to eavesdrop. Pretending to be asleep, she listened for news of the outcome of battles and the progress of the struggle for emancipation, and "when word came that the north had won and the slaves were free," she recalled with utter clarity, "it was I who carried the news to the hundreds of slaves in our section, having crawled to my mother's cabin to give the news. . . . God used me as a bearer of good news to my people."[47] Similarly, Caroline Richardson's mother used her position as a cook in the big house to pass on "war talk."[48] In Missouri, slaves met secretly to discuss "what they had heard about the latest battle, and what Mr. Lincoln had said, and the chances of their freedom, for they understood the war to be for their freedom solely, and prayed earnestly for the success of the union cause. When news came that a battle was fought and won by Union troops, they rejoiced and were correspondingly depressed when they saw slaveholders rejoicing 'for they knew the cause thereof.'"[49] In Mississippi, as runners for "the 4-Ls—Lincoln's Legal Loyal League," they carried word of the Emancipation Proclamation from plantation to plantation, working in secrecy using "knocks, and signs and passwords" and holding small meetings in slave cabins.[50]

Slaveholders tried to prevent the flow of information from within the plantation household to the enemy, a difficult task under the best of circumstances. It was easy to castigate the indiscretion of those who talked openly, "cheek by jowl," in the presence of slaves, wrote Catherine Edmondston, but in the context of open warfare, it was much harder to suppress such talk. In one case, evidence of the cracks in slaveholders' communications came from an unlikely source. In an open letter to the "Gentlemen of Yorktown" on July 4, 1861, an enslaved man who signed himself "C. R. B." alerted slaveholders to the ease by which enslaved people learned details of the war and the means they were using to escape to Fort Monroe. He cautioned slaveholders to make sure that neither the letter nor its contents find their way into the hands of their "wives nor servants," and he advised them to "burn this letter up" after reading it.[51] Slave resistance—the burning of planter homes, murders, conspiracies, and flight—confirmed how much enslaved people knew and understood about the conflict and put their experience as "knowledge brokers" to new use. Keeping their ears to the wind also allowed them to evade slaveholders' attempts to remove them to the interior. With rumors circulating that some Missouri slaveholders planned to move their slaves deeper into the South, two couples gathered their children in a wagon and headed across the border to the free state of Iowa.[52] Enslaved women made their escape during forced marches to the interior. They "called it refugee-ing us," Dicy Windfield stated of the 200-mile trek from Mississippi to the interior of Alabama she and other enslaved people from the Robinson plantation made. Black women laundresses for Confederate officers were well positioned to obtain and pass on information about the war, as John Scott, a free black man from Charlottesville, Virginia, who hired out as an officer's servant in the Mexican War and the Civil War on the Confederate side, learned.[53]

For most slaves, learning what the war meant for them was not easy. They had to assess sometimes conflicting bodies of information, much of it de-signed to convince them that Northerners posed a greater threat to their families and communities than slaveholders did.[54] They were told that Northern soldiers would sell them to faraway lands or kill them. As rumors of war circulated, Jane Williams recalled being unsure about its "real meanin or what to expect" for they were told "all kinds o things." Patsy Mitchner, like many slave children, was frightened enough to hide when the Yankees came.[55] Susie King Taylor recalled hearing similar stories about the Yankees, but her grandmother told her they were patently false, a lesson her parents reinforced. The Yankees were coming to free them and they were praying for the soldiers' success, her parents said.[56] The man who would come to be known as the Great Emancipator was perhaps the greatest enigma. Rumor had it, former slave Edward Jones stated, that the president was a black man and the son of a queen.[57]

For enslaved people less sure of what the war meant for their lives, the behavior of slaveholding women and men, and the deadly dispensations that mark all wars, increasingly clarified matters. Leaving for war, masters called on them to remain loyal. Left alone to manage plantations, jittery slaveholding women suspected plots to take their lives. In the areas occu-pied by Union forces at the beginning of the war, slaveholders fled. Others hid to avoid going to war and asked the enslaved to assist and slip them food. Rachel's master made this request of her, and she apparently did help hide him from Union forces for several months during which time he slept in his house at night and hid in the woods during the day.[58] Each time slave-holders enlisted black people in their efforts to hide from Union soldiers or Confederate enlistment officers or to hide their valuables (sometimes in slave cabins or on the bodies of slave women), they gave up a measure of their aura of invincibility, even when black people kept their secrets. During and after the war, more than a few slaveholders bemoaned the trust they had put in the enslaved.[59]

Black people watched as slaveholding men proudly and confidently marched off to war only to return with crippling injuries, in coffins, or not at all. But they did more than watch; they carefully noted the discrepancy between the slaveholders' declarations of easy victories to come and clear evidence to the contrary. Annie Osborne's brother told her that when the cannons stopped booming, they would be free from their master's beatings.[60] The woman who held Jennie Webb in bondage sent four sons to fight for the Confederacy. As they prepared to leave, the young men asked Webb and the other slaves to take care of their mother and boasted that they would whip the "Yankees hell can scorch a feather." But it was not long before one of the sons returned "in his coffin wid his guns," Webb recalled. Black people remembered how "at the beginning of the war . . . the white folks said that it would not last long and that in the first year of the war they said one southern soldier could whup three Yankee soldiers, but after a while they quit their braggin." Alfred Sligh's master left for the war in similarly jovial spirits in 1861 and over the next two years, Sligh heard many Confederate soldiers brag that they would not stop "fightin til all de damn-Yankees am dead." Thereafter, Sligh noted, "I see more and more of de damn-Yankees."[61]

Black women were not surprised when nonslaveholding white men hid in the bays and woodland pits to avoid conscription into the Confederate army. Jane Lee remembered the woods being full of runaway slaves and deserters from the Confederate army. One of these men held Lulu Wilson in bondage. She remembered that he had sold her mother's children one by one. Now he lay out in the woods and swamps to avoid conscription, and Wilson witnessed his capture by Confederate forces. She saw him taken away in a wagon full of other white men accused of trying to avoid the draft. Some of them, she later heard, did not make it far but were shot in the river bottoms behind the plantation. The Southern social order broke apart as spectacularly when slaves witnessed the execution of Confederate deserters, as on a Mississippi plantation where Confederate general Nathan B. Forrest ordered the execution by firing squad of three Confederate soldiers who refused to fight anymore. Although such executions were designed to deter other potential deserters, for the enslaved, they served as another lesson in the political and social cleavages sundering white Southern society.[62]

Confederate soldiers, happy to be relieved of the burden of cooking and washing, who quietly allowed fugitive slaves—women and men, girls and boys—to remain in or around army camps, aided the slaves' war no less than slaveholders who hid slaves from Union forces and Confederate impressment agents.[63] Every enslaved person in an officer's tent, building a fortification, cooking a private's meal, or cleaning a hospital ward was one less growing food, a point the governor of Florida made candidly in a letter to the Confederate secretary of war: "The maintenance of our armies in the field—of the families of those in Military Service—of the civil Government of the Confederate States and the States separately—in a word, not only the liberty, but the lives of the people of the State, depend upon Agricultural labor."[64] Increasingly, due to the enlistment of black men as soldiers, sailors, and laborers in the U.S. Army and Navy and Confederate conscription of slave labor, that burden fell on enslaved women in the most fiercely contested areas. By March 1865, all but thirty of the enslaved people owned by Virginia planter Thomas L. Preston had escaped; all of those remaining were women and children.[66]

With Federal forces closing in on Alexandria, Judith McGuire prepared to take up the life of a refugee and leave her home in the care of her slaves. Trusting in their promises to be faithful, she turned over the keys, the symbol of her authority over the plantation household, to her cook.[66] Mary Ann Lamar Cobb of Athens, Georgia, left her home in the hands of Aggie, Ben, and Vickey when she flew to the safety of her father's plantation near Macon. They were on their own, she told them, and would to "have to buy their meal and wood," and "take care of the house and lot—and cow and calf and make me a garden in the spring." Her seeming confidence that they would have no problem being on their own was born of past experience. Aggie, an experienced seamstress, was to continue to take in sewing. Cobb expected Ben to work out by the day and Vickey to hire out as a washerwoman.[67] Under such conditions, the everyday power of slaveholders crumbled. Aggie, Vickey, and Ben were no doubt pleased by the turn of events that allowed them to remain among kin and friends in the black community of Athens and for the first time in their lives keep all of the wages they earned. Unlike the hundreds of thousands of slaves who became fugitives in order to secure their freedom, they could remain on familiar ground.

Flight

The passage of the 1850 Fugitive Slave Act and the growing conflict on the borders between slave states and free states led to an escalation in the flight of slaves. As R. J. M. Blackett writes, escapes "were acts of dispossession as

well as profound political statements on the nature and meaning of freedom." News of secession and the impending conflict set more slaves in flight
amid rumors of insurrection.[68] The Civil War not only provided new opportunities, fueling flight, but also provided new destinations. From the first
months of the war, slaveholders found themselves spending a great deal
of time and resources tracking down and punishing fugitive slaves. In November 1861, sixteen-year-old Emma Sams sought information on whether a
group of runaways had "been hung yet."[69]

Mary Barbour was a child when she fled slavery with her family during the
war. Her memory of freedom's arrival would be forever tied to the bushes that
slapped her legs, the wind singing in the trees, and fear of the darkness as
the family made its way to a wagon her father had hidden at a distance from
their cabin. Traveling at night and hiding in the woods during the day, they
finally made it to the Union-occupied town of New Bern, North Carolina.[70]
The mother who made her way at night through the marshes of South Carolina with her two children while hiding during the day also carried into freedom a particular memory of the making of freedom. She had determined to
leave after the man who held her and her children in bondage whipped her
oldest son who he believed planned to run to Union lines.[71] Maria arrived
in Union-held territory at Jacksonville, Florida, having traveled over eighty
miles on foot. Maria had been enslaved in Georgia and first fled in December
1864, leaving her children in the care of her sister. She spent the winter in the
swamp until she finally found a way to get them. As she told her story to Dr.
Esther Hawks, a white woman who had joined her husband as a missionary
in the Sea Islands in the fall of 1862 and went with the army to Florida, she
had braved creeks swollen with rain, "with her little ones clinging to her
neck—her only guide being a paper given her by a colored man with a map
of the road marked out on it by himself—and with this she traversed over
eighty miles of strange country, only losing the road once, and that in trying
to avoid encountering some people." Then there was the enslaved woman
who carried her ten children into Union lines, having concluded that her
husband, a free black man, had made a wrong turn in deciding to side with
the Confederacy. When the opportunity came to leave with U.S. soldiers, she
took it, "leaving him to go his way."[72] Dolly was the only one of the people
Louis Manigault owned who permanently escaped Gowrie Plantation. That
she did so in the more favorable context of the Civil War is instructive and
her example apparently encouraged others. Manigault's overseer feared that
Rose would be among them, prompting a forceful response from Manigault.
"Unless you manage Rose," he wrote, "you need not expect any servant will

stay with you, give her the devil." But when Jenny threatened to run away if separated from her child, Manigault backed off.[73]

Hundreds of thousands of enslaved women made the unauthorized declaration that the Union army and its geographical and political lines of authority were places both of refuge and retribution. Grace Bland's husband had no sooner made his escape and enlisted in the Union army than she began making her own plans to flee with the couple's two children who remained with her. She and another enslaved woman "hired two slave men to build a boat" to make their escape. Together the women secured the lumber to make the boat and carried it four miles on trips during the night. They purchased the tar and hemp to caulk the boat and caulked it themselves. But on the night they planned to leave they discovered that the men they had trusted to help build the boat had used it to make their own escape, leaving them to make the dangerous journey back through Confederate pickets to the plantation. Fortunately for Bland, her husband was simultaneously making plans to rescue his family and had secured permission from the captain of his regiment to recross the river from Liverpool Point, Maryland, to Virginia to rescue them. The captain thought Dennis Bland "mad" but consented and gave "notice of the fact to the commander of the flotilla, to prevent his being fired upon by the gunboats." Bland succeeded, bringing his wife, two children, two other young girls, and a man to the safety of Union lines.[74]

Writing in exile from Beaumont, her home in the North Carolina mountains, Mary Elliott Johnstone was struck by the success of the Union raid led by Harriet Tubman on the Combahee Ferry back in the South Carolina lowcountry. It was not just the raid but learning that "the negroes were packed up ready to leave" that rattled her. "I feel extremely uneasy about all of your people," she wrote her father. "I do not think Jacob's faithfulness will prevent a stampede from Social Hall—and the success at [Combahee] will only renew the wish of the Oak lawn darkies to test freedom for themselves." She thought they must either be removed or sold, stressing to her father that he must not be tempted to do otherwise by the "promise of a crop." At any rate, she suggested, there was the promise of being able to buy less "demoralized" slaves after the war: "If Ralphie sold his people now he might after the war buy some not demoralized—he will think me very officious, however—but while there are people with money to buy I should take advantage of it."[75]

From the upper riverways of Virginia to the Mississippi valley and beyond, enslaved women took the arrival of Union gunboats and armies as a signal for their departure, often to learn that Union lines were not safe or free spaces. They learned that there were Union commanders and soldiers who resented their presence. They learned that a place of safety one day could be a place of danger the next as military lines shifted or became nothing more than the campfire ashes and trash of an army on the move. Edmund Ruffin exulted in the defeat of his slaves who had taken advantage of nearby Union lines to defy his authority and then faced a precarious situation when the Union forces left. With Union soldiers nearby, enslaved people on Ruffin's plantation had moved back and forth between the plantation and the Union camp "at will supposing that the condition of things all around them was general, & Yankee domination completely established throughout," Ruffin wrote, only to be "astonished at the sudden flight & disappearance of their Yankee friends & protectors." With the departure of Union forces, Ruffin wrote, the people returned to "general & complete, if not willing acquies-cence" with the promise of "amnesty . . . for past insubordination." He told them that "in consideration of their former good conduct up to the recent ac-tion, & to their having been deluded & imposed upon by the false statements & false promises of the Yankees, that all past conduct on this score would be overlooked & forgiven" and asked then to "communicate this promise to those who had absconded." Any future such offense, Ruffin made clear, would result in the sale of the offenders.[76]

Ruffin's offer of amnesty, however, proved to be anything but. As pun-ishment for their "misconduct," and collaboration with Union soldiers who they "had accepted and welcomed as friends and guides," Ruffin and his neighbors ordered a reduction in food allowances.[77] The redeployment of Union forces thus could leave slaves more vulnerable to retaliation and give weight to slaveholders' narrative that Union lines were not the places of safety black people supposed them to be. But Ruffin's offer of amnesty stands out for another reason: like many slaveholders, he blamed black re-sistance on outside forces, on the slaves having been "deluded & imposed upon." Black people knew better and could see in Ruffin's choice of words his own delusion.

William Elliott was in bed when he got word that all of his trusted "prime hands," including the women, at his Oak Lawn Plantation "had gone off to the Yankees!" Gathering his son and neighbors, Elliott sought assistance from a nearby Confederate military encampment, where he obtained the loan of a detachment of Confederate cavalry. Led by his son, Capt. Ralph Elliott, the force "arrest[ed] a stampede of negroes from Oak lawn on their way to the Yankees" that included "Walley's whole family (except old Wal-ley)" and to William Elliott's indignation, "Master Bob, with his wife and her brother!" Following their arrest, Elliott had them all whipped and handcuffed and sent two of the men to the Charleston workhouse to be sold. "The rest are being watched and chained at night until the police of the river can be secured as to leave us at liberty to release them," he wrote. Elliott's efforts also partially aborted the plans of the slaves on Edward Barnwell's neighboring plantation, who were said to be part of a larger conspiracy that involved using Barnwell's river flats to make their getaway. Only five managed to escape on the flats. "You will perceive by this that our negroes are utterly demoralized," Elliott concluded, adopting the familiar language of paternalism.[78] Elliott believed that a police state was more necessary than ever before to protect slave property, the white public good, and the Confederate state project.

> Now these negroes are the main sources of our wealth, and the product of their labor is the only fund from which the Confederate States can hope to support the war, and pay the interest of our public debt, immense and still accumulating. More than this, every able bodied negro man who is allowed to go over to the Enemy is not only a valuable producer abstracted from us—but from the unprincipled conduct of our malignant and unscrupulous foe—becomes a recruit in his ranks—and is armed to cut the throat of his former master. It seems to me therefore a matter of life and death—and worth some risk and some actual loss—to prevent so great a calamity.[79]

Slaveholders worried as much about the enslaved who did not flee but remained on the plantations as spies, exposing traitors to the United States. Some slaves had the satisfaction of seeing slaveholding men roused from their beds and arrested or the property of slaveholding women confiscated and the women exiled.[80] The work of black spies led to the arrest of two Maryland white women charged with giving aid and comfort to Confederate forces.[81] Enslaved women were important conduits of information. They used their knowledge of local geography and access to inside information to pass on information about Confederate troop movement, the identities of rebels in Union lines, and the location of valuable military supplies and plantations flush with food crops. The military intelligence that fugitive slave men passed on to Union officers often originated with enslaved women who labored in plantation households. When Gen. Robert E. Lee took tea at the home of a Gloucester County, Virginia, slaveholder, news of his visit and the number of troops in his command was in the hands of Union officers within hours. Overhearing the intelligence Lee confided to the white woman of the home, enslaved people in the household passed it on to a formerly enslaved man who carried it to Union lines. The information confirmed prior intelligence from a Confederate deserter of a planned attack.[82] The slave is "the spy in every household of the enemy," George E. Stephens, an African American correspondent for the New York *Anglo-American*, wrote. "He conveys from every point the information without which the military operations of the United States would be ineffective."[83] The enlistment of black men into the Union army and navy and the quickening of Confederate impressment of slave laborers placed more of the work of making freedom onto the shoulders of black women, who shielded Union soldiers separated from their armies or escaped from Confederate prisons in their cabins, fed them, gave them clothing to disguise themselves and passed intelligence to Union commanders.

In Union Lines

The Civil War provided the space for black women to adapt long-standing strategies of resistance to the revolutionary goal of emancipation. As a result, their lives and the aims and conduct of the war were radically transformed. Yet while their own sense of the war's politics and its possibilities was important, their ability to make freedom more than a claim depended greatly on circumstances of geography, Federal and Confederate policies, the movement of armies, the personal beliefs and attitudes of officers and soldiers, and the actions of slaveholders. These broader circumstances determined, to an important extent, the opportunities available to them to put their weight on the side of freedom and the Union, but their refusal to sit on the sidelines was the critical factor that forced the Union to revise Federal policies that at first paid them no mind.

Enslaved women could not officially take up arms, but in fleeing to Union lines, offering assistance to Union forces, refusing or rendering with the greatest reluctance and inefficiency labor essential to the Confederate cause, and taking up arms as partisans, they changed the gendered and racial dynamics of the war. Having begun their wartime quest for freedom in the most disadvantaged position, they resisted the notion that their exclusion from Union lines was a matter of firm and irreversible policy and worked to see that policy reversed. Changes in Federal policy did not change general Northern opinion that black women refugees were, at best, a nuisance. It did not guarantee fair treatment. Unlike their husbands, fathers, and sons, they could not easily make claims to Federal protection under the provisions of the First Confiscation Act of August 1861, which sought to undermine the ability of the Confederate government to use black men as laborers on fortifications and for other noncombat duties. The measure's gendered notion of what constituted labor in support of the enemy excluded the labor of enslaved women that produced war matériel in the form of clothing and food crops. The Second Confiscation Act of July 1862 declaring slaves of disloyal masters free still offered but a narrow path for black women's emancipation.

While neither the First nor the Second Confiscation Act directly addressed the status of enslaved women, the Militia Act of July 1862 explicitly granted freedom to the wives and children of men employed as military laborers.[84] Yet even the Militia Act represented but a partial victory. It was not applied to African American women in any meaningful way by either officials in Washington or military commanders in the field. These racially gendered Federal policies were obstacles to black women's freedom and, ultimately, a detriment to the Union's ability to prosecute the war. Enslaved women's labor in the fields, in white homes, at salt mines, in Confederate hospitals, and as producers of Confederate war matériel in the form of clothing and food were vital to the Confederacy's ability to wage war. Unlike strong fortifications, the production of war matériel in the form of food and clothing could not stop bullets or armies, but without them Confederate armies were much less ready.[85] The impact was evident during the Vicksburg campaign. "There will be no more planting in this region for a long time to come," Rear Adm. David Porter wrote in March 1863. "The able-bodied negroes left with our army, carrying all the stores left by their masters—for whom they showed little affection—for harder times."[86]

Even after the Federal government began to consider more carefully how the labor of enslaved women enhanced the Confederate effort on the home front and on the battlefield, black men remained the focus of its attention. This was the message Gen. Henry W. Halleck sent to Gen. U. S. Grant in the Department of the Tennessee. "It is the policy of the government," he wrote, "to withdraw from the enemy as much productive labor as possible. So long as the rebels retain and employ their slaves in producing grains, &c, they can employ all the whites in the field." By "productive labor," Halleck clearly did not have in mind the labor of enslaved women. He was concerned, he explained, with labor that which could be used "as a military force for the defence of forts, depts, &c." Adm. David D. Porter concurred: "only single men are wanted," he wrote in November 1862.[87]

The interpretation of Federal policy that Halleck proffered to his commanders in the field was reiterated in the policies that undergird black recruitment efforts. One of the first official acts of Adj. Gen. Lorenzo Thomas, sent to put some teeth in the effort to recruit and organize black troops in the upper Mississippi valley, addressed black women and children refugees. Special Order No. 45 advised that "all children and females of Negro Descent who may hereafter be desirous of seeking refuge within the lines of the United States troops, be advised to remain on the plantations or elsewhere where they have been heretofore in a state of servitude, provided such places be under the control of the Federal troops."[88] Such policies rid the government of responsibility for black women and children refugees and simultaneously placated Unionist slaveholders in the Mississippi valley. Thomas justified the policy on the grounds of "expediency," a rationale that Union commanders increasingly resorted to, but his call for black women and children to return to the plantations from which they had fled was not unproblematic. It refused black women's demands for protection and encouraged Union commanders who preferred to keep their lines closed to black women and children. "As we enlisted the able-bodied, the women and children required care, and contrabands came upon our hands," one officer wrote, "the policy of the Governor and of army officers was to repress their coming into our lines." As they continued to come and crowd "about every army depot" in defiance of Union policies, soldiers' families were placed in deserted chapels, flimsy tents, and simply on the bare ground. In one case, 100 infirm men, women, and children were put on a train to the military post at Chattanooga. There they were "dumped" and "left for hours between the tracks."[89]

By late fall of 1863, as large numbers of black women and children poured into Union lines at Pulaski, Tennessee, headquarters of the Left Wing of Sherman's Sixteenth Army Corps, Gen. Grenville M. Dodge, in an order similar to Lorenzo Thomas's, called for post commanders and provost marshals to return them to the plantations with instructions to slaveholders to receive them and "feed and protect them." In fact, many of the refugees in question had come from the northern counties of Alabama and Mississippi and thus were free people under the terms of the Emancipation Proclamation. Yet Dodge argued that he had no choice because feeding them would strain the resources of his command. When finally forced to acknowledge a major flaw in the plan—the difficulty of returning women and children who had traveled long distances—he ordered that those who fell in this category be placed on deserted farms and left with grain and other supplies. If no abandoned farms were available, Dodge ordered that the refugees "be quartered upon all known rebels."[90] The order effectively meant their re-enslavement. Eviction from Union lines sent black women and children back not only to slavery but to regions rife with rebel guerrillas and wartime slave patrols financed by local county governments to keep "the negroes in order."[91]

The fate of black women in the Civil War was also tied to racist ideas about black female sexuality. Military officials and agents of freedmen's aid societies spent an inordinate amount of time discussing and investigating the subject. The report of the American Freedmen's Inquiry Commission, established by Secretary of War Edwin M. Stanton in 1863 to investigate conditions relating to slaves and former slaves freed by the Emancipation Proclamation, was replete with all manner of rumor and speculation that reflected commissioners' obsession with the subject.

The interests expressed by Samuel G. Howe, James McKaye, and Robert Dale Owen reflected the views of white Northerners.[92] The proceedings document ideas about black women and their bodies that Northerners carried to the South and that normalized sexual assaults on black women by Union and Confederate soldiers. What happened in the Hampton Roads area in the summer of 1862 was not uncommon. "Last night a group of frightened negroes rushed up from their quarters below the hill & said that some soldiers were dragging off a negro girl," wrote Fannie Green, who was no supporter of Lincoln or abolition. The soldiers backed off when "Mr Riley rushed down there with his gun and put a stop to their proceedings in a hurry."[93]

Union soldiers stationed near black settlements and refugee camps were accused of invading the settlements, sometimes on the pretext of recruiting black soldiers, for the purpose of raping girls and women. In the South Carolina lowcountry, Rev. A. Mercherson complained of drunken white soldiers, sailors, and officers raping black women and in general refusing to "behave them selves as men." He contrasted their behavior to that of the black soldiers, who were "faithful in the Discharge of there [sic] Duty."[94] On picket duty on the South Carolina coast in 1862, a Union soldier witnessed an incident that made him "ashamed of America," the rape of a young girl he believed to be seven to nine years old.[95] "No colored woman or girl was safe from the brutal lusts of the soldiers—and by soldiers I mean both officers and men," wrote Esther Hawks while stationed at Beaufort in the South Carolina Sea Islands. She singled out Dr. Charles Mead and his steward of the Fifty-Fifth Pennsylvania Regiment, who she said both "had a pretty colored girl to minister to their private wants." Hawks wrote that "mothers were brutally treated for trying to protect their daughters," and several were shot in the effort. Hawks also noted the speedy conviction and execution—within a day—of three soldiers of the Fifty-Fifth Massachusetts Regiment (an African American regiment) for the rape of a white woman at Camp Finnegan in Florida and wondered why the same offense did not result in a similar punishment for white soldiers. Although Hawks had no way of knowing necessarily, in fact a few soldiers were punished. As Crystal N. Feimster writes, some black women took their rapists to court, and although "no federal soldiers were executed for raping black women, a few were court-martialed and convicted."[96]

In 1864, Gen. Speed S. Fry, commanding at Camp Nelson, Kentucky, opposed the admission of black women into his camp in part, he said, because he feared for their safety among Union soldiers, and that "disgraceful . . . shameful conditions . . . and obscene and brutal practices" would be the result.[97] From his post at Winchester, Tennessee, a Pennsylvania soldier informed his wife that Union soldiers cohabitated with black women. He assured her that he was not among them. "I won't be unfaithful to you with a Negro wench," he wrote, although he found it was "the case with many soldiers. Yes, men who have wives at home get entangled with these black things." In 1863, an Illinois lieutenant, accused of having "a lewd Negro woman in his tent, fornicating with her there, and encouraging a private soldier to do the same in his presence," was tried for "conduct unbecoming an officer and a gentleman." He was found guilty, but a procedural error in the court's interpretation of the charge apparently resulted in informal dismissal of the case.[98]

In Georgia, cavalry troops raped slave women in the presence of white women, and from Louisiana came reports of Union soldiers raping several black women. There were reports of women being "ravished in the presence of white women and children." At Fort Monroe, two Union soldiers raped a black woman in her yard in the presence of her father and husband and, separately, a young woman in her home in the presence of her father and grandfather while two other soldiers stood guard.[99] Reports of rape also followed the train of Sherman's troops in South Carolina.[100] The rapes and the children born from these assaults remain a less-attended aspect of Civil War studies.[101] Ex-slave Lucy Galloway, for example, reported that her father was "a Yankee white man."[102] Betty Powers thanked God freedom had come before she was old enough to be subjected to rape by a master or overseer.[103]

Into the last months of the war, freedom's promise swung back and forth. The movement of the western armies to the east carried with it the kinds of violence and displacement that black women had suffered in the Mississippi valley and it continued after the war. Black people, Rev. John Jones declared, were often "mystified" by their treatment at the hands of Federal soldiers. "Very soon," he wrote in May 1865, "they began to whisper that the said Yankees were only Southern men in blue clothes—that the true Yankees had not come yet."[104] A sense "that the true Yankees had not come yet" would describe the reaction of enslaved people in Georgia as Sherman's army made its victorious march through the state. For slaves in the northwest portion of

Alexander Hay Ritchie, *Sherman's March to the Sea.*
(Courtesy of the Library of Congress)

the state, hemmed in by a strong Confederate military and civilian presence, flight was a treacherous undertaking before Sherman's Atlanta campaign. The Atlanta campaign loosened slavery's grip, but it did so without Sherman's active assistance or encouragement.

Thousands of black women set off to join Sherman's army to find the road blocked as Sherman ordered his officers to turn them back or offer no assistance to them, fearing they would "encumber" his army "on the march." But black people persisted despite the orders, the ill treatment they received, and the ongoing threat posed by Confederate forces pestering Sherman's rear and front.[105] In a letter to Sherman at the end of December 1864, posted "PRIVATE AND CONFIDENTIAL," Gen. Henry W. Halleck, chief of staff of Union armies, suggested that a different rationale motivated Sherman. Rumors were circulating in Washington, he informed Sherman, of his disregard for the rights and humanity of fugitive slaves. Northerners cheered his successful march through Georgia and the capture of Savannah, Halleck told him, but negative press relative to his treatment of black people or, as Halleck put it, the "Inevitable Sambo" problem, threatened to mar the achievement.

They say that you have manifested an almost *criminal* dislike to the negro, and that you are not willing to carry out the wishes of the Government in regard to him, but repulse him with contempt. They say that you might have brought with you to Savannah more than 50,000, thus stripping Georgia of that number of laborers and opening a road by which as many more could have escaped from their masters; but that instead of this you drove them from your ranks, prevented them from following you by cutting the bridges in your rear, and thus caused the massacre of large numbers by Wheeler's cavalry.[106]

Halleck reminded Sherman of the transformation in Union war aims to encompass slave emancipation and urged him to consider reopening his lines to black people. Yet he tried to lighten the condemnation by saying that it was presumed that Sherman had acted out of concern for the need to ensure that the soldiers of his army were fed, concern that he did not have the means to feed the black people following his armies, and concern that they might "embarrass his march."[107] Still, Sherman did not open his lines but did agree to meet with Secretary of War Edwin Stanton and a group of black ministers at Savannah. Four days later, on January 16, 1865, he addressed the problem by issuing Field Order No. 15, which set aside a strip of land on the coast from Charleston, South Carolina, to St. John's River in Florida, encompassing 400,000 acres for the settlement of former slaves. As he organized an army of the Fourteenth, Fifteenth, Sixteenth, Seventeenth, and Twentieth Corps, he focused on his men, ammunitions and provisions, and nothing less than the "complete overthrow" of the Confederacy. The military objectives, he believed, absolutely required ridding his lines of "surplus servants, non-combatants, and refugees." He issued General Order No. 22 prohibiting soldiers from allowing their wagons to be "filled up with negro women and children, or their baggage," as he held out some hope that things might change.[108] "At some future time we will be able to provide for the poor whites and blacks who seek to escape the bondage under which they are now suffering," he wrote.[109] For Sherman, the land set aside under Special Order No. 15 was less a means to provide land to former slaves than a remedy to the problem of refugees following his army.

The command reports of Sherman's officers during the Savannah campaign dramatically capture the impact of his policy on black refugees generally and the disproportionately deadly impact on black women and children refugees. Capt. Eben White of the Sixteenth Illinois Infantry reported that while many had tried, only six slaves, all men employed as officers' servants, made it to Savannah with his regiment. "Large numbers of both sexes and all ages were prohibited from following the command," he wrote, "in obedience to stringent orders issued on that subject from superior headquarters."

Other regimental commanders as well as infantry and division commanders reported only slightly higher numbers, generally ranging from twelve to
forty. The reports of corps brigade commanders showed hundreds of black
people turned away. Gen. James D. Morgan, commanding the Second Division, Fourteenth Army Corps, wrote that he had prevented "near 500" refugees from crossing Buck Head Creek on army pontoons.

Union general Jefferson C. Davis infamously prevented hundreds from
crossing Ebenezer Creek by removing the pontoon bridges after the Fourteenth Corps had crossed. Not only did the black people following the army
have no way to safely cross, but Davis's order also left them abandoned to
Confederate major general Joseph Wheeler's cavalry. More afraid of Wheeler's men than the swift currents of the deep creek, some tried to swim across
and drowned. Some were captured by Confederate guerrillas and executed.
Even some Union officers were enraged, one labeling Davis's action a "disgrace and inhuman" and another "inhuman and fiendish." The disgrace
became a national one as news of the atrocities connected to the removal of
the pontoon bridges made its way to the North. Chief of the Union armies
Gen. Henry W. Halleck blamed Sherman directly.[110] Gen. Henry W. Slocum
estimated that about half of the 14,000 black people who had joined the two
columns of the left-wing command along the march made it to Savannah.
Some commanders took the instructions from headquarters to mean they
should in effect ignore the refugees. Nearly 700 fugitive slaves followed Gen.
Absalom Baird's Seventeenth Regiment, New York Veterans Volunteers, but
"as no notice was taken of them," Baird reported, "nor restraint exercised
over those simply passing along the road, many doubtless disappeared without any account being had of them."[111]

Slaves also found the road blocked by the Twentieth Army Corps. Of an
estimated 6,000 to 8,000 fugitives who joined the coattails of the Twentieth
Corps, some 4,000 to 6,000, unable to keep pace, or directly blocked from
doing so, "disappeared" or perished on the roads leading to Savannah or
among the rank weeds and swamps. No effort was made to drive them away
according to the "Report of the 20th Army Corps." They were simply advised
of the difficulty of trying to follow the corps. Women, children, the elderly,
and individuals too sick for employment made up nearly two-thirds of the
thousands who did not make it to Savannah. Nearly 2,000 were placed in a
colony on the Coleraine plantation on the Savannah River and supplied with
rice. Four hundred of the men found employment as officers' servants.[112]
Thousands more were reenslaved. Confederate general Joseph Wheeler's
cavalry and Confederate snipers attached to other units, reduced to picking
off Union troops bringing up the rear, targeted fugitive slaves one by one

and in large groups. He could not stop Sherman, but Wheeler triumphantly reported that a night attack on the Fourteenth Corps that caused the corps to break camp resulted in the capture of nearly 2,000 slaves. As a result, he reported, "a great many negroes were left in our hands whom we sent back to their owners."[113]

Still black people continued to follow Sherman. They followed him out of Georgia into South Carolina and from South Carolina into North Carolina. But Sherman remained determined to stop them. In March 1865, less than a month before Robert E. Lee's surrender of his armies, Sherman wrote, "I must rid my army of from 20,000 to 30,000 useless mouths." He planned to use captured Confederate steamboats to load "refugees, white and black, that have clung to our skirts, impeded our movements, and consumed our food" and send as many as possible to Cape Fear and others to Wilmington by boat, army vehicles, and captured horses.[114]

In the midst of slavery's destruction, victories for freedom were not always apparent as such.[115] Sometimes they went unobserved except by black people themselves. Many of the women, men, and children who fled Georgia with Sherman's army despite his resistance found sympathy and refuge in black communities in the South Carolina lowcountry. By this point these communities had taken in thousands of refugees from the mainland and from Georgia and Florida like Susie King Taylor. Taylor arrived from Savannah in 1862 at the age of fourteen with her uncle and his family and went on to serve as a nurse, teacher, laundress, and teamster. Refugees arrived constantly from the mainland. A military expedition in 1863, for example, returned to Beaufort with 500 refugees. Newly arrived refugees were warmly welcomed by refugees who had come before and long-time residents who opened their churches to them and welcomed them to their chimneys, as the expression went in the lowcountry.[116]

The efforts of freedpeople to assist each other, however, were not always enough to stave off starvation, sickness, competition for food, or death. "The poor negroes die as fast as ever," Laura Towne, a Northern teacher in the South Carolina lowcountry, wrote in January 1865. "The children are all emaciated to the last degree, and have such violent coughs and dysenteries that few survive. It is frightful to see such suffering among children."[117] The needs of the new arrivals sometimes outstripped the resources of those already settled along the coast. A group arrived from Georgia "frightfully destitute, sickly, and miserable," and some died. After two months, the Georgia refugees had been "nearly reduced to starvation for the want of rations" when a shortage of coal for the steamers delayed the transportation of rations. The food shortages began to wear on the patience of long-time residents, who complained that the refugees were stealing their chickens and other food. The departure of the refugees returning to Edisto Island along with their chickens and pigs added to the problem.[118] There was joy when families were reunited, but many were disappointed in trying to find family members. "Parents are looking for lost children and there are waifs of children without a friend, who have drifted here somehow, and who are so forlorn and dejected and emaciated that it is hard to see them."[119]

Amid the destruction of war, the sickness and death, black women remained dedicated to building new free communities and lives in the low-country and across the South. Sally Anderson was sixteen years old when the war began. Two years later, she fled slavery and married William Anderson, another former slave who became a sergeant in Company I, Forty-Sixth United States Colored Infantry (USCI). They got married in the camp of the Forty-Sixth at Helena, Arkansas, on May 10, 1863, the month after William enlisted. Sally became the company laundress, allowing her to stay close to her husband and to draw rations, but their marriage was short-lived. While commanding a picket guard returning from duty, Sergeant Anderson was struck by a rock thrown by a local white man as the guard marched through his property. Although he suffered a "slight fracture of the skull," Anderson returned to light duty but was soon back in the hospital. He died a year later in August 1864 at Milliken's Bend, not knowing his wife was pregnant with their only child. Anna was born nine months later in June 1865.[120]

Sally Anderson and her daughter would join the thousands of soldiers' wives and children who lost a husband or father in the war. But the wives and children of black soldiers did not have access to the hundreds of organizations available in the North and South that supported the widows and children of white soldiers. The "Report of the Commissioners of Colored Refugees in Kentucky, Tennessee, and Alabama" was a scathing denunciation of the treatment of the families of black soldiers. "White soldiers know that as they leave family and home behind, there are relations and friends, and bounty-paying states to support them. Not so here. They are amidst suffering, and want, and odious oppression. [Black soldiers] leave parents, and children, and wives, with no reliance but promises of public authorities—promises well-intentioned, but too idly made, or promises made in fraud, and broken with little hesitations, and less shame." One Union commander was declared "wholly unfit . . . for any command where the care and safety of colored refuges can, by possibility, become the subject of his official action." The situation, the report concluded, was "an inhumanity to the soldiers' family."[121] After the war, the widows and children of black soldiers continued to receive less aid and support, and their claims for Federal widows pensions drew more intense scrutiny than those for white women.

Black women in the South, however, had made a difference, a difference in the helping to fuel transformations in Union war aims, the conduct of the war, and in contributing to the making of wartime freedom. Throughout the Civil War, they mobilized to support the Union cause and emancipation, taking their stand on the antislavery ground they had sowed for decades as enslaved women. That work had included organizing soldiers' aid societies like the one established at New Bern, North Carolina.[122] The members of the city's Colored Women's Union Relief Association were in every sense Union women and abolitionists. Never unclear about the stakes involved, enslaved women fled to Union lines or fought where they stood whether slaveholders packed up and fled, as in the South Carolina Sea Islands, or not. They turned abandoned plantations not claimed by the Treasury Department into spaces for the making of freedom. The "rehearsal for freedom" in the South Carolina Sea Islands has received the greater part of our attention on this score, most famously in Willie Lee Rose's work,[123] but across the South former slaves engaged in rehearsals for freedom independently without the support of Northern missionaries, teachers, or Treasury Department officials. When Union foragers found former slaves in possession of plantations in the rear of Vicksburg, they were treated to a bounty of foodstuffs—chickens, eggs, butter, bacon, and beef—some of which they bartered for cash and tobacco.[124] On Charles Fore's Cunard Plantation, few black men remained, but the Union soldiers found black women plowing and driving mules, ready to "fight for freedom." One of the women told the soldiers that she was confident that the same God who had led the children of Israel to freedom and protected Daniel in the lion's den would surely rescue her. She knew about the Emancipation Proclamation. Anyone who believed it was not real was simply "wicked."[125]

In June 1865, eight-year-old Maggie Whitehead participated in a celebration of emancipation with other former slaves from her community in Gonzales, Texas. Gonzales was far from the major battlefields of the Civil War, but black people here clearly had some understanding of what was going on in the rest of the country. They lived in a county where in 1860 slaveholders accounted for less than 5 percent of the population and slaves made up some 40 percent, a county that voted overwhelmingly in favor of secession and organized twenty-two volunteer companies, including home guards. Whitehead may have known some of the enslaved men from Gonzales and surrounding counties who were impressed to build a fort to protect the area from Union attacks. She might have seen some of the slave coffles that appeared more frequently on the roads as slaveholders moved their slaves to Texas to prevent their escape to Union lines. From multiple sources that included local slaveholders and nonslaveholders and their fathers and sons who helped build the fort, she and others in her community would have learned about the big battles just to the east in Louisiana and those farther away. Her father's work as a highly skilled blacksmith and her mother's as a midwife favorably positioned them to gain information on the war.[126] What we know for sure is that Maggie Whitehead lived with her parents, John and Temperance Whitehead, in a community of men and women who honored black women Unionists. In 1937 Whitehead was interviewed as part of the Works Project Administration project to record the memories of former slaves. She recalled the celebration they held on June 19, 1866, the first anniversary of their freedom. On their "first Nineteenth," the freedpeople of Gonzales did not neglect to acknowledge black women's contributions to the defeat of the Confederacy. They honored it with a rendition of "The Bonnie Blue Flag" that paid tribute to their community's and the nation's debt to black women and the part they had played in the war.[127] These are the lyrics Maggie Whitehead remembered:

> 'De Blue Bonnet Flag
> Hurrah fo' de Blue Bonnet Flag,
> Hurrah fo' de home-spun dresses
> Dat de colored wimmen wear;
> Yes I'm a radical girl
> And glory in de name—
> Hurrah fo' de home-spun dresses
> Dat de colored wimmen wear.[128]

The song raises important questions. Why did the "colored wimmen" of Gonzales come to see themselves as Union women and abolitionists? What meaning did they attach to "home-spun dresses," an icon that Southern white women took on as an expression of Confederate nationalism and sacrifice? What did it mean that they cheered for the U.S. flag? Why does it matter that the larger community of former slaves incorporated this song as part of their celebration of emancipation? At the very least this celebration of the "radical" dimension of black women's politics captures the critical importance of the antislavery ground enslaved women plowed prior to the war to wartime resistance.

Freedom

Resistance remained critical after emancipation. Its necessity can be traced in the efforts of former slaveholders to prevent black people from exercising their full rights as a free people and citizens. Black people vigilantly identified the threats. The pervasive fear of re-enslavement into the twentieth century recalled and articulated the violence they had suffered during slavery and the war.[129] Agents of the Freedmen's Bureau ridiculed the fear, calling it unfounded, simply more evidence of an ignorant people. They "are so suspicious and fearful that they will again be enslaved that great difficulty is experienced in inducing them to contract as they 'fear it may be signing them back to their masters,' as they express it," one agent wrote.[130] But why should they believe the assistant and subassistant commissioners of the Bureau? They remembered that Union soldiers had trafficked in slaves. In September 1862, for instance, Commodore C. H. Davis, commander of the U.S. Navy Western Flotilla censured and dismissed Master's Mate Sidney H. McAdam of the gunboat *St. Louis* for having "engaged in kidnapping negroes within the lines of the United States Army and running them off to be returned to slavery." For this "scandalous and dishonorable conduct," McAdam was "dismissed from service in the gunboat flotilla with disgrace."[131]

More present threats also emerged. In simple, brief notations, the Freedmen's Bureau agent for Harnett and Moore Counties, North Carolina, documented slavery's continued existence:

Samuel Harrington wants his wife. Dr. John Dongel has his wife as a slave he refuses to give her up.

Andrew Jackson wants his wife Eliza. John Fairley holds his wife as a slave and refuses to give her up.

Gilbert (colored) wants his wife Susey. John McFall holds her as a slave he has been ordered to send Susey to the house of Archy McCrimmon, Gilbert's employer.

It had been over a month since the war ended, but slavery had not ended for Sarah Harrington, Eliza Jackson, and Susey. Nor had it for Jane Stewart's two children, Squire and Mary Jane, whom she fought to gain possession of from one Dickinson Dowd. Manchester Ward Weld, a native of Rhode Island and a graduate of Columbia Law who heard black people's complaints in Harnett and Moore Counties, often dismissed or ridiculed the people and their claims and assertions of the rights of citizens. They were "very much inflated as regards their political powers," he wrote. He supported the arrest of Sallie Harrington for "idleness" after she left the employment of her former mistress. When Benjamin Harrison did not appear when Ward summoned him, Ward wrote that Benjamin Harrison had "lost sight of . . . who shall rule in the Dist [sic]—The United States Government or Mr. Sambo." He did, however, order the children of Jane Stewart returned to her, as she had not consented to their apprenticeship.[132] Into her old age, Lulu Wilson worried that white people still had not given up on the idea of enslaving black people. They had never been any "good," she stated, and she thought it would be a good thing if the president of the United States, who she thought must be a responsible man, were reminded of this. "If I could write to this latest president," she stated, "I would tell him they ain't no good in it and to not listen to the women's clubs that want to bring slavery back." She also wanted the president to know that she had been a Union woman who had helped to spin cloth for the soldiers.[133]

Postwar violence against African Americans also necessitated vigilance and resistance. Black people, former Civil War black soldier Calvin Holley wrote, "were being outraged beyond humanity." Women and children were put out in the cold, "knocked down for saying they are free," and murdered. Holley wrote of two black women found "lying side by side" beside the road "with their throats cut."[134] In Louisiana's Red River parishes the "bloated corpses of Freedpeople" that floated down the Red River and "began washing up in the fields themselves" reminded black people not only of the power of white supremacy after the Civil War but the atrocities endured during the war itself.[135] Postwar violence and the fear of re-enslavement were legacies of wartime violence. The "wave upon wave of protracted violence" during Reconstruction, as John Higginson writes, was "neither serendipitous nor spontaneous"; on the contrary, these "campaigns of terror . . . had notable local precedents."[136] The Civil War constituted one of those precedents. Violence, as Thomas Holt reminds us, is "a deliberate political weapon."[137] Violence surrounded the making of freedom and took many forms.

Enslaved women believed that the Civil War could and should result in their freedom. They understood that the path would not be easy and that some of them would not live to see freedom, succumbing to enemy military and civilian fire or to old age, pregnancy-related mortality, or preexisting illnesses. Others would make it but would lose family members and friends along the way. Still others, like soldiers, would come out maimed. Margaret Ann Ferguson and Missouri Lewis were refugees whose lives reflect the trauma of slavery and the Civil War for African American women. Ferguson, for example, was admitted to the Freedmen's General Hospital in February 1864 with "gangrene of foot and leg." She arrived at the hospital emaciated and with the tibia of one leg "exposed and partially destroyed." A Union surgeon amputated her diseased leg, but gangrene set in again, and she died a few weeks later. Missouri Lewis was one of several women admitted to the same hospital following "a case of abortion." She died three days after her arrival.[138]

Perhaps the women who had abortions were girls who believed they were too young to be mothers; perhaps they were ill and/or alone without kin and could not see how they could care for a child. Perhaps they had been raped. Living in a refugee camp reduced the odds that either they or their babies would survive. They may have asked themselves how they could nurture a baby on weakened breast milk or the one-half ration that children in refugee camps received. Perhaps they decided to end their pregnancy after seeing so many women miscarry, so many mothers succumb to disease after childbirth, so many newborns who died alongside their mothers, and the growing number of orphaned children. What we can say for sure is that they could not know whether the fragile freedom they clung to in refugee camps would last. While refugee camps could be places of hope and were often transformed by black women into spaces for rebuilding community and ties of kinship, they were also spaces of suffering, disease, and death. Freedom and citizenship were on the horizon in 1864, but Missouri Lewis, Malinda Johnson, Mary Miller, Martha Ann Mark, and Ann Hayes could not be certain it would come in their lifetime or what it would look like if it did. In the camps, freedom sometimes hardly looked like freedom. In the camps, they lived "often in overcrowded and unhealthy conditions; some did not live to enjoy their liberty for very long"[139]

To keep a roof over the heads of their own families, slaveholders put more black women and children on the auction block. Stretched budgets and a labor force diminished by runaways made them less tolerant of enslaved women with infants and small children or who were pregnant. "I am very sorry to hear that Betty is getting so *pesant* [sic]," Augustin Taveau wrote concerning the pregnancy of the enslaved woman who worked for his wife. "It is very annoying that she should find herself in that condition just at this particular time, you will be very much inconvenienced."[140] The flight of enslaved women from the plantation household caused particular consternation precisely because their work, and their very presence, was key to slaveholders' beliefs about what womanhood and home, "the bulwark of the Southern social order and as the region's central social institution," meant.[141] The barricaded space that the plantation household represented in a physical sense and ideologically had stood front and center in white Southerners' call to war. "One of the many miraculous things a slave could do was to make a household white," as Walter Johnson writes.[142]

Making households white required their militarization. Understanding black women's resistance to the plantation household and slaveholding women requires attention to the fact that the violence they faced in this space and from these women included the spectacular display of pistols owned by white women. Missing in the literature of slavery and the Civil War is the presence of guns in the homes of slaveholders, for the purpose not of hunting but of intimidating enslaved women. In threatening to shoot a slave woman who refused to deliver "respectful obedience," Georgia DeFontaine exemplified the small-scale but no less terrifying aspect of the larger militarization of the South.[143]

With Sherman's army making its way to Columbia, South Carolina, in 1864, DeFontaine followed the tried but not always true path of thousands of Southern white women during the war. She packed hurriedly, hoping to make it out of the city ahead of Union forces, and called on her slaves to assist. And like many slaveholding women before her, she faced resistance. One of her slaves, Nancy, made clear that she had no interest in fleeing the city and showed, DeFontaine wrote, "unmistakable signs of disaffection." Nancy refused to help DeFontaine pack and laughed appreciatively each time she heard a burst of gunfire from the Union side, taking joy in the approach of Union forces. "Observing this, and fearing that it might demoralize the others who were doing all in their power to help me," DeFontaine wrote, "I quietly walked to the mantle-piece, took down my pistol, and strapping it about my waist, said, 'Nancy, I am still your mistress, and as such I demand respectful obedience from you. If the Yankees take the city and you prefer going with them to remaining with me, you are at perfect liberty to go, but now you must obey me.' Looking first at me and then at the pistol, she accepted the situation temporarily, but made her way to the enemy the next day." Nancy took her chances on the uncertainties of freedom, but her political sensibilities proved in the end far sounder than DeFontaine's.[144] The Civil War fueled an unprecedented militarization of the Southern home front that extended into freedom. "The militaristic nature of plantation production" had always extended to the production of the plantation household. It was now on public view as never before.[145]

Guns and whips were fixtures of the big house. In the kitchens, parlors, and yards of plantation houses, slaves were subjected to violent surveillance no less than in the slave quarters and fields. It does not matter that no jail-like bars ruined the homes' facade and presentation. The open windows and doors—touted as signs of Southern hospitality—masked the military apparatus at the core, designed to protect planter homes from the people who worked in them as slaves. Within, secret stairways sought to diminish the slaves' presence. Slave cabins were also patrolled and militarized spaces of surveillance, as were the South's roads and byways, where slaves were required to show a pass to any white person who demanded that they account for their presence there. These policed spaces were part of the larger police state that the institution of slavery required.[146]

The militarization of the "domestic sanctuaries" of the antebellum South can easily slide from view, but the Civil War cast it into sharp relief. When a loom room caught fire in the home of Kate Stone and her family, the initial blame was cast on Jane, who had recently fled with her children and had a reputation for defying white women who tried to rule her. Fearing Jane might return, Kate Stone picked up a "five-shooter" for protection.[147] Elizabeth Meriwether got her pistol ready to confront, if necessary, a black woman she thought she might have trouble with. Cornelia Lewis [Scales] carried a pistol by her side.[148]The archive of the Civil War is replete with such stories.

During the Civil War, enslaved women transformed personalized, individual, and plantation- and neighborhood-based struggles against slavery into a mass movement to destroy it. They turned what one Union officer called the "Nigger Woman Question" into a question about freedom, citizenship, dignity, and their rights as refugees.[149] Fleeing slavery remained a dangerous enterprise to the very end and, in some respects, more dangerous than it had been before the war. Local wartime patrols did not have the same incentives to return slaves alive or at all. The patrols and regular Confederate troops sold refugees back into slavery or killed them.

Maggie Whitehead heard these stories as a young girl and by passing them on helped ensure their place in the archives of the Civil War and of black political thought. For decades, these archives would rarely be consulted by scholars and thus would remain absent from the historiography. Over time, the archives black people created were so thoroughly wiped out of the history of the war and of black political thought that the erasures themselves became difficult to discern. Yet despite the time and concerted effort devoted to the project of erasure, traces remained because former slaves like Maggie Whitehead remembered, and because we can link their memories to the archives of black people's politics lodged inadvertently among the papers of slaveholders, military commanders, and agents of freedmen's aid societies. Whitehead was too young to have much of a memory of the war itself, but her elders taught her a song chronicling the history of black women abolitionists and unionists. It stuck with her.

Former slaves carried into freedom stories of loss, survival, and triumph that they told over and over to succeeding generations, who committed them to the archives of history. Freedom did not mean an end to lethal and more mundane losses. It did not ensure that black women would no longer be called or treated as animals. In 1866, Harriet Benson quit her job as a cook for the Smith family, a decision her husband supported. This was unacceptable to the employer, Beaton Smith. His wife had just given birth, making Harriet's presence "trebly necessary to us," he wrote. When he demanded that Richard Benson "order" his wife to return, Benson replied "that he'd be G—d d—d if he would, as he wasn't going to have his wife jawed like a dog."[150]

Black women did not fight alone. As soldiers and laborers for the Union army and navy, their husbands and fathers fought policies that banned their wives and families from Union lines. As husbands, sons, and fathers, they protested sexual assaults and stood by their families even when they could not be with them. "I do assure you," one black soldier wrote, "that when three or four thousand brave colored soldiers, who have endured privation and suffering to crush the wicked rebellion, return to their homes in Maryland, it will be rubbed so bright that respectable colored people will be able to walk the street without being insulted. . . . The fact is this; we have been in Egypt, and from the plague of death they have been obliged to let God's people go."[151] It took a long time for that sentiment to grab hold of the nation and become a plank of the Union's war aims. "As things stand," Northerner Abby Woolsey wrote in the summer of 1862, "the South is fighting to maintain slavery, and the North is trying to fight so as not to put it down. When this policy ceases, perhaps we shall begin to have victory, if we haven't already sinned away our day of grace."[152] In the end, the nation did not sin away its day of grace. The ratification of the Thirteenth Amendment ended slavery. Yet even then, black people continued to be sometimes held as slaves long after the war had ended.

PART II

NORTHERN WOMEN

Chapter Four

AM I A SOLDIER OF THE CROSS?

Northern Women's Fight and the Legacy of Slavery

Our nation must be severely punished for its sins, before we can
have perfect peace, and that worst of all, Slavery must be completely
crushed out and the negro acknowledged and treated as a man
before it can be done, in God's own time it will be done.
—DOROTHY L. STEVENS

Poor people have to go to war or starve.
—ARVILLA THOMPSON

IN THE SPRING OF 1859, Jane Eliza Newton Woolsey of New York City
went on vacation in the South with two of her daughters, Mary and
Abby, her granddaughter, and her son-in-law Robert Howland. One day
in Charleston, South Carolina, they had an unforgettable experience. The
"sights and sounds of an auction of slaves," they recalled, had "vexed their
righteous souls." How this Northern abolitionist family ever imagined that
they might escape such a scene in one of the South's largest slave-trading
ports seems hard to fathom. That it seemed to take them by surprise can
only be understood in the context perhaps of nineteenth-century plantation
tourism. "But for that sad insight we might have thought things had a pretty
fair aspect generally. Certainly nothing forced itself unpleasantly on our attention, only every black face in the street reminded us of the system."[1] The
sight of enslaved people reminded them of where they were but did not vex
their souls. Just as white Southerners vacationed in the North, white Northerners vacationed in the South and other "exotic" plantation societies like
Cuba. In the mid-nineteenth century, an estimated 5,000 American vacation-
ers and travelers visited Havana annually. It was one thing to read about slavery or attend abolitionist meetings to hear fugitive slaves and other abolitionists speak and another to see its operation up close, in person. Perhaps it

was that the magnitude of the difference between reading or hearing about slavery secondhand and seeing with one's own eyes and hearing with one's own ears human beings sold like cattle simply made the Woolseys truly realize that the vacation spot they had chosen could not but vex the soul. Jane Eliza Woolsey did have some direct experience with slavery, if not with the auctioning of human beings. Most Northern travelers who witnessed such scenes were not led to condemn slavery. But those who found the experience distasteful would soon have the opportunity to answer slavery's assault on their souls with action.

In 1861, Jane Eliza Woolsey and her children—Abby Howland, Jane Stuart, Mary Elizabeth, Georgeanna Muirson, Eliza Newton, Harriet Roosevelt, Caroline Carson, and Charles William—joined the fight for the Union and the eradication of "the great national sin" of slavery. The daughters would work as nurses at City Hospital on Broadway, Union hospitals on the war front, and with the Hospital Transport Service. The son joined the Union army. For most white Northerners in 1861, a war against slavery was not a goal for which they could fight, but for abolitionists like the Woolsey family, the war would bring an end to the troubling sight and sound of human bondage. The Woolsey home at 8 Brevoort Place "became a sort of headquarters" for family and friends.[2] At social and political gatherings and in the streets, "nothing but politics was talked."[3]

So it was not surprising that members of the Woolsey family would be in the crowd at the Society of the Church of the Puritans—one of the wealthiest churches in New York, pastored by abolitionist Dr. George Cheever—on December 2, 1859, at the hour appointed for the execution of John Brown. They returned three days later for a prayer service for Brown. The church's lecture room was again packed, Abby Woolsey wrote, "crowded with men and women—as many of one as the other—hard-featured, rugged faces, thoughtful faces, some few Chadband faces; plain, quiet women; none that looked like gay, idle, trifling people." A new spirit seemed in the air as they sang "Am I a Soldier of the Cross?" They sang "with a will, and . . . much feeling—some sobs and many hearty Amens."[4] Possibly the sobs came harder when they got to the lyrics that asked if they would "fear to own His cause" or be content to "be carried to the skies on flowery beds of ease while others fought to win the prize and sailed through bloody seas?" Yet even those committed to being soldiers of the cross had a big question before them: What kind of soldiers would they be?

Two weeks later, Abby and Georgeanna Woolsey went to hear Wendell Phillips at Cooper Union Institute.[5] As usual, Phillips drew a large crowd to the Great Hall, giving the kind of speech his audiences had come to expect and on two of his most popular subjects, Toussaint Louverture and John Brown. He had given versions of this lecture on previous occasions and continued to do so during the Civil War before audiences in New York, Boston, and Washington, D.C., where some 2,000 people went to see him at the Smithsonian Institution. With his usual oratorical force, Phillips argued for "the much-despised negro race—that race we trample under foot and declare to be unfit for anything but to carry our burdens—is in every respect equal to the Saxons." He referenced John Brown and praised Toussaint Louverture, the leader of the Saint-Domingue revolution that defeated Napoleon's armies and resulted in the establishment of the independent nation of Haiti under Jean-Jacques Dessalines. Toussaint, he told them, was far from the "fanatic" many people imagined him to be but rather deserved "the name of patriot and martyr." He placed Toussaint in the pantheon of great leaders, comparing him favorably to Oliver Cromwell, George Washington, and Napoleon Bonaparte and placing him above Washington, Brown, Brutus of Rome, John Hampden of England, and the Marquis de Lafayette. They were words Charlotte Forten heard Phillips deliver in December 1857 where he proclaimed Toussaint "the 'First of the Blacks'" and placed him above Cromwell, Napoleon, and George Washington, a president who *"held slaves."*[6]

A year later, as delegates from six Southern states prepared to assemble in Montgomery, Alabama, to form a new nation dedicated to the proposition that all men were not created equal, Abby and Georgeanna Woolsey went again to hear Phillips speak on the Haitian Revolution and John Brown. It was the "perfect treat," Abby Woolsey recalled. She and her sister were "perfectly charmed." Phillips's remarks on John Brown were greeted with "a storm of applause." And to those who questioned the "courage" of black people, Phillips thundered, "Ask the fifty-two thousand of LeClerc's soldiers who died in battle. Go stoop with your ear on their graves! Go question the dust of Rochambeau and of the eight thousand who escaped with him under the English Jack! and if the answer is not loud enough, come home! and (dropping his voice) *'come by the way of quaking Virginia!'"*[7] The reference to Nat Turner's rebellion was inescapable.

Phillips described himself as a man who "could find no place, where an American could stand with decent self-respect, except in constant, uncontrollable and loud protest against the sin of his native land."[8] As he knew, he spoke on radical soil richly seeded by black abolitionists no less than white abolitionists. He stood on the shoulders of a long line of black activists who had for decades "lived an antislavery life" and saw the "leaders of slave re-bellions as activists, true patriots, and messianic agents of God." The most worthy abolitionists, Charlotte Forten wrote, were those who stood for "*radical* antislavery*." Forten, a black abolitionist from the famous Forten family of Philadelphia and a member of the Female Anti-Slavery Society, had long attended Phillips's lectures. In 1847, she went to Lynn, Massachusetts, to hear him speak of the strength of freedom and the evil of slavery and with friends to hear him on the twentieth anniversary of British emancipation. She attended the antislavery convention where Phillips introduced the fugitive slave Anthony Burns, whose plight had aroused abolitionists. She and the black abolitionist Sarah Parker Remond were friends, and she enjoyed hearing Remond speak "strong truths" in "defence of oppressed humanity." In lectures, national black conventions, antislavery conventions and publications like the *Colored American*, Frances Ellen Watkins, Hester Lane, Sarah Parker Remond, Sojourner Truth, Frederick Douglass, and many others had proclaimed the diasporic revolutionary tradition Phillips referenced. "Finding the American Revolution too flawed to stand alone as a usable revolution," they had lifted up Joseph Cinque, Madison Washington, Gabriel Prosser, Denmark Vesey, Nat Turner, Toussaint, Dessalines, and Alexandre Dumas. The frontispiece of the first issue of the *Anglo-African Magazine*, published in 1859, featured an image of Dumas.[9]

The Woolsey sisters and other wealthy Northerners who heard Phillips speak might have found one part of his lecture particularly appealing: his portrait of Toussaint as a man whose first instinct as a revolutionary was to protect the man and woman who held him in bondage from the terror to come. "His first act on taking part with his countrymen for liberty," Phillips said, "was to see to the safety of his master and mistress, whom he put into a vessel, after having loaded it with sugar, coffee, &c., and he then sent them to Baltimore, and never forgot to send them the constant means of support each year as long as they lived." According to a *New York Times* reporter at the event, the account of Toussaint's loyalty drew loud applause. Phillips gave the audience a similar reason to applaud Dessalines. "The lecturer then at some length detailed instances of magnanimity in the negro character, showing how DESSALINES had stood by his master in sickness, and with his own hands dug his grave at his death."[10] It was a story that comforted Northerners, who in almost every other context were being told to fear slave rebels like Toussaint Louverture and Dessalines as fanatics, destroyers of white civilization, and murderers of white women and children. It positioned him not only as a "patriot and martyr" but as a man still capable of loyalty to white people.

For Union or Freedom

The Woolsey sisters joined thousands of Northern women who had felt their souls assaulted by slavery and suffered "persecution" for their views. They had been at the forefront of the abolition movement, organizing antislavery sewing circles, raising money, sheltering and employing fugitive slaves, and turning their homes into miniature factories.[11] They had weathered the ups and downs of tolerance and intolerance of abolitionism in the North, including violent mob action. In 1861, some took the next step, insisting that the war to put down the rebellion in the South encompass the slaves' war for freedom. They answered the long-gnawing assault on their souls with the weapons most readily available to them: giving lectures, placing anonymous posts in newspapers, organizing freedmen's relief societies, and going to the front as nurses, missionaries, and teachers. They represented a minority of Northern women and Northern opinion but they counted.[12]

The vast majority of Northern women joined in support of the war for Union. Few among them believed that the end result need or should be a nation reborn as a land free of slavery or that emancipation need constitute a war aim. Some were women who, like Eleanor Baker of Dorchester, Massachusetts, had come to see Northerners fighting for the slave as "fanatical abolitionists" and "crazy," beliefs confirmed for Baker during a visit with her husband to the South Carolina plantation of his former Harvard classmate. Baker's husband was a successful chocolate manufacturer whose income provided a life of luxury attended to by a coachman and four Irish women who worked as domestic servants in their household in 1850. On a tour of the South with her husband in 1848, she went to hear Henry Clay of Kentucky at the Capitol and applauded his endorsement of the colonization of free black people. She thought he was right to scoff at the idea of black citizenship, quoting him as saying if "all Africans born in the United States may claim to be citizens of the U.S.; and so it might have been claimed that all the children of Israel who were born in Egypt during the captivity were natives of Egypt." The majority of white Northern men shared Baker's views, if they gave much thought to slavery at all. It is not surprising, then, that the cry for Union was the call most likely to enjoin their support for war.[13]

In 1861, the men who enlisted as soldiers in the Union army carried the battle cry of a war for Union to the battlefield. "We have taken up arms to repel the tyrant . . . and *again* to plant the 'star spangled banner' over every city, town and fort from which it has been ruthlessly torn . . . *until every vestige* of treason is swept from our land," declared three soldiers of the Second Regiment, Rhode Island Volunteers.[14] In this they followed their president.

In his famous reply a year later to Horace Greeley's editorial "The Prayer of Twenty Millions," Lincoln challenged those who "would not save the Union, unless they could at the same time *save* slavery." The "paramount object in this struggle *is* to save the Union, and is *not* either to save or to destroy slavery," the president wrote, reiterating a view he had expressed on other occasions. He would take no action in reference to slavery unless he were convinced that it would help "save the Union." In 1861, emancipation was a poor candidate. Lincoln did "*not* believe it would help to save the Union." His "oft-expressed *personal* wish that all men every where could be free," thus, could not be allowed to override his "view of *official* duty."[15] The vast majority of Northern white women, exactly like men, shared the president's sentiment.

Rich and poor, Northern white women turned their parlors into miniature factories. For most, the war's justification would remain restoration of the Union only, even after the official policy of the Federal government changed. At the same time, political differences rent families in the North as they did Southern families. The Woolsey family was not exempt. Though most members of the family were staunch abolitionists, Jane Stuart Woolsey charted a different course. She disagreed vehemently with the idea that a Union victory without slave emancipation was an end not worth fighting for. "Your response to my patriotic fervors gave me a sort of chill. We do not seem *en rapport*," she wrote a friend in Paris in August 1861. For her, the war was "worth what it may cost, although the end be only—*only!* the preservation of the Government and not just now the liberation of the slaves." She was right that people like Wendell Phillips and her sister Abby, who believed "that the war is not justifiable if it means only stars and stripes," held a minority view among white Northerners, an opinion she found disagreeable and wrong. "We think, or to resume the perpendicular pronoun, I think that is enough for it to mean or seem to mean at present. 'The mills of the Gods grind slow,' you know, or, if you will let me requote to you your own quotation, 'you cannot hurry God.' Don't you and Mr. Phillips want to hurry him a little? I would rather, for my part, think with Mrs. Stowe, that the question of the existence of free society covers that other question, and that this war is Eternally Righteous even if it 'means only the stars and stripes.'"[16]

The contingent of Northern white women who stood for Union and emancipation was indeed small, but it was vocal and visible and powerful. From the beginning this determined minority believed the war for Union must also be a war for freedom. "While the flag of freedom waves merely for the white man," Anna Dickinson, a Quaker and abolitionist, said in a public forum, "God will be against us."[17] Their numbers included women like

Dorothy Stevens, the associate manager for the U.S. Sanitary Commission (USSC) in the fishing port town of Castine, Maine, a major shipbuilding and lumber industries center. Stevens stood for the Union cause *and* emancipation, believing the one could not progress without the other. "Our nation must be severely punished for its sins, before we can have perfect peace," she wrote. "*Slavery* must be completely crushed out and the negro acknowledged and treated as a man before it can be done." She was grateful that the war had "knitted together the hearts of all who are truly loyal, as nothing else *ever* could have done." When she lost a son in the war it motivated her to do more. For "although a mother's feelings sometimes almost overpower me," she wrote, "yet I know it is all right, and will not for a moment regret that our precious one died for his country, but will rather rejoice that I was permitted to give such a son for so holy a cause."[18]

Most white Northerners did not go this far in 1861, or ever, but they rose up in a clear majority in support of the flag. Flags and other patriotic emblems floating from homes, shops, and public buildings were a novel sight in cities like New York, so much that the display seemed "foreign." "We all have views now, men, women and little boys," wrote Jane Stuart Woolsey, "from the modestly patriotic citizen who wears a postage stamp on his hat to the woman who walks in Broadway in that fearful object of contemplation, a 'Union bonnet,' composed of alternate layers of red, white, and blue, with streaming ribbons 'of the first.'"[19] The exuberance in the streets reflected sentiments that had been rapidly developing over the past three decades on the question of slavery and its expansion, as well as on the "slave power" and women's activism in the abolitionist movement. That activism now embraced in the most public way ordinary Northerners.

At a mass meeting in Union Square in April 1861, nearly "every individual, man, woman and child, carried the sacred colors in some shape or other, and the ladies at the windows had knots of ribbon, tri-colored bouquets, and flags without number." Maj. Robert Anderson, who had surrendered Fort Sumter, was feted as a hero following his return to New York.[20] "It seems as if we never were alive till now; never had a country till now," Jane Stuart Woolsey wrote. "How could we ever have laughed at Fourth-of-Julys?" With "thousands of flags flying everywhere," it was as if everyone was trying to "make some amends" for the "grievous and bitter insults" the flag had lately endured at the hands of Southerners.[21] The insulted flag at Fort Sumter, whether "all in the interest of slavery" or in the interest of Union, prompted unprecedented patriotism among some women. "Never before," Mary Livermore admitted, had "the national flag signified anything" to her. Now, she wrote, "the dear banner," "this holy flag," "emblematic of national

Oh keep the flag flying!—The pride of the van!
To all other nations display it!
The ladies for union are all to a—MAN!
But not to the man who'd betray it.

"The dear banner." (Courtesy of the David M. Rubenstein
Rare Book & Manuscript Library, Duke University)

majesty became clear to my mental vision."[22] To Jane Stuart Woolsey the new embrace of the flag was part of a new baptismal, patriotic moment in the nation's history. "'Republicanism will wash'—*is* washed already in the water and the fire of this fresh baptism, 'clothed in white samite, mystic, wonderful,' and has a new name, which is *Patriotism*," she wrote in May 1861.[23] "For departing soldiers," Alice Fahs writes, "women and home were the most effective connection to the flag and nation."[24]

The war galvanized Northern women as it did women in the South to work in support of the soldiers to ensure that their material, civic, and spiritual needs were met. In knapsacks destined for the front, they placed small testaments enclosing verses like "Fight the good Fight" and "Endure hardness as a good soldier of Jesus Christ" along with patriotic stationery with the national flag printed in color.[25] Women held "bandage bees" and gatherings to make "beautiful lint" for dressing wounds; knit socks, woolen shirts, and other garments; and dry and can fruit and vegetables.[26] This work became patriotic duty, and women's domestic manufacture would save the lives of countless soldiers. When men applauded the "army of knitters," they adopted "militarized language that itself served to link battlefront and home front."[27] The "army of knitters" was also imagined by many Northerners as an army of middle-class and wealthy women. They became the face of female abolitionism and women's patriotism in the North.

Laboring Women

The vast majority of poor and working-class women from the urban and rural North did not spend the war years as nurses in Civil War hospitals, doing missionary work in the South, or worrying about slavery, even if they worried about the war. Most plowed their own fields, worked in factories, or cooked and cleaned for wealthy Northerners. They suffered disproportionately compared to middle-class and elite Northern women when their husbands, sons, and fathers joined the Union army. Compared to their Southern counterparts, Northern women were less likely to have fathers or husbands in the war. It is estimated that up to 70 percent of Union soldiers were not married and half were farmers or farm laborers. Still, "A number of northern women," writes Judith Giesberg, "experienced the war as a withdrawal of labor from their farms and their rural communities" and "the absence of male labor as a family crisis." That crisis had already begun to make its appearance before the war began, and for some struggling white men in the North, the war was a means to feed themselves and their families. As William Marvel shows, poor men often enlisted because they were poor and "found the promise of regular rations and monthly pay inviting." "It was the same across the North: a plurality if not the actual preponderance of the men who rallied around the flag had recently experienced acute economic need" in 1861. "Young fathers of precarious means and the sons of struggling fathers responded enthusiastically."[28] The impact on the household economies of Northern women was significant. The households of poor and working-class women were especially hard hit. Their economic circumstances also meant that they had less to send loved ones at the front to supplement military rations of food, clothing, and other supplies.

Poor and laboring women stood at a significant disadvantage in their efforts to support the war through the domestic production of war matériel. Struggling to produce enough to feed and clothe their families, whether or not their husbands were soldiers, poor and working-class women had less leisure time for volunteering than wealthy women and fewer resources to commit to the work. They could not easily finance the domestic production of war matériel from their own pockets. In New England, entire towns in Maine confessed "themselves 'too poor'" to help. "The present high price of material for clothing forbid many from doing anything," wrote A. M. Fulton, associate USSC manager in the coastal town of Bluehill, Maine. This did not always mean that they did not wish to do more, and many did, but Eleanor Gardiner believed they could do more. "The difficulty about funds come up in every small town," she wrote, but she thought "the high prices of material ought not to affect them so much for their crops bring equally high process & promised to be very abundant, but they have so little money that a sum seems very large."[29] Gardiner's analysis spoke to class differences that consistently undermined the work of the USSC.

Still, poor and working-class women contributed immensely to the war effort through the domestic production of war matériel as servants in the homes of wealthy employers and in their own homes. Wealthy Northern women often turned the domestic production of war matériel over to servants, just as slaveholders did to enslaved women.[30] At 8 Brevoort Place, three Irish American servants, Mary, Kate, and an unnamed cook, helped knit yarn socks for soldiers that the Woolsey family claimed as its contribution. Kate had a brother in the First Massachusetts, which may have made the burden easier to bear and even enjoyable as it allowed her to contribute in a way she could. At least, unlike enslaved women who were forced to sew and knit for the Confederacy, the wartime work of domestic servants in the homes of the Northern elite did not aid the enemy.[31]

Northern elite women also employed poor and working-class women as a matter of practicality. Like slaveholding women, many were accustomed to employing seamstresses or purchasing store-bought goods and had no sewing experience of consequence. Even those who could sew rarely did. Mary Henderson lamented having to do some sewing herself "in consequence of not having our usual complement of servants." At the time, she was also short-handed in the cooking department beyond the part-time "assistance of a young mulatto girl."[32] Henderson acknowledged that many of her peers lacked the requisite domestic skills, even though they all "say they are all knitting wollen [sic] socks for soldiers." The Philadelphia Summer Street Ladies group to which she belonged had arrived at the point of "talking about knitting," Henderson wrote, but "we will have to learn as none of us know how."[33]

Poor women who did not have the resources to give directly from their own pockets contributed to the Union effort through employment in arsenals and factories that produced for the war and by taking on work that allowed them to work at home or in the homes of wealthy women benefactors who obtained subcontracts from the Federal and state governments. Mary Lowell Gardner Lowell, for example, of the famous Lowell family of Boston, used her family's tremendous wealth and contacts to hire poor women to sew for the war effort. Lowell "puts all others to insignificance," an acquaintance wrote. "She being a lady of means and leisure, took the Government contract for woolen shirts in Massachusetts and is having them cut and made under her own eyes by poor women at good prices, and the sum that would have gone into some wretched contractor's pocket has already blessed hundreds of needy women."[34] In Boston, Harriet ("Hatty") Frothingham Wolcott worked with other women in the U.S. Sanitary Commission to support slaves who fled the plantation during the war and poor white women. She "is entirely devoted," Caroline Carson Woolsey wrote, and "keeps thirty poor women in sewing and runs I don't know how many machines."[35]

The USSC, a precursor of the American Red Cross, grew out of Woman's Central Association of Relief, organized ten days after the war began to direct "the benevolence of the people toward the army" and led to the establishment of the USSC on June 13, 1861, by Secretary of War Simon Cameron with the approval of President Lincoln. The USSC was the major outlet for Northern relief work in support of soldiers, and the work it did was inestimable. In that story, however, the contributions of poor women are sometimes lost. Some of it was through the Industrial Committee of the USSC, which distributed patterns and fabrics to sewing circles and soldiers' aid societies and made them available to poor women, with local benefactors paying their wages. In many small towns, the work of sewing for the soldiers was done almost exclusively by poor and working-class women. Poor and working-class women also acted independently in support of the Union cause. The 10 dressing gowns, 21 shirts, 33 pairs of socks, 19 pairs of slippers, 3 comforters, and assorted magazines and tracts that the Ladies Charitable Society of the Unitarian Parish of Woburn, Massachusetts, shipped in late December 1861 were largely the work of the town's laboring poor women, many of whom held full-time but low-paying jobs in the town's tanneries and boot- and shoemaking shops.[36]

As rural women "confronted the fact that they had depended on male relatives for their very survival," the disparities between their lives and their wealthier neighbors became more obvious and difficult to navigate. From every day, uneventful tasks like chopping wood to more labor-intensive ones like butchering hogs and planting crops, rural women took on more work when adult sons or husbands were gone to war and local markets for surplus produce or homemade clothing dried up.[37] In rural areas and in towns, some found it increasingly hard to pay rent or keep up with farm mortgages. In Pennsylvania, Sarah Heffner and her four children faced eviction from their home. Her husband was a soldier taken prisoner at Fort Wagner, and she heard that he had been captured and imprisoned at Belle Isle, the site of one of several Confederate prisoner of war camps in Richmond, Virginia. Following an illness that lasted through the winter, Heffner owed back rent and, even with some support from her church, feared that she and her children, the family of a soldier, she emphasized, were going to be put "out on the street." She wrote Governor Andrew Curtin for advice and assistance. The Heffner family had depended on the wages Daniel Heffner earned in a gun powder mill as a powdermaker. In 1860, the family listed $300 in real estate worth, which may have allowed them to grow vegetables and other foodstuffs.[38]

Like Southern white women, Northern women called on their husbands to come home and not reenlist. Lt. Col. Daniel F. Griffin left behind a family in New Albany, Indiana. From Gaylesville, Alabama, Griffin penned a letter to his wife, in October 1864, telling her that he was proud of her "goodness and patriotism" and knew he had her support should he decide to reenlist. "I trust the time will come that a happy country may repay you for this disinterestedness and casting aside of selfishness," he ended the letter. Like many soldiers' wives, she would pay a high price. Her husband did not reenlist but in November 1864 returned home, where he died in February 1865 of typhoid fever likely contracted in service.[39] Daniel Griffin considered his wife a patriot, but Northern women's patriotism could not be taken for granted. Northern women formed what Judith Giesberg calls the "army at home," an army of working-class and rural black and white women and immigrant women.

Class Conflict and Organizing the
Fight on the Home Front

Northern women sent thousands of barrels of drawers, shirts, and other clothing, as well as cash donations to soldiers' hospitals and army camps, but they divided over the meaning of what this work meant, what patriotism meant. In the work of the USSC, we see how differently Northern women understood what it meant to be a soldier of the cross, and the ways class and politics determined its meaning. Dozens of women served as USSC branch managers in cities, small towns, and villages. The work put some in the public arena for the first time. For others it represented a continuation of their work in prewar reform movements.[40] All gained important organizational and political skills. At the same time, class and political differences often marred their effort and impaired its effectiveness. Tensions developed among different agencies working for similar causes over means and methods and sometimes who deserved aid and how best to deliver it. The organizational structure of mainline relief organizations lent itself to efficient delivery of food, clothing, and medical and religious care but not necessarily to the needs of the mother or wife who wanted to make sure her son or husband received a package from home. Poor and working-class women fought to make their contribution more visible in a structure of giving that made them virtually invisible to the nation. They complained about perceived biases in relief work and criticized elite women managers and agents.

The USSC had great success mobilizing women in support of the war, but tepid enthusiasm and apathy—often fueled by distance and poverty—distrust of the "Federal" idea of organizing, competition from other soldiers' aid groups, and pro-Confederate sentiment complicated organizing efforts in New England. The work of the New England Women's Auxiliary Association (NEWAA), an affiliate of the USSC with headquarters in Boston, offers insight into these tensions, Northern women's politics, class conflicts, and the advantages and disadvantages of an associational model that relied heavily on local organizing.[41]

Like most aid associations, the NEWAA chose educated women of means to lead its local branches as associate managers. This proved both an advantage and a disadvantage. The associate managers were women familiar with people in their communities and with the social structure; they could call on a network of other elite women and their husbands and fathers. They were women who used the honorific *Mrs.* or, if single, belonged to households that gave them authority and stature. Isa E. Gray served on the powerful executive committee. Though only twenty-one years old, what she lacked in experience she made up for with resources as the daughter of wealthy parents. She remained single and unemployed throughout her life but with substantial wealth at her disposal.[42] The women leaders of the NEWAA brought organizational skills honed in prewar women's associations and societies. Associate managers were responsible for receiving and distributing papers, pamphlets, and reports from USSC headquarters, communicating with women in their districts to mobilize interest in the USSC and with the Boston office. Sometimes they negotiated with railroad officials to get supplies to Boston. They brought sufficient independent means both to travel to meet with women in their districts to explain the USSC's work and to employ other women to take care of their household chores while they worked for soldiers' aid groups. All of this taught them a great deal about what other women thought about the war.

The question of how best to support soldiers became a highly contested and divisive subject within the USSC and its regional affiliates. The USSC's Federal approach seemed to many women cold and indifferent. Rather than sending supplies and money to the Boston headquarters, they indicated their preference for working through their local charitable societies for soldiers from their own communities and on projects that focused on the poor in their own communities who had even less than the soldiers did. As E. H. Dickerson, associate manager at Belfast, Maine, informed Isa E. Gray at headquarters: "Some replied 'we have already organized charitable societies—will do what we can for the soldiers but cannot neglect our own poor &c &c &c.'"[43] Associate managers more often heard that women wanted to focus solely on soldiers from their own communities, men they knew. Reports collected from eight towns filed by Eleanor Gardiner gave notice of similar preferences. Women in the town of Skowhegan sent a barrel of apples to the Maine State agent at Washington, Maine, rather than to the USSC. The women of Corville sent supplies of cotton and linen to the USSC, but only after securing a promise that these would go to men from their families. "We promised the people they should be used for *Maine Soldiers*. That was the best I could do," Gardiner reported in June 1864 after surveying women in eight towns.[44]

Women who preferred to support their "own" soldiers and distrusted the USSC's ability to see to the needs of their husbands and sons held the most strenuous objection to the work of the USSC. Women in the coastal town of Bluehill, Maine, explicitly prioritized the needs of men from their own community. "While we value the great importance of your Commission to our suffering soldiers, and heartily wishing our means only equaled our sympathies for all, we are compelled by our limited resources to confine our contribution to those sick and disabled soldiers gone from *our own* community," they wrote to headquarters. This was a typical response to local manager H. M. Fulton's solicitations—charity began at home, as did trust. Every town in her county had a soldiers' aid society, but sent "their contributions chiefly to their own friends." Fulton acknowledged the high cost of fabric and the limited means of many women as barriers to support of the USSC. Indeed, it became hard to find someone in Bluehill who would agree to represent the USSC.[45] "It is *only* for want of means that our people here decline contributing further to the Sanitary Com.," she wrote. The best many could do was to "occasionally send supplies" directly to their own sons or husbands" and "they feel that beyond that they can do no more while the present prices for clothing are maintained."[46]

Even when women seemed to express full confidence in the Sanitary Commission, it was often a qualified endorsement. For example, as H. B. Chickering, secretary of the Dedham, Massachusetts, Ladies Soldiers' Aid Society, informed the commission, "Our society prefers to send its donations to meet the wants of individual cases, as they are made known to us." This preference, she added, did not stem "from any distrust of the Commission" but reflected the small size of their group, its limited means, its members' finding it "more satisfactory to know specifically, how our benefactions are bestowed."[47] This was a veiled critique of the priorities of the USSC headquarters, just as the oft-cited "lack of interest" was.[48] The emphasis many women in the local chapters placed on soldiers from their own towns reflected a widespread distrust of headquarters, the sense that it was too big and distant to understand and serve their needs. This was the message Fanny Pierce conveyed in a letter to her brother in the Thirteenth Massachusetts Regiment, "the wish to do something personal amidst the vast relief network that had apparently engulfed them all." Their Aunt Susan wanted the pair of "soldier's stocking" she had been knitting to go to him alone, "a soldier she knew, rather than to a vast depersonalized supply network." As Nina Silber writes, "Home-front women resisted the kind of mentality, pervasive in the Sanitary Commission, that wished to efface local peculiarities and attachments."[49]

The USSC competed for attention with a multitude of local groups— from sewing circles to missionary societies to state-run groups and the U.S. Christian Commission, organized by leaders of the YMCA to minister to the religious and spiritual needs of soldiers. Having done little for the USSC in the first months of 1864, women in Concord, Massachusetts, declared in May of that year that "they had worked for the soldiers long enough, and that now they had better work for the missionaries."[50] Some towns wished to give only to hospitals that employed nurses from their town or region. The women of Brunswick announced that they were "interested and occupied in working for hospitals in which are nurses from our own town and in whom we know confidence may be placed."[51] The desire to designate aid to particular hospitals— "so many have their pet regiments or hospitals to send to"—frustrated associate managers, but they were helpless to change the trend. Several sewing circles in Lynn, Massachusetts, even announced their preference for supporting the hospital work of a woman from their own community who had come home to encourage them to send all donations directly to her at the Finley U.S. General Hospital in Washington, D.C., which she would then distribute. The sewing circles liked her appeal, "urging that it is better to send to someone who is known, and who is doing so much good, especially as she says it takes so long to receive through the Commission." M. L. Newhall, the USSC associate manager in Lynn, Massachusetts, encountered many such pet projects and told the Boston office she "did not know what to say in such cases, of which there are a great many."[52] Opponents of the Christian Commission believed it encouraged people "to do for a certain hospital, where there is a friend interested."[53]

Wanting more control over the distribution of the supplies they collected, the secretary of the Calais Soldiers' Aid Society explained the group's decision to switch its support to the Maine state relief agency: "I regret to say that I am not authorized to give any encouragement to hope for aid from us. When we first began to work for the 'Sanitary Commission' there was no organization in our own state through which we could transmit our contributions for the benefit expressly of soldiers from our own state—we therefore sent them to your society but as soon as arrangements were made by which our donations could be thus appropriated a majority of our ladies preferred to send through our state agent & it is for this reason that you have not during the past six months received aid from our association." Instead, they sent boxes of supplies and money to Portland "which have been appropriated to the soldiers from our own state." Some women in the Calais Soldiers' Aid Society appreciated the catholicity of the USSC's "Federal idea." "We have sons & brothers in regiments from many other states besides our own & would like to labor for the *whole army* & feel that the interest is one," the secretary pro tem of the Calais Society wrote. But theirs was a minority opinion, and "in this as in all such cases the majority govern[.] [W]e of course yield."[54]

A few months later the Calais Society voted "unanimously" to support the USSC.[55] It does not appear that the USSC changed its policies on the distribution of goods to accommodate the group. Rather, the change in heart seems to have been precipitated by an attack on women's wartime work. Word had reached the Calais Society that a surgeon had "made an *unsuccessful* attempt to write against the Sanitary Commission," recalling the general opposition of men to women's wartime work. Mary Cooper of the Calais Society requested a copy of the paper from headquarters, believing it would do more to energize women in support of the USSC than dry reports. "That little story will be read and have its influence, where statistics or addresses would be thrown out," she wrote.[56]

Associate managers kept careful track of the mounting opposition to the USSC, but because they seemed unable to fully comprehend the concerns that fueled it, they were unable to see a solution that addressed the concerns. In the small town of Castine, Dorothy Stevens noted the decline in the active membership of the sewing circle. By 1863, the "working" membership consisted of only twelve to fifteen women. Perhaps as important was the change in the class composition of the active membership. The twelve to fifteen "working members" who remained were "not of the wealthiest portion of the community." In contrast to the "many who feel but little, if any, interest, in this good work," these few were "constantly employed in doing for our suffering soldiers."[57] The less wealthy members had their own ideas about who should benefit from their work.

In January 1863, the sewing circle of Castine sent several boxes of clothing, bedding, jellies, preserves, and wine to the Boston office and other towns to be forwarded to Frederick Law Olmsted (the famed landscape architect had taken leave from his work designing New York's Central Park to become the USSC's executive secretary) at the USSC's Washington, D.C., headquarters. But part of the shipment came with explicit directions for its distribution. The donor of the jellies and preserves specifically requested that her contribution be directed to the Department of the Gulf, where several Maine regiments were stationed. Indeed, Stevens wrote, the entire group had a "preference for that portion of our army," as "most of them have sons, brothers, & other friends there," but the group's members "never yet have known whether any Hospital supplies have been sent them."[58]

The efforts of some associate managers to respond to resistance to the USSC's organizational model by working to create "a change in public sentiment" and cultivate a "better state of feeling" toward the commission were largely futile.[59] Dorothy Stevens of Castine acknowledged the concerns over where contributions went and believed they could be resolved by "a plain statement of fact" from the USSC and assurance "of the safe conveyance of their gifts" for the end donors intended.[60] It would not have been possible for the USSC to give such an assurance without revamping its ideology and entire structure, neither of which took into consideration the opinions of poor and working-class women or their politics, and which the organization showed no inclination to change. In addition, Mrs. J. Sumner of Great Barrington, Massachusetts, reminded Annette Rogers at the Boston office, she had to deal with questions about the organization's finances. "We are met on every side with the questions 'What becomes of all the money raised for the Sanitary Commission' & that question implies a doubt in the minds of those who ask it of the necessity of doing anything further."[61]

Resistance to the Boston office and concerns around the question of agency did not go away. The establishment of a General Hospital for soldiers in Augusta, Maine, and the placement there of dozens of wounded Maine soldiers, seemed only to increase the determination of women to focus on soldiers from their own community. "The voice of the people has been so loud & strong to keep our own articles for their use that we dared not disregard it," wrote H. B. Fuller of Augusta. Fuller visited the hospital and was pleased to note that many of the things they had sent "would *not* be needed." She took delight in seeing "the men so comfortable & happy" and "rejoicing at having escaped from the crowded Hospitals of Regiments." Even so, she found "prejudice which still unaccountably exists toward the Sanitary Com."[62]

Women in Solon, Maine, voiced similar sentiments. They had supported the USSC in the past but in 1864 informed the society of the "desire of many to do work for own soldiers" through their state agency. "We have had an appeal from the Maine Soldiers' Relief Association[,] Washington, for special aid for Maine regiments and our ladies are very anxious, indeed feel that we ought to send our next box there," Emeline Coolidge informed the Boston office.[63] The Sanitary Commission also faced competition from foreign missionary societies, the Society of Friends who preferred "working by themselves," and from state agencies in other states. The Massachusetts Relief Society, wrote M. L. Newhall (the USSC associate manager in Lynn, Massachusetts), "takes very largely from the contributions which we should otherwise receive" and was its "strongest competition in the favor of the people."[64]

Andover, Massachusetts, presented a classic case of divided loyalties and determined resistance to control by the Boston office. Andover hosted several soldiers' aid societies that preferred to make their own decisions about where and to whom their contributions would go. They objected to giving their "aid wholly to the Sanitary Commission." The church society, for example, sent supplies to USSC stations in New Bern, North Carolina; Alexandria, Virginia; and Washington, D.C., but also barrels of supplies directly to Fort Albany, Virginia, where a company of soldiers from Andover was stationed, and to the U.S. Christian Commission. Rather than allow the NEWAA in Boston to determine the destination of their contributions, they deferred to the recommendations of individual members. In adopting this decentralized approach, the Andover church society considered itself "perfectly independent of any demands from the San. Com." and no longer "under any obligation to meet any requirements of the Com, except to send articles for the sick & wounded." And this they would do when they were "able to" but would continue "to use their influence for the cause."[65]

A large part of the problem, some associate managers concluded, was disinterest and apathy. D. L. Stevens chronicled the lack of enthusiasm and trust in Castine, Maine. The town sent 80 to 100 men to war, a significant number in a town with only 1,200 residents.[66] But women's support for the war effort remained problematic. "Castine has done well in sending soldiers," Stevens wrote. Yet "notwithstanding that, many of our people manifest an astonishing apathy toward doing anything for the comfort & welfare of those brave & noble men who have sacrificed so much for us," which she thought "ought not so to be." M. L. Newhall thought it was "hard for those who have not friends in the army to realize the constant necessities when all is so bright at home." Stevens rejected that argument. The problem, she wrote, was not that they were "so far from everything that looks like war that many perhaps, can scarcely realize it." This was a poor "apology" for the indifference and not "a very plausible one . . . for we daily have papers," telegrams, and letters from the front, she wrote.[67] Questions more broadly about Northern women's loyalty or indifference led to the formation of the National Women's Loyalty League.

The difficulties associate managers faced in recruiting women to work for the USSC, which they traced to apathy, were at least as rooted in the growing poverty in New England during the war. Towns increasingly sent word that they were "too poor" to help.[68] P. G. Bowman, based in Bangor, Maine, like D. L. Stevens, emphasized the "poverty of many towns." Bowman had some success in the towns of Lebouth, a "rather poor place," and Passadumkey, a similarly poor community. The contributions that came from such communities, a box or two and other small donations, reflected their economic circumstances. Communications from headquarters pressing women to plant more onions and cabbage as a preventive of scurvy, and to send dried fruit rather than jellies to make sure "that not a single article is withheld that could be of service to a wounded man on the field or in the hospital," did not help.[69]

Some women, cognizant of the advantages their class bestowed, worked to facilitate fuller participation by poor women. In Andover, Susan Ellis considered opening a room in her townhouse where work could be given out to women unconnected to any of the soldiers' aid societies and who "have not the means to *furnish the* materials; and where all who may not like to send their humble offerings to any particular society; can blend theirs with those going."[70] The contributions of working-class women also came indirectly through contributions to the cause made by their husbands, fathers, and sons. In December 1861, for example, thirty-three men employed at Alonzo Josselyn's iron foundry in the town of Roxbury, Massachusetts, sent the New England Woman's Auxiliary Association $50.37, "the proceeds of one day's labor," to support sick and wounded soldiers. "It shows that beneath the rough exterior of the hardy mechanic, there dwells the spark of humanity," Josselyn wrote. Ten men from the foundry were in the army.[71]

Associate managers often failed to fully grasp the economic circumstances that made it hard for poor women to contribute labor, money, or time. Their middle- and upper-class women status could easily blind them to the challenges the poor women faced. A faltering economy in Lowell, Massachusetts, fueled an exodus from the town and made it harder for those who remained to support themselves or the troops.[72] Economic woes also affected the work in Lynn, where by the spring of 1864 the aid society "had dwindled to almost nothing." Newhall had "endeavored to rouse the ladies once more; some of them were almost asleep as regards the cause; it is strange what apathy there is." Only twenty-five women had shown up at the last meeting. Giving "up all endeavor to make things better," she closed the society's room. A fund-raiser in March garnered $800, but significant apathy remained. Newhall wondered if other towns were having similar problems or if the situation in Lynn was simply a reflection of their "being so far from the scene of action."[73] Similarly, Mrs. J. Sumner of Great Barrington, Massachusetts, reminded Annette Rogers at the Boston headquarters. "You ladies of Boston with your large organization [and] warm zeal, can scarcely realize the apathy that prevails here," she wrote. She had warned Rogers's predecessor, Isa Gray, not to expect too much from them.[74] Lucy Reynolds, in charge of leading the USSC effort in six towns, could not decide whether the problem was "want of interest, or the right person to lead them."[75]

In addition to poverty, associate managers faced the logistical problem of trying to organize women in widely scattered rural towns. It was not uncommon for women to have to travel six miles to attend weekly meetings. P. V. Bowman thus believed women in small communities like the "wide awake" group at Garland, where two sewing circles took spinning and knitting work, deserved special praise.[76] The distance between towns was also a barrier in recruiting associate managers.[77] Winter weather, especially when roads were closed by snow and ice and the closest railroad or steamer was thirty or more miles away, exacerbated the problem.

In some places, as E. H. Dickerson discovered, it was not worth the effort to try to recruit women to the Union cause because they did not believe in it. Dickerson worked diligently to reach out to towns in her county but obtained mixed results. In some places, she found groups "thoroughly organized and doing a good work for the Commission" and in others, women far "less patriotic." Dickerson's hometown of Belfast was among the better organized and successful in raising funds for the USSC. Belfast was a wealthy shipbuilding town, boasting ornate Federal, Greek Revival, and Italianate mansions, which made it a more fruitful site for recruiting elite women for soldiers' aid work. Dickerson seemed understanding of those who preferred "to work in a less systematic manner, and assist various benevolent objects according as time and circumstances demand." But she was frustrated with women in other "less patriotic" towns who "even neglect to answer my communications."[78]

At the other end of the spectrum were towns like Lincolnville, which Dickerson labeled "*weak & feeble* since the wealthiest portion are '*secesh*.'"[79] The "secesh," Southern sympathizers who supported the copperheads or Peace Democrats, a faction of the Democratic party that opposed a war waged, as they saw it, to destroy the South rather than to restore the seceded states to the Union, just said no. At a mass meeting, New York Democrats declared the war illegal and unconstitutional.[80] The town of Moran, Maine, did not have a soldiers' aid society, and it would make no sense to try to form one because its residents were "Copperheads," Eleanor Gardiner reported. "Coppery" was also alive and well in the town of Salon. "There is a large secession element among us," Emeline Coolidge wrote, "and the feeling prevalent is, that a life so given is not a noble sacrifice but uselessly thrown away. It is this feeling that prevents our doing all we could, ought and are able to for the Soldiers."[81] Soldiers' aid efforts were similarly hopeless in the "copperhead town" of Charleston, Maine.[82]

Local Aid societies rejected the view of the USSC Executive Committee in Boston that the problem was with them, that too many towns simply failed "to come up to the mark."[83] The Boston committee put intense pressure on associate managers to do better, but the comments it got back called on the national office itself to do better. Many women outside of Boston were mystified by the organization's structure and could not understand just what field agents' precise duties were. Attending meetings at the Boston headquarters failed to convince M. L. Newhall that the commission understood the grievances coming from some of the towns. The people she talked to at home believed the USSC needed to do a better job explaining exactly what it did and how it made its decisions. This could be accomplished, she thought, by sending a representative from headquarters to "lecture before the people" "who understands the workings of the whole plan, and who can substantiate, by facts, the advantage of sending through the Commission."[84] Months later, Newhall was still trying to figure out what her job fully entailed and how she should respond to questions about the USSC. She thought prejudice against the Sanitary Commission had declined, but people still wanted and needed to "know better its plans of operations and to understand it more fully, to be convinced of its superior usefulness."[85]

Associate managers struggled throughout the war to understand the USSC's mission and message and their role in it. "I scarcely know just what I ought to do," wrote P. G. Bowman from Bangor, Maine. Bowman had worked hard to organize groups in the towns of her district and encourage their efforts. She sent "reminders of duty" to forty-four towns, some two and three times over. In some towns, she was able to "resalt" groups that had become defunct.[86]

Hannah B. Chickering, an educated woman of wealth and a leader in the reform community of Dedham, Massachusetts, became one of the fiercest critics of the USSC, voicing the complaints of many about the USSC's organizational structure. Writing to Isa Gray at the Boston office, she noted near "entire confidence" of the people in the Sanitary Commission," and that "*a few* have reached what you will consider a 'perfect state' in that they feel that your Society is the *only* channel through which supplies ought to be sent." Yet, while a few were perfectly satisfied, the "prevailing sentiment" was that support for the commission should not be "to the exclusion of other channels for our interest and our benefactions." She questioned whether an "organization of such mammoth proportions, can, in the nature of the case, reach many individual cases, which require *personal* care and assistance—where the material gift may be accompanied with the encouraging word, and the kindly sympathy, which will do more for the 'miracle' of our army than all the shirts and drawers thro' an officials' hands," as important as the latter was. Moreover, "in a country place like Dedham, where the love of doing grace, for its own sake, has not reached its highest stage of development, there needs to be at times, a warming of the heart and a quickening of the hand by a newer approach to the object for which we are working." That required "a diversity of channels, tho' at the same time a oneness of object." She would remain a "firm" supporter of the Sanitary Commission and would continue to circulate its materials but needed to be convinced that she was wrong on the main point of her critique.[87]

The following month Chickering sent "tangible proof" of her group's support of the Sanitary Commission, a list of the supplies it had sent to the commission's rooms. But personally, she remained "*theoretically* incorrigible." Isa Gray tried to convince Chickering of the benefits of centralization of power; Chickering gave her arguments "due weight" but remained skeptical. She and Gray stood differently and must necessarily think differently, she wrote. Her perspective was shaped not only by "viewing the subject more remotely from the centre of action and influence" but by her views on the democratic process. "I cannot but feel that centralization of power, so contrary to the genius of our country and its institutions, is more desirable in benevolent action, than in other departments—and, therefore, as a matter of principle, must object to any organisation [*sic*] not *wholly* Governmental, insisting upon being the *only* medium of the people's benefactions." She believed "that many of those most interested in the Sanitary Commission would be among the very first to agree . . . if the same principle of centralization were brought to bear upon any other subject—or the same subject even,—if their position of deep interest, and knowledge of what they would be glad to accomplish, did not obscure the minor benefits—to be conveyed through inferior channels."

Chickering reiterated her support for the important work of the Sanitary Commission, work no one else was doing, and said she "would urge others, to support it fully and abundantly." Still, she cautioned headquarters, "do not *claim too much*." She continued to question why the commission would "object to the *division of privilege* which allows a loving hand to alleviate the sufferings and cheer the spirit of the convalescent." She had in mind specifically the Christian Commission. Her organization had not given to the U.S. Christian Commission, but surely, she wrote, those who ministered "to the wants of the soul" deserved their support. While not "as 'wholly imbued with Commission ideas' as I am now in my loving interest," she desired to "stand in a *true* light before" the USSC. "Having thus claimed the *right* of free thought and action," she concluded, "I hope our Society may prove faithful and efficient co-workers with you."[88]

S. T. Phelps of Ellsworth in Hancock County voiced similar reservations about supporting the Sanitary Commission rather than the Christian Commission. At a meeting of the Maine Conference of Churches, she heard appeals on behalf of the Christian Commission in preference to all other relief organizations but left unsure of her duty as a Christian. Was she obliged as a Christian to give her support to the Christian Commission? She reached out to the USSC's Boston office for advice. "I have no fault whatever, to find with the Sanitary Commission," she wrote. "But if there is another, which does the same work and adds to it the more precious duty of caring for the soul, what is our duty as Christians?" Her minister had withdrawn his support for the USSC in favor of the Christian Commission, but, whatever her own personal wishes, she doubted she could convince the members of her group to switch its support to the Christian Commission, "for the religious element among us is very small." It was in her "own mind" that she wished to be satisfied.[89]

By the summer of 1864, D. L. Stevens, who in January 1863 had despaired of making much progress, had witnessed a turnaround.

It cheered my heart to hear that boxes were coming in abundantly, and that doubts and objections seem forgotten, in the desire all have to do *something*, it seems to have been the case in our neighborhood too, still we don't yet do half enough, but it is a great thing to have the mass of people become convinced that Govt. can't do *everything*, and we must all open our hearts and purses wider, than we have yet, to relieve the wants and mitigate the sufferings of our brave & noble soldiers, who are willing to suffer and die, if needs be, for their & our beloved country in this struggle for freedom.[90]

Throughout New England and the North more broadly, many white women did answer the call. Mattie Parsons, who worked with the Sanitary Commission in Boston, took in two families left destitute when their husbands and fathers volunteered. The men belonged to a regiment she had helped recruit. In fact, she was credited with recruiting a fourth of them and had made a point of greeting all of them personally. She had "come out in an entirely new character and fairly slaves for the cause," an acquaintance wrote.[91] In the country village of Athens, Maine, Mary W. Bean reported the women doing "all they can for the suffering soldiers." She drew attention to a seventy-five-year-old woman who walked three miles "to have the privilege of giving the widows mite" and hoped this act would inspire the wealthy to give.[92]

Still, money made a difference in women's wartime work. It influenced the forms that work took and who performed it. Wealthy women had more leisure time and were more educated. They had more time to volunteer than poor women struggling just to feed and clothe their families. They had servants to cook, clean, and wash for them. They had connections to powerful men and were able to more easily finance from their own pockets the domestic production of war matériel. Mary Lowell's ability to put poor women to work making shirts on contract to the Federal government was indebted to her membership in a powerful family. She was married to Robert Trail Spence Lowell, whose brother was James Russell Lowell. Like many Northern white women of her class, she employed Irish domestic servants. Twenty-year-old Margaret Reilly lived in her home in 1850. By 1860, Reilly was employed as a servant in the home of a New Yorker who listed his occupation as "Gentleman." Poor and working-class women and soldiers' wives, like their Southern counterparts, also found themselves stigmatized as underserving recipients of charity. Northern states and towns passed laws to support soldiers' wives, but poor women sometimes found themselves up against local officials "who responded with particular parsimony to at least some appeals." Ellen and John Gilbert were poor people. They expected an improvement in their lot when John enlisted in the 3rd New Hampshire Volunteers. They expected that Ellen would receive twelve dollars a month from the town under state law, "but instead of giving her money, the selectmen doled out portions of flour and firewood to her."[93]

The critically important massive relief work Northern women took on in support of the Union cause has rightly drawn the attention and admiration of historians but has left little room or appetite for scholars to question their place in the world or how it had been secured, and little room to explore the class antagonisms and racism that plagued the work of the USSC and other areas of white women's wartime work and the different experiences of

Northern women as soldiers' wives and mothers. The continued ties of many wealthy and most socially prominent Northern white women to slavery and the global economy it spawned is another missing piece of the story.[94]

Cleansed of "the Stain of Human Slavery"

From the nation's earliest history, Northern white women had profited from slavery. Margaret Philips, one of several wealthy women merchants in the Dutch era, "sailed with her own ships," and Northern women continued to profit from slavery long after. Nothing that made the North free soil had extinguished the ties that bound it to slavery. Into the antebellum era, the inherited wealth of many Northern white women continued to include investments that could be traced to the international slave trade and slave-grown commodities and their manufacture. The closing of the Atlantic slave trade in 1808 and slave emancipation in the North did not completely sever the ties Northern women had with the world of slavery. They were the wives and daughters and sisters of men who financed the cotton, sugar, and rice crops, built and operated the factories that turned cotton into cloth and sugarcane into granulated sugar, who financed, built, and operated the ships and railroads that carried enslaved people and slave-produced commodities from New York and Virginia to Europe and New Orleans. The profits that derived from those enterprises accrued to Northern women as well as men directly and indirectly. These ties and profits are fairly invisible in the history of Northern women abolitionists and leaders of soldiers' aid societies. The stories of their lives and politics, their ties to sugar manufacturing concerns, slave plantations in the South and Cuba, disappear, cleansed of "the stain of human slavery."[95] The staunchly abolitionist Woolsey family of New York and Rhode Island had its own cleansing story.

The Woolsey family legacy went in part like this: "When the members of the Woolsey family gave up toys, they took up politics." Brought up by a mother who was born into an old Virginia slaveholding family but who had come to hate slavery, they had walked "in the straight path of abolitionism and would [have] none of the Democratic party."[96] Decades after the Civil War, Jane Eliza Woolsey's children published the family's wartime correspondence with the goal to ensure that their descendants for generations to come would "understand the spirit with which a great multitude, ourselves among them, entered into this struggle" and celebrate "the willing service of the soldiers of the National Army [that] gave you a country worth caring for."[97] The book offered a stirring account of the "straight path of abolitionism" the family had walked from cutting their "political teeth on the *New*

York Tribune" to being "in the right frame of mind to keep step with the steady march to the inevitable through the Kansas perplexities, the John Brown raid and the election of Mr. Lincoln, to the firing of the first gun by the rebels upon the national flag at Fort Sumter."[98] When President Lincoln called for 75,000 troops on April 15, 1861, they had refused to stay "comfortably housed in Washington, while the army marched to danger and death." They had continued that steady march—Jane Eliza's son by joining the army and she and her daughters by helping establish the Woman's Central Association of Relief, and going to the front as hospital nurses. Defying those who said women did not belong in military hospitals or on the battlefield, Jane Eliza Woolsey's daughters "enlisted for the war" and "prepared to move with the Army of Potomac."[99]

Following her marriage to Charles William Woolsey, Jane Eliza Newton Woolsey, the mother who carried her children to Charleston for vacation, moved permanently to the North. By 1861, she was a friend of the slave and the place of her birth seemed immaterial. Charles became a wealthy merchant in the sugar trade and the sugar refinery business located in the heart of Wall Street.[100] His family ranked among the most prominent Northern merchant families, many of whom had strong ties to the abolition and reform movements. And like many of them, the Woolseys had ongoing financial investments entangled with slavery long after the institution had been abolished in the North.[101]

Decades after the end of the Civil War, Jane Eliza Woolsey's children attempted to wipe clean any stain of slavery that might have clung to her and her descendants. The cleansing story removed her—and thus them—from her roots in Virginia, from her ties to Cuba, and from the family's ties to the slave trade and Cuba. Prior to her marriage, Jane Eliza Newton [Woolsey] spent a year with her sister and brother-in-law, Mary and Francis Adams, on the Cuban coffee plantation Adams purchased in partnership with Howland Brothers & Company. According to family lore, Adams named the Cuban property "Mt. Vernon, in memory of Virginia." Francis Adams was also a partner in the powerful merchant firm of Latting, Adams & Stewart, which had a separate partnership relationship with the elite firm of Howland Brothers & Company of Connecticut and New York.[102] One of Jane Eliza's daughters would marry into the Howland family, carrying on the tradition of marriage between the Woolseys and Howlands. Latting, Adams & Stewart also had close ties to James DeWolf of Rhode Island, the largest slave trader in the United States, and his brother George DeWolf. The DeWolfs were also heavily involved in Cuban plantations and owned commercial houses that did business in Cuba. There were ties of other kinds as well, cemented by marriages between wealthy Northern women and Southern slaveholders. Anna Elizabeth DeWolf, for example, was born into the famous slave-trading DeWolf family of Bristol, Rhode Island, and married into one of the wealthiest slaveholding families of South Carolina, the Middletons, whose former plantation, Middleton Place, is a designated National Historic landmark and described on its website as an "American treasure."[103]

The story of Jane Eliza Newton Woolsey's encounter with slavery in Cuba, the account that she passed down to her children and they retold in the family history, meets the definition of what Craig Wilder calls "a tale of decorative servitude." Jane Eliza Woolsey, her children recalled, "always spoke of with bated breath" of this time.[104] Her recollections, as transcribed by her children, included a familiar narrative, slave "loyalty" to white women.

> There had been signs of discontent and half-suppressed mutterings among the slaves of the island for some time, and during one special night the family had listened in terror to whispered plotting under their windows and to the sharpening of knives. Both Mother and Aunt Mary had been kind to the poor blacks in their service, and one man in particular— a servant in the family whose wife had been ill—was most grateful to them for their care of her and his children. It was known for some time in advance when the family of Mr. Adams,—the frightened and unprotected little group of women and children—were to leave the Island. When the time came, *this man* carried the children down in his arms with the greatest care and tenderness, took them on board the sailing vessel which was to take them home, put them in their little berths and took leave of them all, as the other servants did, with great feeling and gratitude. It seemed, Mother said, as though he could not do enough for them.[105]

Jane Eliza Woolsey's children, Eliza Newton Woolsey Howland and Charles William Woolsey, recorded this story in the privately published family history, titled *Family Records*. According to the story, it was only in the weeks following their departure from Cuba that Jane and her sister Mary Adams learned that a slave rebellion had broken out a few days after their departure and that the rebels, on orders from the slave who had helped them escape, had delayed the start of the rebellion until the family had been safely removed. The "terrible insurrection of the negroes" had been "held in check by this man until 'his ladies' were in safety." The slave who had so gingerly carried Mary's children to the ship, they learned, "was the ring-leader who had since distinguished himself by his brutality to the whites and his many murders."[106]

In sum this is, then, a story of a large-scale slave rebellion temporarily halted, "held in check," until the white women of one plantation had been safely removed from the scene. It was similar to the story the Woolsey children heard Wendell Phillips tell about Toussaint Louverture.

One does not have to doubt that slave rebels sometimes acted out of gratitude for some prior kindness extended to them or their families to see the problem such stories raise: The "care" Jane Eliza and her sister extended to a sick slave woman and her children had the effect of disappearing their roles as mistresses in the system of slavery and, more broadly, "the cozy relationship of the northern, southern, and West Indies aristocracies."[107] Jane Woolsey returned to the United States in 1825, the year of the rebellion. It was the year, too, that the commercial house of Latting, Adams & Stewart failed from overexposure in the midst of a bad crop year in Cuba and Russia. Highly overleveraged, Adams was destroyed financially. In February 1825, one of James DeWolf's agents learned that the firm would not be able to fulfill an order for 800 boxes of sugar. Other promised shipments also fell through. Some of DeWolf's trading partners accused Adams of trying to manipulate the financial markets. In the resulting panic, the economy in the port of Bristol, Rhode Island, collapsed and Latting, Adams & Stewart was one of several merchant firms that failed. Francis Adams died on the plantation on May 1, 1825, following an illness, but rumors spread that he had committed suicide.[108]

The story Jane Eliza Woolsey passed on made no mention of the failure of Latting, Adams & Stewart or the rumored suicide. It does, however, draw our attention to the ways families like the Woolseys profited from slavery, and the Cuban trade in sugar was one of the most profitable. As Roland T. Ely writes, "Cuba's commercial class thus formed the vital link in a saccharine chain stretching from the island's sun-drenched canefields to northern counting-houses of merchants like Moses Taylor; thence to grocers or refiners, and finally to the breakfast table or confectioner's shop."[109] In 1827, 87 percent of the 1,053 ships arriving in the port of Havana were American-owned. Prominent families with investments in Cuba included the New York Howland family, whose wealth derived in part from Cuban sugar and coffee plantations and iron and copper mines, and the ancestors of Julia Ward Howe, who owned and operated Cuban plantations starting in at least 1808.[110]

When the Civil War began, slavery's tentacles still reached deep into Northern homes—from the history of abolition that had absorbed racism into its very fabric to complex financial investments in the South and Cuba.

This had important consequences for the wartime struggle for emancipation and equality. The effects were visible in the debates surrounding the capacity of black men to be soldiers and citizens and the capacity of black women to be good mothers and citizens and legitimate soldiers' wives, and in the encounters Northerners had with black people in the South during the war.[111] The philanthropic and reform initiatives of many Northern elite women were made possible by leisure and wealth won from the traffic in slaves and slave-grown commodities, which could not but shape in some measure their interactions with and views about black people. Understanding precisely how requires understanding the ways Northerners continued to traffic in slavery long after the end of slavery in the North.[112]

Whether they called home a plantation in Cuba or a mansion in New York or New England, elite Northern women had longer and deeper personal ties to slavery and profited longer from the system than scholars have generally granted. They were beneficiaries of "cozy" relationships that spanned the globe and enabled the enjoyment of the rewards of slave ownership from a distance. Like slaveholders in the American South, they comprised tight-knit clans linked by marriage, business relationships, and friendship. The Woolseys, for example, were linked by marriage, philanthropic endeavors, and business partnerships to several other influential merchant families, including the Howlands, Aspinwalls, Coits, and Adamses. The marriage of Eliza Newton Woolsey, Jane Eliza Newton Woolsey's daughter, to Joseph Howland, whose father, Samuel, was a principal in the merchant firm of Howland & Aspinwall, deepened the family's ties to the Howlands and Aspinwalls. Howland & Aspinwall was one of the world's largest shipping houses, owned plantations in Cuba and was heavily invested in the sugar trade.[113] The wives and daughters of the men who led this and similar firms inherited tremendous wealth that they controlled in their own right. The links between slavery and homes of wealthy Northerners were largely invisible to the naked eye. But here and there, they poked through to the surface.

Many white women among the most active Unionists, Republicans, and abolitionists who had been liberated by their wealth from having to make a living or earn a wage put this privilege based on wealth that had permitted a distancing of slavery to good use in its destruction. But even then, they were not unaware of either the source of their privilege or the routes to participation in the war that were unavailable to poor women. Georgeanna Woolsey was ecstatic when she went to the New York Medical Committee to seek admission to a training course, to which she was accepted along with ten other women. "We are to learn how to make beds for the wounded, cook food properly for the sick, wash and dress wounds, and other things as they come along in the proper care of the wards—fresh air, etc," she wrote her sister Eliza, who she hoped would join her. She worried about opposition from her parents to her doing this kind of work, but her wealth gave her options. If the opposition to her working at the hospital and her sister going to the front proved too strong, "we shall send substitutes agreeing to pay their expenses."[114] In the end, they had the wholehearted support of their mother and other family members. "Your patriotism is grand," Jane Eliza Woolsey wrote her daughter Eliza in 1865 in celebration of Eliza's wartime work on behalf of Union soldiers.[115] The wealth that backed the Woolseys' wartime work was enormous.

At her death in 1883, Jane Stuart Woolsey, another of Jane Eliza Newton Woolsey's daughters, left a legacy of $53,000 inherited from the estates of her father, the merchant Charles William Woolsey, and her grandfather, a sum that in today's dollars would make her a millionaire. She left the bulk of her estate to her siblings and their children along with generous contributions to charities, including $5,000 to the General Hospital Society of Connecticut in New Haven "to endow a childs [sic] free bed in perpetuity." The investments from which her inheritance drew totaled more than $1.7 million.[116] Her sister Eliza Newton Woolsey Howland held wealth inherited from her father and enlarged by her marriage to Joseph Howland, a benefactor of the estate of more than $11 million left by his father, Samuel S. Howland. To each of his six children, five daughters and one son (Caroline H. Russell, Louisa H. Hoppier, Mary H. Van Renselaer, Emily H. Chauncey, Catherine Clinton Howland, and Joseph Howland), Samuel Howland left a quarter of a million dollars. The hundreds of thousands of dollars inherited by Samuel Howland's daughters, Eliza Newton Woolsey's sisters-in-law, drew from the family's ties to slavery in myriad ways. They included stock in the New York Steam Sugar Refining Company, which processed slave-grown sugar, steamship companies that moved enslaved people along the routes of the domestic slave trade and the products of their labor, shares in insurance companies that insured the bodies of enslaved people, the gas company that kept the major slave importing city of New Orleans lit, and an Alabama bank.[117]

Louisa Meredith Howland, the widow of Samuel Howland's brother Gardiner Howland, drew an annual income of $200,000 from her husband's estate "as long as she is his widow." The Howlands were parsimonious in the legacies they left their servants. To all those in his employ, Gardiner Howland left "a new and entire suit of black."[118] Samuel Howland's will designated that Kate and Ann Mackey, two domestic servants at his farm, receive

$13.75 and $35.00, respectively, and set aside funds to cover the wages of a domestic servant at his Washington Square home for six months. At the same time, he left substantial sums to a wide array of charities, church organizations, and reform organizations, among them the Juvenile Asylum; the American Bible Society; the American Board of Commissioners for Foreign Missions; the American Education Society; the Orphan Asylum Society; the Half Orphan Society; the Colored Half Orphan Asylum Society; the Society for Relief of Respectable Aged, Indigent Females; the Institution for the Deaf and Dumb; and the Institution for the Blind.[119]

The work of scholars over the last few decades has challenged the idea of a hard divide between public and private in nineteenth-century middle-class family life. This scholarship has argued that "behind the public man" were women whose "private labours" provided the foundation "on which new forms of capitalist enterprise were built, new patterns of social life established." The domesticated family, Mary Ryan cogently argues, provided the "cradle" for a new class structure.[120] What we have not detailed are the ways slavery made possible not only the Northern "public man" but also made possible the "private labours" that cradled the new middle class. Wealth enabled some women to more easily enter the public sphere and made a difference in how they responded to the Civil War and to the questions of black freedom and the place of African American women in the nation-state. It made it easier for them to fight for the slave and to fight for women.

The different ways the daughters of Jane Eliza Woolsey confronted and used the privileges of slave-based wealth and abolition reflected the broader contradictions within the abolition movement among Northern elite and middle-class white women. Jane Stuart Woolsey was content to fight for "only the stars and stripes" from the comfort of home. Georgeanna and Eliza Woolsey applauded each step the nation took toward abolition. The performance of Maj. Gen. George B. McClellan in the Seven Days Battles, for example, earned their scorn but did not diminish their belief that slavery's end would come in spite of incompetent generals who "are not even fools, but something less if possible." If it was "God's will to destroy this nation by inches," so be it, Abby wrote. She hoped though that the military defeats and massive loss of life McClellan's army suffered in June 1862 were "intended to drive us, as a nation, to a higher moral ground on the conduct and purpose of this war."[121] She believed this even as she calculated the effect of the war on her family's wealth and as cracks in the Northern economy appeared in everyday transactions.

In July 1862, Stewart's Department Store and Lord & Taylor began "to give

change to their customers in postage stamps." The store gave Caroline Woolsey "a tiny envelope stamped U.S. 50 cts.," as change on a purchase; she
used the stamped envelope in turn to pay for ribbon at another store. As she
surveyed the finances of her immediate and extended family, Abby Woolsey
worried about the impact of McClellan's policy of caution on them. It was
"too expensive a policy," she wrote. "We are bankrupt already. . . . Aspinwalls
and Uncle E. blue as indigo. Don't know what to do about our property and
their own too."[122] Yet, despite the inconveniences and financial losses that
she and her family would suffer, Abby Woolsey remained firm in her support
for the Union and abolition. "I would give every dollar of *mine* if it would
end this accursed war and slavery to boot." She had a lot to give. Her cousin
William Aspinwall of the firm of Howland & Aspinwall actually did just that,
sending a check to the War Department for $25,296.60, his share of the prof-
its on a government contract for arms held by the firm.[123]

While some Northern women used their leisure and resources to raise
money and supplies for Union soldiers, to go to the front as nurses, and work
with freedmen's aid societies, others, like the Northern "secesh," saw the
war as wrong. Still others, as we will see in the next chapter, saw opportunities to join the ranks of nonslaveholding Southern women and satisfy their
yearning to be mistress of a plantation, even if only for a brief moment.[124]
The New York draft riots of 1863, among other events, exposed the degree
to which many white Northerners remained opposed to emancipation and
racial equality and the deep class divisions within Northern society. Fueled
by the conscription law, inflammatory editorials in antiwar newspapers,
economic distress among the working poor, and racism, the riots raged for
several days beginning on July 13. The rioters, mainly Irish Americans, attacked black people in the streets, at their places of employment, and in
their homes and burned down the Colored Orphan Asylum.[125] Employers of
Irish domestic servants suppressed their opposition to the rioters, agreeing
not to allow "a word said against them at table, or within the reach of any of
the servants' ears."[126]

The vast majority of white Northern women and men neither began nor
ended the war as abolitionists, though their ranks grew and deepened over
the course of the war.[127] This was especially true for men like Francis Leland, a surgeon with the Second Regiment, Massachusetts Volunteers, who
encountered slavery for the first time. Leland sent a piece of wood from the
gallows where John Brown died at Charles Town back home to his family to
remind them of what was at stake.[128] It was true for women like Georgeanna
and Eliza Woolsey, who committed themselves even more fiercely to the fight
for Union and emancipation. Those who worked on behalf of freedom for

the enslaved helped shoulder the burden enslaved people carried.[129] "We did not think a year ago that at this time there would be people quarrelling over the contrabands, & almost fighting for places here, but it is so," Julia Wilbur wrote from Alexandria, Virginia, in the fall of 1863.[130] The work in support of black Southerners did gather growing support from Northerners during the war, though never to the extent Wilbur's comment suggested. The views of even the most progressive white Northerners hardly changed.[131]

When Northern white women geared up for war in 1861, they prepared to fight for the Union. The question of slave emancipation and the place of black people in the Union would be at best an ancillary matter. The views of Northern women on the question of emancipation was complex and became more so as their wartime work (as nurses, teachers to freedpeople, and agents of missionary and soldiers' aid societies) brought them into unprecedented, and often intimate, contact for the first time with enslaved and poor white women. The words of a child out with his mother on a "charitable errand through a dingy alley into a dirty, noisy, squalid tenement house" perhaps said it best. He could only think of slavery to contextualize what he saw. "'Mamma,' said he, 'isn't this South Carolina?'"[132]

It was not South Carolina, but the state was never far from the minds of Northern abolitionists. While in Savannah as part of their southern tour, Eliza Jane Woolsey and her children visited the African Baptist Church, pastored by John Cox. As Abby Woolsey recalled, it was communion Sunday and there were some 3,000 to 4,000 people in attendance. She describes Cox as "a slender, meek man in spectacles—a black man you know" and recalled his "many touching words of counsel and passages of scripture" and his assisting minister, "a quiet, excellent speaker." The pastor offered these words to one of the black women in the congregation, she wrote: "'If the Son shall make you free, ye shall be free indeed,' and to another, 'Stand fast, therefore, in the liberty wherewith God shall make you free.'" But Woolsey's racism was deeply ingrained. There were "real darkies and the singing was so like stories I have read, that altogether I had more of a sense of sight-seeing than of worshipping, I am afraid." In fact, Rev. John Cox was a highly respected minister of the Second African Baptist Church, a property valued at $10,000. He was a free black man, having purchased his freedom for $1,100 in 1849. He would be among the black ministers who assembled to meet with Gen. William T. Sherman and Secretary of War Edwin M. Stanton in Savannah on January 12, 1865.[133]

As Northern white women abolitionists strained to embrace wartime emancipation and examine their racism, black women organized in support of the Union and the growing population of freedpeople. In Chicago they formed the Chicago Colored Ladies Freedmen's Association to support refugees in the Mississippi valley and Kansas, raising funds and sending clothing and other supplies. Satirra Ford Douglas, from the Chicago group, went to Kansas as a teacher in 1864.[134] In the nation's capital, Elizabeth Keckley helped lead the effort to organize a Contraband Relief Association. The Northwestern Sanitary Fair of 1864 was one of many fairs organized by black women to support black soldiers.[135]

By performing nineteenth-century domestic ideals to the best of their abilities, the small emerging black middle class in the North had hoped to avoid racial and class stigmatization. But wealth offered even the wealthiest black families, like the Fortens of Philadelphia, only a measure of protection from the most brutal expressions of racism.[136] The majority of Northern black families were not wealthy or even middle-class, and the war placed extraordinary pressures on their households, particularly soldiers' wives. When black soldiers protested unequal pay and refused to accept less, they knew their families would suffer. "No man staying at home can imagine how great and terrible is the wrong done these men, and the distress they suffer," wrote Col. Alfred S. Hartwell, commander of the Fifty-Fifth Massachusetts Regiment. From the men of his regiment he learned of the refusal of almshouses to admit their wives "for their color." Black soldiers' wives "are reduced to degradation that drives the husbands almost crazy," Hartwell wrote.[137]

For a year and a half, the families of black soldiers who had refused to accept less pay than white soldiers had to rely on what wives could scrape together. When the government finally reversed the discriminatory pay scale, black soldiers immediately sent money to relieve their families. The soldiers of the Fifty-Fourth Massachusetts Regiment alone sent $64,000 to their wives and families and the men of the Fifty-Fifth, $65,000, by Adams Express. Some men sent money through private letters.[138]

Black soldiers were rightly concerned for their wives and children. In the public almshouses that did admit them, indigent black women faced such severe racism from poor white "inmates" that some turned for shelter to institutions for the mentally ill. Privately supported institutions for the poor were rigidly segregated or, as in the case of the Boston Home for Aged Women, catered only to "respectable native-born Protestants." In 1860, recognizing the need for a place for indigent elderly black women, some of Boston's leading white citizens, including soon to be elected governor John Andrew, established the Home for Aged Colored Women. "No private institution" in the city "would receive colored women, and the white paupers in the almshouses do not associate with them." Thus, wealthy Bostonians, out of "concern for women who had worked in their families for many years—in one case an elderly inmate had served for four generations of the family," wishing to ensure that "their loyal servants not be forced into public institutions," founded a retirement home for them. But its limited mission prevented the Home for Aged Colored Women from easing homelessness among black soldiers' families.

The home's 1863 annual report lent credence to the concerns of black soldiers' wives about Northern racism. The report acknowledged the nativism that informed the politics and policies of the home's founders and directors. Because the poor houses were filled "with a foreign population, they must be anything but a refuge to our people of color," it stated. Thus, the only solution was segregation. "Whilst we deplore the antipathies that embitter race against race, we must take them into account in our charities," the report read.[139] By the twentieth century, the home's origin story had been substantially revised. The new history stated that the first black women admitted were not domestic servants from the homes of Boston's elite families but women "first gathered from the highways and by-ways of want and neglect" and given "loving care, shelter, warmth and food."[140]

When the USSC turned to black and white Unionists and refugees in the South, it showed compassion especially for white refugees. At New Bern, North Carolina, the USSC used its resources to support black and white refugees, even donating supplies to a smallpox hospital for former slaves. But it devoted most of its time and attention to white refugees, the wives and children of soldiers of the North Carolina Volunteer Regiment, which fought against the Confederacy.[141] Their attitude in this regard was largely shared by the Northern white women who went south as teachers and missionaries to the freedpeople. All had a hard time seeing black women as deserving the full rights and benefits of freedom and citizenship.

Elite white middle and upper class women in the USSC had expressed disdain for working-class and poor women; some had refused to work with them. They made a distinction between "contract nurses" who worked for a living and women like themselves who were "volunteers," taking pride in the fact that they did not require salaries. Within the USSC, wealthier white women—"the Aristocracy of the Commission"—received less dirty and onerous work assignments and "were the darlings of the press." "Upper-crust New Yorker Katherine Prescott Wormeley embraced the elite women who joined her in hospital transport work," women she saw as "wise" and "thoroughbred," and "merry."[142] Wealthy white women also became the aristocracy of the women's wartime abolition movement, and very few Americans at the time or since have questioned much about their ascent, how their wealth enabled their politics, or why their moral outrage could not sustain a politics of the most "*radical* anti-slavery" that Northern black abolitionists like Charlotte Forten and black Southerners themselves demanded. In their encounters with black people during the war, Northern white women often strayed far from a politics of radical antislavery.

Chapter Five

NORTHERN WHITE WOMEN AND THE "GARDEN OF EDEN"

I am here in this garden of Eden of the South
and am perfectly charmed with the prospect.
—HANNAH A. ADAMS

Everywhere you turn you see them—all ages and sizes
and such a degraded set of people you never saw. They really
do not seem like human beings and they are just as
impudent as you please and so obstinate.
—LILLIE DADE

I shall—just think of it!—I shall keep house!
—LAURA M. TOWNE

I gave my services willingly for four years and
three months without receiving a dollar.
—SUSIE KING TAYLOR

THE CIVIL WAR had been over for nearly a year when Laura Towne sat for photographs with three of her students on St. Helena Island, South Carolina. She sent one she labeled the "picture of me with three of my pets" to family and friends back home in the North. The letter that accompanied the image included this description of the children.

The big boy is Dick Washington, my right hand man, who is full of importance, but has travelled and feels as if he had seen the world. He is incorrigibly slow and stupid about learning, but reads bunglingly in the Testament, does multiplication sums on the slate, and can write a letter after a fashion. The little girl with the handkerchief on her head is Amoretta—bright and sharp as a needle. She reads fluently in the Testament, spells hard and easy words in four syllables, and ciphers as far

as nine times twelve on the slate. The other child is Maria Wyne, who is
very bright in arithmetic, but very dull and slow in learning to read. My
face is burnt out so as to do justice to them. Amoretta's head kerchief is
put on as the candidates for baptism wear them.[1]

Amoretta and Maria Wyne are depicted as active and generally successful learners; Dick Washington, "incorrigibly slow and stupid," considerably
less so. The picture and Towne's letter would have arrived in the North at a
time of tremendous interest in slavery and the experiments in freedom that
Northerners like Towne went south to lead. Carte-de-visite photographs of
former slaves were a popular way for Northerners who remained at home
to experience this work. Unlike most of the images of black Southerners
that had circulated in the North via magazines and newspapers—images
of bleeding and scarred bodies and children with visible white ancestry designed to depict the brutality of slavery—that spoke to the problem of slavery, wartime and postwar photographs like Towne's spoke to the problem
of freedom.

Planting the Indelible Stamp of New England Culture

Towne's portrait conveyed a story that was new and newly necessary in the
history of slavery and portraiture featuring white women and black children
in the United States and the visual history of emancipation. Its significance
lies in its attachment of the figure of the white woman as mother to the
black race. That was not how Towne marketed the photograph precisely,
but it is the meaning she intended for her audience. The portrait was symbolically powerful and materially significant and a signal intervention in the
iconography of Southern portraiture. It also presaged the portrait of white
mothering that would become deeply embedded in colonial discourse in
the decades to come.[2] In the accompanying letter, Towne wrote that she
had requested processing that would produce a "burnt out" image, a deliberate blurring of her facial features in order to "do justice" to the children.
Burned-out photographs result in uniform blobs of color where there would
normally be detail. The problem is that the not quite perfectly executed uniform blob of color that is Towne's face does not in fact do justice to the
children. Ironically, not only is her whiteness enhanced by the procedure
but it, together with her description of the children, calls attention to a more
profound absence—the children's mothers.[3] It thus does work quite different from that in photographs and paintings of slaveholders and the enslaved
which trumpeted the racial ideology and paternalism of the antebellum

Feb. 1866—Laura M. Towne, Dick, Maria, Amoretta.
(From the Penn School Collection at the UNC–Chapel Hill
Wilson Library. Permission granted by Penn Center, Inc.,
St. Helena Island, South Carolina)

South, as well as the fiction of "our family black and white." The latter were
intended to buttress slavery and notions of Southern white womanhood;
Towne's sought to buttress a particular notion of freedom and white womanhood different from those slaveholders fixed to the canvas.

Adult slaveholding women rarely sat for portraits with enslaved children.
Typically, white children (babies especially) represented the slaveholding
class in portraits or photographs in which slaves (usually wet nurses and

children's nurses) were also featured. In the less-frequent images where enslaved women are included in white family portraits, they are clearly positioned in relation to white women as inferiors, not family, despite the non-
sense slaveholders peddled about "our family white and black." And they
were not meant for public consumption beyond the parlor walls. Unlike
the images that adorned the walls of slaveholders' homes, Towne's portrait
aimed to reach an audience beyond Towne's own parlor in the South Carolina Sea Islands. It contributed to particular ideas about the making of black
freedom that had been brewing in the lowcountry and in other places in
Confederate-held territory where Northern white women had gone. In the
making of black freedom, Towne seemed to suggest in the portrait, there
would be one family, black and white, and Northern white women would be
the "mothers" to the black race. This view had real consequence for the lives
of black women and children. Celia Howard Wyne, the mother of Maria, one
of the children in Towne's photograph, is absent in the image, though she
was not absent from her child's life. In 1880, Maria and her brother Joseph
were still living with their mother, who by then was a widow.[4]

Winslow Homer's *A Visit from the Old Mistress* (1876) offers an effective
counterpoint to Towne's photograph, to her projection of white mothering. Homer's painting, based on sketches made during his travels through
Virginia, depicts the postwar transformation in the relationship between
women who had formerly been slaveholders and enslaved. There is no obse-
quiousness in the postures of the African American women. One of them remains seated; before the war, she would have been required to stand. Two of
the women stand as equals and look the former mistress directly in the eye,
something they could have been whipped for before the war. Their postures
reflect those of many of the African American women Towne encountered in
Beaufort, South Carolina, though she was good at writing off their politics.

Laura Towne was one of nearly 1,000 Northern women, white and black,
who went south during the war. Most went as nurses, spies, agents of soldiers' aid societies, and teachers and missionaries sponsored by freedmen's
relief societies, and a few traveled in the guise of men as soldiers. Others
accompanied soldier husbands as company cooks or as housekeepers for
husbands who were military commanders, army surgeons and doctors, and
superintendents of freedpeople. Some went in search of a missing relative,
to nurse a wounded father, son, or brother, or to bring his body home. Despite the different causes or urges that carried them South, they generally
united in the belief that enslaved people were at once abused and racially
inferior and lived lives of unrelieved depravity. This view had become cemented in Northern white thought before the war and it affected the nature

of white women's service and encounters with enslaved people in often crippling ways.

The North's own slaveholding history, its continued economic, social, and political ties to the South, its discriminatory laws against free black people, and its strong current of proslavery sentiment informed missionary work to black people during the Civil War. In *Uncle Tom's Cabin*, Harriet Beecher Stowe has a slaveholding woman utter these words: "We mistresses are the slaves down here."[5] It was not a randomly invoked sentiment nor meant as sarcasm. Stowe, like other Northern women, believed it to be true. Northern women in the South during the Civil War were prepared to see themselves, like slaveholding women, as mistresses of a people who were a chore to manage but with a critical difference. Equipped with the "indelible stamp of New England culture," they would be better mistresses. Whatever the evils of slavery, the idea that black people stood "in the plane of vegetable & animal existence," the lowest plane of material existence, and belonged "to the fossil formations," in Ralph Waldo Emerson's words, was resistant to the idea of human equality. Emancipation would not change the "unredeemable African darkness in the hearts of the slaves," Emerson wrote, a view that had many adherents in the North, some quite voluble.[6] "Most found it difficult to fully imagine or reckon with the possibility of a completely free and independent population of former slaves," writes Nina Silber.[7]

Laura Severance Fiske of Massachusetts had moral outrage enough, the kind that sent Northern women to the South as missionaries. She urged her son, Rev. Asa Severance Fiske, who had been recently appointed superintendent of contrabands at Memphis, Tennessee, by Gen. U. S. Grant, to remember that he was raised an abolitionist. She asked him to tell the "poor fugitives" that she "used to weep over the stories of their wrongs" she heard from her own mother and how she had passed her heartache on to her children. Tell them, she wrote, "I brought up all of mine Abolitionists."[8] What this meant on the ground was far from transparent. Who were the women who brought their children up to be abolitionists, the women who could see evidence of women's oppression in Hiram Powers's *The Greek Slave*, who could be touched by the brilliance of Alexandre Dumas, and yet could envision themselves as mistresses? What did it matter if they were wealthy or solidly middle-class and thus had the time and resources to go to the South as nurses, agents of freedmen's aid societies, and wives of Northern men stationed in the South? How did the ideas about gender, race, freedom, and citizenship they carried with them in their roles as missionaries or the wives of Union officers or Federal officials impact their understanding of their mission and their relationship to black people?

Exposed to Danger and Insult

By the end of the war, over 1,000 Northerners had gone to the South as teachers, and most were white women. They included women, like Sarah Ann Dickey from Ohio, who did not come from wealthy families. Sent by the Church of United Brethren to teach in the school it established in Vicksburg, Dickey had only learned to read and write as a teenager. Some, but not all, were avowed abolitionists.[9] Unlike Dickey, they more often came from middle-class and affluent homes and carried the values of their class to the South. Like antebellum travelers, they deployed "the moral language of cleanliness to articulate the sectional differences that were increasingly dividing the nation." As Kathleen Brown writes, "White northerners and foreigners were more likely than white southerners to find the proximity of black bodies disruptive to notions of wholesomeness and cleanliness based on elaborate articulations of domestic hierarchies of dirt."[10] In his introduction to *Letters and Diary of Laura Towne*, published in 1912, Rupert Sargent Holland wrote that the conditions Towne and other white Northerners faced in the South were "little short of those in a savage settlement on the Congo."[11] He, like Towne and many of her peers in the Civil War South, as Sarah Haley argues for another moment in history, saw black women as "sexual and asexual; ideal objects of domestic, industrial, and agricultural labor; shrewdly criminal and daft; maternal and infanticidal; domestically servile and disruptive, docile and irreverent" and "constituted [them] through a series of contradictions that throw stable subject categorization into chaos."[12]

Ideas about enslaved people and Southern slave society dominant in the North contributed to a skepticism that changing the "savage conditions" at the South should even be white women's work. Before they could attend to the "degrading and unprecedented sufferings" of the enslaved, Northern women who went south as teachers and nurses had to convince a skeptical public that activism on behalf of the slave or the soldier that went beyond protests from afar and petition campaigns drafted around kitchen tables and knitting and sewing was the proper work of white women. Women who persisted braved opposition from not only military commanders but also family members and friends. Like many medical professionals, John Brinton, a surgeon in the Union army, objected to what he called the "craze spread among our good people that the women of the country could make themselves very useful by acting as nurses for the sick and wounded." He further demeaned those he had encountered. "Can you fancy half a dozen or a dozen old hags, for *that* is what they were." The idea that women were "well enough in their proper place" enjoyed wide currency.[13]

In general Northerners expressed concern about the wisdom of sending white women to the South in any capacity. Working as nurses would place them in intimate proximity to men and to African Americans and at what cost to their "constitution"? Five days after the start of the war, Sarah Chase wrote to her father, Anthony Chase, requesting his consent to go to the battlefield as a nurse. She assured him that "no one out of the family need know of my going." Like her father, she acknowledged the stigma attached to women who ventured beyond the bounds of acceptable domesticity, "bitter brazen Amazonian philanthropists," Asa Fiske called them.[14]

Anthony Chase couched his reply in the gendered ideology of domesticity and a notion of white women's inferior capacity to bear the hardships of public life. His daughter's desire to lend "woman's soft and delicate hand," and a "look of compassion and soothing words," was a credit to her, he wrote. Still he asked, "Hast thou looked on the other picture? Art thou equal to the incidents of the camp—to witnessing mangled bodies and scenes of agony which no tongue or pen can describe. Is thy experience, thy constitution and health equal to all this?" He also asked her to consider that "experienced nurses" might be better suited. Was there "not an abundant supply of women old in experience ready and willing to do this without pressing into service a young, dutiful and beautiful daughter. . . ?" He worried that she might be "exposed to danger and insults," as army nurses were. In the end, he joined her mother in supporting her wishes. "Loving thee so dearly as we do and knowing how conscientious thee is and how beautifully thee takes up any cross that duty places in thy path, we give our heartiest sympathy," her mother wrote.[15] Sarah, like her sister Lucy Chase, grew up in a Quaker household where abolition was preached. Georgeanna and Eliza Woolsey, who similarly feared opposition from their parents, initially made preparations to go to the front as nurses in secret. After her acceptance by the Medical Committee, Georgeanna began "a month's seasoning in painful sights and sounds." She encouraged Eliza to join her but urged secrecy while there was still the chance of opposition from the family. "I don't want to have to fight my way all through the course, and besides giving a strict account of myself at home," she wrote.[16]

The families of teachers and missionaries expressed perhaps the most concern about the intimate contacts they would have, not with Northern soldiers in hospitals, but with black people. Ellen Noyes worried about her sister, who taught freedpeople in Savannah and St. Helena, in lowcountry South Carolina, putting herself in "great danger" and urged her to come home "at *once* by rail & leave the blacks or drown them or do anything." "It seems too hard that you should be suffering in that horrible place while we are so cool & well among these lovely Mts" of New Hampshire, she wrote.[17] In Thetford, Vermont, Kate Conant's mother worried that she did not hear from her daughter, who taught freedpeople in Beaufort, South Carolina, and later, St. Augustine, Florida, as often as she would have liked. "I feel tonight as if it were of no use whatever to write, in fact, I have not felt so down-hearted before, since you left. I hope you do not feel as badly about it, as I do, & as you say nothing about it, I presume you do not." She asked that Conant at least acknowledge receipt of care packages she sent. Surely, her daughter could write to say "*something* about all those *little things*," which cost her mother "considerable labor & anxiety." When Kate did write, she wrote too little about her own welfare. It was "pleasant to have descriptions of country, & places," but her mother would much "prefer hearing more definitively about yourself, & how you are prospering."[18] Many white Northerners expressed concern about the wisdom of sending white women to the South in any capacity. Not only were they were going into a war zone, they were taking up work none of them had done before.

White Mothers to the Freedpeople

Near the end of the Civil War, Laura Towne took in an orphaned child who was a refugee from Georgia and suffering from typhoid fever. The bacterial infection, spread through contaminated water and food, had already taken the lives of the child's mother, brother, and two aunts. Her only living relative as far as anyone could tell was a young cousin who was hospitalized, but she stated her intention to take her orphaned cousin as soon as she was released. For Towne that moment could not come soon enough. After just a few days caring for the child, Towne was eager to be rid of her. "Our little waif is almost well," she wrote, "but is a sulky, lazy, vicious little piece. We shall not keep her any longer than we can help."[19] Mothering black children had its limits. Towne looked forward to being relieved of the burden but the entire episode, including her depiction of the child as a "vicious little piece," tells us that she was well-versed in the vocabulary of racism and racially gendered and sexualized domestic hierarchies.

By this point, Towne had lived among the people of the Sea Islands for three years, but this had not changed her belief in black racial incapacity and inhumanity in any fundamental sense. The evidence of family affection and kinship exemplified by a sick child's stated intention to "mind" (take care of) her younger orphaned cousin did not sway Towne's judgment. To Towne and other Northern white women in the wartime South, laziness, sulkiness, and viciousness defined the character of black children and their mothers.

Six days after arriving at St. Helena Island, Towne claimed to be amused by the "little darkies tumbling about at all hours." "They swarm on the front porch and in the front hall. If a carriage stops it is instantly surrounded by a dozen or more woolly heads," she wrote. It was a "marvelous" sight. "Clearly, Miss Towne and Miss [Ellen] Murray had much work to do if they were to bring this island culture in line with dominant American norms and values," historian Elizabeth Jacoway concludes.[20] Those "norms and values" were in fact far from dominant in the North. They were the values of the affluent and the aspiring upwardly mobile, as a visit to a Northern rural household would have attested.[21]

White Northerners did not always agree on the best path for integrating African Americans as equals into the nation's body politic and social fabric. However, there came to be general agreement that white women—whether as teachers, missionaries, or agents of freedmen's aid organizations—were key to this effort. In particular, to them would fall the work of mitigating the deficits Northerners believed black women and children carried out of slavery.[22] In the face of concerns about Northern white women taking up work with freedpeople, the notion that they would serve as "mothers" to the black race became a potent argument in support of this work.

Julia Wilbur, sent to Alexandria, Virginia, by the Rochester Ladies Anti-Slavery Society to work on behalf of refugees from slavery, was quite confident of the superior ability of white women. "I have not regretted for a moment that I came," she reported back to the society, as "woman's presence more than any thing is needed among these poor creatures."[23] The black women all around her did not qualify as women and thus could not constitute "woman's presence." Esther Hawks agreed, writing in 1863 that "their [sic] isn't [sic] half a dozen women on the whole island" of Hilton Head.[24] But she did not think much of the few "women" there, and this from a woman who criticized Northern white women teachers. "Many go out as teachers with great ardor to do something, particularly for the souls of these people," she averred to a friend in the North, "but who keep aloof as though they were black spiders."[25]

The views of Northern white women were complex and often contradictory. As a result of their "own experiences as women," Carol Faulkner argues, Northern women were able to see "freedpeople's poverty and dependence as a result of specific historical circumstances rather than as an innate racial characteristic." She sees their efforts as acknowledging "the real privation of freedpeople" and argues that they "endeavored to ameliorate it by public and private charity." Faulkner, however, is not insensitive to the limits of this charity and sisterhood. When Northern middle-class women "portrayed freedpeople as dependents on their aid or as supplicants for their help, thus placing freedpeople in an inferior position," they also revealed that, "in many ways, women's independence rested on the neediness of former slaves," and they "ignored freedwomen's desire for autonomy from whites."[26] In other words, to make their place in the world, to elevate white woman- hood, middle-class white women needed "sulky" black women to rule over. They believed this even when it was contradicted by daily experience. Life among former slaves was full of examples of "the delicacy and tenderness which the Negroes express affection for each other," Lucy Chase wrote. "They know to love, and how to remember."[27]

Given what they believed they knew about slavery and enslaved people, Northern white women were not prepared to see what Chase saw. They be- lieved they would witness degeneracy in the remains of slavery rather than evidence of humanity and viable black family and community life. The be- liefs they carried with them, coupled with the humanitarian crisis they con- fronted, served as "proof of how necessary it is that [former slaves] should have the care and oversight of white people in this transition state."[28] White women deemed themselves best suited to oversee and domesticate black life. Among the black refugees at Craney Island, Virginia, Lucy Chase took the "gift and power" of her control over the storehouse as symbolic of this task. Many were needy, but more were "greedy and lying." She did not stop to try to reconcile this view with her observations of their humanity. As Carol Faulkner writes, "Chase recognized destitution," but "like many missionaries to the slaves she held firmly and adhered to the 'discourse of idleness.'"[29]

White women teachers and missionaries saw their role in part as ridding black people of the vices that were carried out of slavery, "vices which slav- ery inevitably fosters," the "hideous companions of nakedness, famine, and disease." The coming of the Union armies and missionaries, wrote Union surgeon D. O. McCord, meant that "women in travail and children without parents or friends, were no longer permitted to die in the streets or drag out a miserable life of filth and festering disease in wretched dog-kennels where the eye of humanity never penetrates."[30] It seemed natural to Samuel Fiske that his sister-in-law, who had gone to Memphis to be with her husband, Asa Fiske, would be "a mother" to the "poor contrabands."[31] Northern white women in the wartime South fell far short of fulfilling that ill-conceived mission.

Maria Mann, "Sanitary Matron of the colored people" and the only woman agent for the Western Sanitary Commission at Helena, Arkansas, took her whiteness as a mark of privileged womanhood. Samuel Sawyer, the superintendent of contrabands for Arkansas, described her as "a most energetic & efficient co-worker with the friends of this unfortunate race."[32] Yet Mann saw little in the black women and children refugees around her that seemed familiar or admirable, even though she expressed concern for the hardships they suffered. The treatment she received as a white woman confirmed her sense of racial superiority. Although she wrote that it was the last of her dreams that she "should ever be mistress over slaves," she seemed to bask in the privileges that she thought that entailed. "Sometimes," she wrote, "I venture on foot, get where advance or retreat is alike impossible, when some giant of a man either white or colored, passing takes me in his arms & carries me over fences & their private yards to my destination."[33]

Unlike black women refugees, Mann could avoid getting soaked, dirty, and sick from the mud, high water, flooded roads and pathways, and "carcasses, filth & decay" in the streets. Seeing her in these dirt streets, men, white and black, picked her up and carried her over the filth. (That she had no concern about being lifted up into the arms of black men is a story for another day.) It was her job, as "Sanitary Matron," to get black women and children out of those wretched streets, but her instincts inclined first to her own care. The living conditions of the "Ethiops," as she sometimes called black refugees, were "void of comfort or decency." She did not really see how her presence could effect a difference in "personal conditions so deplorable that any idea of change for the better seems utterly impossible."[34]

"Deplorable" was a descriptor that would have appealed to Laura Towne and that she might easily have used. Rescuing black women from themselves animated her sense of what her duties were in the larger project of domesticating former slaves to freedom in the Sea Islands. This effort was led initially by Special Agent Edward L. Pierce, a Boston lawyer appointed by Secretary of the Treasury Salmon P. Chase to oversee the Port Royal expedition of missionaries and cultivation of the 1862 crop in the Sea Islands. Towne saw Pierce as an ally. "When [Pierce] sees a sulky woman he calls upon the ladies for help, and Miss Winsor or I step out and at his command get a smile on the face before we leave it."[35] "Sulky" was one Towne's preferred adjectives for black women and children who defied her governance. How precisely she and Winsor managed to turn resistance into smiles is unclear, but Pierce's turning to them for help in managing black women who resisted doing his bidding is notable.

As leader of the project to transform enslaved people into free laborers, Pierce was responsible for selecting—with the assistance of freedmen's aid societies in New York, Philadelphia, and Boston—some fifty Northern men and women to go to lowcountry South Carolina to supervise operations on the plantations and 16,000 former slaves. The "Gideonites," as they came to be called, were a collection of ministers, teachers, physicians, and women without any previous professional occupations sponsored by freedmen's aid societies in New York, Boston, and Philadephia.[36] Towne, sponsored by the Philadelphia Port Royal Relief Committee, would establish herself as matriarch of the household headed by Pierce at Pope's Plantation on St. Helena Island. The prospect excited her very much. "I shall—just think of it!—I shall keep house!," she exclaimed. "Mr. Pierce needs a person to do this for him. The gentlemen of the company are always coming here for consultation and there will be a large family at any rate—Mr. Pierce, Miss Walker, and we three younger ones, with young Mr. Hooper, who is Mr. Pierce's right-hand man. We shall have visitors dropping in to meals." In addition to the five white women, the "family" included eight domestic servants, five of whom were women.[37] A thick line linked Northern women's view of themselves as mothers to black people and their view of themselves as substitute mistresses. And few proved as aware of their power and the potential to misuse it than Lucy Chase. "I sometimes fancy myself fast growing hard-hearted," she wrote in a letter to her family, having just described to them the "greediness and complaining" she had to deal with. She chastised herself for thinking thus. "I laugh when I realize that I incrust myself in a coarse-grained habit after the fashion of all men who brush daily against the idiosyncrasies of the crowd."[38]

Mistresses at Last

White mothering came with benefits. Black domestic servants were an assumed prerogative of white women working in the South. Laura Towne became the most famous of the white teachers in the Sea Islands and stayed for decades, and like most white women missionaries she took for granted that she would have black domestic help. To "keep house," she relied on a household staff of black men and women. Keeping house after the manner of slaveholding women also meant extending her realm of oversight beyond the interior of the Pope Plantation big house and into the homes of black people. She, fittingly, gave herself the job title "inspector of the huts."[39] The job involved inspecting and overseeing black people's homes, to "keep house" over them too. "I shall have a time of it," she wrote, as she complained of the difficulty of finding good help among so many "untrained field hands,—and worse, very young girls, except the cook." At least the house she lived in was not a hut but the plantation home of the Pope family, a place she described as "pretty."[40] When she wrote the above, Towne had been in South Carolina for less than two weeks. Within a month, she had established that the freed-people were "our people." "We have got to calling them *our* people and lov-ing them really," she wrote in May 1862, establishing a sense of ownership that she would return to in August.[41]

Towne seemed to revel in the fact that she had black women and men to ensure the cleanliness of her home and body and contributed to the rac-ist discourse that encircled them. Her domestic staff consisted of Rebecca, Susanna, Lucy, Jane, Harry, Joe, Dagus, and Rina. "I am housekeeper, with Southern servants, and those irregular, and only half in my control, being at every other body's beck and call," she wrote. So things were hardly perfect: she not only had to sometimes share the men and women who worked for her, but they also were the intractable servants of antebellum lore. In truth, she realized, she had "every comfort except steady servants."[42] Rina was "a real good, old auntie," "the best old thing in the world," yet Rina and the oth-ers constantly tested Towne's "patience." As an example, Towne offered the time when she "told Rina to come up and do our room and [had] not seen her since."[43] One day Towne went to make tea for an unexpected guest but there was no fire, firewood, butter, or milk. At last she was able to offer a cup of tea, hominy, and butter but no bread. She blamed the servants. When the "real good" Rina and other women (and men like Robert) resisted her labor regime, "creating all sorts of household difficulties," Towne wrote them off as "all possessed" by the devil.[44] Towne also saw evidence of the presence of the devil in the ring shout. She had never seen "anything so savage." It could hardly be called "a religious ceremony" but seemed "more like a regular frolic" or "the remains of some old idol worship." Interestingly, the "savage, heathenish dance" Towne witnessed took place in the home of Rina, her washerwoman and chambermaid.[45]

Like Towne, Dr. Esther Hawks had no sooner arrived in the Sea Islands to join her husband, Dr. John M. Hawks, than she began making the house as-signed to them "habitable." "We have a whole family of servants," she wrote, "Joshua, the 'maid of all work,' does the cooking and general housework. Eve, his wife splits the wood and takes care of the horses: while Venus and Appolo [*sic*], the children are supposed to run of errands and do the 'chores."[46] The friends and family Northern women left behind assumed they would have maids. E. B. Sewell supposed that her good friend Kate Conant had "contra-bands to perform the manual labor" in her house. "Some of them are very good help and I should prefer them to the French or Irish," Sewell added. Sewell also hoped that Conant's students understood and were grateful for the sacrifice she "made in going so far to put *sense into them*." Sewell herself had domestic help in her home in the North, "a good girl in the kitchen."[47]

Charles Leigh, a member of the Executive and Finance Committees of the National Freedmen's Relief Association that sponsored Conant, urged her to think of herself as a mother to her freedpeople. Her letters worried him, though, indicating that she thought of white mothering differently from how he intended and implied that it was tainted by racism. While Conant was stationed at St. Augustine, Leigh learned that she made the black children pay for their books. He urged her to reconsider. Forcing the children to buy their schoolbooks might indeed make the books "more valuable to the children, than to receive them as gifts." But he cautioned her not to "carry it to the extent of withholding them from those absolutely too poor to purchase them." He also thought her policy of making the children pay for clothes donated by Northerners was unnecessarily punitive.[48] In establishing this policy, Conant may have drawn on her prior experience in the Sea Islands, where Northern teachers insisted on making former slaves pay for donated clothing, arguing that this was critical to teaching them the value of self-reliance.[49]

The freedpeople could see, however, that such rules did not apply to the Northern teachers, who paid for nothing. "We are at no expense at all here," Towne proudly reported or, rather, boasted.[50] Towne's household economy came with a bonus of free milk, eggs, and butter. She couched her right to them on nearly the same ground that slaveholding women claimed a right to the fruits of black people's labor. "These things belong to the plantation and are necessary to it. We do not pay for them," she wrote.[51] Her rationale makes sense only if the labor that produced the milk, eggs, and butter that "belong to the plantation" is also understood as belonging to her. Towne's view of the matter notwithstanding, that labor no longer belonged to the plantation. Towne's position, following the lead of fellow teacher Susan Walker (from whom Conant may also have learned), was that the free milk, eggs, and butter represented a fair exchange for the donated (free) clothes black people received from the North and should be used in support of the Northern missionaries.

Robert, an elderly former slave, challenged the perversion of free labor ideology the Northern teachers promoted. When he took some of his home-made butter to the teachers, he expected to be paid. He made a point of telling Walker, to whom he presented the product of his labor, how many days he had worked to produce the butter, clearly "wanting pay." Walker, however, quickly disabused him of any notion that he would be paid. "We have paid part in clothes, you know, Uncle Robert, and the Government will take care you have the rest some day." Towne thought Robert should probably be paid something, but this was not her problem. Robert, she explained, is not "our servant, he only makes the butter for us and for sale (which goes to the support of the company expenses) and this is a small part of his work." By this calculated miscalculation, Robert's labor indeed belonged not to him but to the new plantation and constituted part of the "company expenses" of the white ladies from the North.[52]

Edward Pierce disagreed. He supported Robert's claim for wages. Pierce informed Towne that her thinking on the matter, and Walker's, was mistaken. Government rations and donated clothing did not constitute a wage substitute. Robert had a right to be paid, and the teachers "had no right at all to take" the labor of freedpeople "and leave the Government to pay, or to pay . . . servants here out of the goods sent by the commissioners." Prior to the arrival of "Gideon's Band," Pierce had proposed that new clothing be made available to freedpeople who worked for the government at no cost. Once they began receiving wages, he thought a system could be set up to deduct the cost of new clothing from wages but that secondhand clothing "should always be considered a gift."[53]

Towne had thought it acceptable not only to substitute donated clothing for wages but also to deny wages to domestic workers if they received rations of corn (from crops they had cultivated). She claimed to not have known that it was wrong to deny wages to people who received donated clothing or rations. Once she learned that it was, she blamed Walker. "Miss W. it was who told me we were to pay no wages for the work we have done, and at first supposing she knew, I tried to reconcile myself to it by specious reasoning." Pierce agreed to pay the wages for a cook and a driver for Towne to use, but he said that Towne was responsible for wages for all other household help she employed.[54] In fact, Towne seems to have had no trouble at all reconciling herself to the injustice. She had already reasoned that as all the freedpeople were "obliged to work," the "women and young girls unfit for the field . . . are made to do their share in housework and washing, so that they may draw pay like the others—or rations—for Government must support them all whether they work or not, for this summer." As far as she could see, she claimed, the women "are eager to get a chance to do housework or washing, because the Northerners can't help giving extra pay for service that is done them, even if it is paid for otherwise, or by policy."[55] Never mind that a week's ration of a half pint of hominy and three-quarters of a pound of salt pork for adults and a smaller allowance for children was hardly enough for a day.

When Towne got around to paying the domestic workers in her household after Pierce made clear that her failure to do so amounted to wage theft, she offered a pittance. She agreed to pay fifty cents a week "extra" to Rina to wait on her table, wash her clothing, and clean her bedroom—to be dining room

servant, washerwoman, and chambermaid. It was "extra," Towne rational-
ized, because all of the freedpeople, Rina included, received "food" from the
government (corn left on the estate when slaveholders fled the region with
the approach of Union forces on November 9, 1861). Plus, Rina "has her house
as before." While some people might consider this "little," to pay her more
risked making "the field hands and others discontented."[56]

Fifty cents per week was less than a third of the six-dollar-per-month rate
for first-class servants set by the superintendent of contrabands at Beaufort, less than half the rate for second-class workers in the city, and a dollar
short of the rate for child domestic workers.[57] But again, by Towne's logic,
the products of the labor of black people were the government's property
and her own. In effect, if corn rations made cash wages "extra," Rina and
the other laborers were being paid primarily with corn they had produced
by the sweat of their own brow before Towne and the other Northerners arrived. Towne also calculated "free housing" as part of Rina's and the others'
wages. To the freedpeople, the cabins they had lived in as slaves and paid for
many times over with their labor hardly belonged to the government, and
it made no sense that the government would attempt to rent the cabins to
them. Towne made the free rent appear as a welfare benefit from the Federal
government. That the rations they received in corn should "go in part payment of their wages" must have seemed equally unjust to the black people.[58]
Nor must it have seemed just that Northern white women who hired black
women to cook and clean for them should be subsidized by the Federal government. When Towne hired Rina for fifty cents a week, this is exactly what
she acknowledged receiving, a government subsidy. By 1864, in response to
the more competitive market for domestic labor, with some cooks earning
eight to forty dollars a month, "enormous wages" by Towne's view, Towne
had increased Rina's wage to five dollars per month. In addition, she hired a
girl for miscellaneous chores such as scrubbing, waiting on the table, making fires, and running errands for two dollars per month.[59]

Across the South, Northern white women struggled to find a common
bond with black women, to see them as equals or as deserving of cash
wages. The question of whether refugees should pay for donated clothing,
which bedeviled the Sea Island project, surfaced at refugee camps across the
South as agents of freedmen's aid societies and their allies sought to reassure Northerners that former slaves could make the transition to freedom
without becoming a burden on Northern society. Forcing black people to
pay for donated clothes, they argued, would cultivate the necessary work
habits for economic independence and self-respect, though apparently not

their eligibility for waged work. Northern missionaries and teachers "hoped to encourage independence by selling donated cloth and clothing to former slaves, or using it as payment, instead of giving it away."[60] Maria Mann acknowledged that very few black women in the refugee camp at Helena, Arkansas, other than those detailed as washers or "day service to the hospitals, boats & other public places," had any opportunity to earn a living. Even when they found wage labor, they often were not paid. Like her South Carolina counterparts, Mann substituted donated clothing for wages. "I have given liberally from donated clothing, frequently offer it as the pay," she wrote. She too advocated a wage labor system that was antithetical to free labor ideology and black people's conceptions of freedom. She wrote that "nominally no pay is expected, protection & support of families being the equivalent."[61] This was her idea of what black people should expect, not what they expected.

Black Women's Resistance

Black women responded to attacks on their ability to mother their children and their right to just wages with stories of strength and resilience, pride and principle, and love for their children and the members of their larger families and community and resistance. They had shared with Laura Towne the history of their resistance to slavery. Towne recorded some of these oral histories in her diary and letters, and Charlotte Forten was there to sometimes hear them: stories of black women's struggles to protect property they had worked hard to accumulate, their resistance to slaveholders' efforts to move them into the interior when the war began, their flight from inland plantations back to the coast, the lengths to which they had gone to protect their families, and their history of what slaveholders called "impudence." Towne wrote down, for example, Susannah's story about the time she told her mistress that a whipping would do "no good." Susannah explained that she had tried to do what was expected of her but drew the line at anything that violated her sense of what under the circumstances was just. "She spoke continually of doing things from pride and principle," Towne wrote. Lorretta showed Towne the ridges on her back from beatings and told her about the four fetuses that had died in her as a result of the beatings. She recalled being forced to work in the field at her "heaviest" and punishment for being "rather smart in speaking her mind."[62] Yet despite this, despite her three years of residence in the Sea Islands living and working closely with black women and children, Towne resisted the idea that black women might have their own thoughts about the meaning of freedom for their lives, and she resisted their efforts to help her make the transition to a world of black freedom.

Black women also fought back against the condescension and racism some of the teachers showed their children. Children complained of teachers who kept school sporadically or sent them back home without teaching a thing. When questioned about the complaints, one of the accused teachers responded that as far as she was concerned the children "might do as they liked—and she didn't want them and didn't care what they did."[63] Freedwomen also no doubt witnessed or heard about Northern white teachers' contempt for black women teachers and their concern about having to dine or lodge with them. Even Towne recognized the problem. She asked a potential recruit for a teaching position at Edisto Island whether she would mind "messing with a colored lady teacher from the North." She meant "messing" in the military sense, sharing eating and lodging accommodations. Clearly, she was talking about Charlotte Forten, who wrote that while she found kindness in the house where she lived, "congeniality I find not at all."[64]

Even with so much contrary evidence before her, Towne struggled to see black women either as political actors or as caring and thoughtful mothers, wives, sisters, and daughters. After spending a week visiting several plantations "to cheer up and reassure the rather downhearted negroes, or rather the negro women," she said, a task she found "gratifying," though for her "not a cheering thing to do," Towne concluded that she was right all along: black women were grateful for the presence of white women and saw "a white lady a great safeguard from danger, and they say they are 'confused' if there are no ladies about."[65] Some historians have argued that black women found the presence of Northern white women reassuring and regarded them as more trustworthy and "sympathetic" than white men because of "the premium" white women, "too, placed on family bonds and household stability." Some scholars have also suggested that black women in the South preferred Northern white women even to black women missionaries and teachers. Yet nothing in the historical record supports such broad generalizations.

Sojourner Truth's experience showed that freedpeople formed such opinions based more on actions than on gender, or even racial, affinity. Truth's identity as a black woman did not automatically make her an exception. The black women refugees with whom she worked trusted her only so far. On the one hand, they brought to her their complaints about having to pay for donated clothing. "They will tell me for they think a good deal of me," she wrote. They seemed "*delighted*" to hear her talk and applauded when she stood up for them. "I am *needed* here" and "doing good" work, she told her friend Amy Post. When she learned that black refugees at Mason's Island, the contraband camp near Washington, D.C., were forced to pay for donated items, she launched an investigation. "I am going around among the colored folks," she wrote, "to find out who it is sells the clothing to them that is sent from the North." The white Northerners, she concluded, "are only here for the *loaves* and *fishes* while the freedmen gets the scales and crusts."[66] But when Truth's message of uplift seemed more in line with the agenda of white Northerners than former slaves' understanding of what freedom should look like, Truth found herself the subject of black people's ire. When she chastised a group of freedpeople, telling them they were a "disgrace" for "living off the government," they threw her out of the building. Truth responded by accusing them of being content to live by the "vilest of habits."[67] But they had already written her off.

The experience of Harriet Tubman in lowcountry South Carolina also showed the limits of gender and race identity. Some Sea Islanders greeted her initially with a degree of suspicion. The reason, Tubman discovered, was that she, like the white teachers, received army rations at no cost to herself. On this score, in the eyes of the freedpeople, she was no different from the white women. Her response was radically different from that of white women like Laura Towne. She gave up the rations. From that point on, Tubman paid her own way by "keeping an eating house," out of which she sold pies, gingerbread, and root beer that she made at night and other items. In addition, she used her earnings to pay for the construction of a washhouse for women who worked as laundresses for soldiers.[68] And unlike Towne and the other white women on the Sea Islands, Tubman did not have a maid. Tubman did not become a hero to black people in the Sea Islands because she was a woman and an African American but because she incorporated their politics into hers.

Tubman's politics were a better fit for the politics of Southern black women. She was less enamored with Lincoln than Sojourner Truth. She encouraged black women to work for freedom and autonomy; she did not tell them "they must learn to love the white people," as Truth did.[69] In the South Carolina lowcountry black women had a demonstrated history of resistance on the ground of principles that informed their view of the Port Royal experiment and the men and women who had come from the North to lead it. They had stood guard at night to protect their property, and shown over and again their love for their children and extended kin and community. "The long-lost Moses, who walked all the way from Wilmington, North Carolina," to Hilton Head Island two years after the war in 1867 "to find his mother," was but one of thousands of testimonials to these bonds.[70]

When Northern white women spoke of "the safety and integrity" of black families, they did not mean this to extend to the benefits of dominant notions of the domestic ideal white women enjoyed. They did not apply to black women the idea that women belonged in the home taking care of their families and that the primary responsibility for a family's economic well-being and the defense of the sanctity of the home rested with husbands and fathers. Indeed, Towne gained unheard-of authority even over black men's access to the guns they used to defend their homes. After the First South Carolina Volunteers, raised by Gen. David Hunter in 1862, was ordered disbanded by President Lincoln, one company was allowed to remain in arms to defend the refugee camps in the region. On St. Simons Island, for example, where parties of Confederate snipers sneaked onto the island and threatened the safety of a community of 600 refugees, most of whom were women and children and some of whom they carried back into slavery, ninety armed black men went in pursuit of the rebels and forced them off the island. They then evacuated the people to Beaufort.[71] But, Towne wrote, she controlled access to their firearms. "I run up the flag," she wrote, "and the men come for their guns. . . . They drill an hour or so, and then I take the guns again. They are kept in the room next to mine, under lock and key."[72] The gendered dynamics at work here also surface in other areas, as with the use of black men as domestic workers. The "maid of all work" that Esther Hawks delighted in was Joshua, whose wife split wood and cared for the horses.[73]

Northern white women seem to have given little thought to how their actions and words compromised their role as advocates for black women and freedpeople generally. Whereas Tubman worked to pay her way and used her meager earnings to make it easier for other black women to make a living, Towne boasted that she and the other white women lived "at no expense at all here." She did not question how her life, her ability to manage her household, distribute donated goods to the black islanders, and occasionally teach school was supported by a staff of black domestic workers. When she began taking a salary in September 1865, she said she agonized over the decision, fearing it might negatively affect her reputation. "I have got the credit for being a volunteer, all over the country, and to sneak in a salary seems too bad," she wrote. After "a very great deal of worry over it," she concluded that she was unable "to do without it."[74]

Perhaps, but unlike Tubman, she died a wealthy woman. At her death in 1901, after nearly four decades of "sacrifice" for the freedpeople of the Sea Islands, Towne left an estate that included $10,000 in cash (the equivalent of an income value of more than $300,000 in 2017 dollars), a gold watch and other jewelry, six acres of land on St. Helena Island, a half interest in a two-acre lot (the other half interest belonged to her friend Ellen Murray), the Frogmore plantation house purchased from former slaveholder Thomas Coffin in 1868, ownership of the Peoples Graveyard near Frogmore, and assorted household furnishings and goods. Towne left the bulk of the estate (some $5,000, several acres of land, silverware, her dogs, cattle, chickens, and Frogmore) to Ellen Murray and most of the rest to her siblings, William E. Towne and Rosa M. Towne. To each of the domestic workers in her employ, she left ten dollars and to the black teachers at the Penn Normal and Industrial School, twenty dollars each. Perhaps the most perplexing item in Towne's will is the instruction she left for the disposition of the animals she owned. These she left to Ellen Murray during Murray's lifetime. But in the event Murray left the island, Towne ordered, "my horses shall be chloroformed and then shot quite dead, and buried on the farm. My cows and calves and poultry shall be killed and then sold; under no circumstances shall they be sold or given away alive."[75] Perhaps she believed, as many slaveholders professed to, that black people could be no more trusted to take care of animals than of each other.

Northern Black and White
Women Abolitionists in the South

Many black women abolitionists worked side by side, or at least in sympathy, with white women abolitionists before the war and in the trenches with freedmen's aid societies during the war, but it was seldom a relationship of equality. Their work during the war sometimes reopened old wounds and opened fresh ones. The relationship between Julia Wilbur, the corresponding secretary of the Rochester Ladies' Anti-Slavery Society, and Harriet Jacobs, both of whom went to Alexandria, Virginia, to work on behalf of black refugees, exemplified these tensions. Wilbur wrote powerfully about the sorrows and struggles of black refugees at Alexandria, but she was not immune to the racism prevalent in the North. It influenced her initial reaction to Jacobs's arrival to work in Alexandria and handicapped her work among the refugees. She often saw black women refugees as unworthy of her efforts. She referred to them as "the stupid, the obstinate, the lazy, the saucy, the deceitful, & the lying, just what slavery has made them."[76] She wrote this when she had been in the South for only three weeks. Nor did Wilbur fully trust black women who she granted were neither stupid nor lazy; even they might be saucy.

The arrival of Harriet Jacobs to work among the refugees at Alexandria deeply unsettled Wilbur. "Last night I was very much surprised to see Harriet

Jacobs," she wrote. Jacobs arrived with a letter from Benjamin Tatham of the New York Yearly Meeting of Friends, the group that credentialed her work as a matron to the refugees, including the reception and distribution of clothing and other items. "She is to keep a record of the names of all persons & a list of the articles furnished to them to prevent fraud or mistakes," Wilbur noted. Jacobs was given authority to distribute the goods as she desired. The whole arrangement struck Wilbur "very unpleasantly" and "almost like an insult" to her and the Rochester Ladies Anti-Slavery Society. Wilbur described Jacobs as "a very nice person, & well calculated to give personal attention to those people; to nurse the sick & care for them in various ways. . . . She can do these things much better than I can & we want just such a person here. I welcome her with all my heart." But the idea that Jacobs would be given managerial authority, including over goods that up to that point Wilbur had controlled, struck Wilbur as wrong and highly inappropriate. She thought it called into question her integrity and status as a white woman. She was so offended that she informed the New York office to "send no goods to us." Wilbur took the authority invested in Jacobs as a not-so-subtle critique of her own work and judgment in determining which refugees were "needy & deserving" and which items were best "adapted to their wants."[77] For Wilbur more was at stake than the refugees' welfare. "Wilbur's solitary struggle had become a central part of her identity as a freedmen's agent and Jacobs's arrival threatened her position."[78]

There were times when Wilbur and Jacobs worked well together, and over time, Wilbur became less threatened by Jacobs. But more generally, Jacobs's race remained a problem and made her, in Wilbur's eyes, less competent to oversee the management and distribution of supplies to refugees.[79] Wilbur was no doubt rattled by Jacobs's objection to Wilbur's presumption "to speak for freedpeople, positioning herself as their protector."[80] Perhaps it is true, as one scholar maintains, that Wilbur's "patronage was less racial condescension than recognition of the poverty of the freedpeople," but racism lay at its core. British abolitionist Julia Griffiths Crofts believed racism was rife within the Rochester Ladies' Anti-slavery Society. She pressured the organization to place a black woman agent in Alexandria when the conflict between Wilbur and Jacobs first emerged. When a tentative plan to send Rosetta Douglass, Frederick Douglass's daughter, as a teacher was dropped— supposedly to allow Wilbur time to first resolve a conflict with some of the male agents, Crofts was livid. "'I know so fully how nearly every thing American is dyed in 'prejudice against color,'" she wrote Anna Barnes, the Rochester Society secretary, "and how it permeates even *the* best of American

Anti-Slavery Societies, that I feared lest rejection had been on account of color." Crofts, a staunch ally of Frederick Douglass, believed racism was at the heart of the decision to not send Rosetta Douglass or any black woman to Alexandria. "'I cannot my friend, agree in what you say of Miss Wilbur going where no colored woman can go—& doing what no colored woman can do!" she wrote. "A *colored* woman should have had the *opportunity* before any one ventured to say, she could not it!—My views are strong on this subject—& I feel they are the right views. If you send a second teacher, *pray try & find* a suitable colored woman—The New York 'friends' have sent the *right* person in Harriet Jacobs."[81]

Harriet Jacobs was as appalled as Wilbur by the conditions in Alexandria and in refugee camps in Washington, D.C. At Duff Green in the nation's capital, she saw "men, women and children all huddled together without any distinction or regard to age or sex," sleeping on bare floors, poorly clothed, ravaged by disease, and so degraded by slavery that they knew little of "the usages of civilized life." She believed, however, that not just slavery but Northern apathy had "helped to make them what they are" and that they were "as apt to learn as any people that come to you stupid from oppression." Jacobs's perspective also differed in other ways from Wilbur's. She protested when white teachers attempted to take over a school the freedpeople had built without consulting with the black residents. She met with one of the school trustees, who told her that their objection was not to white teachers per se but to the teachers making "all the arrangements without consult- ing them." Saying she "wanted the colored men to learn that the time had come when it was their privilege to have something to say," Jacobs invited the white teachers to a meeting with the trustees. In the end, Jacobs's daugh- ter Louisa and a white woman were chosen as teachers for the school. "I do not object to white teachers," Jacobs wrote Hannah Stevenson of the Boston Educational Commission, "but I think it has a good effect upon these people to convince them their own race can do something for their elevation."[82] Jacobs argued for black autonomy.

Wilbur's unhappiness with black women acting on behalf of black women surfaced again in relation to a black Baptist Society. She was pleased when she first learned that a Baptist Society had appointed a four-woman com- mittee to raise funds to assist the refugees. She loved the fact that it was an antislavery society and attached to a church with several hundred members. "I was encouraged!" she wrote. Wilbur's excitement, however, soon changed to chagrin. "But come to find out," she wrote, "this is a *Cold Church* & this is a committee of *Cold women*," which "alters the case very much." As revealing, she wrote that she was still the "only white woman" in the city "who goes among the colored people." Wilbur felt very much alone, despite the presence of black women refugees, a committee of black church women, and Harriet Jacobs.[83]

Mistresses for a Day

In addition to describing their encounters with slaves and freedpeople, the stories Northern white women conveyed to friends and family back home often revealed their sympathy with the white South and its institutions. Some took this historical moment to embrace long-cherished ambitions of living what they supposed approximated the luxurious life of a plantation mistress. They imagined themselves in antebellum mansions, with an "army" of black servants at their command. Some were happy to have the opportunity to realize these dreams, even if this only lasted for a day or month. Northern abolitionists spoke often of the crippling impact slavery had on black life but much less about racism in Northern society, as Charlotte Forten and other black abolitionists often observed. Forten witnessed it firsthand in the North and in the Sea Islands. They came to believe in what Kathleen Brown terms the "alchemy of southern slavery," that encompassed in part "the strong desire of white southerners to believe that they knew and could trust their enslaved domestics." The use of free black people in Northern homes "gave wealthy Northern households an exotic cachet, enabling masters and mistresses to associate their own social standing with that of the planter aristocracy," Brown writes.[84] To have the chance to actually live in a Southern plantation house and have black women's domestic labor held even more exotic appeal. It was indeed magical racecraft.[85]

A trip to an army hospital in Virginia to visit her brother gave Fannie Green of Pontiac, Michigan, her opportunity to transcend her old life and temporarily experience that of a plantation mistress. "Had an army of colored women cleaning the floors this morning," she wrote from Virginia. A trip along the James River fulfilled a long-standing desire "to visit a real southern home . . . the principle feature being darkies—Little niggers lay around on the piazza and peeped in at the doors and windows—and [the] darkies were numerous."[86] Unlike the women abolitionists discussed in this chapter who supported the Republican Party of Lincoln, Green was a staunch Democrat. She found Lincoln to be a "weak and contemptible executive," leading "a wretched miserable pusillanimous, contemptible, niggardly administration." She opposed the Emancipation Proclamation, believing it would lead to a "more bitter and bloody war" and wished "all the abolitionists could be put in the front ranks of the army."[87] Her animosity for Lincoln and the Republican Party seems to have been matched by her admiration for the South and the ideals of Southern slave society.

The power to command black women in Virginia was a world apart from the life Fannie Green led in Michigan, where her power to command black women and control their movement was severely limited by their status as free people. Back in Michigan in October 1862, her family hired a new cook, "an elderly colored woman" named Elen. Elen was the family's only domestic worker, but Green did not write about her in the derogatory language that characterized her comments about black people in Virginia and Washington, D.C. Rather, she noted, generally without comment, Elen's sense of autonomy. Elen went home when she was not feeling well, as she did on Monday, December 1. She was still out the following Saturday, December 6, leaving Fannie and her mother to do all "the kitchen work." Elen also took time off when her daughter was ill. At the end of December, "Elen was called away in the night to her sick daughter and we have had the work to do today," Green wrote. Elen again did not show up for work in late March 1863 because she had gone to assist in the birth of her granddaughter. This time, the Greens hired Mary Looney as a temporary replacement, and Fannie went to see the newborn whom Elen presented "with great pride." The child was "not very black & has almost straight hair," Green wrote.[88] Elen continued to take time off when she needed to, and the Greens continued to turn to Looney, who appears to have been an Irish servant, in her absence. In May, when Elen again went to Detroit, the Greens "had Mary Looney in her place."[89] For Fannie Green, playing mistress was a fantasy life she lived briefly.

Lillie Dade of Philadelphia also found a fantasy life in the South. For her, it was Beaufort, South Carolina. Dade joined her husband, a Union surgeon, in the Sea Islands and was delighted by what she found, at least the part that appealed to her desire to live the life of a mistress. "Our home—how I wish you could see it," she wrote her sisters back home. "It is as the *old gentleman* says elegant. There is elegance in war times and for Army people it is entirely novel and that I like." She thought it sad that "the inhabitants of these handsome houses were obliged to leave their homes and everything in them," but she would happily take their place. "We have a cook and a waiter," she wrote, and "live in splendid style for this place." Having domestic servants—Laura, who did the washing, housework, and cooking, and Jim, who waited the table—made her life even more delightful. Laura and Jim were refugees from Florida, and she considered herself lucky to have them. They were experienced household workers, unlike the six negro women she found at the hospital when she first arrived. She put the six women to work cleaning the parlor, "went in and tried to talk to them found it was useless for me to waste my breath as they did not understand a word I said." She retired to the piazza and watched them make such a mess that she had to do a "second cleaning" herself. Laura and Jim ultimately proved unreliable as well, it seems. They went to work for Dade in November 1862; before the end of January 1863 they were gone, and Dade had a new cook and washer, Lizzie and her mother. Elizabeth Hand Fiske also went south, to Memphis, to be with her husband, Asa Severance Fiske. In encouraging her to join him, Asa Fiske promised that she would not want for comfort. He had "a very pretty house, nicely shaded by evergreens," waiting for her with "a fine room to ourselves & as a general thing two adjoining opening into each other." Carpet was only a "mere possibility," but she would find her domestic labors greatly reduced. Domestic help was available "in abundance, both for the kitchen & the nursery, and not only abundant but of good quality."[90]

The "help" Asa Fiske offered his wife would come from the ranks of the black women and children refugees under his supervision. Nor would he and his wife want for "society," since there were "a goodly number of officers wives" in Memphis. In addition, she would have a front-row seat to "her country's great labor & sacrifice," including "the beginning of liberty in an enfranchised race."[91] Soon after her arrival, Elizabeth Fiske's comfort was enhanced by the work of "a colored cook" and "several other servants attached to the house," including "a bright little contraband girl who helps me take care of the baby." She did not say how the girl came to be in Memphis or in her household or whether the child was paid. Like Northern teachers in South Carolina, but unlike the thousands of black women and children refugees in Memphis, she and her baby could count on free army rations and free housing. No one complained that they were undeserving or that she should be made to work to help pay for the food they ate and her housing. No one said of her husband, as they did of black men, that he should bear the expenses of feeding and housing his family from his salary. The gratis housing and rations they received were of no small consequence in a crowded city where the cost of housing and board was "enormously high." Because her family only had to purchase "such articles as are not furnished by the government to our bill of fare we do not find our expenses increased" by the move to Memphis," Elizabeth Fiske wrote to her mother, echoing Towne.[92]

When Elizabeth and Asa Fiske lost their son to dysentery—a child described as having a "complexion which was brilliantly white and pure without much color"—"strong men, rough soldiers, came and wept over the little form more than one exclaiming, 'He is too beautiful to be laid in the grave.'" A Northern teacher "dressed him in one of the pretty white dresses he wore in life," and his parents placed his body "in a secure metallic burial basket" and shipped him home to Philadelphia. All around them, black children and their mothers were dying, with seven men on a burial detail having "all they can do to bury the dead," Asa Fisk wrote.[93]

Elizabeth Fiske took the opportunity to witness the "beginning of liberty in an enfranchised race" as a chance to be what she could not be at home, a mistress. In this position she contributed not to the "beginning of liberty" but to the contraction of black freedom at the moment of its birth. She did not see the black women and children around her as people in any way like herself. Her sister-in-law reminded her in an indirect way that they were. Rebecca Fiske encouraged Elizabeth to make her husband's home a place of refuge from the pressures of work and do her "prettiest in keeping him away from the charming contrabands." "When he seems tired," Rebecca Fiske suggested, "write his letters for him, and 'love him up' generally as our chicks say."[94] Rebecca's fear that her brother could be seduced by black women in the South also sounded out racist tropes about black women's sexuality widely accepted in the North. Her views on questions of race mirrored that of most white Northerners. She admired the work of Alexandre Dumas and E. P. Christy, though she thought Christy's Minstrels was "a good deal of low buffoonery" below Christy's talents. She found Hiram Powers's statue *The Greek Slave* intriguing and a statement against patriarchy. In 1849, she had described her admiration for the statue's bare body, the "form exquisitely shaped," the "beautifully formed" chained hands, and the "look of dignity & sorrow & purity" of the face sufficient to "chasten & awe every wrong feeling likely to rise on such an exhibition" of the body of a naked woman. In the "finely chiseled lip" of the statue, she saw "a slight but powerful appearance of disdain at the trafick [*sic*] of her inhuman purchasers."[95] There is no indication that she saw any connection to slavery in her own time, although some abolitionists did. "Whether Powers's sculpture was interpreted as a quintessential slave or a quintessential woman, it was generally understood to valorize a response to oppression that opposed the activism urged by free black and white antislavery feminists," Jean Yellin writes.[96]

Elizabeth Hand Fiske's life in Memphis, with maids, was different from what she was accustomed to. She grew up in a household where, in addition to her studies, she was expected to contribute by ironing, weeding the garden, sweeping, and helping with the general upkeep of the home. "After breakfast I arranged the Chambers in part, for one of my employments is the care of the chambers, & the lower sitting room, & then I sat down to my studies," she wrote in 1849.[97] Then in her early twenties, she was still living with her widowed mother and making a living by offering music and

French lessons three mornings a week, but this did not exempt her from the "demon of housecleaning." "I have been putting down carpets, washing paint & cleaning silver for two or three days," she wrote in her journal in 1857. "My life is pretty uniform. I sweep and arrange the house, assist in baking and ironing—work in my little garden, sew, and study german [*sic*] and practice music moderately." It was not the life she dreamed of, but keeping busy helped to "banish any dreams" for a different sort of life.[98] By the late 1850s, the family's financial circumstances had worsened, and Elizabeth prepared to find a teaching position outside the home. Her mother opposed the plan, but Elizabeth could "see no other way *poverty stricken* as we are" and was unwilling "to be a mere cypher on the world." If marriage, the "crowning glory of womankind," was not to be hers "at present—Then let me work for the good of others at least." Her marriage to Asa Fiske and move to the South would give her the kind of glory she wanted, at least for a time.[99]

The letters Northern women wrote to relatives and friends back home were an important source of information about black people in the South and about white women's relationships to them. The letters captivated Northerners, variously countering and supporting familiar narratives about slavery and race and often recirculating racist ideas. They had the capacity to stymie or bolster the work of making freedom, influence what people thought freedom should look like and how it should be lived. Relatives and friends asked permission to circulate them more widely among acquaintances and publish them in local papers. Kate Conant's letters from Beaufort, South Carolina, and St. Augustine, Florida, circulated widely in Thetford, Vermont. "The universal question" she was asked, Conant's mother wrote, "is, what does she say about the capacity of the coloured people to learn, & I am most happy to tell them." She carried the letters with her when visiting relatives and friends, reading them "to eager listeners" and saw their potential to shape the views of Northerners less interested in the former slaves, people whose "doctrine heretofore [had] been to let the Negroes alone," including an elderly male acquaintance. She thought the letters could "be the means of making him an abolitionist." Conant's mother thought Northerners responded best to accounts written by people they knew: "All seem to feel they should rely more implicitly on what you write."[100]

Austa Malinda French's 1862 book, *Slavery in South Carolina and the Ex-slaves; or, The Port Royal Mission*, showed that even works written for a wider public found a large audience in the North. The widespread interest in "the coloured people" made a publishing hit, "lent all the time, & engaged two or three deep, in advance." Charlotte Forten sent her journal of life as a teacher in the Sea Islands to a friend hoping she would share it as "almost anything from this region w'ld [sic] be interesting to people." John Greenleaf Whittier, to whom she was close, published a letter she wrote to him in the *Boston Evening Transcript*, giving her work an even larger audience.[101]

Correspondence between those who went to the South and those who stayed at home also shaped a growing demand for black domestic labor in the North. Northern white women who did not go to the South seized opportunities the war opened up to ease their domestic labors and be mistresses of black labor. They could import black domestic help from the South. Libby Bowler besieged her husband "to try to get a nice little negrow [sic] boy to bring with you."[102] In Minnesota George Nourse sought help from his friend Asa Fiske in obtaining "a 'cullud gal' to do housework" for his wife. "Can you send me a smart one that can cook, wash & iron & will be pretty sure to stay," he wrote. "We would like one that knows how to cook nicely; but one that cannot do that, but is smart, neat, & quick to learn would be better than one that has learned the slow shiftless ways of slaves, even if the cooking has to be taught after she comes. I would advance the fare of such a girl, whom you know to be neat, smart, & willing, if sent up as soon as the river opens."[103]

George Nourse was an antislavery man. He had opposed petitions calling for a prohibition on black migration to Minnesota, Illinois, and Indiana and worried about the "poor darkey" in the South. "For God's sake," he urged Asa, "stand up for the oppressed race." Nevertheless, he sought his friend's help in greasing the wheels to get black domestic help for his wife and other white women in St. Paul who were weary of having to negotiate with Irish women who, he wrote, "are ruling us with a rod of iron & all hands are sick of it." In St. Paul, Irish "house girls" demanded eight to twelve dollars per month and their husbands who worked as field hands, twenty to twenty-six dollars per month. "No one can afford" such wages, Nourse added. One of his neighbors, Mrs. Dayton, offered to act as an agent to bring male and female "colored laborers" to St. Paul. She was confident that she could place ten of each sex immediately and would "go about among the ladies and engage any number that might be sent up." Nourse believed he could "dispose of at least one hundred of the two sexes for home work & field work" and probably place 500 easily.[104]

The Civil War gave Northern white women access to a new pool of domestic servants and a new platform to exhibit what many considered the superiority of white womanhood. Northerners had worked hard to dismiss the notion that emancipation would lead to a "flood" of unwanted black immigration to the North, but certain migrants were acceptable. Black women domestic servants headed that list and thousands were taken or sent north for this purpose, many of them teenagers. While stationed at Coffin Point

Plantation in the Sea Islands, Harriet Ware had a young black girl named Rose as her maid. On one of her trips back to the North, she took "an extremely pretty mulatto girl," rumored to be the daughter of Clarence or Eddings Fripp, the sons of planter John Fripp of St. Helena Island. Rose and Amaretta seemed to have been widely shared among the women missionaries, including black abolitionist Charlotte Forten. Rose also served Forten. Forten described her as "our little maid-of-all-work" and Amaretta as their cook, washer, and ironer.[105]

The Pennsylvania Abolition Society (PAS) shipped hundreds to the North.[106] "I should like a woman who understood cooking, washing and ironing and would be obliging and willing, age between 25 and 35 without children," one woman wrote to the PAS. Another solicited a "couloured [sic] Girl from 12 to 14 years of age of rather dark coulor of sprightly appearance" and "well calculated for general housework in the country." Another preferred a black boy, twelve to fourteen years old, who could milk a cow. The only other stated requirement was that he not be "a yellow boy, but as black as he can be."[107] Laura Towne approved of this traffic in black domestic laborers. "I wish you could have the comfort the Heacocks have in the little darkies they sent North," she wrote. "The two young girls are large and strong and able to do pretty much all the work of the house. They work without wages till they are of age, but are to have the privilege of schooling. The experiment has been a perfect success, and every few weeks some one sends to them for another girl or boy, and all have given satisfaction so far."[108] It seemed not at all extraordinary to Towne that she would favor a system in which black children worked without wages for the "privilege of schooling." And despite her complaints about Rina's service and religion, Towne hoped to one day carry Rina back to the North.[109]

Mary Phinney von Olnhausen, a Northern nurse stationed at Fort Monroe, had similar plans for the "capital contraband" servant she planned to take home when she left the South. Perhaps a relative might also want one. "I am sometimes tempted to send you a nigger," she wrote. As Nina Silber writes, "Northern white women were reluctant to imagine the former slaves as fully independent beings and assumed that their liberation did not completely release them from the shackles of dependency." Rather, they "imagined themselves as the new recipients" of the allegiance they imagined black people felt toward slaveholders.[110] Northern soldiers also carried black women to the North. The colonel of a New Hampshire regiment returned home with a former slave woman who had fled slavery with her husband and found work with the regiment.[111]

No doubt there were black women who welcomed the opportunity to go north to work as domestic servants. Sojourner Truth supported the effort to place former slaves in Northern white homes and worked especially hard to place mothers with children. Her efforts, which continued into the postwar era, helped to send hundreds of former slaves to the North and West. In April 1867, she carried a group of men, women, and children to Rochester, part of a larger group she planned to transplant with the assistance of the Freedmen's Bureau. "I am coming with them & shall come back for the rest," she wrote.[112]

The efforts to get black domestic workers from the South spoke to the dominant Northern ideologies on race, gender, and class. The Northern free labor economy accorded middle-class Northern women like Elizabeth Fiske, Eleanor Baker, and Laura Towne class and race privilege. On this privilege they rested their claims to womanhood and access to idealized notions of domesticity. But middle-class women increasingly viewed the work of domesticity—at least that part involving the preparation of meals, house cleaning, and laundry—as beneath them. Those not wealthy enough to hire help aspired to. Those able to hire a domestic servant or two typically still had to perform at least a part of the domestic labor in their own households, but that was better than no maid at all. They experienced the troubles that beset all households with domestic workers. The women they hired rarely pleased them. Before the war, Ravella Balch's mother hired and fired servants often. There was Catherine, who proved to not "know how to cook much" and was fired. To replace Catherine, Balch's parents went to the nearby town of Newburyport, Massachusetts, and hired "the girl" Jane, who seemed "quite pleasant." In less than three months Jane gave notice, so the search was on for a replacement, this time in Boston. They returned with Hannah, described by Ravella Balch as "very fat and red."[113]

By their words and actions, Northern white women often discounted or demeaned the struggles black women waged on their own behalf and in support of their families, communities, and the Union. Those struggles were present in the movement of black women across the landscape of the wartime South, carrying when they could "their little movables, frying pans, old hats; and bundles," seeking safe places of refuge, fighting off sexual assault by Union soldiers—black and white. To white observers, they did not look like people with any understanding of politics or freedom or what it meant to be a woman. Observing a group of black women and children picked up by a Union gunboat, Georgeanna Woolsey saw in them "no appearance of anxiety or excitement." Even she, reared in abolitionism, could not resist a smear. Attired "in their gayest dresses and brightest turbans," they appeared to her "like a whole load of tulips for a horticulture show." Similarly when she observed a group of black women "quietly nursing their children, and singing hymns," the scene conjured up in her mind a kind of serenity but one that bordered on uncaring. "The day of their deliverance had come," she judged, "and they accepted this most wonderful change with absolute placidity."[114] Woolsey ignored the effort and courage it had taken the women to get this far.

Woolsey joined a chorus of Northern voices who declared efforts by black women to present themselves in the best clothing they owned ludicrous and to whom black women remained caricatures of true womanhood. She mistook their confidence in their own strength and courage for a lack of political consciousness and made light of their humanity.

Hannah Adams also made fun of them and their attempts to live free lives of dignity. The "darkies" attired in "good clothes" amused her. Fannie Green was dismayed to encounter "colored gentlemen in kid gloves escorting their lovely and richly dressed Dinahs" promenading along Pennsylvania Avenue in the nation's capital.[115] While at Newport News, Virginia, to nurse her wounded brother, Green attended the wedding of a black couple out of "a curiosity to see the darkies at their festivals and ceremonies as described in works of fiction." She described the bride and "her three sable bridesmaids" all dressed in white, and the bride adorned additionally with "a brown tissue veil thrown over her face." The groom and groomsmen were also smartly dressed, but Green was not impressed with any of it. She found the effort of the groom to place a wedding ring on the finger of his bride, "after a good deal of pushing and screwing," amusing. So too the "Dinahs present with their sable escorts—and all dressed in their best finery." Green and her companions, two Union doctors, did not stay to the end, having "concluded that it was too warm and fragrant for us to stay any longer."[116] Catherine P. Noyes, a teacher in the South Carolina Sea Islands, described a group of former slaves on their way to church one Sunday morning in 1864 as attired "in the most ludicrous toiletries." It was a common response of white Northerners.[117]

The ways white Northerners thought about enslaved and formerly enslaved women and judged how they talked and talked back, how they looked and dressed, how they cared for their children, and how they worked drew on long history of racist ideas. What was ludicrous on the body of black women was beautiful on the bodies of white women. To Eleanor J. Baker, white "ladies in their spring dresses looking like butterflies" was something to admire. There was no hint of scorn or sarcasm in this description or in her reaction to Robert Weir's painting *Embarkation of the Pilgrims*.[118] The painting depicting the Pilgrims on the deck of the *Speedwell* prior to their departure from Holland in 1620 features women dressed in bright and even fanciful clothing. Viewing *Embarkation of the Pilgrims* made her "heart ache." Among the refugees pictured in the painting, the one who most held her gaze told of "the patience & faith of woman's heart which enabled her calmly to embark with her languid sick child in her arms for an unknown desolate shore."[119]

In 1862, Edward Pierce laid out what he believed to be the most important qualification to be a missionary to the freedpeople: "To both the Boston and New York Committees, I have said that persons accepted must have in the first place profound humanity—a belief that the negro is a human being and capable of elevation and freedom."[120] For white women who went south, this was a difficult mark to reach. Refusing a sisterhood of equality with black women, they helped to refurbish the racial ideology that had defended slavery and would work to constrain black women's lives for decades to come. Laura Towne's reliance on black women domestic workers continued into the postwar period. Increasingly, like former mistresses, she too had to accommodate freedwomen's demands for change in the delivery of domestic service. The women who did her washing and ironing demanded to do it at their own homes. She still kept a black child in her home, "a nice little girl, who seems very honest and capable," she wrote in June 1865. White women teachers and missionaries gave little indication that they understood how their occupation of the homes of former mistresses spoke to racial hierarchies, no less than their assumption that they like mistresses would have black women and children to cook and clean for them. As Barbara Fields writes, "The personal may be political but the political is not necessarily personal."[121]

PART III

THE HARD HAND OF WAR

Chapter Six

UNDER THE RESTLESS
WINGS OF AN ARMY

Fallen Angels

I am here the Stern & Cruel tyrant, slave of a Despotic Master, Lincoln.
Hundreds of children like yourself are daily taught to curse my
name, and each night thousands Kneel in prayer & beseech the
almighty to consign me to Perdition. Such is War. The People here
look on us as invaders come to rob them of home & property and even
life. We tell them we want nothing they have. We don't want their
houses, their farms, their niggers, anything they have, but they don't
believe us, and I fear that this universal bitter feeling will cause
the very result they profess to dread.
—WILLIAM TECUMSEH SHERMAN

I am sometimes weary and long for my family once again. . . . I have
seen the ladies in this vicinity only when flying from the enemy, and
it caused me acute grief to witness their exposure and suffering.
—ROBERT E. LEE

"SURELY OF SHERMAN, God himself will say, 'Let him be accursed!'
and ages to come shall roll up the deep 'Amen.'" So wrote Confederate Kentuckian Lizzie Hardin, invoking 1 Corinthians 16:22. "I know
not the number nor the heinousness of the crimes committed within sound
of the bugle where this modern hero slept," wrote Zillah Haynie Brandon of
Alabama, who had four sons in the Confederate army, two of whom died in
service. "Widows were robbed of their last meal, their furniture crushed, the
beds on which their fatherless children slept ripped open and their feathers
thrown to the winds."[1] Women like Hardin and Brandon took their fight to
the Union armies and the Union armies fought back.

More than any other Union officer, William Tecumseh Sherman came
to personify the view that the Union armies, deliberately and without

provocation, waged a war against Southern women and Southern homes. "Sherman the theif [sic]" and "the Prince of Bummer," were among the milder epithets hurled at him.[2] With Sherman at Savannah and poised to move into South Carolina, Kate Crosland, the daughter of a small slave-holder, believed she knew the man. He "now squats there looking over into South Carolina with vengeful eyes," she wrote, "on what he imagines is the dead carcass of Georgia," and he "vows to spare no age, sex, or condition" in South Carolina, "this noted rebel state where first we breathed the pure free air and saw the sweet light of heaven." Crosland prayed he would not get that far, that "surely Georgia is not dead." Surely Georgia would respond to the "cry of her fair daughters driven to a madhouse by brutal outrage and she *will* drive the insolent from her soil or perish *all* in the conflict."[3] But as Crosland must have known, Sherman had already kept his promise to "make the inside of Atlanta too hot to be endured," that whether his army got "inside of Atlanta or not, it will be a used-up community when we are done with it."[4] It was too late to drive him from Georgia soil. Across the border in the northeast corner of Alabama, Zillah Haynie Brandon had watched Sherman's movements in Cherokee County. "This deplorable invasion swept over our whole country," she wrote. Her daughter Melvina Symer had gone to Sherman to ask that the mill belonging to her husband and father be spared "for the sake of her aged parents." He told her he would burn them before he left. Burning with indignity, Melvina turned away with the emphatic words, "We will live, and live here, too."[5]

Historians have often agreed that Sherman and his men were often worse than "bummers." As Sherman's army moved across Georgia and into the Carolinas, "mothers and children suddenly became military targets as the distinction between combatant and noncombatant blurred," George Rable writes.[6] "No longer would sex provide immunity from the horrors of modern war, for the invaders not only tore up furniture and devoured food, they also tore at the sinews of faith and devoured hope."[7] In a perhaps more measured interpretation, Mark Grimsley argues that while the policies adopted by the Union armies did aim to demoralize Southern civilians and to undermine the Confederate economy, those armies did not engage in indiscriminate war against the home front.[8] The hot words of Union commanders like Sherman, Mark Neely writes, were often little more than "sound and fury, signifying nothing," more "barometers of the intensity of national feeling" than reflections of "marching orders and policy papers."[9] This was certainly sometimes the case. The actions Union commanders took against Confederate women that diminished the line between soldiers and civilians were

also grounded in clearly delineated policy. Sherman was hardly its only prac-
titioner and Atlanta hardly the only site of its enforcement.

The convergence of home front and battlefront began with the start of the
war and escalated as the war wore on. And from the beginning Confederate
women made it a central story of the war. In letters, diaries, and journals,
some never intended to be made public, they presented themselves as victims of an inhumane war that targeted their homes, livelihoods, and bodies.
Sherman was but a "modern Hannibal," Brandon wrote, and Union soldiers
"Woman Exterminators," Sarah Morgan would add.[10] "When the history of
this War is written impartially there will be scenes to record of atrocity and
inhumanity unequalled save in the barbarous war fare of the darkest ages
of the world. Scenes *here* in *Tennessee* which will call forth scalding tears
from the eyes of the gentlest and cause the hearts of her strong and free
sons almost to burst with indignation," wrote Eleanora Willauer of Tennessee.[11] In her diary of the war years, Willauer chronicled the mundane as-
pects of daily life in Middle Tennessee—courting, parties, visiting friends
and relatives, meeting Nathan B. Forrest, and resistance among enslaved
people—but never lost sight of the sacrifices of the Confederate people. The
war had produced "pain, anguish, despair" and "many noble, brave" men
had "poured out the last treasured drop of their life tides, have sacrificed
themselves on the altar of their native land their sunny southern homes."
Willauer reminded herself of the duties of Confederate women, how "*good*
and *pure* our women should be when our men are so brave and patriotic."
Counteracting the "toughening influence of camp life" called for "increased
gentleness and refinement on our part." In the end she would conclude that
the price paid had been too high. "So fair a land and so brave a people is
a fearful sacrafice [*sic*] to Negro Liberty. . . . a strange *philanthropy* in the
white race to sacrafice so *proudly* and so *gladly* its own kind to the inferior
race—*black*—and by the curse of God."[12]

For Willauer and other Confederate women, the "record of atrocity and
inhumanity" extended into the postwar era. Many Northern commanders
and soldiers branded them all "secesh." It was a brand Confederate women
took pride in, as they did in their opinion of the men of the Northern armies.
"I know I hate them," Kate Foster wrote in the summer of 1863.[13] Union commanders often seemed to respond in kind and Sherman had a lot to say
about the subject. In a letter to his daughter, he acknowledged the widely
shared view of him by white Southerners but disputed their perception of
his motives: he was not, he told her, the cruel tyrant they imagined.[14] But
he feared that the extreme bitter feelings against him would only lead to

the result they came to believe he had preplanned. This story is told in this chapter through the eyes of Southern white women adherents of the Confederacy, and intentionally through the eyes of the men they blamed for the war on the home front. The two stories are inextricably tied together. In some parts of the Confederacy, the wives and families of guerrillas suffered deliberate violence, but such instances were infrequent and exceptions to the general rule that women did not qualify as combatants. The treatment Union commanders and soldiers accorded Southern white women Unionist refugees contrasted sharply with their treatment of enslaved women and black women refugees, who suffered deliberate harm.

All the Women Are Secesh

In letters to loved ones and friends and in official reports, officers and soldiers testified copiously to Confederate women's ferocious patriotism. The women he encountered in Louisiana, Gen. Thomas Williams wrote, were "for the most part almost violent, threatening to spit in the faces of Union officers. Such venom one must see to believe. Such unsexing was hardly ever before in any cause or country so marked and so universal. I look at them and think of fallen angels."[15] Federal soldiers and Confederate women alike remarked on the frequency with which each subjected the other to verbal and, sometimes, physical abuse. Southern women cursed the Yankees, calling them beasts, devils, "fiery flying serpents," and worse. Phenie Finly wrote dramatically that she hoped to see Abraham Lincoln "burnt by piece meales [sic]."[16] Francis Springer cringed at the "devilish fury," "violent fits of weeping & exclamatory utterances," and "madness in a number of ladys [sic]" he encountered in Arkansas and Missouri. It marked "a wide departure from the calm & modest dignity of the female character," he wrote.[17]

Union soldiers saw less and less reason to defer to gender conventions. "It is truly a terrible thing to have a hostile army pass through a country," a soldier from Iowa wrote to his wife. The recognition that the war was "hard for the women and children" did not change another soldier's opinion that "rebellion must be put down and we are doing it." When an elderly woman begged an Ohio corporal "to leave her just enough corn to live on," he had little sympathy. "I told her they brought it on themselves."[18] When Confederate women from Donaldsonville, Louisiana, arrived at a Union hospital in New Orleans looking for wounded prisoners and "making their sympathies a little too apparent," Francis Bacon, director of the medical Department of the Gulf, turned them away. "This kind of cats [sic] I pretty uniformly exclude now," he wrote, and "as a consequence, when they find themselves baffled,

I have some highly dramatic interviews with them, almost at the risk of my eyes, I sometimes feel."[19]

When Confederate women spat out their hatred of the North and Northern armies, often literally, Union soldiers became even more convinced that the women had "forfeited their exemption as ladies and noncombatants." This view increasingly found expression in the treatment of Confederate women, whom the wife of one Northern soldier described as "female hyenas."[20] Sherman never resorted to such language, but he agreed that such women were enemies. "When one nation is at war with another, all the People of the one are enemies of the other" and "all the women are secesh," he wrote from Memphis in 1862.[21] He believed it would have been better to acknowledge this from the outset and "the Rules [made] plain and Easy of understanding." It was also "wrong longer to be misled" by a view that the home front was off limits when its people carried the war.[22] The mistake had led the Union to adopt policies that encouraged military engagement on an unsustainable premise.

Sherman never wavered subsequently from this conviction, shared over the course of the war by a growing number of ordinary soldiers and other officers. "We have treated them as misled long enough," one soldier wrote to his family, instead of as "the Rebels they are." Brig. Gen. Alvin P. Hovey agreed. "The great error that the Federal officers have committed during this war has been their overkindness [sic] to a vindictive and insulting foe," which he contrasted to the disgraceful "treatment that helpless Union families" had received from rebels in Memphis.[23] As early as 1860, there were calls in the North for a war of destruction that would encompass the home front and make "the south a desert," as Senator Benjamin Wade of Ohio put it. "We must starve, drown, burn, shoot the traitors," Judge Levi Hubbell of Milwaukee stated in a speech in Philadelphia in 1861. "Northern expressions of support for intensified war-making," Charles Royster argues, "assumed that the Confederate army was an instrument of the Southern populace and that the populace was a legitimate object of attack."[24] Sherman remained one of the most persistent critics of a policy of appeasement.

The weakness in the Union policy of appeasement was in fact evident everywhere the Union armies landed in 1861. In South Carolina slaveholders did not stick around to receive the notices from Washington declaring a policy of nonintervention with slavery. Catherine Edmondston was not impressed when she heard about the proclamation Gen. Ambrose Burnside issued upon his arrival in North Carolina "assuring the people he was civilized & a Christian, that he came to restore order & bring them back to the bosom of their Mother, that he did not intend to molest citizens in the enjoyment of their rights but to protect them in it." He similarly found no takers.[25] The Unionist drive everywhere brought poor results.

Responding to the complaint of a group of Warren County, Mississippi, slaveholders in September 1863 concerning his army's treatment of civilians in rebellion against the United States, Sherman was blunt: "Your preamble starts off with a mistake. I do not think any nation ever undertook to feed, supply and provide for the future of the inhabitants of an *insurgent district*." He described just what "an insurgent district" looked like:

> I know it is the purpose of the controlling Generals of this war to con-
> duct it on the most humane principles of either ancient or modern
> times, and according to them, I contend that after the firing on our
> steamships navigating our own rivers, after the long and desperate re-
> sistance to our armies at Vicksburgh [*sic*], on the Yazoo and Mississippi
> generally, we are justified in treating all the inhabitants as combatants,
> and would be perfectly justified in transporting you all beyond the seas,
> if the United States deemed it to be to her interest. But our purpose is
> not to change the population of this country, but to compel all inhabit-
> ants to acknowledge and submit to the common laws of the land.[26]

By this point in the war, Sherman was convinced of "the bitter enmity of the women of the South," of their part in Southerners' "long and desperate resistance," and he had concluded that the laws of war supported his right to seek retribution.[27] Gen. U. S. Grant reached a similar conclusion about Memphis. It seemed to have all the marks of an "insurgent district," a perfect site for reprisal.

With the occupation by Union forces on June 6, 1862, Elizabeth Meriwether wrote, "All Memphis seemed sorrowful and mourning. I drove into town and saw the streets thronged with women and children; all seemed as if at a funeral—it *was* the funeral of our hopes."[28] Hundreds of the city's white residents fled the occupied city. Many who remained demonstrated to successive Union commanders continued rebellion against the lawful authority of the United States. Soon after taking command of Memphis, Gen. U. S. Grant ordered the evacuation of disloyal women. Confederate brigadier general M. Jeff Thompson protested that the order targeted "helpless women and children" who would "be turned out of doors." Yet he acknowledged their disloyalty to the United States. Nine-tenths of the city's residents were enemies to the United States and thus came under Grant's order, Thompson wrote, with "scarcely a respectable family in that city who have not a father, husband, or brother in our army, or who are the widows and orphans of those who have fallen bravely for our cause."[29] In the "cause of humanity,"

Thompson asked the Union army's cooperation in either establishing a point between the lines where "the fathers, husbands, brothers, sons, or friends of the exiles can go in safety to meet them," or extending the deadline for families to leave the city to allow transportation to be arranged. Surely, he wrote, Grant did not "propose that the little feet that will thus be driven from their homes and birth-spots should plod the weary distance of 30 miles."[30]

Brig. Gen. Alvin P. Hovey succeeded Grant and increased the pressure on Confederates in the city, ordering male residents between the ages of eighteen to forty-five to take an oath of allegiance to the United States or leave the city limits within the week. Elizabeth Meriwether sought to avoid both evacuation and the confiscation of her property in the city that Hovey's successor, Sherman, would order. Meriwether went to Sherman hoping to get him to rescind the order confiscating rents on property, which affected the house she and her husband owned in Memphis and rented out while they lived in a house just outside the city. She left the meeting in tears. As long as her husband was in the Confederate army, Sherman told her, the rent would be confiscated. According to Meriwether, he further insulted her by suggesting that if she needed money, she might try working for a living. "I would give you a set of shirts to make for me if I hadn't already given the order to a woman who says I have robbed her of everything she has," she said he told her. But as he did not need more shirts, he could do nothing for her. "I felt this as an insult not only to me," Meriwether wrote, "but to the womanhood of the South."[31]

Sherman also rejected Meriwether's claim to be the sole owner of the rental property by virtue of a deed her husband signed before he left for Confederate service. The document that "construes the property to be substantially that of the absent husband," he wrote, was nothing but a ruse, and he refused to recognize its legality. By "Law and common sense the transfer of property to a wife at such a time and under such circumstances is simply an evasion, and therefore void," he argued. He was "willing to stretch the Rule as wide as possible to favor distressed women and children," but the risk of "a single departure from the Rules of severe justice may lead us into many inconsistencies and absurd conclusions." He also ruled against Meriwether's attempt to avoid being exiled from the city by "taking or making a parole." Again turning to the law, Sherman argued that this was impossible because she was a woman and "in war the parole of a woman citizen is not good, from them an oath should always be exacted, for the parole is a word of honor which according to the old feudal code, a soldier alone could make." Sherman would send Meriwether behind enemy lines and confiscate her property.[32]

Sherman took over command of Memphis after Hovey and endorsed a policy of less kindness to committed foes, regardless of gender. When a group of Memphis doctors appealed to him for the relief of white women and children, he sent a curt reply: "It is now sunset, and all who have not availed themselves of Gen'l Hovey's authority are supposed to be loyal and true men." The sex of the disloyal was immaterial. "I will say only," Sherman wrote, "that I cannot allow the personal convenience of even a large class of ladies to influence me in my determination to make Memphis a safe place of operations for an army, and all people who are unfriendly should forthwith prepare to depart in such direction as I may hereafter indicate."[33] He also warned the men to step carefully. While doctors were "not liable to be made prisoners of War . . . they should not reside within the lines of an Army which they regard as hostile." To stay would place all in too "delicate" a situation.[34] Over the course of the war, Union commanders and soldiers alike increasingly agreed that the Union army needed to better police a hostile population of Southern women.

In August 1862, having suffered repeated attacks on Federal gunboats from Confederate regular as well as militia and guerrilla forces from the Mississippi River towns of Plaquemine and Donaldsonville, Louisiana, Union officers acted. Adm. David Farragut, having sent a warning that "a repetition of the offense would result in the destruction of their town," when the attacks continued, ordered Union gunboats to "stop at Plaquemine and Donaldsonville and give them notice to send their women and children out of the towns, as it is my intention to destroy those places on my way down, for firing into our vessels."[35] In a blunt message "to the people of Donaldsonville, La.," he stated, "Every time my boats are fired upon I will burn a portion of your town." When the attacks continued, he made good on the promise. "I therefore ordered them to send their women and children out of the town as I certainly intended to destroy it on my way down the river, and I fulfilled my promise to a certain extent," he reported to Secretary of War Gideon Welles. Union forces burned the town's hotels, buildings on the wharf, and at least one home and other property belonging to Phillippe Landry, believed to be the captain of a local guerrilla unit. They also liberated a dozen of his slaves and occupied the town.[36]

All along the Mississippi River, "from New Orleans to Vicksburg, on both sides of the river," a Union naval officer wrote, "all the residents are hostile to the United States and in arms against us," and only the "most energetic and severe measures" would "reduce these people to subjection and obedience to the laws of the United States."[37] As guerrilla activity along the Mississippi River continued, Union commanders ordered the evacuation and destruction of additional towns, prompting appeals both from Confederate women and military commanders. Following attacks on Union gunboats above Vicksburg in February 1863, a delegation of white women from Greenville went to Union lines asking that they be provided advance notice of a Union response but got no satisfaction. "I answered that when the rebels fired on us from that town it would be their note of warning," the Union naval officer wrote. The following day he received a Confederate officer who accused him of firing on unarmed citizens and frightening women and children and promised to exact revenge on Union prisoners and burn cotton that might fall into Union hands.[38] Attacks on Union vessels from Greenville continued. At the end of March 1863, Sherman sent an expedition to Deer Creek, Greenville, and Lake Washington with orders to clear the area of guerrillas and Confederate soldiers. The "planters and inhabitants on Deer Creek" should be made to "see and feel that they will be held accountable for the acts of guerrillas and Confederate soldiers who sojourn in the country for the purpose of firing on our boats passing Greenville and the section of the Mississippi thereabouts." He made clear that he was determined to have "unmolested navigation" of the Mississippi River, even "if all the country within has to be laid waste."[39] The expedition also opened the ways for slaves from the region to make their way to Union lines.[40]

Union officers like Lt. F. A. Roe, commander of the Union gunboat *Katahdin*, who opposed the policy of firing on insurgent towns and districts were increasingly a minority voice. Roe protested the pillaging of a home in Donaldsonville by Union troops and the part he believed he was forced to play. It was "disgraceful and humiliating . . . to be ordered upon guard duty of soldiers employed in pillaging ladies' dresses and petticoats," he wrote. He requested to "be relieved from such services" that required him to "prostitute the dignity of my profession." Roe's argument that the guerrillas along the river were simply trying to protect their homes against pillage drew a sharp rebuke from Gen. Benjamin Butler. "If true," Butler responded, the pillage was "without palliation or excuse," but he went on to upbraid the young officer. Wanton acts of pillage, he informed the lieutenant, were "no more to be justified than this improper, bombastic, and ridiculous rhodomontade of a sublieutenant of the Navy."[41]

Enemy Women and the Laws of War

Union soldiers and commanders came to see the politics, actions, and activities of Confederate women as evidence that they had not only lost God's grace but subjected themselves to the laws of war.[42] The laws of war permitted women to be turned out of their homes and, if necessary, authorized the burning of those homes and the crops that sustained them. The War Department's General Orders No. 100, "Instructions for the Government of Armies of the United States in the Field" (1863), bolstered the position that enemy women should be treated as enemies. "War is not carried on by arms alone," read Article 17. "It is lawful to starve the hostile belligerent, armed or unarmed, so that it leads to the speedier subjection of the enemy." Articles 21 and 24 were even more explicit. According to the former, "The citizen or native of a hostile country is thus an enemy, as one of the constituents of the hostile state or nation, and as such is subjected to the hardships of the war." Article 24 referenced the "almost universal rule in remote times," still applicable to "barbarous armies, that the private individual of the hostile country is destined to suffer every privation of liberty and protection and every disruption of family ties." A qualifying clause in Article 22 advised "that the unarmed citizen is to be spared in person, property, and honor as much as the exigencies of war will admit."[43]

As John Witt writes, Francis Lieber, the principal author of the code, was interested in formulating a law of war that did not separate "the regulation of conduct in war from the justice of war's aim."[44] Justice seemed to dictate a more punitive policy. Only two clauses in Lieber's code referred explicitly to women, Articles 19 and 37. Article 19 stated that "commanders, whenever admissible, inform the enemy of their intention to bombard a place, so that the non-combatants, and especially the women and children, may be removed before the bombardment commences. But it is no infraction of the common law of war to omit thus to inform the enemy. Surprise may be a necessity." By Article 37, the United States would "acknowledge and protect, in hostile countries occupied by them . . . the persons of the inhabitants, especially those of women; and the sacredness of domestic relations. Offenses to the contrary shall be rigorously punished."[45] Both articles aligned with policies Union army and navy commanders had already begun to adopt and would continue to use. "Insurgent districts" would not be spared simply because women were present in them. Indeed, women's presence defined them.

The Confederate people could not expect the enemy they fought against to wage war according to "the usages of war, of humanity, and of civilization," when they violated such usages at every turn, Adm. David D. Porter argued. He would treat those captured in the act of firing on Union vessels as no more than "highwaymen and assassins." He would punish his men caught pillaging private homes but would not allow "parties who are overseer civilians one day (trading with our people) and soldiers the next, to be traveling around the country firing upon hospital vessels and river steamers." Union crews had been "killed in cold blood" by men who jumped aboard their vessel, the kind of men who "lurk in the woods without a flag or distinguishing mark and fire at any human being they may see on the deck of a steamer . . . and this we are called upon to recognize as civilized warfare." If "this savage and barbarous Confederate custom" continued, Porter wrote in February 1863, "we will try what virtue there is in hanging."[46] The following month, Confederate women in the region began taking the path of others before them. Black people fleeing to Union lines reported white people fleeing in the opposite direction. The evidence lay on the roads and in the fields: "Carts and plows with mules are to be seen scattered here and there just as they left yesterday," one officer noted, along with a rich supply of chickens, hams, eggs, butter, quilts, and other items.[47]

It made no difference whether the aid Confederate women rendered the Confederate cause was direct or indirect. When Confederates concealed themselves not only "under the cover of the woods" but under the skirts of women, this entailed an act of complicity on the part of women.[48] It was also an act of cowardice on the part of men who, rather than fight like men, left "their women in their residences, and relying upon their feebleness to protect them and their property from the righteous punishment which should await them for their treason." By firing on Union gunboats from the safety of treetops, woods, and levees, and from under the skirts of women, they placed white women and children at greater risk.[49] It was a damning indictment: The men at Donaldsonville stood accused of using white women as shields and making them homeless.

Union commanders argued that Confederate women endorsed such usage by voluntarily opening their skirts and homes to hide contraband goods and rebels and commit other treasonous acts, willingly allowing themselves to be used as shields and actively assisting rebel forces in other ways. On the Missouri border, LeeAnn Whites shows, women with husbands "in the bush" were "willing suppliers of the guerrilla war." Their homes were "key outposts" used to signal the alarm at the approach of Union troops.[50] In Virginia, Mary A. Seddon, wife of Confederate secretary of war James Seddon, was among the residents "suspected of sending signals to rebels at night by lamps" and was warned to stop. Seddon denied the charge but not her loyalty to the Confederacy, "a cause to which I would willingly sacrifice my life, but not my honor," she wrote. She remained "unswerving in her loyalty to the rebel cause."[51]

War Is Not Carried on by Arms Alone

Confederate women's expressed hatred of Northern armies did not stop them from seeking help from those armies. Confederate women besieged the lines of Union forces in the Mississippi valley, requesting and demanding assistance and protection from Union commanders and soldiers. Capt. E. W. Sutherland of the Union ram *Monarch* complained of being constantly besieged by "wronged and outraged women asking for protection." Union officers generally "discouraged wanton pillaging" and often stationed soldiers at white homes as military protection, as they did for Mary Seddon, but sometimes the fierce allegiance of Confederate women to the Confederate cause made them less sympathetic figures.[52] At one point, Sherman became so exasperated with having to take up so much of his time fielding the complaints that he moved his headquarters to "a camp a little way out on purpose to avoid the crowd of curious women who always flock about to represent absent husbands. There must be about 2000 men in the Southern army from Memphis whose mothers & sisters not only expect us to protect them as long as they the mothers & sisters stay indoors, & sew & write letters to their absent sons, & husbands but actually to hunt up their lost niggers, horses, hogs & [illegible]."[53] In Memphis, they were everywhere playing the "old game," he wrote to his wife: "Every nigger has run off, and of course I am supposed to be in immediate possession. . . . Miss Nancy raised in her mistress's bosom and nursed like her own children, has run off, and the whole family must rush to Gen. Sherman. Father brother and all gone to fight us, but of course I must neglect business to catch Miss Nancy—Cases of that kind occur fifty times a day, besides real ones."[54] Even when the widow of an old military buddy from Ohio came to him in search of a runaway, Sherman turned her away. She "presumed on my favor which she did not get," he wrote.[55]

Former slaves rejoiced when Union officers turned aside the pleas of mistresses seeking to stay in Union lines or to have black people returned to their ownership. One formerly enslaved woman who had made her way to Memphis recalled her former mistress's attempts to persuade her and others to return to the plantation. When they refused, the former slaveholder went to General Grant, who declined to interfere. She then again tried to convince the former slaves to go with her, but "not one would go," at which point she went back to Grant and "begged an' cried" to at least be given her cook. The cook feared Grant would change his mind but was thrilled to hear "the General say, 'I can't help you, madam; if your cook wants to go wid you she can, but she is free, an' can do as she likes about it.' An she went off cryin'; and we

George Caleb Bingham, *Martial Law or General Order No. 11.*
(Courtesy of the State Historical Society of Missouri)

could jus' kiss de groun' General Grant walks on."[56] This slaveholder learned
the lesson Sherman had tried to teach the group of Warren County planters, that in "rebelling against the only earthly power that insured them the
rightful possession" of enslaved people they had "practically freed them."[57]

Following the passage of Confiscation Act of 1862, Sherman issued General Orders Nos. 60 and 67 in July and August 1862 providing for the employment of black people in his lines at Fort Pickering and around Memphis.
They were to be given clothing and rations and paid wages. The wages, however, were to be withheld until the courts decided, Sherman said, whether
or not black people were free by law. In the interim, the names of slaveholders would be entered in the record in case the pay should go to them.[58] Not
having yet received instructions for implementing the act, he felt "forced to
lay down certain rules for my own guidance." The constant interruption of
slaveholders "so thronged my tent as to absorb my whole time and necessity
compelled me to adopt some clearly defined rules, and I did so," he wrote.
He worried that his actions might not be "legal and just."[59]

Prior to informing Secretary Chase of the action he had taken, he sought
the advice of his father-in-law, Thomas Ewing, Sr., a member of the Ohio

bar, "to know if I have guessed right at the Law points." It was not only the throngs of Southerners who came to him for help with reclaiming black people as slaves or seeking protections for white women that moved Sherman to act by late summer of 1862. He had already concluded that "changing the opinions of the People of the South" was "impossible" and went so far as to suggest that "they must be killed or dispossessed." The war's second stage, which he called "the real struggle of conquest," he believed, must involve the confiscation of "Negro property and personal property" as "fair objects of conquest" and the repopulation of the South with white Northerners. Only that would bring real change.[60]

Unladylike Conduct

Union commanders were not totally unsympathetic to Confederate women and helped them in many ways, such as posting soldiers to protect them and their homes, and to keep their slaves from escaping. The grudging thanks they sometimes received was often laced with vituperation. Women's sometimes violent and "unladylike" conduct bothered some Confederate women who called for more "ladylike" conduct in keeping with notions of female propriety.[61] Julia LeGrand tried to draw a line between dignified protest and resistance to the Northern "invasion" and plain rudeness. She opposed women's public expressions that seemed to put them beyond the protections of white womanhood, "for rudeness in a woman is always vulgar." This did not mean that Confederate women should extend hands of friendship to the enemy, as she counseled two young women who came to her concerned that they might have damaged their reputations by entertaining a Union officer. LeGrand let them know that even though they had their father's permission, what they did was wrong, for "friendly intercourse with those against whom four of their brothers are in arms was inappropriate." The girls had suffered the condemnation of their neighbors, although one of them saw this as overreaching, for "no one had a right to speak of what they pleased to do." The young woman said that "she had read of instances where passages of romantic love had passed between rebel ladies and English officers (always officers) in our first revolution." This did not make it right, LeGrand told them, and they "should avoid carefully any show of entertaining union feelings; besides it is scarcely decorous to take a hand in friendship which is red with Confederate blood." "No woman's smile should cheer these invaders," lest it be taken as "tacit acknowledgment of want of self-respect."[62]

LeGrand could also sympathize with Union soldiers' wives, mothers, and daughters. She wanted an independent Confederate state, but she also understood the impact that the war had on the mothers, wives, and children of Northern soldiers. Her joy in Confederate military victories was tempered by her sympathy for Northern women. For "even a great victory to one's side" was "a sad thing to a lover of humanity." Union soldiers also had "many to mourn them at home, and their love of life was as ours." She was told that this was an "unnatural" position to take and accused of being "'half Yankee.' I am thought wavering in my faith to the Confederate cause because I can still pity the slain foe." This did not signal a waning of her support of the Confederate cause. She refused to take an oath of allegiance to the United States and criticized those who did for the selfish reason of holding onto their slaves when they should be devoting their efforts instead to "prove that Louisiana is not a loyal State."[63]

After reading a letter written by a Northern soldier's wife to her husband that by chance came to her hand, Mary Rhodes expressed similar misgivings and sympathy. Old enough to remember the horrors of the Revolutionary War, she had watched preparations for the Civil War with dread. "As long as it was only the dress parade, barbeques, balls, and presentations of honor, it was well enough," but "the reality of the thing that was upon us made many a poor woman's heart beat—the sickening dread that to-day the call might come." Her husband and brothers were soldiers in the Confederate army, and, like other Confederate women, she waited anxiously for mail from the nearest post office four miles away and sent someone every day to the nearest telegraph office, which was twenty miles away, to check for news. This made her even more sympathetic toward Northern soldiers' wives. The letter showed her how much they had in common. It was no different from most letters from the home front, filled with "the minutia of her everyday life," the "pain she was suffering," and concern for her husband's safety. Rhodes empathized with the Northern woman's plea to her husband to resist the call to reenlist and instead come home. "If I thought you never would come back I'd die, and pray I may die before I ever hear it," the Northern woman wrote, adding that his pay could never compensate "for all this pain."[64]

For the first time it seemed to occur to Rhodes that Northern women might dread Confederate soldiers as much as Southern women dreaded Federal soldiers. The letter conveyed the Northern woman's "horror of the South" and her belief that the rebels "were so many demons." It drew Rhodes's sympathy. "I often thought of her," she wrote. "She so far away was suffering the same that I was, but for the pay for which he was fighting. To us it was a novel idea. We did not know whether our men were being paid or not—that was the last thing we ever thought of—certainly not in that light."[65] Union soldiers took note of those moments when Confederate women responded as fellow human beings, when, for example, they nursed wounded Union soldiers. "I was glad to see one thing I never saw before," Charles Francis Adams Jr. wrote his father, "women caring for our wounded. They were Virginians, and only the week before our regiment searched their house for one of their two brothers in the Confederate Army; but now we found the old father and four daughters, two miles this side of their home, doing what they could for one of our Sergeants, who had fallen by the road-side."[66] In the end, the ambivalence some Confederate women felt about the war and the aid some rendered to Union soldiers were overshadowed by the legendary stories of their anger, disdain, contempt, and hatred for Federal soldiers.

Confederate women spoke and wrote often of "the prowling Yankee[s] who like the tigers consume the prey they find." They spread, Zillah Haynie Brandon wrote, "over our valley like blood hounds, occasionally lighting the torch that consumes the storage of our citizens."[67] Southern white women also had to deal with violence and destruction from the hands of men in their own armies. Confederate soldier George Butler was appalled by "how much wickedness is carried on in the army." It was not just the cursing, swearing, and lying of his fellow soldiers, "as if they had no consciences," but the wanton destruction and thefts he found so objectionable. "It has been no uncommon sight to see hogs lying about in the woods and along the roadside, where the soldiers have shot them dead and gone off and left them there to waste," he wrote. "Some of the citizens say that the soldiers have robbed them of their last hog and left them not a mouthful to eat. Our soldiers are worse here than they were in Pennsylvania. They try to excuse themselves by saying that the people are nearly all Union and ought to suffer. I do not mean to say that all or even a majority of our soldiers are thus wicked, but it prevails to an alarming extent."[68]

Wronged and Outraged Women

The war on and against the Southern home front was part of the long history of women and war in America. America's past wars were important touchstones for the Civil War. Long before the war on the Southern home front in the Civil War—along the Mississippi River; in the Shenandoah valley; in Arkansas, New Orleans, Memphis, Atlanta, and Columbia, South Carolina—Americans had experienced the home front as a battlefield, most prominently in the Revolutionary War. Even as Zillah Haynie Brandon watched nervously the movement of Sherman's army on northeast Alabama, she recalled the stories of her ancestors' experience during the Revolution, when "the devastating course of war like an avalanche from the mountains came sweeping over the emigrants, and drove the men from their quiet homes and well-cultivated fields, to turn their plough shares into weapons of death . . . while their wives and children were forced to take shelter in a fort to save themselves from the scalping knife of the Indian; and the no less savage treatment of the Tory." Her grandfather had lost his life in battle, leaving behind a widow and two infant daughters, one of whom was Brandon's mother.[69] Now her son and his family were refugees. As Kirsten Wood writes, "Memories of wartime abuse lingered for decades."[70]

In many respects, the Civil War indeed was profoundly novel, but Americans had experienced elements of war waged against the home front before. They recalled the "brutality of the British and Tories in sacking houses, carrying off cattle, abducting slaves, insulting the defenceless [sic], and sometimes burning the dwellings of those who were particularly obnoxious to them." Samuel DuBose recalled the particular experience of white women.

> No pen can adequately describe the anguish of mind constantly endured for the fate of husbands and sons, exposed not merely to the dangers of the tented field, but to all the horrors of a civil war, in which life was every moment in peril from every quarter. . . . the instances of barbarous rudeness which they experienced from a remorseless and an exasperated soldiery, whose discipline was purposely relaxed by the stern policy of our unrelenting foe. No one can adequately portray those heartrending troubles which afflicted the lonely and isolated mothers with their tender offspring to support, not secure that even the meal in actual preparation would appease their craving appetites, for even this was often the prey of the robber soldier. . . . All these trials were endured with fortitude which none but women can exhibit. Often in childhood have I hung upon a mother's lap and listened with astonished wonder to the recital of tales of misery like these.[71]

In the years after the Civil War, Southern women would recite such tales again. White women on the road as refugees, the destruction of homes and crops, ordered evacuations of cities, and prisoners of war were part of the Revolutionary story that reverberated on into and helped shape the Civil War experience.[72] Memories of stragglers and deserters and assaults on the home front were still alive in 1861. "Many now living," Frederick A. Porcher wrote, "recollect that persons rarely ventured to travel the Goose Creek road without arms."[73] Southerners also recalled the confiscation of property by both sides during the American Revolution. On June 19, 1778, patriot forces occupying Philadelphia confiscated the property of leading loyalists and ordered the evacuation of loyalist wives and children upon pain of being placed "in a workhouse until they could give security that they would leave the state and never return."[74] The Revolutionary War, as a growing body of scholarship reminds us, was "quite simply a civil war" and "routinely described as such by contemporaries on both sides of the Atlantic."[75]

Revolutionary-era women experienced exile—voluntary and involuntary—and life as refugees. In the North and South, they saw their homes burned or turned into military barracks and hospitals and lost male and female kin.[76] The war in Georgia "precipitated a mass exodus of whites from Georgia and from South Carolina." Slaveholders abandoned their plantations, some taking "refuge in the swamps" with their slaves. Others "fled to the safety of St. Augustine."[77] Regular and irregular warfare on the Georgia-Florida frontier brought widespread devastation and destruction to plantations between the St. Johns River in Florida and St. Marys River bordering the states of Georgia and Florida.[78] Like Confederate women decades later, loyalist women proved fierce enemies. In March 1777, Mrs. Tomas Robie of Massachusetts wrote that she hoped to live long enough to return from forced exile to "find this wicked rebellion crushed, and see the streets of Marblehead run with Rebel blood." It was a not uncommon loyalist sentiment.[70] Women voiced similar sentiments during the American Civil War—an understanding of how easily the war front could bleed in the home front.[80] They also recalled the loss of slaves—those who ran away, often with enemy encouragement, or were confiscated by the British during the Revolution and the War of 1812.

When John Jay, a member of New York's Commission for Detecting and Defeating Conspiracies, reached out to an old friend, prominent landowner Beverley Robinson, hoping to convince him that the time had come to cross the Rubicon and join the patriots, he took his argument to Robinson's wife, Susanna. To back the loyalists, he told her, would be to back a government that "claims a right to bind you & your children in all Cases whatsoever." By refusing to take an oath declaring that he owed no allegiance to the king or crown of Britain, her husband "put his own, and the happiness of his family at hazard." Famine and "incessant anxiety" would be the result. Jay painted a dismal portrait of the life she and her children would face as refugees buffeted by "contending armies" in the besieged city of New York. "Should it be evacuated," he wrote, "where & with whom & in what manner are you next to fly?" He asked her to imagine what it would be like "living under the restless wings of an Army." He regretted to bring up such "delicate" matters but acted to help her avoid the worst possible fate: "Will you ever Madame be able to reconcile yourself to the mortifying reflection of being the Mother of Slaves."[81] Jay's decision to appeal directly to Susanna Robinson and the domestic realm was not accidental, and neither was the call to defend the home and women in the Confederacy's call to war.

Memories not of what she had personally experienced but what had been passed down to her haunted Mary Rhodes. "A child of the Revolutionary War," she remembered "hearing the tales told by the family and the old negroes of hair-breadth escapes and the terrible cruelty of both 'Redcoats' and 'Tories.'" She had thus "imbibed a horror of it, and from my earliest years dreaded lest I too might live to see one. The deeds of daring which made the boys wish there might be another war, for me had only the dark and suffering side. . . . It was therefore with all the old childish dread intensified, that I read and heard the constant predictions of a civil war—one much more to be dreaded than the other."[82]

None of this history, however, rescued Sherman's reputation. Sherman's infamous march from Atlanta to Savannah in 1864 was just one of the last phases of the war against the home front, but that theater had already been opened as early as 1862. It was also part of the history of U.S. warfare. Yet, despite the important ongoing revisionist work of the past two decades, the debate about hardships women endured during the Civil War continues to proceed largely as if the nineteenth-century Civil War were America's first and only conflict that enveloped the home front.[83] Even as revisionist scholarship challenged the long-dominant narrative that focused on battles, generals, and regiments and left little room for the home front and women, the imprint of the battle-centric focus has proved hard to dislodge.[84]

Sherman also viewed his job within the broader context of his ideas about the future of America and the place of the Mississippi valley, in particular, in that future. He had come to believe "that the interest of the great valley of the Mississippi must control the destiny of America, and Memphis, occupying its centre, like the heart, must regulate the pulsation of life that runs throughout the more remote arteries and veins."[85] "I do not pretend to See daylight ahead yet," he wrote, "but I assume you all mistake[n] who expect to convert the South, to reconcile or subdue them. I can imagine no sure process but the same that began in the colonization of America." He made the same argument in a letter to his brother, John Sherman. "My full belief is we must Colonize the Country *de novo* beginning with Kentucky & Tennessee, and should remove five millions of our people at once south of the Ohio River taking the farms and plantations of Rebels. I deplore the war as much as ever, but if a thing has to done let the means be adequate. Don't expect to overrun Such a Country or subdue such a people in our two or five years, it is the task of half a century. . . . We must colonize & Settle as we go south for in Missouri there is as much strife now as ever."[86]

Battlefields "Void of Interest to the Soldier"

In the Civil War as in other wars in American and world history, the space of men and guns intersected repeatedly with the ideologically cordoned-off spaces of women, children, and the elderly. At the Wilderness, Gettysburg, Vicksburg, Atlanta, Stones River, and any number of other battlefields, formal battlefield plans and the arrangement and movements of powerful armies arrayed against each other could suggest the containment of warfare to designated spaces—whether through deliberate planning or the exigency of the moment. But the spaces where soldiers fight are difficult to limit to formal battlefields and inevitably ripple out into the spaces of women and children. Armies on the move or of occupation can erase for all practical purposes the line between combatants and noncombatants, between armed men and unarmed women. New offensives, victories, and defeats redraw and sometimes completely erase the most carefully mapped battlefield lines, dissolving in real time the theoretical distinction between home front and battlefront. Sherman's March to the Sea was in a military sense battle-free, "void of interest to the soldier," one Union officer wrote.[87] His army waged no major fixed battles between Atlanta and Savannah, but the destruction of roads, homes, depots, railroads, and bridges along its path, foraging by soldiers of both armies, and the trail of black refugees following it, turned the countryside into a battlefield. For civilians and noncombatants along the way, the sight of an army of 60,000 men comprising four corps arrayed across sixty miles, moving at a pace of 15 miles a day along four roads, and accompanied by 3,200 wagons that alone occupied five miles or more of road, would have suggested nothing less than a battlefield.

Sherman carried to the East views honed in the West. He continued to make no bones about war's realities. Reporting to Gen. Henry W. Halleck the day before Christmas 1864, having just occupied Savannah, he reiterated that he was "not only fighting hostile armies, but a hostile people and must make old and young, rich and poor, feel the hard hand of war."[88] By this point, the hard hand with which he waged war was a weapon much used by both sides. Long before Atlanta and his march to Savannah, Columbia, and on to North Carolina, Sherman and other Union and Confederate commanders had waged war against enemy women.

Women across the divides of race, region, and class had experienced the

hard hand of war as Civil War armies repeatedly crossed the lines that supposedly separated the space of men and guns from the "home front" of
women, children, and the elderly, most without either guns or battlefield
plans, or in the words of Confederate Sarah Morgan, "women, carrying babies instead of guns."[89] Millions of women in the South faced a borderless
battlefield. Labeling women "civilians," D'Ann Campbell and Richard Jensen
have ventured, "is a technicality."[90]

When Confederate women declared their willingness "to sacrifice everything for independence," they spoke with deep knowledge of war and its
harms. They understood that the sacrifices might include the loss of fathers,
sons, and husbands. They knew that their job included supporting and encouraging their fathers, husbands, sons, brothers, and neighbors to enlist
and to stay in the fight. As one woman wrote, "Every man's duty now is at
his post."[91] At the same time, some women were ready to at least save the
men they loved even as they continued to support the goal of an independent
Confederate nation.

Mary Maxcy Leverett did not cease to support the war, but by the end she
urged her own son to *"Resign, if there is no other better step to take."* She
had already lost one son in the war. Over the course of several months,
she pleaded with him to resign or at least find a less-dangerous unit, like
the Reserves. "You have been under fire long enough and could with honor
take a safer position." She chastised him for not being aggressive enough in
seeking one: "Do you expect an office to be thrust into your mouth?" She also
worried about the "cold-blooded wretch Sherman and his crew." She was
angry that friends and relatives were refugees, some, like the Coffins, hiding
out "the whole night in the woods." She wanted to save her son but also the
Confederacy. "If our men never fought before, tell them I say they must do
so now: if they give up, or their knees shake, I won't count them as men, but
as dogs who deserve to, deserve to die."[92]

Women knew that the home front was a critical component of the machinery of war. Despite their exclusion from formal politics and their subjectiv-
ity to the authority of men, in their patriotism throughout history, Abigail
Adams wrote, women equaled "the most Heroick."[93] The gendered duties
that defined the domestic sphere that white women controlled on a day-
to-day basis should not confuse us. Though most did not show their hands
publicly during the secession debates, there was every reason for men to
know that they would "have to contend with the women," black and white,
rich and poor.[94]

The history of what had come before dictated that much. Women's race
and class identities, however, made a difference in how they faced war and

how hard it hit them. It mattered whether they were black, white, or Native American, rich or poor, free or enslaved.[95] All learned that "an army, any army, does poison the air."[96] Confederate women were not the only women to breathe its air. It reached into the cabins of enslaved and the homes of poor and nonslaveholding white women, pushed them too onto the public road and followed them on the road to freedom.

Chapter Seven

BLACK WOMEN REFUGEES

Making Freedom in Union Lines

Young children, only five or six years of age, were found skulking
in the cane brake with wounds, while helpless women were
found shot down in the most inhumane manner.
—COL. SAMUEL J. NASMITH

One negro was killed, and two families of the refugees carried off.
—HENRY BOOBY, acting ensign, Mississippi Squadron

I N THE WINTER OF 1863, a family of twenty survived the journey from
slavery to Union lines, arriving safely at Helena, Arkansas. Some found
work, and for a time the family seemed to do well. But it was not to
last. Their hopes of finding freedom within the lines of the Union army were
quickly disappointed. Robbed of their clothing and bedding by Union soldiers, they were left exposed in winter. Thirteen members of the family died.
It was at this moment that the man who had held them in bondage arrived,
hoping to persuade the survivors to return to slavery. They decided to go
back with him.

It is difficult to imagine the decision of these people to re-enslave themselves. We know that to keep their families together and for myriad other
reasons, countless slaves had made this hard choice before the war. This
moment, however, was different. They had made it to freedom as a family.
The slaveholder who went to the refugee camp at Helena did not have the
kind of leverage slaveholders held before the war. Still, in the truest sense of
the word, there was nothing voluntary about their decision. "They did not
want to go," wrote Northerner Maria Mann, an agent of the Western Sanitary Commission stationed at Helena. They "faltered, changed their minds
daily, for a week," she wrote, "we encouraging them all we could," but "as
destitution, persecution & death stared them in the face the sad sufferers
went back."[1] When freedom in the making looked so much like slavery,

others also retraced their steps and turned back toward slavery.[2] Chaplain Samuel Sawyer, the superintendent of contrabands at Helena, reported that the abused refugees "seek for passes through the lines & hundreds of them return[ed] to their old home."[3] The camps at Helena and outlying farms also suffered repeated Confederate attacks, sometimes due to weak Union picket lines and sometimes due to the success of Confederate arms. By the spring of 1863, Helena had become a graveyard for Union soldiers as well. Mann asked Sawyer to move the people to the camp at President's Island near Memphis, but she had come to have little faith in him. She considered Sawyer a nice man but found "his total incapacity to carry out a system effectively" problematic. "He is an excellent man, a true friend to the race, an untiring worker," she wrote, and "has afforded then great aid & succor, but has no system in his nature to work out a large plan, no executive power to control such a colony."[4]

Across the Mississippi valley and the larger slave South, enslaved women acted on the belief that the war was about slavery and that their freedom lay in the balance. Enslaved women pleaded with Union forces to rescue them and give them shelter. They persisted in their efforts to build communities that could stand as critical sites of resistance, both to Confederate attacks and to Union policies that discouraged their coming and sought to limit their freedom. They made clear that they were ready and willing to fight for their own freedom and the Union cause.[5] Louisa Alexander, enslaved in the border state of Missouri, lived only sixty miles from the Union stronghold at St. Louis, but her master kept a close watch on her. Alexander was convinced that her freedom would come only "at the point of the Bayonet," a resolution she welcomed. "I dont see how I can ever get away except you send soldiers to take me from the house as he is watching me night and day," she wrote her husband, Archer Alexander.[6] He and three of their children had already made it to St. Louis and he would indeed find a way to get his wife out. Their son died in battle as she was making her way to freedom.[7]

Long before Lincoln drafted the Preliminary Emancipation Proclamation of September 1862, enslaved women helped put emancipation on the nation's wartime agenda by making their own "actual freedom."[8] To the end of the war, their journey to Union lines remained a dangerous enterprise. Many experienced it as another migration in a long history of migrations for the enslaved, even though this time, they moved on their own volition. Memories of the domestic slave trade that had carried a million enslaved people from the Eastern Seaboard states to the new cotton and sugar fields of the Mississippi valley before the war were fresh in 1861. The work of reconstituting families and communities torn apart by the trade was very much still underway when war brought new separations and trauma. The difference now was the possibility that such separations and trauma would forever end. By the end of the Civil War, black women and children constituted the war's largest refugee population. Refugee camps dotted the landscape, particularly in areas of heavy fighting between the two armies and with large concentrations of enslaved people before the war, and rarely afforded protection or safe refuge. Black people, one Union official wrote, "have a dread of the Freedmen's Camp, in which so many have suffered and died."[9] It was not an unfounded fear.

Building on the pioneering insights of W. E. B. Du Bois, the work of scholars over the past three decades has forced a reassessment of the history of wartime flight and resistance. Historians have explored in rich detail the unevenness of freedom's arrival, its precarious and protracted nature.[10] This scholarship has illuminated slaves' politics, the impact of the exodus that Du Bois termed "The General Strike" on Union and Confederate policy, and some of its gender dynamics.[11] In Civil War refugee and labor camps, the gender dynamics of the making of freedom come squarely into view. In refugee camps and on plantations, black women sharpened the politics of freedom born in slavery. Before the war, the vast majority of fugitive slaves were men and boys. Now, women and children figured prominently among the fugitives. By the spring of 1863, the refugee camp at Corinth, Mississippi, housed 2,999 women and children and 668 men; the Grand Junction, Tennessee, camp, 1,355 women and children and 353 men; and a Memphis camp, 1,021 women and children and 361 men. Rations reports for the camps also make visible the disproportionate representation of women and children. In January 1863, for instance, of the 1,700 rations issued per week at Memphis, less than 150 went to boys and men between the ages of sixteen and fifty.[12]

On the war's battlefields the refugees moved to the rhythms of slaveholders in flight, massing armies, the decrees of governments and military commanders, and their own political imperatives. The battlefield was sometimes the plantation where slaveholders remained in residence, sometimes a Union military or refugee camp, sometimes an abandoned plantation leased by the Federal government. It was sometimes the traditional battlefield with opposing armies arrayed against one another. On each, new regimes of power were being mapped out.

The outcome of military battles effectively defined the geographical perimeters of where black women could make freedom. Congressional legislation and resolutions marked its arbitrary political parameters. Within those borders, the views of Union commanders and soldiers, Treasury Department officials, and agents of freedmen's and soldiers' aid societies—on whether or not black women had political or moral standing in the war—conditioned the kind of freedom black women could pursue. Confederate patrols and the use of Confederate military forces to police the countryside, raids on the camps in which they took refuge, and slaveholders' dragnets that carried them deeper into the interior further squeezed the perimeters and terrain of freedom.

For those who took the chance to flee to freedom, luck could make all the difference between success and failure. Emeline Anderson, and her husband, Robert, just barely escaped removal in the coffle their master James Berry drove to Texas in 1863. Another family who lived on a different plantation owned by Berry was not so lucky. Charles Washington escaped the dragnet but his wife and three children were among the people Berry carried to Texas. He never saw them again.[13] On the other end were people like Louisa and Israel Smith and Lutitia and Henry Taylor, who caught a ride to freedom on a Union gunboat, and fourteen-year-old Cynthia Hobson, who followed the Union army to freedom in April 1863 and secured a job as a chambermaid on the steamer *Hannibal City*.[14] When the *Hannibal* docked at Vicksburg on July 4, 1863, the day the city fell to Union forces, she left the boat and took up residence in the city. Hobson took advantage of the region's steamboat and river economy, which before the war employed thousands of enslaved and free black women and men, enabling them "to daily reproduce the networks of affiliation and solidarity" that they again turned to during the war.[15]

When black men were recruited directly from the plantations as laborers and soldiers, their families were often left behind. On the Messenger Plantation in March 1863, for example, the men "parted with their relatives and friends without a tear, others begging to be taken also," an officer wrote.[16] Those who remained behind might rejoice knowing their brothers, sons, fathers, and husbands would be fighting for them. Yet the departure of black men to join Union forces left women and children more vulnerable to revenge by slaveholders. The flight of slaves from Washington County, Mississippi, fueled greater repression from slaveholders. In the area just west of Lake Washington, where slaves were reported to be "very insubordinate," leading slaveholders called on Confederate military forces to help stem the flow of fugitive slaves and "bring out a lot of the most unruly, and place them at work inside our lines." A Confederate commander threatened to "hang every negro that he could catch going or coming off [Union] boats" along the river.[17] The path to "actual freedom" crisscrossed ground both fertile and inhospitable to the work of making freedom. That path was also deeply gendered. Orders from Union commanders and congressional policies stipulated gendered terms that placed boundaries on the kind of freedom black women could pursue. These policies sent enslaved women along a path to freedom distinctly different from those taken by enslaved men.

The Gendered Path to Freedom

Louisa and Israel Smith set out for freedom in 1863 as a married couple. They had married on Christmas Day 1856, surrounded by friends and family, knowing that their union was bereft of legal protection. They knew that they and any children they might have could be separated, sold, beaten, starved, or killed. They would have understood that any number of factors—the death of the person who held them in bondage, a disappointing crop yield, a gambling debt, or the purchase of a piano or a wedding dress—could spell disaster for their marriage and their lives. They no doubt dreamed of a time when they would no longer be subject to market forces that could send them to the auction block or the caprice of a slaveholder that could without warning result in assault and battery against a loved one or friend. Even in a decade that witnessed a Supreme Court decision that in declaring black people permanently ineligible for citizenship cradled the dreams of slaveholders, the rise of the Republican Party and the escalating debate over the expansion of slavery allowed for cautious optimism. That optimism buoyed their commitment to marriage, community, and freedom.[18] The coming of the Civil War seemed to confirm the justifications for those hopes. And so they left slavery joined by other people from the plantation where they had been enslaved, as well as people like Lutitia and Henry Taylor, a married couple with two small children, who lived in the neighborhood.

The Taylors and Smiths walked away from slavery in Washington County, Mississippi, together. A Union gunboat picked them up and carried them on to freedom but did not land them there together. After leaving slavery the women would travel separate and disparate paths to freedom and citizenship from those their husbands followed. Downriver at Goodrich's Landing, Louisiana, women, children, and men deemed unfit by age or ill health for military service were placed ashore. The boat moved on, carrying Israel Smith and Henry Taylor and the able-bodied men some fifteen to twenty miles away to Lake Providence to enlist in the Union army. On May 1, 1863, Israel Smith and Henry Taylor mustered into the Forty-Seventh USCI along with several other formerly enslaved men from Greenville, Lake Washington, and Deer Creek in Washington County.[19] None of these men and women could have safely predicted just a few years before that the nation would go to war over slavery or that they would play a role in its destruction. Yet, in 1863, in the heart of the cotton kingdom in the Mississippi valley they joined the flight of hundreds of thousands to Union lines and a new world in the making, sometimes aided unwittingly and sometimes proactively by the operations of the Federal army.

Emancipation, together with "the use of colored troops," President Lincoln argued, "constituted the heaviest blow yet dealt to the rebellion."[20] Without it, "we can not longer maintain the contest," he wrote. But it was manly *"physical force"* that Lincoln trusted most and that helped him justify the use of black men as soldiers and laborers. As he often stated, his support of black enlistment was grounded in the conviction that it helped save the Union: Not "sentiment or taste," but *"physical force, which may be measured, and estimated as horsepower, and steam power, are measured and estimated."* The husbands, fathers, and sons of enslaved women earned by the "physical force" they offered to the Union side a contested but clear-cut path to freedom.[21] Enslaved women faced a far more complicated and arduous path. The physical force that went to the side of the Union was physical force removed from the Confederate side. This calculation did not include enslaved women, a view at least some people at the time challenged. The use of enslaved men to help build fortifications and to perform fatigue duty, by "thus relieving the Confederate soldier from labor, and enabling him at all times to swell the ranks at short notice," gave the Confederates a huge advantage, the Contrabands' Relief Commission of Cincinnati, among others, noted. The relief commission gave equal attention to the slaves "on the plantations engaged in agricultural pursuits, furnishing the food and means of sustaining the army in the field."[22] The number of black women and children fugitives grew with the mobilization of black men as soldiers and laborers in the Union army.

Though gendered as a male attribute, the Federal government also came to rely on and demand "physical force" from black women—as plantation laborers and as cooks and nurses. This was plainly evident in the Federal government's plans to rent abandoned plantations to private citizens and corporations. George B. Field, one of the three "Commissioners of Plantations" appointed by Lorenzo Thomas in April 1863 to establish a system of leasing abandoned plantations, emphasized the gains to be had by employing "noncombatants . . . in cultivating the soil." The noncombatants he had in mind were mainly black women and children.[23] Yet if the application of physical force would earn freedom for black men, the Federal government envisioned no similar opening to freedom to compensate the physical force of black women's labor.

The arrival of Union forces in Washington County, Mississippi, was pivotal in breaking the bonds of slavery in Greenville, Lake Washington, and Deer

Creek. By early April, a division of troops was stationed on Deer Creek immediately above Lake Washington. When it left, the town of Greenville was in ruins and plantations and cotton in the region had gone up in flames.[24] Another expedition to Deer Creek in the summer of 1863 carried away 300 slaves along with hundreds of cattle and a few rebel prisoners.[25] The Union campaign in Washington County, part of Grant's second campaign to take Vicksburg in the winter and spring of 1863, enhanced the opportunities for enslaved people to escape, underscoring the importance of the Federal army in helping to actualize black freedom. But Union policies also presented obstacles to freedom.

Enslaved women challenged the conflicting and sometimes incoherent Union policies, often devised on the spot in the face of their unanticipated flight to Union lines. In their flight and in building refugee communities, they defied the notion that the Civil War was a fight that only concerned white Americans and the question of Union with or without slavery. They defied the notion that if black people were allowed to have a role in the Union war, they would be men. The decision to allow black men to serve as laborers and soldiers in the Union army did not lead automatically to policies that expanded the grounds upon which black women could contribute. The grounds upon which they could make claims upon the state to freedom and citizenship more often contracted despite congressional policies that should have had the opposite effect.

The "Act to Suppress Insurrection, to Punish Treason and Rebellion, to Seize and Confiscate the Property of Rebels, and for Other Purposes" of July 1862 (commonly referred to as the Second Confiscation Act) offered freedom to enslaved men and women under certain conditions that technically should have made it harder for Union commanders to rid their lines of black women. Section 9 defined three classes of fugitive slaves who would fall under the rubric of "captives of war" and be "forever free of their servitude, and not again held as slaves": slaves whose owners were in rebellion against the U.S. government and who came into Union lines as refugees ("Taking refuge within the lines of the army"); slaves captured from traitors or deserted by them "and coming under the control" of the United States; and "all slaves found on [or] being within any place occupied by rebel forces and afterwards occupied by the forces of the United States."[26] Implementing the policy was another matter and depended heavily on the views of military commanders.

On the ground, the actions of military commanders could help or hurt. Enslaved women who found themselves within the command of the Twenty-Second Wisconsin Infantry would learn that soldiers of the regiment would go out of their way to protect them.[27] More frequently, black women on the run faced Union commanders more committed to stanching the flow of refugees and constraining the freedom of those who made it to Union lines. A special field order issued by Grant in December 1862 called for the removal and encampment of "Negro women and children and unemployed men," with the exception of authorized laundresses, hospital nurses, and officers' servants. John Eaton, appointed by Grant as superintendent of contrabands in November 1862 "to take charge of the contrabands that came into camp" and a year later made General Superintendent of Negro Affairs for the Department of the Tennessee, viewed the presence of black women and children in Union lines as a positive "menace to soldiers which it is difficult to overestimate."[28] He was convinced that unless they were removed, the result would be "the demoralization and infection of the Union soldiers and the downfall of the Union cause."[29]

Northerners who went to the South to help the freedpeople often shared this view. Chaplains were among the strongest critics of military policies that left black women and children homeless and defenseless, but the rationale they offered for better treatment laid the blame as much on black people as on the incompetence and racism of Union soldiers. Chaplain James B. Rogers, chosen to oversee the camps at Corinth and Cairo, described in detail the "ill-treatment" of the refugees by Union soldiers and the many "kinds of deception . . . practiced upon them." His description of the refugees as a people, however, would not have inspired confidence in their capacity to be free citizens. "The town [of Corinth] was infested by them and in many instances they had not only proved a great annoyance to the citizens but were corrupting and demoralizing the soldiers." Rogers unequivocally supported emancipation, the "last great struggle." He did not wonder, though, that "the self-reliant, energetic men of the North should feel disgusted at the utter shiftlessness and childishness of those whom generations of bondage have almost despoiled of the last vestige of manhood."[30] Perhaps nowhere was the impact of Union policies affecting fugitive slaves more greatly felt than in the Mississippi valley, where at one point in early 1863, more than 50,000 refugees crowded a narrow strip of the banks of the Mississippi River. Many would make their way to towns and cities and find employment as domestic servants, cooks, and nurses; a few found land to work independently. The largest number would end up in the dozens of refugee camps or as laborers on abandoned plantations.[31] It would fall largely to black women to turn refugee camps—imagined by agents of the Federal government and freedmen's aid societies as spaces of containment—into spaces capable of sustaining life.[32] They had great successes and disappointing failures.

Refugee Camp, Helena, Arkansas.
(Courtesy of the Nebraska State Historical Society)

Refugee Camps

Formerly enslaved women entered a wartime space of displacement and violence with long experience in dealing with crippling impediments to the survival of their families and communities. The domestic slave trade and slave
hiring had forced enslaved people to constantly "reconstruct their families
and communities" and develop "a strong sense of identity and community
ethos."[33] As they made their way across the landscape of war—pushed forward by wartime exigencies and their own analysis of the war's meaning—
and settled in cities and refugee and labor camps, black women used this
history of reparative work as ballast and drew strength from networks of kin
and community formed during slavery.

To survive the war, migration to the Union lines, and the challenges of
refugee camps, black women refugees used well-honed survival skills that
placed a high premium on family and community ties and the bonds of
gender, reconstituting them on the ground of freedom. On the road to freedom and in the camps, they took in orphaned children and unrelated elderly
men and women. "Hounded by poverty and short of decent housing," Dylan
Penningroth writes, "many black people in the late 1860s took in nieces,
nephews, elderly parents, aunts, and uncles. Others came up with new living

arrangements that bent traditional notions of what a household looked like. It was not unheard of for middle-aged men to move in together and 'go to farming,' for married couples to share rooms with bachelors, or even for newlyweds to take in the groom's ex-wife as a boarder for a while to make ends meet."[34] Black women in refugee camps also turned to these and other kinds of nontraditional arrangements during the Civil War. Widows of black soldiers moved in together, women took in elderly people and orphans and established households with men to whom they were not married and had none but a financial relationship, establishing new household patterns that scholars have tended to see as a postwar phenomenon.[35] The wartime innovations established important precedents.

In the refugee camp at Goodrich's Landing and in the camp of the Forty-Seventh USCI, the men and women from Washington County reconstituted the bonds of kin, friendship, and community that had helped sustain them in slavery.[36] Refugees who had known each other before the war, escaped together from the same or neighboring plantations, or met and formed ties on the road from slavery may have had the best chance of surviving the camps and the war. The presence of friends and family was no substitute for inadequate medical care, nor could it provide complete protection from soldiers who had no qualms about selling refugees back into slavery. Yet it could make an enormous difference in one's ability to survive the camps.

Louisa Smith, Louisa and Malinda Johnson, Lutitia Taylor, Cynthia Hobson, Emeline Anderson, and Susan Taylor all grew up on neighboring plantations in Washington County, Mississippi, and were bound together by a number of other overlapping connections. Smith, Anderson, and the Johnson sisters had been enslaved on the same plantation. As Louisa and Malinda would recall after the war, they had known each other since they "were small children" and were "raised" together. They also attended Louisa and Israel Smith's wedding in 1856. With the exception of Anderson, they all ended up in the same refugee camp at Goodrich's Landing. During the war and into the twentieth century these women supported each other. As their lives crossed again and again, they turned to ties of kin and community they carried out of slavery and new ones made on the road to freedom to build free lives. Their ties embraced the men with whom they fled slavery, several of whom enlisted in the Forty-Seventh USCI—Louisa Smith's husband, Israel Smith; Lewis Robinson, the minister who married Louisa and Israel at John A. Miller's Lake Washington Plantation in northeast Mississippi; Robert Anderson; Henry Taylor; Sam Christmas; and John Hampton.[37]

Nurturing old ties and building new ones, black women in refugee camps banded together to share resources, support each other in sickness, and bury those who did not make it.[38] When her husband became sick from dysentery and after his death, Louisa Smith found comfort in the company of women at Goodrich's Landing with whom she had long-standing ties and others she met in the camp. When Israel Smith was hospitalized in the Regimental Hospital at Snyder's Bluff, their childhood friend Malinda Johnson accompanied Louisa to visit him.[39] Israel Smith enlisted on May 1, 1863, at Providence Island and died on July 27 at Milliken's Bend. Thus within three months of fleeing slavery with her husband, Louisa was a widow. She mourned her loss in the supportive company of old and new friends, some of whom, like Sally Kiger and Lutitia Taylor, were also war widows. Louisa and Sally met at Goodrich's Landing. Over a decade later, Kiger testified in support of Louisa's application for a widow's pension.[40] After Louisa Smith moved to Vicksburg, she reunited with Malinda Johnson.[41]

In the relationship between Lutitia Taylor, Emeline Anderson, and Cynthia Hobson, we can also see the ways the ties black women formed during slavery and their escape from it supported them in freedom. Hobson had been enslaved on a plantation owned by Mary Yerger on Big Deer Creek in Washington County that was two to three miles from the plantation belonging to a widow where Taylor and her husband were held above Lake Providence. They first met, Anderson stated, "during war times away up the Mississippi River when they were gathering up colored men to make soldiers of them near Lake Providence, La." Anderson secured a job as the regimental cook and laundress for the Forty-Seventh USCI, which allowed her to be near her husband, who was also a soldier in the Forty-Seventh. Taylor, however, "did not go with the regiment but staid [sic] about Goodrich's, La."[42] The women kept in touch, and Anderson served as a courier for Lutitia Taylor and her husband, Henry. "I used to go back & forward from the regiment," she recalled, "& I carried Lutitia's money from Henry Taylor."[43] Stationed at Vicksburg with her husband's regiment, Anderson did not have to go back and forth between the refugee camp and Vicksburg. She could have easily let go of her friendship with Lutitia Taylor. Instead she used her mobility and access to the military post at Vicksburg to support a woman she barely knew but who was also a soldier's wife. Taylor was twenty-one years old when her husband died in December 1863, less than a year after they fled slavery, of complications from measles, pneumonia, and diarrhea. The women in the camp provided emotional support and helped Taylor care for her children, Alberta and Amanda, during her time at Goodrich's Landing.[44] The refugee population at Goodrich's Landing increased dramatically after January 1, 1863. By early February 1863, an average of 100 refugees arrived daily. At Lake Providence, in the first two weeks of February, the population increased by some 1,250; of this number, 700 were men who, a Union officer wrote, "wo'd gladly take arms & often *beg* the privilege."[45]

As they had in slavery, black women in the camps grieved together the loss of a husband or child. They helped each other to get the day's work done—work now demanded by a military commander, Northern lessee, or a slave-holder with "loyalist" credentials—and put food on the table. The potential for women like Leah Black to build free lives was even greater at Camps Fiske, Shiloh, and Dixon because of their proximity to the city of Memphis. Despite having children to care for, Black used the wages she earned washing and ironing to support other camp residents and black soldiers. She cooked for the men in the Third U.S. Colored Heavy Artillery Regiment stationed at Memphis's Fort Pickering and carried the food to their camps.[46] Black women carried the reconstituted networks of family, kin, and community into the postwar era. The widowed Lutitia Taylor shared a home with two other war widows, Kittie Carter and Susan Taylor, after the war. Together, the three women cared for Bob West, the elderly father of Clay West (a black soldier who died during the war) and grandfather to Lutitia's child with Clay. They had all been enslaved on the same plantation in Washington County.[47]

Black women found myriad ways to make refugee camps more than they were intended to be and, in the process, laid claim to freedoms they were not intended to have.[48] By the end of the war, Lutitia Taylor, Cynthia Hobson, Sallie Anderson, and Louisa Smith had all moved to nearby Vicksburg, where they remained a part of each other's world. When they fled slavery in 1863, Lutitia and Henry Taylor left their two girls behind. Henry died of dysentery in Vicksburg in 1863 shortly after enlisting in the Forty-Seventh USCI and never saw his children again. But after the war, Lutitia sent for the children, who joined their mother in Vicksburg.[49] Her long-standing friends were there to help her.

A growing body of research has begun to explore the ways preexisting ties of kinship and community and the camaraderie that soldiering fostered increased Civil War soldiers' chances of survival. These studies show that Civil War soldiers—white and black—who served with men they knew before the war were more likely to survive the conflict than those who did not. Black soldiers, for example, "who knew their fellow soldiers prior to enlisting" and came "from the same plantation, were less likely to desert, go AWOL, or be arrested."[50] Similarly, women's ties were critical to their survival in refugee camps and after the war remained important to the larger work of reconstituting kin and community. Still, the obstacles remained formidable.[51] Despite the efforts of black women, most refugee camps were not hospitable to building free homes.

Conditions in the camps along the Mississippi River varied greatly. Some camps like Shiloh boasted sturdy houses (Shiloh had over 300 houses and 2,000 residents), churches, schools, saloons, lunchrooms, and barbershops. Some like Camp Dixon were profit-making enterprises. At Dixon, the refugees cultivated 300 acres in cotton in 1863.[52] By contrast, Helena, Arkansas, was known as a "sickly, pestilential, crowded post" where disease and mortality felled Union soldiers and black refugees. Starvation, violence, and inadequate housing marked black life in the so-called Camp Ethiopia. Shortly before the arrival of the family described at the beginning of this chapter, in one night alone three black men had been murdered, "two for their money, & one for his cabin." Another refugee, a hospital employee, had been arrested and returned by a Union soldier to a woman from the town who claimed ownership of him. When Chaplain Samuel Sawyer protested this act of treachery and re-enslavement, "the guard *our soldier* told him, he'd rather shoot an abolition[ist] any time than a secessionist."[53] Sawyer's protest meant little at a post where Union soldiers, officers, the medical director, and post surgeons were "proslavery" and "all brutal," Mann wrote, and some sold people back into slavery for a profit. "The barbarities from *our soldiers* are unparalleled," wrote Western Sanitary Commission agent Maria Mann, adding, "There is not a cordial feeling here among officers or soldiers on the subject of emancipation; there are many traitors here aiding masters in catching slaves. When they do capture, as in case on that gunboat, they treat them cruelly & rob them. Many want to go back because of faithlessness of soldiers who promise when they take them, & severity, after they get here, from others. No redress for any wrongs. Go to the officers in their behalf, they sneer at you."[54]

Mann's complaints were echoed in reports by Gen. B. M. Prentiss, military commander of the District of Eastern Arkansas; the Chaplains Association of the Army of the Eastern District of Arkansas; Samuel Sawyer, chaplain of the Forty-Seventh Indiana Regiment who was placed in charge of the refugees at Helena as superintendent of contrabands in January 1863; and Col. Cyrus Bussey during his brief stint as military commander of the post. The refugees, "disabled men, women, and children," Prentiss wrote, "deserve care and kind treatment at our hands" but at the same time were "a burden and an encumbrance to the army and the cause." Still, he considered their ill-treatment "a great source of embarrassment."[55]

A letter to Gen. Samuel R. Curtis from a committee of chaplains and surgeons adopted by the Chaplains Association called "loudly for the intervention of authority" to address the oppression and neglect of the refugees at Helena. "In a great degree," the committee wrote, "the contrabands are left entirely to the mercy and rapacity of the unprincipled part of our army . . . with no person clothed with Specific [sic] authority to look after & protect them." Rather, they were "waylaid by soldiers, robbed, and in several instances fired upon," or given counterfeit money for their labor. Wives were "molested by soldiers to gratify their licentious lust, and their husbands murdered in endeavoring to defend them." The guilty parties were known but suffered no consequences. The hospital for black people, the report noted, "had become notorious for filth, neglect, mortality & brutal whipping," such that the refugees "would almost as soon as go to their graves as to their hospital."[56] Col. Cyrus Bussey, when briefly commanding the District of Helena, tried to remedy the situation for the soldiers and the thousands of refugees "who had been neglected." He ordered that the refugees be gathered at one spot, appointed a surgeon for them, and provided medicines. He dismissed the hospital steward and a contract surgeon, but Bussey soon left the post, wanting an assignment with more military action.[57]

Little had changed when Sawyer took charge the following month. He came into a post riddled with poor management, fraud, and systemic abuse of the refugees. A new staff had been put in place by Col. Bussey during his command of the post from January 10 to January 25, but when Gen. Willis Gorman's expedition returned to Helena, his men claimed the cabins of fifty refugee families, who were turned out "into the wet & mud." Black men still labored in the mud without shoes along the river, loading and unloading government supplies. Soldiers stole what little they had.[58] As Chaplain James Rogers noted of the refugees, many "kinds of deception [were] practiced upon them."[59] It was a "poor place" for "colonizing" or resettling former slaves, Mann concluded, but there were few other options in the region. The camps at Helena were the only ones below Memphis, which was also crowded, but at least there was "*nominally* an army to protect & furnish food & employment."[60]

Refugee camps varied in size and in the duration of their existence. Some held fewer than twenty people and some held hundreds. Some were open a few months, some two to three years.[61] Inadequate housing was a perennial problem at the camps and consisted mostly of tents or structures constructed from whatever material was readily available. Environmental hazards made life even more precarious. The vast majority of refugee camps were in the Mississippi River valley. Those built along the river were particularly vulnerable to river overflows. Levees built before the war to control flooding were mostly neglected during the war, and when the river overran its banks, refugees' tents and shanties became uninhabitable, exacerbating the housing crisis.[62] The housing crisis sometimes factored into the decision of refugees to turn around and go back to the plantations. Eighty-two refugees dropped off at Helena by a Union gunboat in the winter of 1863, "so abused & starved already" were so disheartened "that they wished themselves back" on the plantation. Mann thought that if they could at least find decent shelter, "it would encourage them, but Govt has much to do, & here there is little interest manifested."[63]

Union occupation of Memphis had forced Sherman to deal directly with black women in addition to the white "*female* humanity." Located on the Chickasaw Bluff just south of the confluence of the Wolf and Mississippi Rivers, the city had been the largest slave-trading city in Tennessee before the war. Union occupation turned it into one of the largest sanctuaries for African Americans in the South. By the time Lincoln issued the Emancipation Proclamation on January 1, 1863, thousands had already taken refuge in and around the Memphis. Predominantly women and children, some made their way to the city on their own through heavily militarized territory. Military exigencies pushed others to the city. With the loss of Holly Springs, Mississippi—a critical supply line in Grant's initial attempt to take Vicksburg—in December 1862, Union forces moved refugees from the area to Memphis.[64] The establishment of a major recruiting station for black soldiers at Memphis further fueled the growth of the city's population of black women and children refugees who followed their fathers, husbands, brothers, lovers, and friends to freedom. Brig. Gen. Alvin P. Hovey, however, did not count them among the "helpless Union families" who he believed had been violated by Confederate forces and Confederate sympathizers.[65]

The appointment of Asa Fiske to take charge of the refugees at Memphis brought some order but no great improvement in the lives of the refugees. By August 1862, Sherman was convinced that the first phase of the war, which had embraced a policy of reconciliation, of seeking and fostering Union sentiment in the South, had failed. By this point, tens of thousands of slaves had taken their own freedom and entered Union lines. Some 2,000 were within Sherman's own lines, 4,000 were within General Curtis's line at Helena, Arkansas, and "vast numbers" were with other Union armies. "We have a place full of women & run away niggers, not a very interesting set," Sherman wrote his wife.[66] Sherman knew that "by encouraging" their flight "and agreeing to protect families," he could easily have 30,000 within thirty days, but he did not intend for things to get to this point. He could not "afford to feed such hordes," he wrote, and suggested colonization as a solution. "They must be colonized and that near at hand," he wrote, and Arkansas seemed "a fair place to do this" for the time being.[67]

For most of the tens of thousands of refugees in the Department of the

Tennessee, refugee life was precarious, with constant turmoil and movement between refugee camps and between the camps and military posts. Leah Black's life exemplified the long journey many black women made from slavery to freedom and numerous stops along that road. Black fled to Union lines with her four sons after the murder of her husband by Confederate forces in 1862, fearing they would kill her and her four sons if she stayed. She traveled first east to Bolivar, a distance of twenty-four miles. After two to three weeks there, she moved twenty-six miles south to La Grange, where she stayed until July 1, and then moved twenty-four miles east to Camp Dixon on President's Island for about six months before moving to Camp Shiloh in the city of Memphis. She had traveled nearly eighty miles.[68]

Sometimes the journey was forced by the movement of armies, the occupation of territories and the loss or evacuation of territory. At nearly the same moment that enslaved women from Washington County were making their way to refugee camps in the spring of 1863, military exigencies caused women already in camps to be moved. When Union armies evacuated a town or area, refugees might also be left behind. More often, military commanders ordered nearby or attached camps closed because they could not be protected. The residents were either simply abandoned or moved en masse to a new or existing camp. In March 1863, refugee camps at Cairo and Columbus were "broken up" and the people removed to Island No. 10, a one-mile-long, 450-yard-wide island in the Mississippi River strategically located at the boundaries of Tennessee, Kentucky, and Missouri. They had barely settled in before they were forced to move again. The camp at Cairo had only been open for a few months, from autumn of 1862 to the spring of 1863. With the abandonment of Corinth, Tennessee, nearly 3,000 refugees were moved nearly 100 miles to Memphis in March 1863.[69] Camp closings came amid increasingly restricted access to Union lines. In the spring of 1863 access to Union lines was again tightened. As General Grant stated in a special field order, "The nature of the service the army is now called to perform, making it impracticable to transport or provide for persons unemployed by Government, the enticing of negroes to leave their homes to come within the lines of the army is positively forbidden." Those already within Union lines, however, would not be turned out. It may very well have been the case at that moment that Grant could not provide transportation or food and shelter for the refugees. Inadequate transportation was a problem that commanders complained about constantly. For example, Gen. Clinton B. Fisk charged that a lack of adequate transportation had resulted in two hundred of his men being "murdered outright by crowding them into dirty, rotten transportation as closely as slaves in the 'middle passage.'" He called what had happened to his men "a crime against humanity."[70]

Louisa Smith was working as a laundress for Company D, Fiftieth USCI, in Jackson, Mississippi, when black women and children were ordered removed from the regiment's lines. In response, the soldiers of Company D, including Charles Anderson, the soldier with whom Louisa lived at the time, built houses for their wives, children, and lovers on the commons.[71] Union commanders opposed such efforts. "The innumerable huts of contrabands in the vicinity of the camps and fortifications," Col. Hermann Lieb, the commander of a black regiment, wrote, "are a nuisance besides being an expense to the Government." He called for greater restrictions on black women's access to soldier husbands and fathers that allowed them the "opportunity of obtaining Rations and clothing from the Soldiers, notwithstanding the Strict watchfulness of officers and the heavy penalty inflicted upon the offender."[72] "Slaveholders and their allies," as Stephanie Camp explained, "were not the only ones interested in confining enslaved people; many Union officers shared some values with the planters, among them the importance of containing and controlling the human contraband of war." Lieb's claim, however, that the refugees had been enticed to Union lines was a dodge, the kind slaveholders had long used to deny the capacity of black people to think for themselves and make their own rights claims. Union commanders could not make those rights claims go away, but they could make them harder to achieve.[73]

The plantation system set up by the Federal government made it particularly difficult for black women to carve out the life of freedom they imagined. The Federal government's threefold effort sought to turn abandoned plantations into profit-making enterprises, nurse Unionist sentiment, and relieve the burden refugees placed on military commanders. Refugee camps became little more than holding stations for the controlled dispersal of people to plantation labor camps.[74] Claims that the refugees were "out of all control" supported this initiative, as did concerns Union officials expressed about the burden of feeding and caring for the "roaming hordes" of black women and children refugees. Corralling them on abandoned plantations seemed to many the most effective, and profitable, solution. In the unfolding humanitarian crisis, it became increasingly difficult for black women and children refugees to find a place of safe refuge or asylum. Along an eighty-mile stretch of the Mississippi River north of Vicksburg from Lake Providence to Lake Sherman in July 1863, some 10,000 women and children remained homeless, "roving about without adequate support or protection."[75]

Defying Union policies outlined in the 1862 Confiscation Act, the Emancipation Proclamation, and the Lieber Code of 1863, some Union commanders simply refused to recognize black refugees as legitimate refugees or free people or did their best to ignore black refugees altogether. Some believed the status of refugee should be reserved for white Southern Unionists.[76] Brig. Gen. Thomas W. Sherman believed the best solution was simply "to get rid of the negroes."[77] Union officers and soldiers who tried to help often became discouraged by the weight of the forces arrayed against them. With 500 refugees on his picket lines, many "entirely destitute," Gen. John McClernand declared the situation before him one of "urgent humanity," but few satisfactory options for redress presented themselves to him. The most popular option—placing the refugees on abandoned plantations and hiring them out to Northern lessees or Southern Unionists, McClernand argued, had "led to the most atrocious frauds and outrages."[78]

One of the outrages came in the form of a tax on the wages of freedpeople, ostensibly to cover the costs of their rations, the clothing they received, and for the support of orphaned, elderly, and indigent refugees. "In the case of the sick and dependent," John Eaton wrote, "a tax was laid on the wages of workers." Eaton praised the freedpeople at Grand Junction, Tennessee, who, he wrote, "freely acknowledged that they ought to assist in helping bear the burden of the poor, and were flattered by having the government ask their help. . . . Five thousand dollars was raised by this tax for hospitals, and with this money tools and property were bought."[79] Abundant evidence attests that where possible, freedpeople generously supported each other during the war, but one may doubt that they were "flattered" by being taxed in a way no other Americans were.

A special fund, called the Freedmen's Fund, was set up to hold the monies generated in large measure from taxes deducted from the wages of black laborers and court fines they accrued. The "taxes on salaries of colored employees retained in some instances during the war to support the destitute, the sums from taxes on cotton, where freedmen were interested, from fines in the provost courts, and from donations or small amounts raised in any lawful manner for the benefit of the freedmen, were considered by us as a *single fund*, and we named it 'The Freedmen's Fund,'" Gen. Oliver Howard, head of the Freedmen's Bureau, later explained.[80] The fund was used to purchase medicines and clothing and bedding for freedpeople, for example, but also for purchases that had nothing to do with their support. An unsuccessful effort was made to use it to pay the wages of black hospital nurses and hospital attendants and surgeons assigned to black hospitals.[81] The defeat

of this initiative meant that those black women nurses and hospital attendants went unpaid.

Union officials continued to insist that unpaid black workers were "flattered" at being asked to help the Union cause by having their wages taxed
and did not complain. Surgeon D. O. McCord further argued that "the colored attendants have not suffered so much as might be supposed and have
been reasonably satisfied and contented from the fact that we have constantly assured them that the Government would pay them eventually, and
that they have been supplied with comfortable quarters, good rations and
a limited supply of clothing." At any rate, McCord continued, they were better off because they performed less physically taxing labor. "Many of them
being physically unfit for hard labor and the rough fare usually meted out to
colored people in this country, have done better than they might have done
in other situations." To his credit, McCord did not think that this should
"lessen the obligations of the government to them," though he, like many
Northerners, apparently believed that freedom did not give black people immediate access to wages.[82]

Even as they taxed the labor of black women and men, Federal officials
denied women and children the right to wages earned by deceased husbands
and fathers. In 1864, black men who worked on fortifications in Tennessee
had earned $112,292.17. Most had not been paid and the total owed them
amounted to $96,394.62. Some of the men died before they were paid, but
the government refused to give their wages to their widows. At the Huntsville, Alabama, camp, an officer reported, "If a wife come in with a certificate
issued to her deceased husband for labor, we have to refuse payment, for
the reason there is no one authorized to sign his name to the receipt-roll. I
know of no way in which I can pay those claims, unless the person who did
the work, and to whom a certificate may have been issued, presents said
certificate, and is satisfactorily identified as the person who did the work,
and to whom the certificate issued."[83] The government thus denied $96,000
in unpaid wages to the deceased soldiers' families and retained hundreds of
thousands more in taxes from wages and bounties. The communities black
refugees built against the odds were made more fragile by the imposition
of taxes, withheld wages, nonpayment of wages, and the establishment of
wage rates below the rates for agricultural laborers in the North, as well
as the refusal to distribute laborers' wages to their families. It is unclear if
workers whose wages were withheld just in case slaveholders won the war, or
won a settlement that would have allowed them to maintain the institution
of slavery, were ever paid.

With Union officials focused on ridding their lines of black refugees and the U.S. Treasury Department determined to use the refugees as laborers on abandoned plantations, the freedom and safety of black women and children remained tenuous. Even when the flow of refugees to Union lines resulted from evictions by slaveholders, Union commanders floundered. One clearly exasperated officer pleaded for directions on what to do when a slaveholder evicted the wife of a black soldier and their two-year-old child and sent them to Union lines. "What is proper for me to do?" he asked. "What are we to do with the women and children?"[84] The answers coming from the War Department were hardly encouraging. Responding to the complaint of a black regimental commander arrested for refusing to carry out the order of a superior officer to return the wives and children of black soldiers to slavery, the adjutant general's office responded that although the "law prohibits the return of slaves," it "does not provide for their reception and support in idleness at military camps."[85]

Slaveholders reveled in any evidence of signs of a weak Union commitment to black freedom. "The Yankees have the impudence to send a petition to the planters to come and take their negro women & children as they were now starving. What consummate fools and knaves these Federals are," Confederate Kate Foster wrote.[86] Days later, she boasted that while black people were "flocking to the enemy in town . . . the Yanks are cursing them and saying they wished they had never seen a negro. They are all tired of them. None of ours have gone from here yet but Billy & I hope they will *all* prove faithful to the end."[87] That was in July 1863. Before the month was over, Amy, Kizzie, Sally, and Matilda had denied Foster that satisfaction. "Old Amy and Kizzie left Sunday morning and that night old Sally decamped with all her 'traps,'" wrote Foster at the end of July, calling her former slaves "a set of ingrates" whom God would punish, for "God punishes us for ingratitude as much as for any other sin," and "the sooner we are rid of them the quicker we will whip our enemy." Two days later, she wrote that Matilda had also left and Rose stopped working, leaving Foster to do much of her own housework, including "taking out the slops" and helping with the ironing. Foster was left to hope that "some of them will be faithful for if they are not I shall lose entire faith in the whole race." The black women and men she claimed as property continued to give Foster reason to know her faith was ill-placed. Those who stayed "do no work," she wrote. In August, Celia left, taking her two children with her. "She was very [cool] evil about it had a wagon to come out for her things." Celia's leaving put Foster in her own kitchen, and in November, Sarah's departure put her at her own washboard.

Foster no longer pretended that she enjoyed the work. Doing the laundry for six weeks "came near ruining" her. "I was too delicately raised for such hard work," she concluded. Having to work left no time for her to write in her journal.[88] Amy, Kizzie, Sally, and Matilda, Celia, and Sarah likely found their way to the Union lines and the refugee camp at Natchez, where 6,000 fugitive slaves had gathered by August 1863.[89] Like refugees in camps all along the Mississippi River, this would have left them vulnerable to a series of raids by Confederate forces on refugee camps and plantations along a broad swath of the Mississippi valley in the late spring and summer of 1863, exposing the tenuousness of their freedom.

Violence

Louisa Smith was at Goodrich's Landing when the attack on that camp came. She recalled that they had "worked on the land until the rebels captured some colored people and took them off." She was among the survivors who "scattered."[90] William D. Butler, a special agent of the Western Sanitary Commission and a delegate with the U.S. Christian Commission, observed the refugees fleeing "in terror to the river's banks for safety" and "crouching in groups . . . at the water's edge in evident dread lest their pursuers should find them." Butler saw mothers clinging to their children and watched as some secured a small boat and moved themselves two to three at a time to a sand bar on the Mississippi side of the river, where they put up makeshift brush shelters. They "beckoned despairingly to be taken on board" the Union gunboats that passed, but the boats did not stop: "We passed on," Butler wrote. "What became of these negroes I know not."[91]

Butler may not have ever learned the fate of the people he saw injured that day, but what he saw after landing in Vicksburg shortly thereafter surely gave him an inkling. He arrived amid an army-ordered removal of refugees from the city. Citing fear of an outbreak of disease, military officials dispatched twenty wagons to handle the job—one wagon dedicated solely to hauling the dead. The army removed the "well" with the "sick, and dead." He saw a woman dying alone behind a fence and witnessed the recovery of the bodies of six refugees from a building occupied by small children, the children "sitting and lying around" the dead, "apparently unconscious of their situation." The job of searching out, removing, and burying the dead on the banks of the river took over two weeks. Some 3,000 survivors, many infected with smallpox, were "removed to the low grounds opposite Vicksburg" and left in the weeds without shelter. The death toll continued to mount, averaging fifteen to twenty per day; another 400 soon died. Some of the people, Butler remarked, "would crawl off into the woods and die, where their bodies could be found out by the stench which arose from their decay."[92]

Refugee and government-sponsored plantation labor camps were easy targets for regular and guerrilla Confederate forces, scouts operating in detached units, wartime slave patrols financed by county governments, and "citizens who mount a horse for an hour a night—or a few days" and then returned home.[93] Irregular and detached bands were a particular problem. Even when commanders of these units held commissions from the Confederate War Department or acted under the "special authority" of local, regularly commissioned commanders, operationally, they generally acted independent of any formal command structure.[94] Their "detached" status allowed them to operate as guerrilla forces, which could be useful to regular forces and slaveholders but also made these units uncontrollable. Complaints about the activities of groups like Wingfield's Partisans operating around Port Hudson, Louisiana, came from commanders and slaveholders alike.[95] Confederate commanders cited irregularities in the organization of detached companies and the commanders' "incompetency" [sic] and "ignorance of military laws and regulations." The murder of a group of black men who had returned from Union lines for their families was apparently so heinous it prompted a complaint from a Confederate inspector general. The murders, he wrote, constituted an "execution," "a piece of barbarity." Reports by Union officers and soldiers also documented cases "of cold blooded murder" and re-enslavement.[96]

Attacks by Confederate forces turned refugee camps into battlegrounds, resulting in deaths, the destruction of refugee housing, and re-enslavement. In an attack fifteen miles outside of Helena, Arkansas, in late April 1863, "several colored families were captured" from a settlement of people who had been independently supporting themselves.[97] In June, several hundred Confederate soldiers raided at Lake Providence, tearing up the camps, leveling refugee housing, and carrying hundreds of refugees back to slavery. They left behind an untold number of casualties. On June 29 at Goodrich's Landing—where small camps of family groups intermingled with larger camps—Confederate cavalry and artillery forces easily overpowered and captured two companies of black soldiers.[98] That attack left in its wake "burning mansions, cotton gins, and negro quarters as far as the eye could reach." An estimated twenty plantations went up in flames and the casualties included an undetermined number of women and children, some of whom died in the fires. The "main object" of the raiders, Gen. Alfred W. Ellet wrote, was "being to secure the negroes stolen from the plantations along the river, some hundreds of whom they had captured." Some 1,200 people were reported captured and returned to slavery. A Union marine brigade arrived the following morning to find a shocking sight of the "charred remains of human beings who had been burned in the general conflagration." In his report to Adm. David D. Porter, brigade commander Gen. Ellet wrote that his men saw evidence "that human bodies had been burned in several of the cabins, destroyed by fire," but he could not say "whether [they had been] killed and burned, or burned alive, or [whether they were] simply the charred corpses, of the unburied."[99] Ellet wrote that he witnessed "five such spectacles" on three other plantations and "did not doubt that there were many others on the 20 or more other plantations burned in similar manner" he did not visit.[100] A report two days later by Col. Samuel J. Nasmith gave additional details of the terror that had been unleashed along the riverfront:

> Scenes of a character never before witnessed in a civilized country . . . such as the pen fails to record in proper language. They spared neither age, sex, nor condition. In some instances, the Negroes were shut up in their quarters, and literally roasted alive. The charred remains found in numerous instances testified to a degree of fiendish atrocity such as has no parallel in either civilized or savage warfare. Young children, only five or six years of age, were found skulking in the cane brake with wounds, while helpless women were found shot down in the most inhumane manner. The whole country was destroyed, and every sign of civilization was given to the flames.[101]

By this point in the war there had been even more horrific losses of life on the Civil War's battlefields. What most distinguished these raids was not the number of casualties but that so many were unarmed women and children.[102]

Two weeks prior to the attack at Goodrich's Landing, a Confederate Texas cavalry unit mounting 2,000 men launched a raid before daylight at Milliken's Bend, Louisiana, capturing 150 refugees and 50 black soldiers.[103] Another raid on June 4 at Lake St. Joseph resulted in the capture and reenslavement of some sixty women and children.[104] Hundreds of refugees were returned to plantations from which they had fled or been sold to new owners as far away as Texas.[105] "Some of their proceedings," Lt. George Hanks wrote of Confederate raids at Plaquemine, Mound Plantation, and Donaldsonville, Louisiana, "were too atrocious to be believed."[106] In a report filed on July 10, 1863, Gen. J. G. Walker, commander of the Confederate Arkansas cavalry, confirmed the reports of atrocities. His men, he wrote, had "broken up the plantations engaged in raising cotton under Federal leases from Milliken's Bend to Lake Providence capturing some 2,000 negroes, who have been restored to their masters with the exception of those captured in arms, and a few the property of disloyal citizens of Louisiana." Three white officers and 113 black soldiers were "captured in arms." Walker considered it "an unfortunate circumstance that any armed negroes were captured" rather than killed, but he had accepted the Union officers' offer to surrender on the condition that they be treated as prisoners of war and that the black soldiers be allowed to surrender unconditionally. In addition, Walker reported that he was "engaged in burning all the cotton I can reach from Lake Providence to the lower end of Concordia Parish" and had "instructed the cavalry to burn all subsistence and forage on abandoned plantations," ensuring further hardship for any who survived.[107] The raid cheered white Southerners on the home front. "We drove the Yankees to near three miles of Lake Providence capturing 1500 negroes," wrote Kate Foster.[108]

Prior to the raids, refugees at places where the raids occurred, like Milliken's Bend, had already endured periods of starvation, and black women's efforts to obtain passes that would allow them to enter Union military lines to find employment as laundresses had been rebuffed. Inadequate shelter, health care, food, and clean water had fueled "fearful mortality" all along the river by April 1863. More women miscarried, and the number of orphaned babies and children grew.[109] A chaplain's report published in the *New York Times* stated that not less than 35,000 refugees at one point gathered on the banks of the Mississippi River, only 500 of whom were men. Newborn babies died alongside mothers who succumbed to disease, childbirth, and military fire. At Helena, Arkansas, a pregnant young mother of two young children (ages six and two) died soon after arriving. Her youngest child died shortly thereafter.[110]

The violence and relocations that had characterized much of refugee life in 1863 continued nearly unabated into 1864 with the capture of some 1,000 black people in the districts of Helena, Vicksburg, and Natchez who were resold.[111] Preparations for Sherman's Meridian, Mississippi, campaign in early 1864, a Confederate commander reported, had led to the removal of an estimated 1,000 to 1,500 black women and children from one side of the Mississippi River to the other side. They were taken to Carolina Landing in Washington County, where they reestablished their refugee camps.[112] At the battle of Mark's Mill, Arkansas, on April 25, 1864, some 300 black refugees were caught on the battlefield. "Large numbers of contraband," a Confederate officer admitted, were "shot down where captured" and "inhumanly butchered." Excessive violence sometimes shocked even Confederate officers, some of whom tried unsuccessfully to restrain their soldiers.[113] Of the refugees captured at Mark's Mill, a Union brigade commander reported learning that "a large number of the dead at Mark's Mill were Arkansas refugees" and, he wrote, "I am informed were inhumanly butchered by the enemy, and among them my own negro servant." Summary executions added to the misery. Following an order from his brigade commander to execute four refugees, a "soldier quietly sitting on his horse, shot them down as so many pigs."[114] That fall, Confederate forces captured another 1,200 refugees following a raid on the Wilkins Plantation near Goodrich's Landing.[115] Disease continued to take a toll in refugee camps and on leased plantations. Thousands died in the summer of 1864 at Young's Point, repeating scenes from the previous year at Memphis.[116]

Meanwhile enemy raids on leased plantations continued to set thousands of black refugees adrift.[117] Rev. Asa S. Fiske, sent by the Western Sanitary Commission in 1864 to investigate conditions on leased plantations, found only 165 of 450 leases that had been taken for the year still in operation. From the "nine[ty]-five safest" of these, Confederate raiders had taken 966 refugees and "resold them into bondage."[118] Whether in regard to leased plantations or the refugee camps, Federal response remained haphazard. Some officers continued to express uncertainty as to their authority to assist black families, including black soldiers' wives and children, "even for a short period."[119] Some continued to order African American women and children out of Union lines and returned to slavery.[120] Changing military fortunes constantly redrew battle lines, triggering new disruptions and fostering environments conducive to Confederate guerrilla and regular army attacks. In the meantime, conflict escalated between Union military officers who viewed the plantation system as a wasteful expenditure of resources in time, men, and supplies, and Treasury Department agents focused on the profits to be derived from black labor on abandoned plantations.[121]

Following the disaster at Milliken's Bend in July 1863, Capt. Abraham Strickle, one of three commissioners appointed to supervise the leasing of plantations, accused military officials with thwarting the work of the Treasury Department. Strickle's main concern was to protect "the agricultural and commercial interests involved in this region," not the black refugees.[122] That priority led to the adoption of policies to help protect the lessees from financial loss. Planters who suffered losses due to guerrilla raids could file claims with the Federal government for reimbursement. No similar mechanism existed for plantation laborers, except possibly through the planters. A. Winchell & Company, one of the major Northern planting enterprises operating in the Mississippi valley, filed a detailed claim for nearly $10,000 in losses. The company noted that the laborers had also suffered a "large loss" but that it did not see "fit to include" a tabulation of these losses or a request for compensation.[123]

As the crisis unfolded, some white Americans joined enslaved people in calling for more radical and just approaches. Insisting that "the freedmen would require efficient protection to preserve his freedom during the existence of the rebellion," the Contraband Relief Commission of Cincinnati proposed the confiscation of rebel property, the establishment of a Bureau of Emancipation, and the designation of "certain points in each State as a place of rendezvous for freedmen and their families."[124] In the aftermath of the raids in the summer of 1863, some Union officers, like Adm. David Porter, also called for change.[125] The government must either commit to providing additional material resources and personnel, Porter wrote, or else end the plantation lease system. He recommended that the "leasing of property in the river be stopped."[126] The fact that Federal authorities knew of orders Confederate commanders carried to break up refugee camps and military posts where black soldiers were stationed, and to destroy plantations "in cultivation by agents or contractors of the United States Government," made the continuation of the plantation system even more indefensible.[127]

While news reports of the attacks and the humanitarian crisis they fueled filtered out to Northern audiences and fostered increased support from freedmen's aid societies, they never triggered much in the way of national outrage. This was in contrast to the outrage occasioned by reports of atrocities against black soldiers. In the summer of 1864, two families of refugees near Helena were re-enslaved, "carried off" by Confederate forces after a skirmish. The primary official reports of the skirmish reported the casualties as one U.S. soldier killed and four wounded, and twenty-four Confederate soldiers killed or wounded. They did not mention the families re-enslaved.[128] In general, the reports about plantation attacks failed to convey the full extent of the problem or focus on the noncombatant casualties. A *New York Times* article on the raid at Milliken's Bend noted that the raid "did not turn out to be as serious an affair [as] was first supposed," even as it reported the capture of 150 refugees.[129] Lorenzo Thomas's October 1863 report to Secretary of War Edwin M. Stanton, reprinted in the *New York Times*, focused on the losses lessees suffered by the raid. Thomas made clear that his main concern and priority was to round up the scattered laborers who had survived and convince them to return to work. The report said not a word about the devastation the refugees had suffered.[130]

The reports of agents of freedmen's relief societies and superintendents of contrabands and refugees, reprinted in national papers like the *New York*

Times and circulated in private correspondence, revealed the humanitarian crisis under way but also failed to generate national outrage. With tens of thousands of refugees, predominantly women and children, gathered along the banks of the Mississippi between Natchez, Mississippi, and Helena, Arkansas, a group of chaplains at Helena protested a military order calling for their removal from Union lines. It was tantamount, they wrote, to sending "them to starvation and death." Further, they reasoned, "if we can feed the rebel soldiers that fall within our hands, fighting to destroy our government, it would seem that some method might be devised to take care of these people, who are our natural allies, and have done the best they could to serve us."[131] The protest underscored the refugees' statelessness. Even John Eaton, who had once described the refugees as a "menace," was increasingly appalled by the conditions he saw among 20,000 refugees in Vicksburg, the sick and the "disheartened" all crowded together. An additional 10,000 refugees were scattered on the opposite side of the Mississippi River. Up and down the Mississippi, refugees were dying on the banks of the river, on the streets of its port cities, and in refugee and plantation labor camps.[132] Meanwhile, the United States was removing cotton to help fund the war. The Union gunboat that dropped off eighty-two refugees at Helena also carried bales of cotton they had cultivated. The cotton continued on up the river for sale, but the profits would not benefit the "abused & starved" refugees.[133] None of these problems curtailed expansion of the plantation lease system.

The 1864 growing season dawned with reports that guerrilla forces had commenced "their depredations, frightening lessees, and the Freedmen." The raids on camps and plantations, re-enslavement, and loss of life notwithstanding, Lorenzo Thomas termed the 1863 experiment in leasing plantations in the Mississippi valley a "complete success" and prepared to expand the plantation lease system in 1864.[134] The number of refugees moved from camps to plantations increased dramatically that year, as Eaton ordered rations for "all able bodied, not disposed to labor voluntarily" cut in half.[135] By February 1864, more than 600 applications had been made for plantations embracing over 400,000 acres in the districts of Helena, Arkansas; and Skipwith's Landing, Vicksburg, and Natchez, Mississippi.[136] With the resulting increased demand for laborers, the role of refugee camps as temporary receiving and holding grounds and hiring depots for plantation labor grew in importance.[137] In one week in early March 1864, 3,700 people were removed from refugee camps to plantation labor camps.[138] Increased raids and depredations by Confederate forces accompanied the uptick in the number of government lessees.

James Yeatman, president of the Western Sanitary Commission, had once expressed the hope that things would improve with greater protection of the refugees. Instead, refugees were still being "carried off, [with] some outrageous cruelties reported to have been practiced." The Western Sanitary Commission had been working in support of Union soldiers in the Western armies for two years when it appealed to Lincoln in early November 1863 to be allowed "to extend our labors to the suffering freed people of the South-West and South" as a work of "philanthropy" and "equally of patriotism." Yeatman worried that the humanitarian crisis would be the source of "increasing reproach against the Union cause," whereas "lessening the difficulties of emancipation, would materially aid in crushing the rebellion." But the practice of supplying lessees with laborers from the camps continued with all of its attendant problems. By the summer of 1864, thousands of refugees labored on a line of plantations stretching from Lake Providence to Natchez. In the area around Lake Providence and Vicksburg, some 4,456 workers cultivated 30,970 acres of cotton on fifty-one plantations.[139]

From the moment they began their journey, black women faced overwhelming odds. Their race, gender, and statelessness made them more vulnerable to the apathy or active hostility of Union commanders. Some left children or parents and other loved ones behind, planning to return for them. Some lost traveling companions on the way, to exhaustion, hunger, disease, or violence. In Union lines and camps, they remained largely unprotected; armies are armies, and in the Civil War, black women and children refugees got in their way and triggered efforts to push them out of Union lines. But claims of military necessity made it easy for Union commanders and soldiers and agents of freedmen's and soldiers' aid societies to fall back on racist views as they sought to contain the movement and freedom of black women. It made it easy to dismiss, miss, or ignore the ties of kin and community that continued to form the ballast for black people's survival and the particular strengths that women brought to the struggle for freedom and Union.

IN THE END, there were too few places of safe refuge, too few Union commanders willing or able to help, too many policies that varied in their implementation from one command to the next, and too much silence and inaction from Washington. Yet relationships from the past renourished, and new ones forged, on the battleground of war enabled more black women and children to survive the Civil War than otherwise would have. As Steven Hahn has argued, refugee camps, far from being "mere collecting points for slaves who had rebelled against the authority of their masters . . . became the first great cultural and political meeting grounds that the war produced."[140] Black women refugees' intellectual work was critical to the making of these "political meeting grounds." In no way did it lessen the losses, pain, and exploitation they suffered, but it did help them survive the losses and continue to fight. Leah Black suffered multiple losses. In April 1862, a party of Union soldiers came to her home in Fayette County, Tennessee, and carried away two horses, corn, fodder, chickens, geese, and cows, and meat from hogs her family killed at the property rented by her husband, James Black, a free black man who had purchased his freedom a few years earlier. Next came Confederate guerrillas or soldiers, she did not know which, who murdered her husband, leaving her a widow with four sons to feed and protect and all of the family's carefully husbanded resources stolen. Black remained undaunted by the struggle ahead, committing herself to the intellectual and political work black women refugees understood as vital to their survival and to winning and maintaining their freedom. As she fed black soldiers from her own wages, she gave encouragement to other black women refugees and supported the larger freedom struggle. As Fountain Day, who had known her before the war, recalled, when he met her again at the camp in Memphis, she told him that "she wished her sons could grow up and go into the service" as Day had.[141]

After the war, Louisa Smith and women she had known at Goodrich's Landing and up the river during slavery lived as neighbors in the corral at Springfield, a community of refugees that grew up in the shadow of Vicksburg during the war. Cynthia Hobson, who had been enslaved in the same neighborhood as Louisa Smith and Lutitia Taylor, was there too, helping transform a camp of refugees into a neighborhood of free people. "I belonged to Mary Yerger on Big Deer Creek, Washington Co.," Hobson recalled, while "Miss & Letitia & her husband belonged to the widow West and the quarters of the places were two or three miles apart." She remembered that Lutitia and her husband, Henry, had been "older," and out of respect, she and the other children "called them Uncle Henry and Aunt Telia."[142] Decades after the war, Hobson came forward to testify in support of Aunt Telia Taylor's Civil War widow's pension claim.

Into the twentieth century, women who worked together to build free lives and communities in refugee camps and on abandoned plantations continued to rely on each other as they faced new challenges and the persisting legacies of slavery and the war. Black soldiers' wives who became wartime widows supported each other in their efforts to obtain federal widows' pensions. In October 1908 the commissioner of pensions rejected Lutitia Taylor's claim under the Act of April 19, 1908, "on the ground of no title under said act, as the soldier was never discharged from the service," even though she had previously been granted a widow's pension.[143] In response, several former slaves from the widow West's plantation and neighboring plantations in Washington County, Mississippi, stepped forward to vouch for her. Their affidavits testified to the critical importance of slave neighborhoods before and during the war. Ann Dunbar, Susan Taylor, and Lutitia Taylor, "fellow slaves" before the war, testified that they lived as close neighbors after the war until Lutitia Taylor "went up the river." John Hampton, who had been enslaved on a neighboring plantation, vouched for the woman he had known for eight years before the war.[144]

Holding tightly to ties of kin and community, black women fought to do more than survive, the minimum prerequisite for building the new world of freedom for which they risked their lives. Their efforts helped propel the nation toward emancipation and an entirely new world of freedom.[145] Many did not live to see the acts of defiance embodied in their flight from slavery and struggles for just treatment ratified in Thirteenth and Fourteenth Amendments. The traces of those acts, however, nourished in refugee camps, persisted in the communities they helped build, the spaces of violence they transformed into spaces of freedom-making. Refugee camps like Springfield became the founding ground for postwar black neighborhoods.

The story of black soldiers in the Civil War—the salary discrimination they faced and protested, their gallantry under impossible odds, the massacres at places like Fort Pillow—has been detailed in historical accounts and film. But black women also died on the battlefields at places like Fort Pillow, Mark's Mill, Milliken's Bend, Goodrich's Landing, and Petersburg. They were captured on those battlefields and from within Union lines, as if they were enemy soldiers. They were re-enslaved and impressed as laborers. They were viewed as enemy combatants even when the designation was not formally applied to them and even when they lacked either battlefield plans (at least of the type recognized by the state) or guns. The battlefield plans they carried to war were largely invisible to Union commanders, statesmen, and even abolitionists and, largely, have remained so in the historiography.

CONCLUSION

It is expected that you will show in a free South
that cotton is more of a king than ever.
—BRIG. GEN. AND MILITARY GOVERNOR
RUFUS SAXTON to the Freedpeople, 1864

B Y 1865, Americans had endured a war that had lasted longer than
any of them could have imagined in 1861. With military casualties approaching 1.5 million, it was the deadliest war in American
history. Women bore that cost in the loss of fathers, husbands, sons, and
more, an experience they shared regardless of where they lived, what political party they supported, whether they were rich or poor, free or enslaved.
When war came, women geared up to support it. Most did so from the comfort of their homes or in association with neighboring women, putting their
talents to sewing and knitting and making bandages to support soldiers.
Others moved out into the larger world as teachers and missionaries, sponsored by freedmen's aid and relief societies, and as nurses, soldiers in disguise, and spies. They left the confines of home in defiance of the notion that
women had no place in the public sphere. "I was born to be a missionary,"
Ester Hawks wrote.[1] Most American men, however, would have agreed with
David Outlaw, a lawyer, planter, and antebellum congressman from North
Carolina, who wrote that "ladies had no business to be present where men
contended for victory & empire any more than they had to be in a military
camp," else they risked becoming "he-women," a phrase he claimed to have
coined.[2] Millions of women disagreed, enslaved women included.

Enslaved women's fight took place in their cabins, in the fields and slaveholders' homes, and on the road as they fled to Union lines. It took place
within Union lines in regimental and refugee camps and on plantations
run under the auspices of the U.S. government. Enslaved women's fight also
met with unsurpassed violence when compared to other American women,
with the possible exception of Native American women. The experience of
black women like Anna Ashby and Maria West were exceptional. Enslaved

when the Civil War began, Anna Ashby became free during the war. In 1864, she was a new mother living with her husband in the heart of war-torn Mississippi, far from her place of birth in Kentucky. Together with seven other adults and twelve children under the age of fourteen, they worked independently on an abandoned plantation, formerly the property of Jacob Sartorius, confiscated by the Federal government. Her husband, William, managed the place with another former slave, William West. Because they lived and worked on a plantation managed by their husbands, Anna Ashby and Maria West occupied an enviable position for freedwomen in the Mississippi valley. Across the Mississippi River in Louisiana, forty-year-old Hannah Duke worked on the Pt. Celeste plantation in the Parish of Plaquemines, another abandoned plantation administered by the Federal government but leased to a Northerner. Hundreds of miles away, and in many ways a world away, forty-nine-year-old Silvia (Sylvia) Evans, formerly enslaved in Jacksonville, Florida, had run away and claimed her freedom in the South Carolina lowcountry.

In the historiography of the Civil War, these women are as invisible as Louisa Smith, who worked to build a free life in a refugee camp in the Mississippi valley. None of them lived their lives during the war as inert casualties of war, or simply as the beneficiaries of Northern missionary largesse or even the sacrifices of black soldiers. Nor were they simply the "problem" of Union armies. Anna Ashby, Maria West, Hannah Duke, Sylvia Evans, Louisa Smith, Letitia Taylor and hundreds of thousands of others like them were wartime refugees, women who fled their enslavement and sought refuge within Union military lines and Federal zones of occupation in the South. Their experiences would differ in as many ways as they were similar, differences that were a function of precise configurations of place and geography, the individual circumstances of their enslavement, and the resources they carried into freedom, among other factors. All of these things played a part in determining their wartime experience, including their chances of surviving the war. It made a difference that Anna Ashby and Maria West labored alongside their husbands on a plantation that their husbands jointly managed. It mattered that Hannah Duke was a survivor of the antebellum domestic slave trade that had carried her from Virginia to Louisiana, and that she had the responsibility of caring for two children as she made her way to freedom and worked on an abandoned plantation leased not by men she knew or from her community but by Northern investors. It mattered that Sylvia Evans fled slavery with her family intact—her husband and two young children, ages four and nine in 1864—and other family and kin from the Florida plantation, and that Louisa Smith was a soldier's wife. But in every instance, they were subject to arbitrary Federal policies and sometimes vicious treatment at the hands of Federal officials, Union commanders and soldiers, and agents of freedmen's aid societies. Yet they contributed immensely to the Union war effort and the fight for emancipation, contributions that are lost in the way historians tend to view women's contributions to the war. We are more inclined to see these contributions in the work of women who knit and sewed for the soldiers like the Woolsey sisters.[3]

From the Woolsey home at 8 Brevoort Place in Brooklyn came an impressive amount of supplies for the support of Union army hospitals. A partial list compiled by Abby Woolsey showed 667 flannel and cotton shirts, 134 pairs of drawers, 165 wrappers (nightgowns), 628 pairs of sock, 1,144 handkerchiefs, 1,036 towels and napkins, 121 pillow sacks, 58 pieces of mosquito netting, large quantities of tobacco, dozens of boxes of cologne, hundreds of toothbrushes, combs and pocket mirrors, condensed milk, tea and crackers and jellies, canned tomatoes, and farina and oatmeal, among other items. The list, intended for the descendants of the Woolsey family, provided another measure of how hard the Woolsey sisters had worked for the Union cause—had fought for home, freedom, and nation. For the historian, it is an important archival source of the wartime production of just one household. But the historian can say more than the Woolseys did about this list. The historian can relay the labor of millions of other women that made possible the material production that came from 8 Brevoort Place, the hidden labors and costs not visible in the list but that contributed to the Union cause: the Irish women who cleaned and cooked for the Woolsey family; enslaved people who grew the cotton for the shirts and sacks, nightgowns, towels, and handkerchiefs; the women who labored in home sweat shops in the North to turn cotton into cloth.[4] These facts disappear from lists like the one Abby Woolsey kept and from the lists kept by the thousands of USSC societies in the North of the more than $50 million in goods and funds they supplied in support of Union soldiers and the cause of Union and nation and, sometimes, the cause of freedom.

THE CULTIVATION OF COTTON in the South did not cease with the outbreak of war, nor did the cotton trade. The Federal government did all it could to ensure that it did not and to retrieve and transport to the North as many bales of cotton as possible that Union or Confederate armies did not burn. Black women refugees put to work growing cotton on abandoned plantations leased out or managed by the Federal government were central to this project. This history, too, is as invisible in the scholarship on women in the war as are other contributions black women in the South made to the

U.S. treasury that helped to keep the war machinery running. The cotton that black women cultivated and picked on abandoned plantations leased by the Federal government, and the taxes they paid on the wages they earned, no doubt more than matched the monetary value of the contributions made by the USSC. In 1865 alone, the Federal government collected nearly $500,000 from the labor of black people. Over $900,000 dollars remained in the account of the Refugees and Freedmen's Fund in 1867. Commonly called the Freedmen's Fund, it comprised money from taxes paid by black laborers, the sale of cotton grown by black people, rents on confiscated Confederate properties, bounties due to black soldiers but not paid, and taxes on planters. Laborers made the largest contribution to the fund. The invisible history of black women's wartime labor and their fight for home, freedom, and nation was made more so by the history compiled by Confederate women.

"Delicately nurtured women, unaccustomed to labor, toiled the livelong day for the soldier. . . . Fairy fingers, used alone to toy with delicate embroidery, boldly seized and made the coarse garments of the soldier." And they had "No 'Sanitary' or 'Christian Commission,' heavily endowed by leading capitalists or government funds," to back their efforts, to help them take "nourishing food and medicine to the wounded or fever-stricken Confederate, South of the Potomac. It was the mission of woman to attempt, and in hundreds of thousands of cases, to successfully perform, this self-imposed and unprecedented task."[5] In the end, although their cause had been defeated, they had "throughout all the horrors of the Reconstruction era" continued to hold it in "boundless love and reverence and regret."[6] This is how the Daughters of the Confederacy of South Carolina remembered the contributions of the state's white women to the Confederate cause. Following in the steps of their ancestors in the American Revolution, they had "gloried and exulted in the name of Rebel women." There were Southern white women who might have disagreed, whose experience of the war for Confederate nationhood and the Southern white home was vastly different, like the mountain women of North Carolina and small slaveholders like Sarah Espy of Alabama.

Espy identified and supported the Confederacy, though she was hardly a fairy-fingered woman. She and her husband enslaved two adults in 1860, down from five in 1850. They thus belonged to the largest class of Southerners who owned slaves: the 15 percent of slaveholding families who owned one to six slaves in 1860; the vast majority owned none at all. Although not poor (she had a son attending college in 1860), and despite owning slaves, she categorized herself among the "working classes," listing her occupation in 1860 as seamstress. However, Espy shared wealthier slaveholders' view of abolition. Espy had hailed the execution of John Brown and his associates as just punishment for their "fanaticism." On December 2, 1859, the day Brown was hanged, she wrote, "may the women and children of the South be saved from their Northern murderers."[7] Instead of the peace she hoped the death of Brown and his followers would enable, a war whose bloodshed was unprecedented in the history of the young nation had erupted. She sent two sons to fight for the Confederate cause. But she became a more discerning chronicler of her world and, perhaps, as Drew Faust writes, "newly aware of class differences in the South."[8] Near the end of 1863 she left this remark in her diary: "There is a great wrong somewhere, and if our Confederacy should fall it will be no wonder to me for the brunt is thrown upon the working classes while the rich live in ease and pleasure."[9] She watched as slaveholders trying to get away from the war increasingly passed her home with enslaved people. She had little sympathy for them and certainly not for those who complained they were "distressed about leaving home." At least they had a place to go, Espy wrote. They had "wealthy friends" with whom they could seek shelter, whereas she "and many others, have no friends and our children even barely boys, are taken from us and put into the service."[10] By the end, the war had taken one of her sons, and she had joined the ranks of slaveholders hiding enslaved people or taking or sending them into other Confederate-held areas to keep them from running to Union lines and, in her case, from joining the rumored "insurrectionary" movements in nearby Wills Valley.[11]

In the final year of the war, Espy would witness "droves of refugees from Wills Valley." She would deal with the mundane affairs of everyday life, some of which she believed were less likely to trouble wealthy women. When her hogs found their way into the cornfields of a neighboring woman and were badly injured by the neighbor's dogs, Espy protested, but her neighbor stood her ground; her dogs did what they should—protected her cornfields. Espy thought the problem was not in the trespass of her hogs but the neighbor Mrs. B's "sorry fence," which she should have repaired over the winter.[12]

Espy is not easy to place in the categories we traditionally use to assess Southern white women's loyalties in the Civil War. It angered her that wealthy slaveholding women seemed to have an easier time of it, a view poor white women who encountered slaveholding women refugees shared. Her critique of the rich, however, did not necessarily mean that she sympathized with the tribulations of the poor, but she could understood the reasons that pushed four "Mountain-women" to commandeer seventy bushels of threshed wheat from a neighbor's farm. It was "bold thing," and she believed the suffering of the poor would trigger more such actions.[13] In the end, like all slaveholding women, Espy lost her right to own other human beings, and like them, she resisted this reality as long as she could. She apparently had not fully accepted it when her son who survived the battlefield returned home in June 1865. He "thinks the slaves are free unconditionally," she wrote. It was only the following month that she "contracted with Jane and Dick to serve the remainder of the year, such being the federal law." In return for their labor, they would receive just what they had gotten as enslaved people: "their victuals and clothing, the proceeds of their patches and they are to perform their duties as heretofore." She was not yet willing to grant that they were free. "The freedom of the negroes will not be ratified until Congress meets which will be in October," she wrote.[14]

Women understood that when "men contended for victory & empire," their own lives and "business" were very much involved. However much men might worry about the contamination of white women in the public sphere, when men went to war, they put women in the public sphere, in the fight. War put women on the roads fleeing armies in search of shelter and freedom and in unprecedented numbers on factory floors. It put them on the battlefield as nurses and refugees. It put them in each other's path, often moving in opposing political and geographical directions. War carried contending men to women's parlors and cabins and contending women to the battlefield.

Men's business was women's business. Women could not vote or hold office, but they crowded the galleries of statehouses and the U.S. Senate and Congress before the war, during the secession crisis, and when war came. They knew that their support and labors would constitute a vital part of the war's political and military machinery. When the war began, women who had never before addressed a letter to a public official wrote Abraham Lincoln and Jefferson Davis and their governors seeking redress for crops confiscated by armies and relief from poverty exacerbated by the enlistment of fathers, sons, and husbands, and dignified treatment of black soldiers captured by Confederate armies. Regardless of their public statements to the contrary, men also understood that their business was women's business.

Men went to war expecting that women would play a vital role in keeping up morale with good cheer and supplementary supplies of food and clothing, and policing the space where men acknowledged that women had "business": the home. "We appeal to the women of the land. If they would keep our fair South free from the curse of negro equality; would keep forever the slave in the kitchen and the cabin, and out of the parlor, and encourage their husbands, sons, and brothers to vote for secession," urged the *Augusta Daily Constitutionalist* in January 1861."[15] Slaveholding women—who had slaves in the kitchen—were the clear target of such appeals, but the reference to the "curse of negro equality" enlarged the potential audience for such appeals to include nonslaveholding women. When Southern white men went to war, they made the defense of the home the main selling point for the conflict. Yet the separation of affairs of the home front from other more public affairs of the family had never been clear-cut, even in the South.

In the North, the appeal to women were made pointedly on the ground of patriotism. "Patriotism is a great ingredient of Northern blood and I think our country has nothing to fear in regard to the loyalty of her sons and daughters," Emilie Quiner of Madison, Wisconsin, wrote two days after the attack on Fort Sumter. "The great uprising among men," Northern Civil War nurse Mary A. Livermore agreed, "was paralleled by a similar uprising among women. The patriotic speech and song, which fired the blood of men, and led them to enter the lists as soldiers, nourished the self-sacrifice of women, and stimulated them to the collection of hospital supplies and to brave the horrors and hardships of hospital life."[16] Yet as William Marvel argues, economic motivations inspired the enlistment of poor men at times more than patriotism. When it was all over, women would talk about their sacrifice in the lofty language of "exquisite suffering" and "heroism." They had "throughout the country" answered the call, "forcing their white lips to utter a cheerful 'good-bye,'" when their hearts were nigh breaking with the fierce struggle," Mary Livermore wrote. The wives and daughters of poor white men who joined the army for the salary it brought did not have the luxury of looking back to a time of "exquisite suffering."[17]

Livermore also saw "exquisite suffering" and "heroism" exhibited by black women, but lacking "white lips" could their sacrifice be the same? She wrote, for example, of the "poor contraband mother from Lake Superior" who sent socks she had knit in support of a soldiers' fair and whose son had enlisted in the Union army and died on the battlefield. The text makes clear, however, that this woman was in fact not a "contraband" but a person who had escaped slavery before the war with her son. In general, Livermore was inclined to see black refugees as a degraded people, "half-imbruted."[18] Like most Northern white women who went south, she considered white women far superior. The narratives of heroic and suffering black Union women were less visible to the eyes of white women no less than white men. Women like Ann Bradford (Stokes), who enlisted as a nurse on the U.S.S. *Red Rover*, a naval hospital transport, at Memphis on January 1, 1863, Louisa Smith and other black women who fled slavery and fought for their freedom, for the right to a home and nation, and black women who organized aid societies for black soldiers and their families have had a harder time finding a place in the historical narrative of women's fight in the Civil War.[19] Yet they insisted and demonstrated that they were a vital part of the "silent army of heroines."[20]

The public and ideological staging of the war at the center of the call to arms by the United States and the Confederacy and strategies for mobilizing men, materials, and patriotic support cordoned off combatants from noncombatants, citizens from noncitizens, free people from the enslaved, and women from men. This staging had important implications for women's fight. When the war began, Northern white men opposed fighting alongside black men or for emancipation, and the North's strategies for mobilization positioned black people outside the parameters of the nation-state and its concerns. The position of the United States was clear: the Southern *rebellion* against the authority of the United States was a matter to be settled "privately" by citizens, including those who had declared their disloyalty and treason. The seeming simplicity of the pronouncement, however, did not make it clear policy.[21]

White Americans, North and the South, staked their lives in 1861 on a union with or without slavery or disunion with slavery. For them, the war had little if anything to do with black people—at least in any sense that required white Americans to seriously consider black people's politics. Certainly, compared to Northerners, Southerners were less naive about these matters, less sanguine that slaves would volunteer to maintain a position of neutrality and more knowledgeable about slaves' politics. Where Northerners prevaricated, white Southerners admitted the value of the labor of the enslaved to their project. They did not expect or desire that black men would fight for the Confederacy, but they did expect that black men and women would play a vital role in their fight to maintain slavery. This expectation was central to their military strategy. But no matter, black people staked their ground on revolution to bring about a new union based on universal freedom. This understanding informed this resolution of black people in Boston: "Resolved, That the colored woman would go as nurses, seamstresses, and warriors, if need be [to] crush rebellion and uphold the Government."[22]

THE WORK OF THE ENSLAVED played a large role in the steady erosion of the principle that the war between the North and the South was merely a commotion, a family dispute among white people that concerned only white freedom, the white home, and the white nation. As put by Gen. George B. McClellan, "the true issue for which we are fighting is the preservation of the

Union." The armies of the United States, Gen. John A. Dix proclaimed to the rebels of Northern Virginia, come "among you as friends." Black people embarrassed the pervasive sentiment among white Americans that their participation would tarnish an otherwise principled contest. Early in the war, Gen. John Dix argued that receiving fugitive slaves into Union lines would "taint" the "holy" cause of Union: Intermingling the questions of slavery and Union would subject the North "to the imputation of intermeddling with a matter entirely foreign to the great question of political right and duty involved in the civil strife." "In regard to the Negroes," he concluded confidently in January 1862, "they are of no use to us. I would therefore have no more to do with them than is absolutely necessary to comply with the act of Congress."[23] In June of that year, Gen. William T. Sherman felt sure enough of the Union policy of nonengagement with slaves to issue an order to the officers and men in his command asserting that "the well settled policy of the whole army is to have nothing to do with the negro."[24] That proposition failed but Unionist black women refugees would never be accorded the same treatment as Unionist white women refugees. Rather, they were disparaged as "women of bad character," charged fees for permits to move about on their own free will, and forced to pay taxes on their waged labor.[25]

This book traces a part of the story of women's business during the Civil War, their struggles and victories in the fights they waged as they came into contact with each other across borders previously closely restricted and policed by law and custom on the basis of class and race. Tearing down those borders inspired the work of countless women. Other women had worked to strengthen the borders that divided women. The Civil War brought concrete and often transformative changes to women's lives, but it left the borders that had separated them fairly intact. In the years to come, the goal of keeping those borders intact fueled the activism of many women and created unseemly partnerships. Former white women abolitionists made common cause with Southern white women to push for women's right to vote at the expense of African American men and women. At the same time, white women in the South worked to put themselves back on the pedestal, with black women restored to their kitchens. With her husband, a former Confederate officer, in Egypt trying to earn a living to keep from losing his family's home and farm, Margaret Graves took seriously her husband's command to not become a "household drudge." Though poor enough to have no fingers but her own to wash her clothes, she paid a washerwoman and, true to her training, "counted out the wash clothes" to make sure none was stolen by the washerwoman.[26] White women refugees, historian Mary Elizabeth

Massey wrote, had been churned, tossed, and bruised as no other people in the history of the nation.[27] She exaggerated, but it was close enough to the way white women in the South felt.

Ellen Cook Whitehurst remembered being on the road with her mistress—who sat on top of the wagon "with the family silver and jewels tied in bag under her close"—when they heard the news that Roanoke had fallen to the Union. They were in Tarboro, North Carolina, when the Union took the town and burned the bridge over the Tar River. From there they fled to Oxford, where Ellen Whitehurst's mother, Nancy, died before she could experience life as a free person.[28] The dreams of the woman who claimed ownership of her that somehow the Confederacy might survive, also died there but not her dreams of a domestic sanctuary.

With the defeat of the Confederate South's bid for independence, slavery was destroyed, but the meaning of freedom, nation, and home remained contested, and the fight for free homes and full citizenship rights continued. In the midst of that fight, many of the nation's preeminent scholars and thinkers portrayed African Americans as "the cause of wasted property and small crops" who "had impoverished the South, and plunged the North into endless debt," as "funny, funny—ridiculous baboons, aping men" and de-gendered women.[29] This took place as memoirs and reminiscences documenting the role of white women in the war took center stage, where they were to remain for decades to come. They offered a partial, misleading, and often untruthful narrative. In the narratives of black women filed as testimony in widows' pension claims, as oral interviews in the 1930s, as claims before Union commanders and soldiers, in disputes with Northern missionaries, and as testified to in the letters and diaries of slaveholders lies another rich and compelling story of the history of women in the war. In the stories of poor white women lies another.

ACKNOWLEDGMENTS

THIS BOOK SOMEHOW found its own way after a long, circuitous journey. Its completion took longer that I had imagined, to the understandable dismay of my editors and publisher, though they never quite put it that way. Gary Gallagher and T. Michael Parrish, the editors of the Littlefield Series, and Mark Simpson-Vos, my editor at the University of North Carolina Press, were unstintingly patient and suffered through several drafts with care and brought to it incredibly helpful insights. I was fortunate to work with an extraordinarily talented staff at the press. All of these people saved me from errors large and small. They did their best, and I am responsible for any errors that remain.

Gary brought the idea of this project to me many years ago, too many to decently recall. Over the years, other projects took my immediate attention, but this one always maintained a presence, becoming at last the primary focus of my research and writing.

Over time, the archival notes grew and the pages of writing took on the semblance of a manuscript. Still, wrangling a book from my notes proved daunting. This book enters a field defined by fierce debates and fine scholarship, including in the area of the book's core concern—American women and the Civil War. It is interested especially in the places and spaces—intellectual, political, social, and physical—where women's lives intersected across space, time, race, and class and continues my ongoing interest in the idea and meaning of home as a political as well as economic structure. Writing this book was made easier because I could call on the vibrant literature on women in the Civil War that has emerged in recent decades.

This book would not have been possible without the intellectual and funding support of the deans of Trinity College of Arts and Sciences and Duke Law School and the Office of the University Provost. The work on black women refugees that appears in this book is part of a larger project financed in large measure by the National Institutes of Health. For bringing me into the world of the NIH, I am indebted to colleagues in sociology, public policy, and demography: Seth G. Sanders, Angela O'Rand, and Linda K. George.

The work and friendship of colleagues in the History Department, Duke

Law School, and the Duke Population Institute continues to inspire me; to them I owe much. The generous comments and critiques of colleagues at conferences and seminars on parts of what appears in this book offered opportunities to rethink and revise. Thank you for inviting me to share my work at your institutions and for the conversations that helped me to think through many of the ideas in this book at symposia, seminars, conferences, and keynote addresses: Africana Studies Program Lecture Series, Rhodes College; Alexandrian Society, Virginia Commonwealth University History Department; American Philosophical Society; Annenberg Seminar, Department of History, University of Pennsylvania; Center for Civil War Research, University of Mississippi; Center for Historical Analysis and Black Atlantic Seminar Series, Rutgers University; Center for the Study of the American South, University of North Carolina at Chapel Hill; Charles Warren Center, Harvard University; Civil War Institute, Gettysburg College; Clemson University; Clough Center for the Study of Constitutional Democracy, Boston College; College of Charleston; Department of Women's Studies, University of Maryland; DePaul University; Emory University; Hampton University; Havens Center for the Study of Social Structure and Social Change, University of Wisconsin–Madison; Hebrew University of Jerusalem; History of the Military, War, and Society Seminar, Duke University; Indiana State University; Institute for African American Research, University of South Carolina; Institute for Research on Women and Gender, University of Michigan; Interdisciplinary Workshop in the Global Nineteenth Century, New York University; Johns Hopkins History Department Seminar; Langford Lecture, Duke University; Lincoln Forum; Maryland University Libraries Symposium, University of Maryland; National Constitution Center; National Trust for Historic Preservation, Lincoln Cottage; Program in Race, Law, and History, University of Michigan; Nineteenth-Century U.S. History Workshop, Georgetown University; Program in the Humanities and Human Values, University of Illinois–Urbana-Champaign; Robert Fortenbaugh Memorial Lecture; Tulane University; University of Alabama Libraries; University of Alabama, Tuscaloosa; University of Buffalo Humanities Institute; University of Chicago; University of Connecticut; University of Massachusetts, Amherst; University of Missouri–Kansas City; University of North Carolina at Chapel Hill; University of South Carolina; University of Tennessee; University of Virginia; University of Texas at Austin; University of the Witwatersrand; Vanderbilt History Seminar; Villanova University; Wake Forest University; Wake Forest University and the Oxford Character Project; Washington and Lee University; Woodrow Wilson Center; Works in Progress Seminar, New York University; Yale University; and the meetings of the American Historical Association, the British

American Nineteenth–Century Historians (BrANCH) Conference, the Organization of American Historians, the Southern Historical Association, and the Society for Civil War Historians. The work of librarians and archivists underpins this book and allowed it to grow.

Graduate students Alisha Hines (now Professor Hines) and Sarah Amundson and the inimitable Alisa Harrison have been a source of much joy. I have learned from them, the members of the Graduate Working Group on Slavery, Gender and War at Duke, and students in my graduate and undergraduate history seminars and law school courses. I also thank the wonderfully talented administrative staffs in the History Department and Duke Law School and the librarians and archivists at Duke and other institutions.

Friends, colleagues, and students at other institutions have inspired and helped to keep me going in numerous ways. Among the many who have blessed me with their friendship and collegiality—often over great meals in far-flung places—are Darlene Clark Hine, Nikky Finny, Lorin Palmer, M. Giovanna Merli, Giovanni Zanaldo, Susan Thorne, Sarah Deutsch, Paula D. McClain, Maggie Lemos, Doriane L. Coleman, Steve Hahn, Katherine Brophy Dubois, Evelyn Brooks Higgenbotham, Sharon Harley, Bill and Lorna Chafe, Ira and Martha Berlin, Claudia Koonz, Alice Kessler-Harris, Mary Kelley, Rebecca Scott, Martha Jones, Sarah Haley, Kendra Taira Field, Leslie Rowland, Barbara J. Fields, Karen Fields, Julia Saville, Catherine Clinton, Jim Downs, Val Littlefield, Bill Hine, Linda Kerber, Crystal Feimster, Joseph P. Reidy, Yael Sternhell, David Roediger, Michael Honey, Richard Blackett, Thomas Holt, Ta-Nehisi Coates, Tamika Nunley, Tommy DeFranz, Bert Johnson, and Sasha Turner. And a special thank you to Evelyn Higginbotham and Darlene Clark Hine for the gift of sacred spaces to write and think at Martha's Vineyard and Union Pier.

My children—Morgan, Kristal, and Sebastian—read not one page of this book, but every page bears their imprint. Life without them is really unimaginable. I adore the brilliant, funny, and loving adults they have become and the dreams they imagine possible for our world.

NOTES

ABBREVIATIONS

AAS   American Antiquarian Society
ADAH   Alabama Department of Archives and History
AFIC   American Freedmen's Inquiry Commission
AQM   Assistant Quartermaster
BRFAL   Bureau of Refugees, Freedmen, and Abandoned Lands
DMo   Department of Missouri
DU   Duke University
EU   Emory University
FSSP   Freedmen and Southern Society Project, University of Maryland,
          College Park, Md.
HSP   Historical Society of Pennsylvania
LOC   Library of Congress
LR   Letters Received
LS   Letters Sent
NARA   National Archives and Record Administration
NEWAA   New England Women's Auxiliary Association Archives
NPS   National Park Service
NYPL   New York Public Library
OR   U.S. War Department, *The War of the Rebellion: A Compilation of
          the Official Records of the Union and Confederate Armies*, 128 vols.
          (Washington, D.C.: Government Printing Office, 1880–1901)
ORN   *Official Records of the Union and Confederate Navies in the War of the
          Rebellion*, 30 vols. (Washington, D.C.: Government Printing Office,
          1894–1922)
PAS   Pennsylvania Abolition Society
RASP   Rochester Anti-Slavery Society Papers, William L. Clements Library,
          University of Michigan
RG   Record Group
SCHS   South Carolina Historical Society
SCL   South Caroliniana Library, University of South Carolina, Columbia,
          South Carolina
SHC   Southern Historical Collection, Wilson Special Collections Library,
          University of North Carolina at Chapel Hill

UNC   University of North Carolina
USCC   United States Colored Cavalry
USCHA   United States Colored Heavy Artillery
USCT   United States Colored Troops
USSC   United States Sanitary Commission Records
UT   University of Tennessee
WPA   Works Progress Administration

INTRODUCTION

1. Women of Maryland, "An Appeal," University of Maryland Library. In addition to Lee, Johnston, Beauregard, and Davis, Scott's officers at Cerro Gordo included George B. McClellan and Ulysses S. Grant.

2. J. S. W. [Jane Stuart Woolsey] to Cousin Margaret Hodge, February 7, 1861, in Bacon and Howland, *Letters of a Family*, vol. 1, 33–34, quote on 34; Glymph, "Invisible Disabilities."

3. Western Freedmen's Aid Society Commission, Cincinnati, February 12, 1863, Rubenstein Library, DU.

4. The terms *refugees* and *displaced persons* are important to this discussion and applicable to white and black Southern women who fled, seeking refuge from warring armies. The first usage of *displaced persons* to refer to slaves who ended up in refugee camps that I have found was by Henry L. Swint in his edited collection of wartime letters by Northerners who went to the South as teachers. Swint, *Dear Ones at Home*, 6. See also Sterling, *We Are Your Sisters*, 256; and Faust, *Mothers of Invention*, 40–41.

5. This historiography includes Bleser and Gordon, *Intimate Strategies of the Civil War*; Bynum, *Unruly Women*; Campbell, *When Sherman Marched North from the Sea*; Cashin, *The War Was You and Me*; Clinton and Silber, *Divided Houses*; Faust, *Mothers of Invention*; Frank, *The Civilian War*; Giesberg, *Army at Home*; Leonard, *Yankee Women*; McCurry, *Confederate Reckoning*; McPherson, *For Cause and Comrades*; Mitchell, *The Vacant Chair*; Rable, *Civil Wars*; Silber, *Daughters of the Union*; Vinovskis, *Toward a Social History of the Civil War*; and Whites and Long, *Occupied Women*. For a review of portions of the literature, see Glymph, "The Civil War Era."

6. See, for example, Glymph, *Out of the House of Bondage*.

7. Duyckinck, *National History of the War for the Union*, 2:115.

8. Nolan and Redmond, "Civil War Cartography Then and Now."

9. Holt, *Children of Fire*, 141. For a similar analysis, see Hartman, *Scenes of Subjection*, 5.

10. See Silber, *Daughters of the Union*.

11. Quotes from Bacon and Howland, *Letters of a Family*, vol. 1, viii; Women of Maryland, "An Appeal," University of Maryland Library.

12. D. L. Stevens to Mrs. [A. L.] Endicott, May 27, 1864, USSC, NEWAA, Manuscripts and Archives Collection, NYPL; Oates, *A Woman of Valor*, 157–58.

13. E. H. Dickerson to Miss [Isa E.] Gray, May 24, 1863; Ursula M. Penniman to Mrs. [A. L.] Endicott, June 15, 1864; Mrs. J. Sumner to Miss [Annette P.] Rogers, March 9, 1864, USSC, NEWAA, Manuscripts and Archives Collection, NYPL.

14. Though it often succumbed to standard race and class tropes, Mary Elizabeth Massey's *Bonnet Brigades: American Women in the Civil War*, published in 1966 (and republished in 1994 as *Women in the Civil War*), attempted the first systematic study of women across regional divides and included a chapter on black women. See Glymph, "The Civil War Era," 179–80.

15. Jordan, *Black Confederates*, 269. For an elaboration of these points, see Glymph, "I'm a Radical Girl."

16. Brown, *States of Injury*, 128.

17. See Williams, "Letters of General Thomas Williams," 325. Bill of Sale, Columbia [S.C.], February 22, 1864, Augustin Louis Taveau Papers, Duke University; no. 78, March 21, 1863, Manumission of Slave, Lismene, by Marie Joseph Sarcy alias Victorine, State of Louisiana, Parish of Orleans, City of New Orleans, Acts 18, pp. 168–69, New Orleans Notorial Archives.

18. LeeAnn Whites and Alecia P. Long describe this phenomenon as "household-based war." See Whites and Long, *Occupied Women*, 12.

19. Faust, *The Creation of Confederate Nationalism*, 6–7, 16, 21.

20. Hsieh, "Total War," 398. Hsieh writes that historians have treated the U.S. Civil War as "a profound discontinuity not only in the history of the United States but the larger history of the modern world." While I disagree with Hsieh's argument that cultural and material constraints meant that "Civil War armies placed serious limits on the violence that could be unleashed on civilians"—it is at least an overly broad assessment—I think he is right in asking that we unlink the rhetoric contemporaries used from the "ground truth" of wartime violence. Hsieh, "Total War," 396, 397, 400–401.

21. Holt, *Children of Fire*, xvi–xvii.

22. Sterkx, *Partners in Rebellion*, 24–25; Genovese and Fox-Genovese, *Fatal Self-Deception*, 23.

23. *Holston Salt & Plaster Co. v. Campbell et al.*, 274. During the war Palmer worked with Confederate general James Ewell Brown ("Jeb") Stuart to consolidate the saltworks in the Holston River Valley. See also Hall, *Mountains on the Market*, 115; New York Census, 1855, Onondaga County, Syracuse City, Ward 4; and U.S. Census, 1860, Smyth County, Va. See also Kurlansky, *Salt*.

24. U.S. Sanitary Commission, *Hospital Transports*, xi.

25. Sterkx, *Partners in Rebellion*, 24–25.

26. William C. Green to Fannie Green, Ann Arbor, April 22, 1861, Green Family Papers, folder 5, box 1, Stuart A. Rose Manuscript, Archives, and Rare Book Library, EU.

27. J. S. W. [Jane Stuart Woolsey] to Cousin Margaret [Margaret Hodge], April 1861, in Bacon and Howland, *Letters of a Family*, vol. 1, 45–46.

28. A Charleston Woman, "In the Cradle of the War," in *Our Women in the War*, 281.

29. For insight on the association of childhood with vulnerability and suffering, see Duane, *Suffering Childhood in Early America*.

30. Woods, *Development Arrested*, 40–47, quote at 45.

CHAPTER ONE

1. Margaret Ann Meta Morris Grimball Diary, December 15, 1860; December 5, [1861], and March 6, [1862], SHC. Hereafter cited as Grimball Diary. Journal of Meta M. Grimball (Née Morris), December 1860-February 1866, typescript available at SCHS.

2. Grimball Diary, December 15, 1860; December 5, [1861]; and March 6, [1862], SHC. In the lowcountry, the flight and resistance of slaves and "exultation" at the arrival of Union forces on November 7, 1862, put slaveholder John DeSaussure in a "state of abject fright" and turned him into "absolutely a lunatic," wrote Mary Chesnut. Woodward, *Mary Chesnut's Civil War*, entry for November 11, 1861, 233. Drew Gilpin Faust addresses some of these complexities in *Mothers of Invention*, 30–52; see also Rose, *Rehearsal for Reconstruction*, 11–17.

3. Horn, "Nashville during the Civil War," 9; Ravenel, *The Private Journal of William Henry Ravenel*, December 10, [1864], p. 205; Defontaine, "Stirring Days in Chester," in *Our Women in the War*, 86–87.

4. Rable, "Despair, Hope, and Delusion," 49.

5. See, for example, Faust, *Mothers of Invention*; Fox-Genovese, *Within the Plantation Household*; and Glymph, *Out of the House of Bondage*.

6. Hammond, "Speech of Hon. James H. Hammond, of South Carolina, on the Admission of Kansas, under the LeCompton Constitution: Delivered in the Senate of the United States," March 4, 1858, Washington, D.C., AAS.

7. *Green v. the State*, 58 Al. 194, 1877, Lexis 204, December 1877. The case at hand turned on the question of interracial marriage and a defense of women and home grounded in antebellum understandings of the meaning of home.

8. A Puritan [George Bourne], *The Abrogation of the Seventh Commandment, by the American Churches*, 3.

9. Hall, "The Sweet Delights of Home," 49.

10. Dew, *Apostles of Disunion*, 76, 80; Oakes, *Freedom National*.

11. See Robinson, *Bitter Fruits of Bondage*, 164–65; and Fox-Genovese and Genovese, *The Mind of the Master Class*, 383–406.

12. Hartman, *Scenes of Subjection*, 5.

13. Furry, *The Preacher's Tale*, 96–97.

14. Bercaw, *Gendered Freedoms*; Du Bois, *Black Reconstruction*, 55–83; Edwards,

Scarlett Doesn't Live Here Anymore, 149–85; Glymph, *Out of the House of Bondage*; Weiner, *Mistresses and Slaves*, 207–33.

15. This statistic is from Ayers, *Thin Light of Freedom*, 184.

16. An estimated 200,000 to 250,000 white Southerners, most of whom belonged to the slave-owning class, fled their homes. By comparison, an estimated 500,000 enslaved people, or some 13 percent, became refugees. Both estimates, though widely cited, are fairly unreliable. Firm numbers and attribution for the estimates are impossible to come by. Historians tend to cite each other with the circle inevitably returning to Mary Elizabeth Massey, who put the number of white refugees at "tens of thousands" but provided no documentation to support the estimate. Massey, *Refugee Life in the Confederacy*, 282. The Freedmen and Southern Society Project, following Du Bois, also puts the number of fugitive slaves at 500,000. To get to this number, one would have to add to the 200,000 black soldiers Du Bois counted (179,000 black men served in the U.S. Army and 10,000 in the Navy); the "perhaps 300,000 other black laborers, servants, spies and helpers" he estimated were part of the mutiny of enslaved people during the war. (Du Bois, *Black Reconstruction*, 80; Glymph, "Du Bois's Black Reconstruction," 492.) I am currently working on a project that aims to arrive at an estimate of the number of black refugees. The estimated 300,000 Du Bois gives clearly omis the hundreds of thousands of enslaved women and children.

17. Clinton, *Tara Revisited*, quote at 23.

18. The labor of the lowcountry's black majority meant enormous wealth before the war. The prevalence of absentee slaveholders also had a negative impact on the ability of slaveholders to put up an effective resistance to the disintegration that hit in the fall of 1861. On the importance of the nature of the crop, and demographics, see Berlin, *Many Thousands Gone*.

19. Massey, *Refugee Life in the Confederacy*, 68–94, quote at 4; McGuire, *Diary of a Southern Refugee*.

20. East, *Sarah Morgan*, August 7, [1862], May 31, [1862], 199, 95.

21. Faust, *Mothers of Invention*, 10–12, quote at 10; Ayers, *Thin Light of Freedom*, 114–16. Stephanie McCurry argues that in not formally soliciting white women's opinions, white men made a cardinal mistake. McCurry, *Confederate Reckoning*.

22. Harriett Warren to J. B. M. [James Blount Miller], Columbus, Miss., September 6, 1844, Miller-Furman-Dabbs Family Papers, SCL.

23. Tyler, "To the Duchess of Sutherland," 120. During the war, the widowed Julia Tyler went to live with her family in New York. She returned to Sherwood Forest following the war.

24. Tyler, "To the Duchess of Sutherland," 122, 123, 124.

25. East, *Sarah Morgan*, May 30, [1862], 90.

26. East, *Sarah Morgan*, May 30, [1862], 89, 90.

27. East, *Sarah Morgan*, May 30, [1862], 90–95, quote at 91.

28. Lee, *Recollections and Letters*, 86.

29. East, *Sarah Morgan*, August 7, [1862], 199.

30. Manigault, *A Carolinian Goes to War*, 9.

31. Thomas Ravenel Journal, entry for January 2, 1861, SCHS. On the early efforts to put the state on a military footing, see Edgar, *South Carolina*, 358.

32. Thomas Ravenel Journal, entries for December 31, 1860, January 2, January 8, January 12, and January 24, 1861, SCHS; Berlin et al., *The Destruction of Slavery*, ser. 1, vol. 1, 664–65.

33. R. Oswald Sams [Robby] to [Caroline Oswald Sams], November 27, 1861, Montgomery, Ala., Sams Family Papers, SCL.

34. Thomas Ravenel Journal, entry for November 10, 1861, SCHS. Clearly not all slaveholders grasped the urgency of the changed reality. A meeting on January 24 to organize a local volunteer militia drew so few men that the election of officers had to be postponed. When they tried again five days later, a fight broke out over the elections and one inebriated delegate "had to be put under arrest." Thomas Ravenel Journal, entries for January 24, 1861, and January 25, 1861, SCHS.

35. Thomas Ravenel Journal, entry for November 10, 1861, SCHS. On Thomas Chaplin's plantation, Tombee, see Rosengarten, *Tombee*.

36. Grimball Diary, entry for October 19, [1861], SHC. Union military forces landed at Bay Point on November 7, 1861. It appears that Grimball simply kept writing under the October 19 dateline.

37. Grimball Diary, entries for March 16, 1862, and [December] 15, [1860], SHC.

38. Thomas Ravenel Journal, entry for May 13, 1861, SCHS.

39. R. Oswald Sams to My Dear Ma [Caroline Oswald Sams], November 17, 1861, Montgomery, Ala., Sams Family Papers, SCL; R. Oswald Sams to My Dear Ma [Caroline Oswald Sams], October 10, 1861, Montgomery, Ala., Sams Family Papers, SCL.

40. *Congressional Globe*, 37th Cong., 1st Sess., 31: 222–23.

41. R. Oswald Sams to My Dear Ma, Montgomery, Ala., November 17, 1861, Sams Family Papers, SCL.

42. Lee, *Recollections and Letters*, 88.

43. Ravenel, *The Private Journal of William Henry Ravenel*, June 10, [1862], p. 147.

44. Grimball Diary, [December] 15, [1860].

45. Kate D. Foster Diary, entry for September 28, [1863], near Natchez, Miss., Rubenstein Library, DU.

46. Scott, "Social Facts, Legal Fictions."

47. Morgan, *Civil War Diary*, June 1, [1862], 96–97.

48. Moore, *The Diary of Keziah Goodwyn Hopkins Brevard*, November 18, 1860, 52.

49. Morgan, *Civil War Diary*, June 1, [1862], 97.

50. *OR*, ser. 3, vol. 2, p. 784. Applications went through the Office of the Judge Advocate General, established on July 17, 1862, as the legal advisor to the secretary of the army and all army offices and agencies and successor to the judge advocate of the army. On the establishment of the office, see also Leonard, *Lincoln's Forgotten Ally*, 158–64. To evade the passport system, some Southern white men took desperate measures. In 1862, a group of Confederate prisoners of war escaped

by disguising themselves in blackface (*OR*, ser. 2, vol. 4, p. 24). On efforts to control the movement of women across the borders of the North and South, see also Sternhell, *Routes of War*, 128–40; Taylor, *The Divided Family in Civil War America*, 92–97; and Massey, *Refugee Life in the Confederacy*.

51. As quoted in Côté, *Mary's World*, 193.

52. Sternhell, "Papers, Please!"; Thomas Ravenel Journal, entry for May 15, [1862], SCHS.

53. Oldham, *The Rise and Fall of the Confederacy*, 127, 129, 130–31.

54. F. G. DeFontaine, "Stirring Days in Chester," in *Our Women in the War*, 87.

55. Mrs. Blackford, University [University of Virginia], March 6, 1865, in Blackford, *Letters from Lee's Army*, 281.

56. Sullivan, *The War the Women Lived*, 56.

57. Faust, *Mothers of Invention*, 4.

58. On the usages of paternalism, see Genovese, *Roll, Jordan, Roll*, 3–7.

59. Anna O. [Oswald] to Dear Sister, Wednesday, November 20, 1861, Sams Family Papers, SCL.

60. Edmondston, *"Journal of a Secesh Lady,"* 242.

61. For a discussion of the making of free homes, see Glymph, *Out of the House of Bondage*.

62. Phillips, *Plantation and Frontier Documents*, 44–45.

63. Chaplin, *An Anxious Pursuit*, 125–26.

64. C. M. S. [Caroline M. Sams] to My Beloved Manny [Marion W. Sams], Lawtonville, December 2, 1861; H. D. D. [Rev. H. D. Duncan] to My dear Caroline [Mrs. Caroline M. Sams], November 23, 1861, Sams Papers, SCL.

65. C. M. S. [Caroline M. Sams] to My Beloved Manny [Marion W. Sams], Lawtonville, December 2, 1861, Sams Papers, SCL.

66. Emma L. Sams to Dear Pa [Miles B. Sams], Barnwell, November 28, 1861, Sams Papers, SCL.

67. Slaveholding men feared leaving enslaved men behind who could be enlisted by the Union army as military laborers and, after 1863, as soldiers. They also believed black men could be put to work more effectively on distant plantations and more easily hired out as farm laborers and at saltworks or other industries like turpentine.

68. U.S. Census, 1860, District of Beaufort, South Carolina; Miles B. Sams, Statement of Losses, March 21, 1862, Rebel Archives, Confederate Papers Relating to Citizens or Business Firms, 1861–1865 (Confederate Citizens File), War Department Collection of Confederate Records, NARA M346, RG 109. See also Schwalm, *A Hard Fight for We*, 93.

69. Holland, *Letters and Diary of Laura M. Towne*, August 23, [1862], February 28, 1864, December 5, 1864, February 23, 1866, 86, 131, 143, 169, 171. Pope eventually captured Bella as a result of the duplicity of another slave but she apparently managed to escape. Elizabeth also had money from the earnings of her soldier husband, Jack Brown, who died during the war.

70. Wm. Elliott to Ralph [Ralph Emms Elliott], December 15, 1861, Elliott-Gonzales Papers, SHC; Thom. R. S. Elliott to Mother [Ann Hutchinson Smith Elliott], [1861], Elliott-Gonzales Papers, SHC. One of Robert E. Lee's assignments prior to taking command of the Army of Northern Virginia was as commander of the Department of South Carolina from November 8, 1861, to March 3, 1862.

71. "List of Negroes, furniture, goods & effects of Mrs. Ann B. Oswald of Beaufort, So Car., now in the possession of the public enemy," March 7, 1862, Confederate Citizens File, Rebel Archives, War Department, RG 109, NARA, Fold3 Database. Oswald listed the value of the property as $9,518 with the furniture and other goods accounting for $2,500 of the total. On Oswald's wealth, see 1860 U.S. Census, where she is listed in the household of planter John Bell. Matilda and Ann were also listed as full field hands. In 1860 Ann Oswald's wealth in real estate and personal assets, respectively, was valued at $2,500 and $5,500.

72. Claim of Andrew Johnstone, State of South Carolina, Georgetown District, No. 103, Entered May 21, 1862; Record of Court of Pleas & Quarter Session, January 8, 1862.

73. "Report of the Auditor of South Carolina on Claims against the State for Slaves Lost in the Public Service," December 3, 1864 (Columbia, S.C.: Charles P. Pelham, State Printer, 1864), Rubenstein Library, DU. Joint resolutions passed by the South Carolina General Assembly in January 1863 directed that claims for slaves lost in the public service (impressed by the state for labor on military fortifications) "whose death or loss has been occasioned by reason of said service," be presented to the state auditor. The December 1864 report listed a total of 261 claims representing the loss of 267 slaves valued at $570,250. Of these, 218 were allowed in the amount of $452,150.

74. Mary [Elliott Johnstone] to Mamma [Ann Hutchinson Smith Elliott], Beaumont, March 2, [1862], Elliott-Gonzales Papers, SHC.

75. Mary [Elliott Johnstone] to [Ann Hutchinson Smith Elliott], Beaumont, Sunday, [June] 21, [1863], Elliott-Gonzales Papers, SHC; Taylor, Matthews, and Power, *The Leverett Letters*, 284.

76. Mary [Elliott Johnstone] to William Elliott, Beaumont, June 14, 1863, Elliott-Gonzales Papers, SHC. The Hugers leased their plantation in Louisiana for $12,000 along with the enslaved people who worked it. On J. Fraser and company, see Hagy, *Charleston, South Carolina City Directories*.

77. Stone, *Brokenburn*, January 25, 1863; March 2, 1863, 168–69, 170. Amanda Stone and her husband, William, who died in 1855, owned twenty-one slaves in 1850. By 1860, the family's wealth in slaves had thus increased by nearly 60 percent. U.S. Census, Slave Schedule, Carroll, La., Ward 1, 1860; U.S. Census, 1850; U.S. Census, 1860.

78. Stone, *Brokenburn*, May 2, 1863, 204; May 3, 1863, 205; U.S. Census, 1860. The term *"planteress"* is from the description of Amanda Stone's occupation in the U.S. Census.

79. Hattie [Harriett Elliott] to Emmie [Emily Elliott], Charleston, February [1865], Elliott-Gonzales Papers, UNC.

80. Thomas Porcher Ravenel Diaries, vol. 2, September 25, 1863, SCHS.

81. Grimball Diary, March 25, [1862], May 21, [1862], SHC.

82. [Mary Elliott] to Emmie [Emily Elliott], Beaumont, Sunday, [October] 26, [1862], Elliott-Gonzales Papers, SHC.

83. Cuthbert, *Flat Rock of the Old Time*, 31; Lockley, "The Forming and Fracturing of Families," 3.

84. Hattie [Harriett Elliott] to Emmie [Emily Elliott], Charleston, February [1865], Elliott-Gonzales Papers, SHC. Drew Gilpin Faust argues that the term *displaced persons* best describes white families forced to leave their homes by military action. Faust, *Mothers of Invention*, 40–41.

85. Faust, *Mothers of Invention*, 9–29, 43–44; Emma [Sams] to mother [Caroline Sams], Barnwell, November 28, 1861, Sams Papers, SCL.

86. H. D. D. [Rev. H. D. Duncan] to My dear Caroline [Mrs. Caroline M. Sams], November 23, 1861, Sams Papers, SCL.

87. Mother, C. M. S. [Caroline M. Sams] to My Beloved Manny [Marion W. Sams], Lawtonville, December 2, 1861, Sams Papers, SCL.

88. Grimball Diary, March 25, [1862], May 12, [1862], SHC.

89. Mother, C. M. S. [Caroline Sams] to My Beloved Manny [Marion W. Sams], Lawtonville, December 2, 1861, Sams Papers, SCL.

90. As quoted in Cuthbert, *Flat Rock of the Old Time*, 39.

91. Mary P. to Emmie [Emily Elliott], Cokesbury, April 18, [1862], Elliott-Gonzales Papers, SHC.

92. Stone, *Brokenburn*, April 24, 1863, 194; Morgan, *Civil War Diary*, 97.

93. Mother, C. M. S. [Caroline M. Sams] to My Beloved Manny [Marion W. Sams], Lawtonville, December 2, 1861, Sams Papers, SCL.

94. H. D. D. [Rev. H. D. Duncan] to My dear Caroline [Mrs. Caroline M. Sams], November 23, 1861, Sams Papers, SCL.

95. By 1864, these problems had become even more urgent. See, for example, Faust, *Mothers of Invention*, 70–71.

96. Diary of Miss Sue Richardson Recorded at "Rose Hill," Front Royal, Va., December 3, 1863, EU.

97. Diary of Miss Sue Richardson, October 1, 1863; Monday, [October] 5; Saturday, [January] 2; Thursday [April] 14, EU.

98. Diary of Sue Richardson, October 1, 1863; Monday, [October] 5; Saturday, [January] 2; Thursday, [April] 14, EU. U.S. Federal Census, 1840, 1850, 1860, 1870; U.S. Federal Census—Slave Schedules, 1850, 1860. The family owned 13 slaves in 1840, 17 in 1850, and 29 in 1860. According to the 1850 census, the family held $21,600 in real estate wealth. Richardson's son William died in battle in 1864. Richardson survived the war in better shape than many of her neighbors. In 1870, she held assets of over $22,000, but she was no longer farming on a large scale.

In 1870 Richardson emplyed one farm laborer, a young mulatto man, and one domestic servant.

99. Saville, *The Work of Reconstruction*, 12.

100. William [Elliott] to Emmie [Emily Elliott], Georgetown, January 4, 1864, Elliott-Gonzales Papers, SHC. Allston was a member of the Soldiers Board of Relief. He died in April 1864.

101. Rable, "Despair, Hope, and Delusion," quotes at 149, 138, 148, and 139.

102. Rable, *Civil Wars*, 163; Woodward, *Mary Chesnut's Civil War*, entry for March 3, 1864, 577–78. LeConte, *When the World Ended*, January 18, 1865, 12–13.

103. As quoted in Sherman, *Memoirs*, vol. 2, October 17, 1864, 635.

104. Henry Butler to Emma Butler, Hd Qrs Cooke's Brigade, near Petersburg, Va., October 10, 1864, in Huckaby and Simpson, *Tulip Evermore*, 48.

105. Ravenel, *The Private Journal of William Henry Ravenel*, December 10, [1864], p. 205.

106. F. G. DeFontaine, "Stirring Days in Chester," in *Our Women in the War*, 86.

107. F. G. DeFontaine, "Stirring Days in Chester," in *Our Women in the War*, 86–87.

108. Cumming, *Journal of Hospital Life*, entry for March 9, 1865, 169.

109. Cuthbert, *Flat Rock of the Old Time*, 43.

110. Reed, *A Faithful Heart*, 10–11, 16, 30, quotes at 16.

111. Reed, *A Faithful Heart*, entries for Friday, April 14, [1865], Saturday, April 15, [1865], and Sunday, April 9, [1865], 37, 38, 27. At the approach of Sherman's army, the Confederate printing office at Columbia had been moved to Anderson, where it was housed in the Johnson Female Seminary, founded in 1848 by Reed's father (xxviii). On the relocation of the Confederate Treasury office to Anderson, see also Russell, "Sketch of Old Confederate Treasury."

112. Rubin, *A Shattered Nation*, quote at 66.

113. Rubin, *A Shattered Nation*, 54.

114. Rable, *Civil Wars*, 154. On the impact of the mobilization for war on the gender demographics on the home front, see also Faust, *Mothers of Invention*, 30–32.

115. Edmondston, *"Journal of a Secesh Lady,"* May 7, 1865, 708.

116. Susan Leigh Blackford to Charles Blackford, March 6, 1865, in Blackford, *Letters from Lee's Army*, 282. One of the professors who hoisted the white flag was Thomas L. Preston.

117. Susan Blackford to Capt. Charles M. Blackford, March 11, 1865, in Blackford, *Letters from Lee's Army*, 287. U.S. Census, 1860, Washington, D.C. Six dormitories built in 1859 for students at the University of Virginia comprised the original Dawson's Row. On the composition of the Maury household, see U.S. Census, 1850, Ward 1, Washington, D.C., and U.S. Census, 1860, Charlottesville, St. Anne's Parish, Albemarle County.

118. On Taveau's efforts to avoid service in Virginia, see, for example, Augustin Taveau to Delphine Taveau, March 26, 1864, April 29, 1864, May 26, 1864, Augustin Louis Taveau Papers, Rubenstein Library, DU.

119. Augustin Taveau to Delphine Taveau, April 5, 1864; June 12, 1864; June 16,

1864, Augustin Louis Taveau Papers, DU. The Taveaus had moved to a farm in Abbeville, South Carolina, in late 1861 but broke up this establishment after Augustin joined the Confederate army. See Augustin Taveau to Delphine Taveau, June 12, 1864, Taveau Papers, Rubenstein Library, DU.

120. Augustin Taveau to Delphine Taveau, June 21, 1864, June 22, 1864; Elias Ball to Augustus [*sic*] Taveau, August 14, 1864, Augustin Louis Taveau Papers, Rubenstein Library, DU. See also Glymph, *Out of the House of Bondage*, 106, 126–28.

121. Mrs. Dr. Shaver of Atlanta, "War Scenes in Richmond," in *Our Women in the War*, 307; Glymph, *Out of the House of Bondage*, 97–136.

122. Hattie [Harriett Elliott] to Emmie [Emily Elliott], Charleston, February [1865], Elliott-Gonzales Papers, SHC.

123. See Faust, *Mothers of Invention*.

124. Mrs. O. T. Porcher to my dear children, April 3, 1865, Octavius Theodore Porcher Papers, 1829–73, SCL.

125. Southerners would mount no more serious filibustering or secession efforts. The South's success in securing an accommodation with the nation that allowed it to build a new nondemocratic society that would withstand constitutional challenges for decades to come played no small part in this outcome.

126. Mrs. Mary Rhodes, "War Times in Alabama," in *Our Women in the War*, 277.

127. M. [Mollie] M. Houser to Dear Cousin [James W. Houser], February 28, 1864, [Greenville, Augusta Co., Va.], John F. Houser Papers, 1863–1879, Rubenstein Library, DU. On the Houser family income, see U.S. Census, 1860; and 1870, for Samuel Houser.

128. Mary [Elliott] to Mamma [Ann Hutchinson Smith Elliott], June 8, [1862], Beaumont, Elliott-Gonzales Papers, SHC.

129. Mrs. Mary Rhodes, "War Times in Alabama," in *Our Women in the War*, 277.

130. Mrs. Mary Rhodes, "War Times in Alabama," in *Our Women in the War*, 277.

131. On the "Lost Cause," see Blight, *Race and Reunion*; Brundage, *The Southern Past*; Brundage, *Where These Memories Grow*; Cox, *Dixie's Daughters*; Foster, *Ghosts of the Confederacy*; Gallagher and Nolan, eds., *The Myth of the Lost Cause and Civil War*; Goldfield, *Still Fighting the Civil War*, and Wilson, *Baptized in Blood*.

132. Caroline Seabrook to her cousin Mary Maxcy Leverett, Hodges [Abbeville District, S.C.], July 1, 1865, in Taylor, Matthews, and Power, *The Leverett Letters*, 299.

133. Verner, *Mellowed by Time*, 24.

134. Stone, *Brokenburn*, 110.

135. Taylor, Matthews, and Power, *The Leverett Letters*, 399.

136. Cuthbert, *Flat Rock of the Old Time*, 53–54, 59–60. See also 38, 40, 43, 44, and 63. "The Reminiscences of Captain Thomas Pinckney: Postscriptum," in Cuthbert, *Flat Rock of the Old Time*, 53. Charles Cotesworth Pinckney, the owner of Piedmont, died in 1865.

137. "The Reminiscences of Captain Thomas Pinckney: Postscriptum," in

Cuthbert, *Flat Rock of the Old Time*, 54. The identification of poor whites as the culprits by former slaves may have spoken to tensions between these two groups.

138. "The Reminiscences of Captain Thomas Pinckney: Postscriptum," in Cuthbert, *Flat Rock of the Old Time*, 54, 58.

139. Grimball Diary, February 20, 1866, SHC.

140. Plantation Journal of Thomas B. Chaplin (1822–1890), January 1, 1866, in Rosengarten, *Tombee*, p. 713.

141. H. Landsdale Boardman to his parents, Sunday, June 19, 1862, Bolivar, Harpers Ferry, Landsdale Boardman Civil War Letters, 1862, NYPL.

142. Harriette H. Branham Diary, December 21, [1861], December 4, [1861], December 20, [1861], Rubenstein Library, DU.

143. Branham Diary, March 19, March 31, May 1, [1862], DU.

144. Branham Diary, [January] 31, [1862], March 8, [1862], DU.

145. December 21, [1861], Branham Diary, DU; U.S. Census, 1860 and 1870. Sarah Branham is listed in the 1860 census as a farmer with $22,300 in real estate and $16,000 in personal wealth. At her death in 1863, her daughters inherited the farm and slaves, some of whom they sold. Henrietta and Ellen each held $4,000 in real estate wealth in 1870 and $300 in personal wealth.

146. Branham Diary, January 8, 1863, DU. See also entries for February 8, 13, and 14 [1863]. On refugees, see entries for March through August 1862.

147. Faust, *Mothers of Invention*, 5.

148. As quoted in Fox-Genovese and Genovese, *The Mind of the Master Class*, 385.

149. Edmondston, *"Journal of a Secesh Lady,"* 666, 692.

150. Hammond, "Speech of James Henry Hammond," AAS.

151. Bonner, *Mastering America*; Karp, *This Vast Southern Empire*; McCurry, *Confederate Reckoning*.

152. One of its least remarked-upon consequences was the narrowing of opportunities that made possible the reproduction of the planter class. For example, it became immensely more difficult for slaveholders to endow their daughters with dowries and their sons with sufficient property to marry as they wished and marry well. For one of the most forthright sources on the war's impact on white marriages, see, for example, Grimball Diary, December 1860–February 1866, SHC.

153. LeConte, *When the World Ended*, Sunday, January 21, [1865], 14.

154. Rable, "Despair, Hope, and Delusion," 150.

155. Dew, *Apostles of Disunion*, 76, 80.

156. Woodward, *Mary Chesnut's Civil War*, entry for November 17, 1861, 238.

157. Gallagher, *The Confederate War*, 5–6, 44–45, 75–80. Gallagher cites the case of a poor white woman John J. Trowbridge encountered in Richmond in 1865 as evidence of the support of working-class women even after Appomattox. Despite her poverty and the severe wounds she suffered while working in a munitions factory, she stated that had no regrets because the cause was a "good" one (164–65).

158. W. D. [William Dudley] Gale to [Katherine Polk Gale], March 26, 1864, Gale and Polk Family Papers, 1815–1940, SHC.

159. Gallagher, *Becoming Confederates*, 2. Cumming, *Journal of Hospital Life*, 169.

160. Massey, *Refugee Life in the Confederacy*, 246.

161. Massey, *Refugee Life in the Confederacy*, 253.

162. Grimball Diary, March 8, 1862, March 25, 1862, April 1, 1862.

163. Grimball Diary, entries for March 6, [1862], and April 1, [1862], SCHS; 1860 U.S. Census for Ward 6, Charleston, S.C. U.S. Census, 1790; U.S. Census, 1820. George A. Trenholm, the son of Elizabeth Irene de Griffin Trenholm, a Haitian emigrant, and William Trenholm, was one of the wealthiest men in the antebellum South and the Confederacy. His father owned four slaves in 1790. The family's fortunes apparently declined, as the census for 1820 lists no slaves owned by William Trenholm. This may have accounted for his son's decision to leave school and take a job as a clerk with Fraser & Company, the firm he would take over in 1854. Renamed Fraser & Trenholm, it became one of the most powerful merchant firms in the South. By 1860, George Trenholm owned real estate worth $90,000, personal property worth $35,000, and thirty-nine enslaved people labored in his Charleston home alone. Trenholm's investments included steamships, hotels, wharves, and plantations. His commercial house had branches in New York and Liverpool. The latter proved instrumental during the war when he ran a successful blockade-running enterprise with sixty vessels making millions of dollars. Clark, *Last Train South*, 32; Nepveau, *George Alfred Trenholm: The Company That Went to War*; Nepveau, *George A. Trenholm, Financial Genius of the Confederacy*.

On Fraser & Company, see Hagy, *Charleston, South Carolina City Directories*. Trenholm was appointed secretary of the Confederate Treasury Department in July 1864 and was arrested by the Union in June 1865. By 1870 he had recovered much of his wealth to the tune of $300,000. U.S. Census, 1870.

164. Woodward and Muhlenfeld, *The Private Mary Chesnut*, entry for [March 18, 1861], 42.

CHAPTER TWO

1. Furry, *The Preacher's Tale*, 100.

2. Furry, *The Preacher's Tale*, 100, 71–75. Although Springer included Native Americans in his appeal for help, he saw them as an inherently inferior people. He described a group of Indian families he encountered while on a march with soldiers from the fort as "frightened & deluded creatures, toiling along the dusty road with their crazy wagons & lazy oxen," "a pitiable spectacle of human degradation."

3. Sterkx, *Partners in Rebellion*, 142.

4. On the politics of poor Southern women, see esp. Bynum, *Unruly Women*. On the politics of yeoman farmers and nonslaveholding white people, see Hahn, *The Roots of Southern Populism*; McCurry, *Masters of Small Worlds*.

5. Boddie, *History of Williamsburg*, 365.

6. McCurry, *Confederate Reckoning*, 135; Wm. W. Hooke to Robert Hooke, Burke's Mills, Va., July 4, 1861, Robert W. Hooke Papers, Rubenstein Library, DU.

7. Eliza Fulgham to [President Davis], November 11, 1863, in Crist, Williams, and Dillard, *The Papers of Jefferson Davis*, 10:65.

8. On the phrase "domestic sanctuaries," see chapter 1.

9. Fields, "Slavery, Race and Ideology," 111; Woodman, "The Profitability of Slavery," 304.

10. Ayers, *In the Presence of Mine Enemies*, 162–63.

11. Furry, *The Preacher's Tale*, 53. See also, Ash, *When the Yankees Came*; Fellman, *Inside War*; Sutherland, *Guerrillas, Unionists, and Violence*; Sutherland, *A Savage Conflict*; and Whites and Long, *Occupied Women*.

12. Bynum, *Unruly Women*, quote at 149; McCurry, *Confederate Reckoning*. A large body of scholarship has explored the question of class divisions and dissent in the Confederate South. Much of this discussion has focused on the impact of class divisions on the defeat of the Confederacy. See, for example, Blair, *Virginia's Private War*; Ayers, *In the Presence of Mine Enemies*.

13. Phillips, "The Origin and Growth of the Southern Black Belts"; Hahn, *The Roots of Southern Populism*; Burton and McMath, *Class, Conflict, and Consensus*; Johnson, *Toward a Patriarchal Republic*; Thornton, *Politics and Power in a Slave Society*; Ford, *Origins of Southern Radicalism*.

14. Faust, *Mothers of Invention*, 40.

15. "Editorial," *Daily Journal* (Wilmington, N.C.), April 17, 1862, North Carolina Collection, Wilson Library, SHC. The act extended the terms of currently enrolled soldiers to three years from the date of enlistment and made all white male citizens of states in the Confederacy between the ages of eighteen and thirty-five subject to national military service for a term of three years. It also included the unpopular provision that allowed men subject to conscription to hire a substitute from the ranks of those normally exempt leading to controversy over the categories of exemption and charges of widespread abuse. The exemption granted to slaveholders or overseers of plantations with twenty or more slaves proved the most objectionable. A law passed in January 1864 required that men who had hired substitutes report for duty either as volunteers or inductees.

16. Lockley, "The Forming and Fracturing of Families," 5. In 1860, Andrew Johnstone's property real estate was valued at $125,000 and his personal estate at $150,000. U.S. Census, 1860; Cuthbert, *Flat Rock of the Old Time*, 2–3. The Barings founded St. John in the Wilderness Episcopal Church (the oldest Episcopal church in western North Carolina), which became the church of the lowcountry elite in the mountains. Susan Baring became the focus of much gossip among planter families in the lowcountry. Her brother-in law accused her of "luring" her first husband, the wealthy James Heyward, into marriage. The marriage deprived James's brother of a substantial inheritance and, hoping to find a way to invalidate it, he sent an investigator to London to pry into Baring's background. Baring inherited three plantations in the lowcountry from James Heyward, but the questions raised by her brother-in-law about her lineage and morals apparently resulted in her being ostracized by some lowcountry families and triggered a permanent

move to Flat Rock (Cuthbert, *Flat Rock of the Old Time*, 3–4). After her death in 1846, her second husband remarried and moved with his new wife, Constance Radcliff Dent, to the Colleton, South Carolina, plantation that had belonged to Susan prior to their marriage. He was back in Henderson, N.C., at the time of the 1860 census. Susan Baring Will, 1845, Henderson, North Carolina, Wills and Probate Records, Ancestry.com. https://search.ancestry.com/cgi-bin/sse.dll?dbid=9061&h =639540&indiv=try&o_vc=Record:OtherRecord&rhSource=60525; U.S. Census, 1850, St. Paul's, Parish, Colleton, S.C.; U.S. Census, 1860.

17. Blackmun, *Western North Carolina*; Cuthbert, *Flat Rock of the Old Time*, 12, 16, 234–35.

18. Woodward and Muhlenfeld, *The Private Mary Chesnut*, entry for [June 3–4, 1861], 77–78.

19. Porcher, "Historical and Social Sketch of Craven County," 129. The slaveholders from Charleston with places at Flat Rock included Judge Mitchell King, who had donated the land for the county seat at Hendersonville and was one of Andrew Johnstone's business partners. See also Inscoe, *Mountain Masters*, 33.

20. See, for example, Glymph, "Rose's War."

21. Mary [Elliott Johnstone] to Mamma [Ann Elliott], Beaumont, August 3, 1862, Elliott-Gonzales Papers, SHC.

22. Earlier migrations to the mountains were facilitated by the completion in 1827 of the Buncombe Turnpike, which linked Greenville, S.C., to Buncombe County. Within a few years it extended to Asheville, North Carolina, and Greenville, Tennessee. The town of Hendersonville was laid out on seventy-nine acres near Mud Creek on land donated primarily by Judge Mitchell King of Flat Rock and Charleston. King, who owned twenty-two slaves in 1840, died at Flat Rock in November 1862. Mountain towns like Flat Rock also attracted a small class of merchants, clerks, lawyers, and other professionals. Inscoe, *Mountain Masters*, 25–58; Lockley, "The Forming and Fracturing of Families," 5.

23. Mary [Elliott Johnstone] to Mamma [Ann Elliott], Beaumont, July 13, [1862], Elliott-Gonzales Papers, SHC.

24. U.S. Federal Census, 1860, Slave Schedules, Prince George Parish, Division 2, Georgetown, S.C.; Wm. C. Johnstone, "Memorandum and Evaluation of Property," State of South Carolina: Georgetown District, January 8, 1863, Confederate Citizens File, Fold3 Database. Confederate treasury secretary George A. Trenholm purchased the Annandale plantation in 1863; National Register of Historic Places, Registration Form, Annandale Plantation, Georgetown County, S.C., September 18, 1973, http:// www.nationalregister.sc.gov/georgetown/S10817722007/S10817722007.pdf.

25. Mary [Elliott Johnstone] to Mamma [Ann Elliott], Beaumont, August 3, [1862], Elliott-Gonzales Papers, SHC. Johnstone referred to the whites as "natives" on other occasions as well, writing later in the same letter, for example, that "the natives are so vexed at the conscript they are trying to get some excitement—but Mr. L is quite confident in his ability to protect his property, so I don't feel at all uneasy."

26. Woodward and Muhlenfeld, *The Private Mary Chesnut*, entry for [November 18, 1861], 203; Nomination for Flat Rock Historic District, Office of Archives and History Department of Cultural Resources, N.C. State Historical Preservation Office, National Register of Historic Places, Flat Rock Historic District, Boundary Increase, Boundary Decrease, and Additional Documentation, https://www.ncdcr .gov/press-release/national-register-adds-18-north-carolina-places. Farmer's Hotel opened in 1850, financed by ten summer residents who contributed $1,000 each. Mary Chesnut visited Catherine Miller at Dunroy in August and September 1862; Woodward and Muhlenfeld, *The Private Mary Chesnut*, 218.

27. Mary [Elliott Johnstone] to Mamma [Ann Elliott], Beaumont, July 13, [1862], Elliott-Gonzales Papers, SHC; quote from Cuthbert, *Flat Rock of the Old Time*, 62.

28. Cuthbert, *Flat Rock of the Old Time*, 23.

29. Cuthbert, *Flat Rock of the Old Time*, 40.

30. Saville, *The Work of Reconstruction*, 12.

31. Mother [Frances Ann Devereux Polk] to my dear child [Katherine Polk Gale], August 19, [1862], [before 1863] [*sic*]; Mother [Frances Ann Devereux Polk] to [Katherine Polk Gale], July 12, 1863; Mother [Frances Ann Devereux Polk] to Harriett Polk, November 27, 1863; Mother [Frances Devereux Polk] to my dear Kate [Katherine Polk Gale], Asheville, December 17, [1862]; "Recollections of Katherine Polk Gale," undated, 32, 34, 35, 36, 46, 47; Gale and Polk Family Papers, 1815–1940, SHC. Inscoe and McKinney, *The Heart of Confederate Appalachia*, 5; Cashin, *A Family Venture*; Massey, *Refugee Life*, 272–73

32. Cuthbert, *Flat Rock of the Old Time*, 57–58, quote at 57.

33. Ralph [Elliott] to Mrs. A. H. Elliott, Charleston, June 15, 1864, Elliott-Gonzales Papers, SHC. Andrew Johnstone was also able to fire a round of shots at the men before he died. See Cuthbert, *Flat Rock of the Old Time*, 53–58; and Inscoe and McKinney, *The Heart of Confederate Appalachia*, 128–29.

34. Cuthbert, *Flat Rock of the Old Time*, 27–28; Harriott Middleton to Susan Miller, August 7, 1862, August 19, 1862 in Cuthbert, *Flat Rock of the Old Time*, 27, 28. Harriott Middleton and Mary Johnstone were sisters.

35. Ralph [Elliott] to Dearest Mother [Ann Elliott], Charleston, June 15, 1864, Elliott-Gonzales Family Papers, SHC.

36. Taylor, Matthews, and Power, *The Leverett Letters*, 322, 335.

37. Augustin Taveau to Delphine Taveau, June 16, 1864, Augustin Louis Taveau Papers, Rubenstein Library, DU.

38. Cuthbert, *Flat Rock of the Old Time*, 41, 52, 53.

39. Cuthbert, *Flat Rock of the Old Time*, 59.

40. Cuthbert, *Flat Rock of the Old Time*, 53.

41. Taylor, Matthews, and Power, *The Leverett Letters*, 131; Inscoe and McKinney, *The Heart of Confederate Appalachia*, 6.

42. Zebulon Vance, "Proclamation against Deserters," May 11, 1863, in Mobley, *The Papers of Zebulon Baird Vance*, 2:27–29. Vance and other Southern governors

continued to rail against deserters until the end. See Rable, "Despair, Hope, and Delusion," 148.

43. Cuthbert, *Flat Rock of the Old Time*, 43, 46–47. I found no evidence that this rebellion ever materialized.

44. Captain Blackford to Mrs. Blackford, January 18, 1865, in Blackford, *Letters from Lee's Army*, 232–33.

45. A Charleston Woman, "In the Cradle of the War," in *Our Women in the War*, 282.

46. A Charleston Woman, "In the Cradle of the War," in *Our Women in the War*, 282.

47. Hahn, "The 'Unmaking' of the Southern Yeomanry." Hahn, *The Roots of Southern Populism*.

48. Mrs. Blackford, University [University of Virginia], March 6, 1865, in Blackford, *Letters from Lee's Army*, 280.

49. Stone, *Brokenburn*, 238.

50. Hundley, *Social Relations in Our Southern States*, 262, 264, 251.

51. Mary [Elliott Johnstone] to Mamma [Ann Elliott], Beaumont, July 13, [1862], Elliott-Gonzales Papers, SHC.

52. Bynum, *Unruly Women*, 133–35; Massey, *Ersatz in the Confederacy*, 55–73.

53. Wm. W. Hooke to Robert Hooke, Burke's Mills, Gloucester, Va., July 4, 1861, Robert W. Hooke Papers, Rubenstein Library, DU.

54. Johnston, *The Papers of Zebulon Baird Vance*, 1:308.

55. Kimball, "The Bread Riot in Richmond," quotes at 150, 152, and 153. For a fuller discussion, see McCurry, *Confederate Reckoning*.

56. Gertrude Thomas Journal, entry for April 4, 1862, Atlanta, Rubenstein Library, DU.

57. Massey, *Refugee Life in the Confederacy*, 242–62, quote at 244.

58. E. A. Catron to [John Catron], November 20, 1861, in Metcalf, *The Irrepressible Conflict*, 3; U.S. Census, 1860. This letter was one of many that soldiers from each side took from the battlefield. It was found in a rebel camp at Roanoke Island and appears to have been taken by or ended up in the hands of Private Edwin M. Wheelock of the Twenty-Fifth Regiment, Massachusetts Infantry, which fought at the Battle of Roanoke in February 1862.

59. E. A. Catron to [John Catron], November 20, 1861, in Metcalf, *The Irrepressible Conflict*, 3.

60. Johnston, *The Papers of Zebulon Baird Vance*, vol. 1, 308; McCurry, *Confederate Reckoning*, 133–77.

61. McCurry, *Confederate Reckoning*, 135, 178–217, quote at 135.

62. McCurry, *Confederate Reckoning*, 135; Massey, "The Free Market of New Orleans," 201–5, 208, 210, 216, quote at 204; Massey, *Women in the Civil War*, 170–71. Rhodes, "War Times in Alabama," 276. Free markets were established in Memphis, Natchez, Charleston, Montgomery, Atlanta, Mobile, and Richmond modeled

after the New Orleans program, but the markets in Richmond and Mobile were established after the riots in those cities. Interestingly, a fancy ball organized by a black porter raised over $600 to contribute to the New Orleans fund. Massey, "The Free Market of New Orleans," 212–13.

63. Deiler, *The Settlement of the German Coast*; Forsyth, *German "Pest Ships."*

64. U.S. Census, 1860, First Ward, New Orleans; U.S. Census, 1860, Eleventh Ward, New Orleans.

65. [George S. Denison] to Jimmy, Custom House New Orleans, July 6, 1862, Denison Papers, LOC. By October 1862, the local relief board in Charleston supported some 600 families. See McCurry, *Confederate Reckoning*, 194, 198, 201–6.

66. Denison to Jimmy, July 6, 1862, Denison Papers, LOC.

67. Bynum, *Unruly Women*, 145–46, 148.

68. McCurry, *Confederate Reckoning*, 133–77, 178–217, quotes at 179, 180, 185, and 198. On bread riots in the North, see Massey, *Women in the Civil War*, 171–72.

69. McCurry, *Confederate Reckoning*, 180–85, quotes at 185, 180 and 182, respectively.

70. McCurry, *Confederate Reckoning*, 191. The tactics soldiers' wives adopted—from the strategies of mobilization to the kinds of weapons used to the strategic invocation of the war as a rich man's war—also ironically echoed those used in the best-known urban slave rebellions.

71. McCurry, *Confederate Reckoning*, 191.

72. Anna O. [Oswald] to Dear Sister, Wednesday, November 20, 1861, Sams Papers, SCL.

73. Massey, "The Free Market of New Orleans," 215; Rowland and Croxall, *The Journal of Julia Le Grand*, 38.

74. Mrs. Mary Rhodes, "War Times in Alabama," in *Our Women in the War*, 276. See also Bynum, *Unruly Women*, 145–47.

75. Rhodes, "War Times in Alabama," 276.

76. Rhodes, "War Times in Alabama," 276.

77. Rhodes, "War Times in Alabama," 276; Massey, "The Free Market of New Orleans," 215.

78. "War Reminiscences of Alicia Hopton Middleton, 1865," entries undated, Middleton Family Papers, 1820–65, SCHS; Diary of Sue Richardson, entries for November 2, 1863, November 3, 1863, January 16, 1864, April 14, 1864, and April 19, 1864, EU.

79. On desertion in the Confederacy, see Moore, *Conscription and Conflict in the Confederacy*; Ramsdell, *Behind the Lines in the Southern Confederacy*; Robinson, *Bitter Fruits of Bondage*; Sheehan-Dean, *Why Confederates Fought*, 92–97, 145–47; Tatum, *Disloyalty in the Confederacy*; and Wesley, *Collapse of the Confederacy*.

80. Rhodes, "War Times in Alabama," 276–77.

81. Rhodes, "War Times in Alabama," 276–77.

82. Minutes of Greenville Ladies' Association, Saturday, October 3, [1862]; November 28, [1864], Rubenstein Library, DU.

83. Minutes of Greenville Ladies' Association. August 13, [1862], August 27, [1862], September 17, [1862], January 3, 1863, April 17, [1865], Rubenstein Library, DU. At its general meeting on October 4, 1862, the organization also appropriated $1,000 for hospitals in Virginia.

84. Rhodes, "War Times in Alabama," 276–77.

85. Henry Lea Graves to mother [Sarah Graves], Steamer *Savannah*, Savannah, Ga., August 20, 1863, Wartime Letters, 1861–1865, of Henry L. Graves, C.S.A., Mt. Pleasant, Newton County, Ga., One Time Private, Army of Northern Virginia, Later, Lieutenant of Marines (typescript copy), Graves Family Papers, EU.

86. Huckaby and Simpson, *Tulip Evermore*, 35. The North Carolina soldiers were from Daniel's Brigade, commanded by Junius Daniel, a West Point graduate from Halifax County. The Arkansas soldiers belonged to the Third Regiment, Arkansas Infantry.

87. Huckaby and Simpson, *Tulip Evermore*, 35, 41, 45.

88. Robinson, *Bitter Fruits of Bondage*, quotes at 68 and 77.

89. Robinson, *Bitter Fruits of Bondage*, 77.

90. Bynum, *Unruly Women*, 143. See also Ash, *When the Yankees Came*; Fellman, *Inside War*; Paludan, *A People's Contest*; Sutherland, *Guerrillas, Unionists, and Violence*; Sutherland, *A Savage Conflict*; and Whites and Long, *Occupied Women*.

91. Myers, *Rebels against the Confederacy*, 121. Yokely and a party of Unionists rescued the men. On Chloe Yokely, see U.S. Census, 1850 and 1870.

92. U.S. Census, 1860. https://www.measuringworth.com/calculators/uscompare /relativevalue.php.

93. Barrett, *The Civil War in North Carolina*, 184–201, quotes at 185.

94. Bynum, *Unruly Women*, 142.

95. [Mary Elliott Johnstone] to [Ann Elliott], Beaumont, July 13, [1862]; Mary [Elliott] to Mamma [Ann Elliott], August 3, [1862], Elliott-Gonzales Papers, SHC.

96. Bynum, *Unruly Women*, 130, see generally 130–50. See also McCurry, *Confederate Reckoning*, 124–26. Estimates of desertions of North Carolina soldiers range from 14,000 to 23,000.

97. Younce, *The Adventures of a Conscript*, 2, 4, 9.

98. Robinson, *Bitter Fruits of Bondage*, 80.

99. Robinson, *Bitter Fruits of Bondage*, 81–83.

100. Robinson, *Bitter Fruits of Bondage*, 140–41.

101. Bynum, *Unruly Women*, 144.

102. Younce, *The Adventures of a Conscript*, 58.

103. Robinson, *Bitter Fruits of Bondage*, 140–41; Glymph, *Out of the House of Bondage*, 128–29.

104. For an in-depth discussion of this point, see McCurry, *Confederate Reckoning*.

105. Robinson, *Bitter Fruits of Bondage*, 58–83, quote at 61.

106. Edmondston, *"Journal of a Secesh Lady,"* 243. Edmondston does reference the Lamentations on at least one occasion (69).

107. Rable, *Civil Wars*, 159.

108. Bynum, *Unruly Women*, 131, 133.

109. Bynum, *Unruly Women*, 132, 144–45.

110. Edmondston, *"Journal of a Secesh Lady,"* February 10, 1861, April 11, 1865, 35, 691–92.

111. Faust, *Mothers of Invention*, 234–54, quote at 238.

112. Sterkx, *Partners in Rebellion*, 243–46.

113. G. B. Fleece Supt. to Maj. A. [Albert] S. Smith, January 2, 1862, Bowling Green, Memphis & New Orleans Steam Packet Co., Bidders, vol. 20, p. 37, Confederate Papers Relating to Citizens or Business Firms, [Citizens File], roll 0677, compiled 1874–1899, documenting the period 1861–1865, RG 109, NARA, Fold3 Database.

114. Minutes of Greenville Ladies' Association, September 18, [1862], Rubenstein Library, DU. The women called on a prominent local man to protest on their behalf.

115. Harriott Middleton to Susan Middleton, February 29, 1864, March 4, 1864, in Cuthbert, *Flat Rock of the Old Time*, quotes at 48, 49.

116. Harriott Middleton to Susan Middleton, March 10, 1864, April 2, 1864, in Cuthbert, *Flat Rock of the Old Time*, 48–52, quotes at 49, 50, 52.

117. Lt. Col. Daniel F. Griffin, letter to his wife, October 22, 1864, in Funk, "A Hoosier Regiment in Alabama," 92. Hood replaced Joseph E. Johnston as commander of Army of Tennessee on July 17, 1864, while Johnston was fighting the Battle of Atlanta. On September 2, Sherman occupied Atlanta and Hood retreated to mountains of northwest Georgia and then into Alabama.

118. Rable, *Civil Wars*, 159.

119. Baptist, *Creating an Old South*, 277.

120. Bynum, *Unruly Women*, 131.

121. Edmondston, *"Journal of a Secesh Lady,"* July 8, 1861, 87, 88.

122. War Reminiscences of Alicia Hopton Middleton, 1865, SCHS; Mississippi Valley Sanitary Fair, Freedmen and Union Refugees Department of the Mississippi Valley Sanitary Fair, St. Louis, Mo., March 17, 1864. Digital Collections, U.S. National Library of Medicine, Bethesda, Maryland, https://collections.nlm.nih.gov /ext/mhl/101156144/PDF/101156144.pdf. Alicia Hopton Middleton's mother, Anna Elizabeth DeWolf Middleton, was a member of the famous slave-trading family of Bristol, Rhode Island, with whom she remained in contact during the war.

CHAPTER THREE

1. LeConte, *When the World Ended*, entry for January 18, [1865], 12–13, On the commodification of black bodies, see, for example, Berry, *The Price for Their Pound of Flesh*; Johnson, *River of Dark Dreams*; Johnson, *Soul by Soul*.

2. Sterling, *We Are Your Sisters*, 244.

3. Mrs. Mary Rhodes, "War Times in Alabama," in *Our Women in the War*, 277.

4. Stone, *Brokenburn*, 170–71, 180. Jane was believed to have attempted to slowly poison Stone's aunt.

5. The only full-length study of black women in the Civil War examines their experience "through the prism of the experience and actions of African men." Black women, Ella Forbes asserts, "would not have found this insulting. Rather, they achieved a certain nobility by playing a supporting role to their husbands, fathers, sons, and brothers." Forbes, *African American Women during the Civil War*, vii.

6. Giesberg, *Army at Home*, 9; Ginzberg, *Untidy Origins*, 10, 12; Brown, "Negotiating and Transforming the Public Sphere." On slaves' politics, see Du Bois, *Black Reconstruction*; Hahn, *A Nation under Our Feet*, 13–61; Hahn, *The Political Worlds of Slavery and Freedom*, 1–114.

7. McGuire, *Diary of a Southern Refugee*, entries for May 29, 1861, and October 3, 1862, 22, 164.

8. Dr. George Washington Buckner, *Indiana Narratives*, vol. 6, pp. 28, 30, quote at 28. Buckner became a medical doctor and served as a diplomat to Haiti in 1913. The narrator mentions that Buckner is a mulatto and learns that his siblings are as well. It is possible that both his grandmother, who was the cook for the plantation owner's family, and his mother may have been raped by a white man. For information on the military service of William Buckner and John Buckner, see the NPS Soldiers and Sailors Database, https://www.nps.gov/civilwar/soldiers-and -sailors-database.htm. On the health of enslaved women, see Fett, *Working Cures*; Schwartz, *Birthing a Slave*; Savitt, *Medicine and Slavery*; Owens, *Medical Bondage*.

9. The phrase is from Burkhead, *History of the Difficulties of the Pastorate of the Front Street Methodist Church*, 44. Burkhead was appointed pastor to Front Street in 1865 only to confront massive resistance to his leadership from the church's overwhelming black majority membership. The black church leaders labeled him a rebel preacher and demanded full control of the church.

10. Royster, *The Destructive War*, quote at 344; Glymph, *Out of the House of Bondage*, 106.

11. George Washington Albright, *Mississippi Narratives*, supp., ser. 1, vol. 6, pt. 1, p. 11. For additional information on Albright, see Hahn, *A Nation under Our Feet*, 41, 223.

12. Bruce, *The New Man*, 85–86, 99–100, quotes at 86, 99, and 100; Wilson Temple, *Mississippi Narratives*, supp., ser. 1, vol. 10, pt. 5, p. 2372.

13. *OR*, ser. 1, vol. 51, pt. 1, p. 384. The repression of the attempted insurrection came in the immediate aftermath of Arkansas's formal admission to the Confederacy on May 18, 1861. Arkansas passed a secession ordinance on May 6. Long, *The Civil War Day by Day*, 70, 75.

14. Colored Women's Union Relief Association of Newbern, North Carolina, Edward W. Kinsley Papers Correspondence; Edward W. Kinsley Papers, 1863–91, Rubenstein Library, DU; Joseph E. Williams to Edward Kinsley, August 19, 1863;

James J. Holbrook to Edward Kinsley, September 3, 1863; Holbrook to Mrs. [Calista] Kinsley, September 12, 1863, Edward W. Kinsley Papers, 1863–91; Special Collections and University Archives, University of Massachusetts. See also Cecelski, *The Fire of Freedom*, 69–70, 86–89; Glymph, "I'm a Radical Girl."

15. Liza Strickland, *Mississippi Narratives*, supp., ser. 1, vol. 10, pt. 5, p. 2066; Litwack, *Been in the Storm So Long*, 18–21.

16. Taylor, *Reminiscences of My Life in Camp*, 31–32.

17. Chana Littlejohn, *North Carolina Narratives*, vol. 15, pt. 2, p. 58; Minnie Davis, *Georgia Narratives*, vol. 12, pt. 1, p. 257; Temple Wilson, *Mississippi Narratives*, supp., ser. 1, vol. 10, pt. 5, p 2373; Litwack, *Been in the Storm So Long*, 21–27. The extent to which slaves kept apprised of news cannot be precisely determined, but many remembered newspapers as an important source of information and the risk that reading them entailed. Indeed, as Union victories occupied more and more Southern territory and cut rail communications, large sections of the South were almost completely cut off from communications. Newspapers were even more treasured, and in an ironic twist, slaveholders increasingly relied on the enslaved people's communications networks for information on everything from troop movements and the outcome of battles to the fate of relatives.

18. Mary Anne Patterson, *Texas Narratives*, vol. 5, pt. 3, p. 171.

19. Hanna Fambro, *Ohio Narratives*, vol. 5, p. 341; "The Story of a Contraband," *Minnesota Narratives*, supp., ser. 1, vol. 2, pp. 125–28, quote at 125.

20. Robert J. Cheatham, *Indiana Narratives*, vol. 5, p. 48; Cindy Mitchell, *Mississippi Narratives*, supp., ser. 1, vol. 9, pt. 4, p. 1511.

21. Henry Webb, *Indiana Narratives*, vol. 5, p. 232. According to the narrative of Ben Wall, Union soldiers stopped sacking the home of a Confederate woman after she gave the Masonic sign. Ben Wall, *Mississippi Narratives*, vol. 10, pt. 5, pp. 2163. The headmistress of a girls' school, Barhamville Academy in Columbia, S.C., is said to have saved the school by placing a Masonic emblem on its door. Massey, *Women in the Civil War*, 228. See also Wiley, *The Life of Billy Yank*, 357.

22. William Irving, *Texas Narratives*, supp., ser. 2, vol. 5, pt. 4, pp. 1869–74; cited passages, 1866–67. See also Fields, *Slavery and Freedom on the Middle Ground*, 90–130. William Irving's narrative on the political views of Alexander Stephens and the organization of the Confederate government is one of the most detailed slave narratives on the Confederate state.

23. Holland, *Letters and Diary of Laura M. Towne*, May 12, 1862, 58.

24. Holland, *Letters and Diary of Laura M. Towne*, April 28, 1862, 27–28.

25. For recent work on fugitive slaves, see Blackett, *The Captive's Quest for Freedom*; and Sinha, *The Slave's Cause*, 381–420.

26. Bacon and Howland, *Letters of a Family*, vol. 1, March 1859, 12–14, 8–9; Thomson, "A Great Slave Auction." See also Bailey, *The Weeping Time*.

27. Bailey, *The Weeping Time*.

28. Thomson, "A Great Slave Auction." On slave market valuations, see Berry, *The Price for Their Pound of Flesh*; Johnson, *Soul by Soul*.

29. Johnson, *Soul by Soul*, 162–88, quotes at 176 and 164.

30. Simkins and Roland, *A History of the South*, 19. Scholars have cited various versions of this quote. See, for example, Genovese, *Roll, Jordan, Roll*, 456.

31. Holland, *Letters and Diary of Laura M. Towne*, 32.

32. On slaveholding women and the slave market, see Jones-Rogers, "Nobody Couldn't Sell 'Em but Her."

33. Dave Lawson, *North Carolina Narratives*, vol. 15, pt. 2, p. 46–50.

34. Victoria Perry, *South Carolina Narratives*, vol. 3, pt. 3, pp. 260–61.

35. Lulu Wilson, *Texas Narratives*, vol. 5, pt. 4, pp. 191–92; Lulu Wilson, *Texas Narratives*, supp. ser. 2, vol. 10, pt. 9, p. 4194. Wilson's narrative appears in two volumes of the WPA narratives.

36. Fannie Moore, *North Carolina Narratives*, vol. 15, pt. 2, pp. 130–31; Celia Robinson, *North Carolina Narratives*, vol. 15, pt. 2, pp. 218–19.

37. Schwalm, *A Hard Fight for We*, 93.

38. Holland, *Letters and Diary of Laura M. Towne*, 34.

39. Holland, *Letters and Diary of Laura M. Towne*, 27.

40. *ORN*, ser. 1, vol. 20, p. 721.

41. *ORN*, ser. 1, vol. 24, p. 494. On one plantation, a woman slaveholder, Mrs. Messenger, took the rare stand of refusing to allow the Confederate military forces to put enslaved people on her plantation to work placing obstacles in the river to block Union vessels, and she paid a price. Confederate forces burned her cotton and seized and sold her furniture. They further "stigmatized her as a Yankee, and her relatives by marriage (though the rankest rebels in the country) could do nothing for her."

42. *ORN*, ser. 1, vol. 20, p. 798.

43. Sterling, *We Are Your Sisters*, 238–39.

44. *ORN*, ser. 1, vol. 24, p. 494.

45. Report of Col. R. D. Massey, Colonel, 100th USCT, Commissioner, Organization Colored Troops, Nashville, Tenn., Headquarters Commissioner Organization U.S. Colored Troops, August 14, 1864, in Hood and Bostwick, "Report of the Commissioners of Investigation of Colored Refugees," in Senate Executive Documents for the Second Session of the Thirty-Eight Congress of the United States of America, 1864–'65, 17.

46. "The Story of a Contraband," *Minnesota Narratives*, supp., ser. 1, vol. 2, p. 125.

47. Elizabeth Russell, *Indiana and Ohio Narratives*, supp., ser. 1, vol. 5, p. 180.

48. Caroline Richardson, *North Carolina Narratives*, vol. 15, pt. 2, 199.

49. Bruce, *The New Man*, 99–100.

50. George Washington Albright, *Mississippi Narratives*, supp., ser. 1, vol. 6, pt. 1, pp. 11–12. The Loyal League that Albright remembered was a precursor to the Union League movement organized during the war to build morale in opposition to the copperhead movement and became a major political arm of the Republican Party in the postbellum South. Albright was correct in his understanding that the league was organized at the behest of President Lincoln to inform the slaves

about the Emancipation Proclamation. Frederick Douglass recalled the meeting at which the president made the request and agreeing "at his suggestion . . . to undertake the organizing a band of scouts, composed of colored men, whose business should be somewhat after the original plan of John Brown, to go into the rebel states, beyond the lines of our armies, and carry the news of emancipation, and urge the slaves to come within our boundaries." The course of the war and the success of Union forces quickly rendered the plan moot, Douglass wrote. Albright's testimony, however, reveals that in some places the plan did go forward. Douglass, *Life and Times of Frederick Douglass*, 358–59. Albright also believed the idea had originated with a committee of six composed of Douglass, John Langston, James Lynch, Henry Ward Beecher, Charles Sumner, and Harriet Beecher Stowe. Albright, *Mississippi Narratives*, supp., ser. 1, vol. 6, pt. 1, pp. 12–13.

51. Edmondston, *"Journal of a Secesh Lady,"* entry for August 6, 1862, 232; *OR*, ser. 1, vol. 2, p. 966. The man to whom C. R. B. was enslaved was on the staff of Confederate general J. B. Magruder, who enclosed the letter in a report to Col. George Deas, assistant adjutant general of Richmond, on July 7, 1861, clearly not heeding the advice to burn the letter after reading. *OR*, ser. 1, vol. 2, pp. 964–66.

52. Hodge, *The Civil War Diary of Betty Herndon Maury*, April 25, 1862, p. 52; Faust, *Mothers of Invention*, 57–60; George Johnson, *Minnesota Narratives*, supp., ser. 1, vol. 2, pp. 116–17. George Johnson's father regularly hauled grits from Missouri across the state line to Iowa and used the wagon and the knowledge of the geography and the habits of white people on his route to get his family out of slavery. The family's escape reminds us that there were many people like Robert Smalls who used their knowledge of land, sea, rivers, and white people to escape slavery. Smalls famously steered a boat past Confederate sentries in the Charleston harbor to Union lines with his and another enslaved family on board.

53. Dicy Windfield, *Mississippi Narratives*, supp., ser. 1, vol. 10, pt. 5, pp. 2382–85, quote at 2382; Hattie Rogers, *North Carolina Narratives*, vol. 15, pt. 2, pp. 227–29. Charles Minor Blackford, the officer for whom John Scott worked, noted that he and Scott were reading William Francis Patrick Napier's popular six-volume *History of the Peninsula Wars*, published between 1828 and 1840. It was "very curious literature for a negro servant," Blackford wrote without further comment. Charles Minor Blackford Journal, January 18, 1864, in Blackford, *Letters from Lee's Army*, 233.

54. Numerous slave narratives document this point. See, for example, the account of Millie Williams, *Mississippi Narratives*, supp., ser. 1, vol. 10, pt. 5, p. 2349; Wright Stapleton, *Mississippi Narratives*, supp., ser. 1, vol. 10, pt. 5, p. 2023; *North Carolina Narratives*, vol. 15, pt. 2, pp. 346–47; see also, Berlin, Reidy, and Rowland, *The Black Military Experience*, 234.

55. Jane Williams, *Mississippi Narratives*, supp., ser. 1, vol. 10, pt. 5, pp. 23–24; Patsy Mitchner, *North Carolina Narratives*, vol. 15, pt. 2, p. 119.

56. Taylor, *Reminiscences of My Life in Camp*, 31–32.

57. Edward Jones, *Mississippi Narratives*, supp., ser. 1, vol. 8, pt. 3, p. 1207. Making

Lincoln the son of an African queen may have had special meaning. In the slave narratives, slaves who are of direct African descent are revered and often depicted as rebels. Ann Parker stated that she had no father because her mother had been a queen in Africa and "queens doan marry." The other slaves, Parker stated, always bowed to her mother after she told them and adhered to her mother's admonition about telling white people who she was and bowing in the presence of the owners. So, "when de is out of sight of de white folkses dey bows down ter her an' does what she says." Ann Parker, *North Carolina Narratives*, vol. 15, pp. 156–57; see also Lucy Galloway, *Mississippi Narratives*, supp., ser. 1, vol. 8, pt. 3, pp. 803–4, 807–8; Virginia Newman, *Texas Narratives*, vol. 5, pt. 3, p. 148. Also interesting are the reported sightings of Lincoln. Lincoln did not travel in the South during the war, but several ex-slaves reported that he had come to talk with them or had appeared in the South in various disguises before and during the war. Elizabeth Russell claimed to have met Lincoln in Atlanta while he was on a "secret" tour of the South before the war, at which time, she stated, he told her he hoped that black people would one day be free. Sam Mitchel insisted that President Lincoln had come to Beaufort, S.C., before the war and had dinner with Col. Paul Hamilton at the Oaks plantation. This too was a secret trip. No one knew he had been there, Mitchel stated, until he wrote asking for the return of a gold-headed walking cane left behind. Charlie Davenport stated that Lincoln had come to Mississippi and gone "all through de country jest a rantin and preachin 'bout us bein his black brudders. Old Marse didn't know nothing 'bout it 'cause hit was sorta secret like." As a result, Davenport noted, slaves were encouraged to run away. Elizabeth Russell, *Indiana Narratives*, vol. 5, pp. 184–85; Sam Mitchel, *South Carolina Narratives*, vol. 3, pt. 3, p. 203. See also, for example, Charlie Davenport, *Mississippi Narratives*, supp., ser. 1, vol. 7, pt. 2, p. 562; Henry Gibbs, *Mississippi Narratives*, supp., ser. 1, vol. 8, pt. 3, pp. 815–17. In *Lincoln in American Memory*, Merrill D. Peterson sees these remembrances as nothing more than folk tales, part of a culture of worship surrounding Lincoln for his role in emancipation. See also Hodes, *Mourning Lincoln*.

58. Holland, *Letters and Diary of Laura M. Towne*, February 28, 1864, 131.

59. Lulu Wilson, *Texas Narratives*, vol. 5, pt. 4, p. 193; *Mississippi Narratives*, ser. 1, vol. 10, pt. 5, p. 2253; Rosengarten, *Tombee*, addendum to entry of January 29, 1852, made after the war, 559. After the war, Thomas Chaplin noted his frustration with a former "head man," Robert. Robert had disappointed him by hanging out with Union soldiers and failing to save "a single thing" for Chaplin. "He proved an old rascal," Chaplin wrote in an addendum to the journal entry from January 29, 1852.

60. Annie Osborne, *Texas Narratives*, vol. 5, pt. 3, pp. 158.

61. Jennie Webb, *Mississippi Narratives*, supp., ser. 1, vol. 10, pt. 5, p. 2253; Frank Magwood, *North Carolina Narratives*, vol. 15, pt. 2, pp. 91–92; Alfred Sligh, *South Carolina Narratives*, vol. 3, pt. 4, p. 92.

62. Hattie Rogers, *North Carolina Narratives*, vol. 15, pt. 2, p. 227; Sallie Paul,

South Carolina Narratives, vol. 3, pt. 3, pp. 234–35; Henry Gibbs, *Mississippi Narratives*, supp., ser. 1, vol. 8, pt. 3, p. 825; Jane Lee, *North Carolina Narratives*, vol. 15, pt. 2, p. 52; Lulu Wilson, *Texas Narratives*, supp., ser. 2, vol. 10, pt. 9, p. 4196.

63. Berlin et al., *The Destruction of Slavery*, 680–82, 698–99.

64. Berlin et al., *The Destruction of Slavery*, 746, 748–54, quote at 746.

65. Charles Minor Blackford Journal, March 11, 1865, in Blackford, *Letters from Lee's Army*, 287. In 1850, Preston owned over 100 slaves, most employed at his saltworks. He sold the saltworks to George Palmer in 1862. U.S. Census, 1850.

66. McGuire, *Diary of a Southern Refugee*, entries for May 10, 1861, and May 25, 1861, 13–14, 19. Federal troops took Alexandria on May 24, 1861.

67. Thomas, *A Portrait of Historical Athens and Clark County*, 89–95, quotes at 95–96.

68. Blackett, *The Captive's Quest*, 139–40; Blackett, *Making Freedom*; O'Donovan, *Becoming Free in the Cotton South*; Jordan, *Tumult and Silence*; Schwalm, *A Hard Fight for We*, 92.

69. Emma Sams to Dear Pa [Miles B. Sams], Barnwell, November 28, 1861, Sams Papers, SCL. The story of the lowcountry "experiment in freedom" has been amply told by numerous historians. See, for example, Rose, *Rehearsal for Reconstruction*; Foner, *Nothing but Freedom*; and Saville, *The Work of Reconstruction*.

70. Sterling, *We Are Your Sisters*, 238.

71. Holland, *Letters and Diary of Laura M. Towne*, April 28, 1862, 24.

72. Hawks, *A Woman Doctor's Civil War*, 18–21, 26, 31–33, and entries for May 1, 1864, March 15, 1865, 69–70, 119–21, quote at 70.

73. Dusinberre, *Them Dark Days*, 166–67.

74. Yacovone, *A Voice of Thunder*, 186, 205. Dennis Bland was one of hundreds of black laborers at Liverpool Point, Md. Bland entered the service as a private and was promoted to first lieutenant; his brother was promoted to captain.

75. Mary Barnwell Elliott Johnstone to William Elliott, Beaumont, June 14, 1863, Elliott-Gonzales Papers, SHC. Ralphie was Elliott's brother, Ralph Emms Elliott, a captain in the Confederate army who died in 1864 and was buried at Hollywood Cemetery in Richmond. Grimball Diary, entry for June 1863, SCHS.

76. Scarborough, *The Diary of Edmund Ruffin*, entry for July 4, 1862, 2:367–68.

77. Scarborough, *The Diary of Edmund Ruffin*, entry for July 4, 1862, 2:368.

78. Wm. Elliott to William Elliott, Adams Run, August 25, 1862, Elliott-Gonzales Papers, SHC. Oak Lawn was located at Parkers Ferry in Charleston County, about thirty miles west of Charleston. William Elliott owned several rice and cotton plantations in the Beaufort and Colleton districts in South Carolina and on the Ogeechee River in Georgia. At least five of these plantations he obtained through marriage: Balls (1,083 acres); Social Hall, the Bluff, and Middle Place (totaling approximately 3,400 acres); and Pon Pon, later called Oak Lawn (1,750 acres) on the Edisto River. He also owned Myrtle Bank plantation on Hilton Head Island; Bee Hive and Hope tracts on the Edisto River; Ellis, Shell Point, The Grove, and Bay Point plantations in Beaufort District; Farniente, a mountain house in Flat Rock,

N.C.; and houses in Beaufort and Adams Run. According to the 1860 slave schedule, Elliott possessed 103 slaves in St. Helena parish and 114 slaves in St. Paul parish.

79. Wm. Elliott to Genl. [August 1862], Elliott-Gonzales Papers, SHC.

80. *OR*, ser. 1, vol. 51, pt. 1, pp. 97–98.

81. Yacovone, *A Voice of Thunder*, 175.

82. *OR*, ser. 1, vol. 51, pt. 1, supp., p. 991.

83. Yacovone, *A Voice of Thunder*, 203–4. Stevens was also a soldier in the famous African American 54th Massachusetts Regiment.

84. *U.S. Statutes at Large, Treaties, and Proclamations*, 319, 589–90, 597–600. For a full discussion of these measures, see Berlin et al., *The Destruction of Slavery*, 1–56.

85. Food crops produced by slaves were also important to Union victory. Sherman's army would have suffered greatly if not for the abundant supply of corn and other food crops and animals they confiscated during the "March to the Sea."

86. *ORN*, ser. 1, vol. 24, pp. 475–78, quotes at 474 and 478.

87. Berlin, Reidy, and Rowland, *The Black Military Experience*, 143; *ORN*, ser. 1, vol. 23, p. 478.

88. Adj. Gen. L. Thomas, Special Orders No. 45, August 18, 1863 [V-17]; Hood and Bostwick, *Report of the Commissioners of Investigation of Colored Refugees in Kentucky, Tennessee, and Alabama*.

89. Report of Col. R. D. Massey, Colonel, 100th USCT, Commissioner, Organization of Colored Troops to Hon. Thomas Hood and Hon. S. W. Bostwick, August 14, 1864, in *Report of the Commissioners of Investigation of Colored Refugees in Kentucky, Tennessee, and Alabama*, 17.

90. *OR*, ser. 1, vol. 31, pt. 3, p. 198; Massey, *Women in the Civil War*, 273.

91. *OR*, ser. 1, vol. 32, pt. 2, p. 568.

92. See, for example the Testimony of Henry A. Judd and A. D. Smith, AFIC. [K-74 and K-71]; Glymph, "Black Women and Children in the Civil War."

93. Thursday, [July] 10, 1862, Fannie Green Diary, EU.

94. Rev. A. Mercherson to Maj. Gen. J. G. Foster, August 12, 1864, M-826, LR, ser. 4109, DS, RG 393 [C-1327].

95. As quoted in Wiley, *The Life of Billy Yank*, 115.

96. Hawks, *A Woman Doctor's Civil War*, October 16, 1862; undated entry at 55; [February 1864], 34, 55, 61, quotes at 34, 55. On rape, see, for example, Feimster, "Rape and Justice in the Civil War"; Feimster, "General Benjamin Butler and the Threat of Sexual Violence"; Feimster, *Southern Horrors*, 20–22, quote at 22.

97. Fry as quoted in Massey, *Women in the Civil War*, 173. *OR*, ser. 1, vol. 32, pp. 195, 338; *OR*, ser. 1, vol. 31, p. 68; S. S. Fry to Robert Breckinridge, November 28, 1864.

98. Wiley, *The Life of Billy Yank*, 115, 117–18, 213–14. According to Wiley, officers and enlisted men commonly assaulted black women and girls. He also noted that some were punished. See also Lucinda Hall Shaw, *Mississippi Narratives*, supp., ser. 1, vol. 10, pt. 5, p. 1929. Shaw made clear her feelings on the matter: "I never did remire [admire] white mens an' I didn't have nuthin' to do wid dem."

99. Sterling, *We Are Your Sisters*, 239–40.

100. Simms, *Sack and Destruction of Columbia*.

101. Important exceptions include Clinton, "Southern Dishonor"; Jordan, "Sleeping with the Enemy"; Faust, *Mothers of Invention*; Hodes, *White Women, Black Men*; Murphy, *I Had Rather Die*; Feimster, "General Benjamin Butler and the Threat of Sexual Violence"; and Barber and Ritter, "Dangerous Liaisons"; Feimster, "Rape and Justice in the Civil War"; Feimster, *Southern Horrors*.

102. Lucy Galloway, *Mississippi Narratives*, supp., ser. 1, vol. 8, pt. 3, p. 801; Evans, *Sherman's Horsemen*, 297; Mitchell, *The Vacant Chair*, 106–10; Royster, *The Destructive War*, 23. See also Mohr, *On the Threshold of Freedom*, 93–95.

103. Betty Powers, *Texas Narratives*, vol. 5, pt. 3, 192.

104. John Jones to Mrs. Mary Jones, August 21, 1865 in Myers, *The Children of Pride*, 1292.

105. McPherson, *Ordeal by Fire*, 462; Mohr, *On the Threshold of Freedom*, 93–96; Glymph, "This Species of Property," 71.

106. *OR*, ser. 1, vol. 44, p. 836.

107. *OR*, ser. 1, vol. 44, pp. 836–38. Halleck, never an enthusiastic supporter of fugitive slaves or emancipation, was sympathetic to Sherman's philosophy, so similar was it to his own. However, not wanting to see Sherman's military triumphs marred by the bad press and more sensitive than Sherman to the transformation that had taken place in Washington at the highest levels of the government, he emphasized the importance of obedience to congressional and government policy. See, for example, his letter to Gen. U. S. Grant in 1863 cautioning him against allowing his men to turn back fugitive slaves. Berlin, Reidy, and Rowland, *The Black Military Experience*, 143.

108. For Special Fields Orders, No. 119, November 8, 1864, see Sherman, *Memoirs*, vol. 2, 651; for General Orders, No. 22, see *OR*, ser. 1, vol. 44, p. 502.

109. Special Field Orders No. 119, Kingston, Ga., November 8, 1864, in Sherman, *Memoirs*, vol. 2, 651, 654.

110. Marszalek, *Sherman*, 312–13; Glatthaar, *The March to the Sea and Beyond*, 64.

111. For Sherman's Savannah Campaign command reports cited here, see *OR*, ser. 1, 44, pp. 159–225. Information cited from Capt. Eben White's report is at 187, James D. Morgan's at 184, Gen. Henry W. Slocum's at 159, and Gen. Absalom Baird's at 205; Jefferson Davis's at 166.

112. *OR*, ser. 1, vol. 44, pp. 211–12, 190. The Colerain Plantation, located on the banks of the Savannah River, belonged to the Potter Family of Savannah, Georgia, and Princeton, New Jersey. John Potter, the son of owner James Potter, a soldier in the Confederate army, was at the battle of Atlanta and died of wounds near Marietta, Georgia. The 2,000 people settled by Sherman at Colerain would have joined the more than 300 slaves owned by the Potters. See James Potter Executor for the Estate of John Potter, U.S. Census, 1860.

113. *OR*, ser. 1, vol. 44, pp. 406–10; *OR*, vol. 46, pp. 898, 979; McPherson, *Battle Cry of Freedom*, 809; Glatthaar, *The March to the Sea and Beyond*, 58.

114. *OR*, I:47, pt. 2, p. 803.

115. Berlin et al., *The Destruction of Slavery*.

116. Taylor, *Reminiscences of My Life in Camp*, 33; Holland, *Letters and Diary of Laura M. Towne*, 148, 110.

117. Holland, *Letters and Diary of Laura M. Towne*, January 26, 1865, 153–54.

118. Holland, *Letters and Diary of Laura M. Towne*, March 12, 1865, 158.

119. Holland, *Letters and Diary of Laura M. Towne*, January 21, 1865, 149–50.

120. Affidavits of Julia Ann Wright, Betty Brett, Edward Allcorn, and Marshall Dawson, Sworn May 22, 1868. The marriage ceremony was performed by Lt. Col. A. T. Wood of the First Indiana Colored Infantry. Julia Ann Wright and Betty Brett were midwives at Anna's birth. Sally Anderson Pension File.

121. Hon. Thomas Hood and Hon. S. W. Bostwick, "Report of the Commissioners of Investigation of Colored Refugees in Kentucky, Tennessee, and Alabama," quotes at 20, 18, and 21, respectively.

122. Glymph, "Invisible Disabilities."

123. Rose, *Rehearsal for Reconstruction*.

124. *ORN*, ser. 1, vol., 24, p. 494.

125. *ORN*, ser. 1, vol. 24, pp. 493–94.

126. Maggie Whitehead, *Texas Narratives*, supp., ser. 2, vol. 7, p. 2623; Wilson W. Whitehead Will, Mississippi Wills and Probate Records, 1780–1982, *Transcribed Record of Wills*, vol. 1, *1833–1888*, 74–75, filmstrip 69–70. For a fuller discussion, see Glymph, "'I'm a Radical Girl.'"

127. Maggie Whitehead, *Texas Narratives*, supp., ser. 2, vol. 7, p. 2623.

128. Maggie Whitehead, *Texas Narratives*, supp., ser. 2, vol. 7, 2625. Construction on the fort had ceased by November 1864, and it was never used or completed. "Gonzales County," Texas State Historical Society Online, https://tshaonline.org /handbook/online/articles/hcg07.

129. On the question of reenslavement, see Oakes, *Freedom National*, 422–29.

130. A. [Brobst?], Report of 1865, BRFAL, RG 105, M826, roll 30.

131. *ORN*, ser. 2, vol. 23, p. 339.

132. Manchester Ward Wald Papers, Journal entries for Friday, May 26, 1865, and May 29, 1865, December 10, 1867, pp. 3, 7, 42. Rubenstein Library, DU. In June, Sarah was arrested "for idleness" after she ran off from the McDougald home. Duncan McCormick to the Provost Marshall, June 26, 1865; Ward Papers, entry for December 10, 1867. Ward here misspells the name of J. C. McDougald as "Dongel." See U.S. Census, 1860. At least by 1870, Sarah and Samuel Harrington were together. U.S. Census, 1870.

133. Lulu Wilson, *Texas Narratives*, supp., ser. 2, vol. 10, pt. 9, pp. 4191–92, quote at 4191.

134. Pvt. Calvin Holley to Maj. Gen. O. O. Howard, December 16, 1865, BRFAL, Mississippi, LR, M826, roll 10, RG 105, NARA.

135. Black Southerners' concerns about white intentions after the war were clearly a legacy of this violence. John Higginson's comparative studies of terror

and collective violence in the Reconstruction South and South Africa after the Civil War and the 1899–1902 Anglo-Boer or South African War yield important insights into the question of wartime violence. Higginson, "Upending the Century of Wrong," 11–12, 24, 48–49; Higginson, "A Tale of Two Counties."

136. Higginson, "Upending the Century of Wrong," 11, 16. See also Ortiz, *Emancipation Betrayed*; Rosen, *Terror in the Heart of Freedom*; Woodruff, *American Congo*.

137. Thomas Holt, Reconstruction Symposium, University of North Carolina at Chapel Hill, October 1, 2005 (author's notes).

138. Register of Patients General Hospital for Freedmen, Vicksburg, Miss., Roll of Patients General Hospital, M1914, RG 105, NARA.

139. Quote in Parish, *Slavery*, 156; see also Downs, *Sick from Freedom*, 18–41.

140. Augustin Taveau to Delphine Taveau, February 22, 1864; William Whaley to Augustin Taveau, February 16, 1864; Augustin Taveau to Delphine Taveau, May 17, 1864, and June 18, 1864; all in Augustin Louis Taveau Papers, DU.

141. Faust, Epilogue, *In Joy and in Sorrow*, 253.

142. Johnson, *Soul by Soul*, 90

143. F. G. DeFontaine, "Stirring Days in Chester," in *Our Women in the War*, 85.

144. F. G. DeFontaine, "Stirring Days in Chester," in *Our Women in the War*, 85.

145. Woods, *Development Arrested*, 40–71, quote at 45.

146. Glymph, *Out of the House of Bondage*. The extent to which slaves were used to spy on other slaves as part of the apparatus of surveillance is an important but largely unexplored subject. For a recent work on violence within the slave community, see Foret, *Slave against Slave*.

147. Stone, *Brokenburn*, 171–72. An interesting question is how many pistols were owned by slaveholding women.

148. Meriwether, *Recollections of 92 Years*, 83; Feimster, *Southern Horrors*, 19.

149. The phrase is Gen. S. S. Fry's. He was not the only commander to use it.

150. Beaton Smith to Lieutenant McDougall, September 5, 1866, Letters Received, ser. 3053, RG 105 [A-7210].

151. Redkey, *A Grand Army of Black Men*, 228.

152. A. H. W. [Abby Woolsey] to E [Eliza Woolsey], Saturday, July 5, 1862, in Bacon and Howland, *Letters of a Family*, vol. 1, 49.

CHAPTER FOUR

1. Bacon and Howland, eds., *Letters of a Family*, vol. 1, 2–3; Pérez, *Slaves, Sugar and Colonial Society*, 22. See also Sophia Peabody Cuba Journal, 1833–35, Peabody Collection, NYPL. I am indebted to Nina Silber for pointing me to this archive.

2. A. H. W. [Abby Howland Woolsey] to E. [Eliza Woolsey Howland], April 19, 1861, and A. H. W. [Abby Howland Woolsey] to E. W. H. [Eliza Woolsey Howland], April 14, 1861, in Bacon and Howland, *Letters of a Family*, vol. 1, 38–39.

3. J. S. W. [Jane Stuart Woolsey] to Cousin Margaret Hodge, February 7, 1861, in Bacon and Howland, *Letters of a Family*, vol. 1, p. 34.

4. A. H. W. [Abby Howland Woolsey] to E. W. H. [Eliza Woolsey Howland], 8 Brevoort Place, December 2 and 5, 1859, in Bacon and Howland, *Letters of a Family*, vol. 1, 15–16, quote at 16.

5. Abby [Woolsey] to Eliza [Woolsey], December 17, 1859, in Bacon and Howland, *Letters of a Family*, vol. 1, 17.

6. Phillips, "Toussaint L'Ouverture"; Phillips, "The War for the Union." For a discussion of Phillips's speech at the Smithsonian and the Southern reaction, see Clavin, *Toussaint Louverture*, 1–2; Forten, *Journal*, December 16, 1857, p. 112.

7. A. H. W. [Abby Howland Woolsey] to Eliza [Woolsey], February 1, 1861, in Bacon and Howland, *Letters of a Family*, vol. 1, 31–32. Charles Leclerc was a French general and brother-in-law of Napoleon Bonaparte, who sent him to Haiti to put down the Revolution. Although he captured Toussaint and deported him to France (where Toussaint died in prison), Leclerc failed to reestablish French authority and, like many of his troops, died in Haiti of yellow fever. The vicomte de Rochambeau succeeded Leclerc as leader of the French expedition in Haiti. He would surrender to Haitian general Jean-Jacques Dessalines and was captured by the English on his way home to France.

8. Phillips, "The War for the Union," 8.

9. Ball, *To Live an Antislavery Life*, 109–31, quote at 115; Forten, *Journal*; Quarles, *Black Abolitionists*; Blight, *Frederick Douglass*; Sinha, *The Slave's Cause*.

10. Phillips, "Toussaint L'Ouverture." The story of Toussaint and his mistress also appears in Beard, *Toussaint L'Ouverture*, 48–49; and in the introductory materials to Toussaint Louverture, *Memoir of Pierre Toussaint*, 7. On Toussaint's reported affairs with white women., see Girard, *Toussaint Louverture*; and Toussaint Louverture, *Memoir of Pierre Toussaint*; Bell, *Toussaint Louverture*, 198–200; Dubois, *Avengers of the New World*, 187, 279.

11. Historian Julie Roy Jeffrey tells this story in Jeffrey, *The Great Silent Army of Abolitionism*, 211.

12. Attie, *Patriotic Toil*; Silber, *Daughters of the Union*; Giesberg, *Army at Home*.

13. Mrs. Eleanor J. W. Baker Journal, 1848, undated entry, DU.

14. Jos. M. Wood, Geo. W. Wilcox, and Lowell C. Cook to Myles J. Geo. Metcalf, Henry A. Aldrich, and Geo. Ransom, Second Regt. Rhode Island Volunteers, Camp Brightwood, Washington, D.C., February 1, 1862 in Metcalf, *The Irrepressible Conflict*, p. 7; McPherson, *For Cause and Comrades*; Mitchell, *The Vacant Chair*.

15. A. Lincoln to Hon. Horace Greeley, Executive Mansion, Washington, D.C., August 22, 1862, reprinted as Lincoln, "A Letter from President Lincoln."

16. J. S. W. [Jane Stuart Woolsey] to a friend in Paris, Brevoort Place, August 8, 1861, in Bacon and Howland, *Letters of a Family*, vol. 1, 167–68. This difference in opinion may explain why Jane Stuart Woolsey did not attend Phillips's lectures with her sisters.

17. Jeffrey, *The Great Silent Army of Abolitionism*, 210–15, quote at 215; Venet, *Neither Ballots nor Bullets*.

18. D. L. Stevens to Mrs. [A. L.] Endicott, May 27, 1864, USSC, NEWAA, NYPL.

Women either used their husband's names or their initials but increasingly in the nineteenth century, women began using their own full names. Mary A. Hedrick of Lowell, Massachusetts, wrote of her transformation. "When I first sent to the Commission, I used my initials only, not wishing to be individually known but after sending *for* the *ladies*, wishing that they should be informed of the reception of the articles I added my name, and shall continue to use the same, though I will enclose my card." From that point on she signed Mary A. Hedrick, rather than M. A. Hedrick. Mary A. Hedrick to [Hannah] Appleton, November 25, 1862, USSC, NEWAA, NYPL.

19. A. H. W. [Abby Howland Woolsey] to E. [Eliza Woolsey Howland], April 19, 1861, and A. H. W. [Abby Howland Woolsey] to E. W. H. [Eliza Woolsey Howland, April 14, 1861, in Bacon and Howland, *Letters of a Family*, vol. 1, 39, 67.

20. J. S. W. [Jane Stuart Woolsey] to Cousin Margaret, April 1861; A. W. H. [Abby Howland Woolsey] to E. [Eliza Woolsey Howland], April 17, 1861, in Bacon and Howland, *Letters of a Family*, vol. 1, 41–42, 45–46, 49–50.

21. J. S. W. [Jane Stuart Woolsey] to a friend in Paris, Friday, May 10, 1861, in Bacon and Howland, *Letters of a Family*, vol. 1, 67, 68.

22. Livermore, *My Story of the War*, 91–92. Livermore fiercely advocated for Union soldiers in her work with the U.S. Sanitary Commission, which took her to army camps and field hospitals. See Giesberg, *Army at Home*, 17–22 and Giesberg, *Civil War Sisterhood*.

23. J. S. W. [Jane Stuart Woolsey] to a friend in Paris, Friday, May 10, 1861, in Bacon and Howland, *Letters of a Family*, vol. 1, 71; O'Leary, *To Die For*, 20–25.

24. Fahs, *The Imagined Civil War*, 123.

25. J. S. W. [Jane Stuart Woolsey] to the Sisters Abroad, [1861] in Bacon and Howland, *Letters of a Family*, vol. 1, 56, 57.

26. J. S. W. [Jane Stuart Woolsey] to a friend in Paris, Friday, May 10, 1861, in Bacon and Howland, *Letters of a Family*, vol. 1, 68. On "bandage bees," see H. B. Chickering to Miss [Annette P.] Rogers, April 23, 1864, USSC, NEWAA, NYPL.

27. Fahs, *The Imagined Civil War*, 120.

28. Silber, *Daughters of the Union*, 17; Giesberg, *Army at Home*, 18–22, quotes at 19, 21; Marvel, *Lincoln's Mercenaries*, see especially 20–73, quotes 25, 23, respectively.

29. A. M. Fulton (Mrs. Dr. Fulton) to Miss [Isa] Gray, February 17, 1863; Eleanor Gardiner to Mrs. [A. L.] Endicott, June 14, 1864, USCC, NEWAA. See also Silber, *Daughters of the Union*, 162–93.

30. Edmondston, *"Journal of a Secesh Lady,"* 57, 60.

31. A. H. W. [Abby Howland Woolsey] to G. [Georgiana Woolsey] and E. [Eliza Newton Woolsey], July 22, 1861, in Bacon and Howland, *Letters of a Family*, vol. 1, 121–23, 124, 125, 127, 128–31. In 1850, the Woolsey household, then based in New York City, included three female servants, all born in Ireland: twenty-three-year-old Mary J. Taylor, twenty-three-year-old Ellen Mooney, and twenty-two-year-old Martha Moran. U.S. Census, 1850, New York Ward 7, District 2; Silber, *Daughters of the Union*, 166.

32. Mary P. Henderson to Laura [Henderson], Philadelphia, April 5, 1859, Mrs. Irving H. McJesson Collection, no. 1542, Henderson Letters, 1851–1891, HSP.

33. Mary Henderson to Laura [Henderson]. Philadelphia, September 18, 1861, Henderson Letters, Mrs. Irving H. McJesson Collection, no. 1542, HSP.

34. A. H. W. [Abby Howland Woolsey] to G. & E. [Georgeanna and Eliza Woolsey], July 22, 1861, in Bacon and Howland, *Letters of a Family*, vol. 1, 127.

35. C. C. W. [Caroline Carson Woolsey] to G. & E. [Georgeanna and Eliza Woolsey], Boston, January 13, [1862], in Bacon and Howland, *Letters of a Family*, vol. 1, 249.

36. List of Items Sent by Women's Societies, December 21, 1861, USSC, NEWAA, NYPL. Woburn had a population of just over 6,000 in 1860. U.S. Census, 1860.

37. Silber, *Daughters of the Union*, 55–56, 58–59, 61, quote at 55; Etcheson, *A Generation at War*, 66–67; Giesberg, *Army at Home*; Giesberg, *Civil War Sisterhood*.

38. Giesberg, *Army at Home*, see esp. 45–67, 119–22, quotes at 45, 46. If Daniel Heffler survived Belle Isle, he would have been among the prisoners transferred to the new Confederate prison at Andersonville, Georgia, which opened in February 1864, the month Belle Isle closed.

39. Funk, "A Hoosier Regiment in Alabama," 93–94.

40. The definitive work on the USSC is Giesberg, *Civil War Sisterhood*. The U.S. Sanitary Commission played an important role in providing support for Northern soldiers. Its Sanitary Fairs raised millions for sick and wounded soldiers. By the end of the war, an estimated 7,000 soldiers' aid societies had been organized in the North and Midwest and women had gained valuable organizing skills. As the efforts to build support reveal, however, the mission, organizational structure, and managerial style of the Sanitary Commission came in for much criticism. The critique by women reveals a lack of consensus around the organization's mission and key political and class divisions. On women and the abolitionist movement, see Jeffrey, *The Great Silent Army of Abolitionism*; and Sinha, *The Slave's Cause*.

41. The NEWAA was established on November 28, 1861. Four men nominally headed the NEWAA, but the bulk of the work was conducted through three committees—Industrial, Finance, and Executive—chaired by women. It recruited women in local communities as associate managers. Associate managers were tasked with identifying sewing circles and soldiers' aid societies within their districts and encouraging them to associate with the USSC and organizing societies in towns where there were none.

42. U.S. Census, 1850, 1860, 1870. Isa Gray's mother was the daughter of Caleb Loring and held a trust in her own name in the amount of $60,000 in 1870. That census year, her father reported real estate property valued at $326,000 and personal property at $75,000. Isa Gray remained an activist for the remainder of her life and used the money she inherited for good causes. She contributed to a fund to help build a school for the children of former slaves in Knoxville and to the NAACP Antilynching Fund. On the latter, see *The Crisis* 2, no. 5 (September 1916): 219.

43. E. H. Dickerson to Miss [Isa] Gray, August 13, 1863, USSC, NEWAA, NYPL.

44. Eleanor Gardiner (Gardiner, Me.), to Mrs. [A. L.] Endicott, June 16, 1864, USSC, NEWAA, NYPL. Two dozen relief associations had been established in Washington, D.C., of which some sixteen were, like the Maine Soldiers' Relief Association, state-sponsored relief societies (*Daily Morning Chronicle*, Washington, D.C., November 6, 1862).

45. A. M. Fulton to Miss [Isa E.] Gray, February 17, 1863, USSC, NEWAA, NYPL.

46. Miss A. M. Fulton to Miss [Isa] Gray, April 7, 1863, USSC, NEWAA, NYPL. Fulton ultimately declined the invitation to serve as associate manager for her county and informed the Boston office that she had had no luck in finding anyone else to take the job.

47. [Miss] H. B. Chickering to Miss [Isa] Gray, November 21, 1862, USSC, NEWAA, NYPL.

48. Miss E. A. Gray to Miss Isa [E.] Gray, Bowdoinham, Mass., August 1863, USSC, NEWAA, NYPL.

49. Silber, *Daughters of the Union*, 179–81.

50. Lucy M. Reynolds to Miss Rogers, May 9, [1864], USSC, NEWAA, NYPL.

51. Frances A. McKeen to Miss [Isa] Gray, February 16, 1863; McKeen to Gray, April 22, 1863, USSC, NEWAA, NYPL.

52. M. L. Newhall to Miss [Isa] Gray, Lynn, January 23, 1863, USSC, NEWAA, NYPL.

53. Mary A. Hedrick to Miss Rogers, September 29, 1864, USSC, NEWAA, NYPL.

54. H. C. Green, to Miss Isa E. Gray, December 29, 1862; January 10, 1863, USSC, NEWAA, NYPL.

55. Mary J. Cooper to [Isa] Gray, May 11, 1863, USSC, NEWAA, NYPL.

56. Mary J. Cooper (of Calais) to My dear Miss [Isa] Gray, May 11, 1863, USSC, NEWAA, NYPL. For a discussion of the opposition to women's work, see Giesberg, *Army at Home*; Giesberg, *Civil War Sisterhood;* Schultz, *Women at the Front*.

57. D. L. Stevens to Miss Abby W. May [Gray], November 2, 1862; January 2, 1863, USSC, NEWAA, NYPL. U.S. Census, 1850, Castine, Hancock County, Me.; U.S. Census, 1860.

58. D. L. Stevens to Miss [Isa] Gray, January 21, 1863, USSC, NEWAA; D. L. Stevens [Mrs. Dr. Stevens] to Miss Abby W. May, November 22, 1862, USSC, NEWAA. In addition to his work as an architect, Olmsted is known for his two-volume work on his travels in the antebellum South, *The Cotton Kingdom*. See also Horwitz, *Spying on the South*.

59. E. H. Dickerson to Miss Gray, May 24, 1863, USSC, NEWAA, NYPL.

60. D. L. Stevens [Mrs. Dr. Stevens] to Miss Abby W. May [Gray], November 22, 1862, USSC, NEWAA, NYPL.

61. Mrs. J. Sumner to Miss [Annette P.] Rogers, March 9, 1864, USSC, NEWAA.

62. H. B. Fuller (Augusta, Me.) to My dear Mrs. [A. L.] Endicott, June 16, 1864, USSC, NEWAA, NYPL.

63. Emeline E. Coolidge to Mrs. [A. L.] Endicott, June 21, 1864, USSC, NEWAA; *Report of the Maine Soldiers Relief Association*, Washington, D.C., October 1866.

64. M. L. Newhall to Miss [Isa] Gray, Lynn, June 19, 1863, USSC, NEWAA, NYPL.

65. Susan L. Ellis to dear Madam [Isa Gray], Andover, April 22, 1863; Harriet K. Webb on behalf of Mrs. Ellis [Susan Ellis] to Isa E. Gray, June 6, 1863, USSC, NEWAA, NYPL.

66. D. L. Stevens [Mrs. Dr. Stevens] of Castine, Me., to Mrs. Dr. [Joseph L.] Stevens, November 22, 1862, USSC, NEWAA, NYPL.

67. M. L. Newhall to Miss [Isa] Gray, Lynn, June 19, 1863, USSC, NEWAA, NYPL; D. L. Stevens to Miss Abby W. May [Isa Gray], January 2, 1863, USSC, NEWAA, NYPL; U.S. Census, 1850, Castine, Hancock County, Me.; U.S. Census, 1860, Castine, Hancock County, Me.; Giesberg, *Army at Home*, 122, 124–26.

68. E. H. Dickerson to Miss [Isa] Gray, August 13, 1863, USSC, NEWAA, NYPL.

69. P. G. Bowman to Mrs. [A. L.] Endicott, June 25, 1864, USSC, NEWAA, NYPL; A. L. Endicott to My Dear Miss [Juliette F. Gaylord], United States Sanitary Commission, May 4, 1864, Juliette F. Gaylord Collection, Clements Library; Marvel, *Lincoln's Mercenaries*.

70. Harriet King Webb to Miss Isa E. Gray, Andover, May 3, 1863; E. H. Dickerson to Miss [Isa] Gray, November 5, 1863, USCC, NEWAA, NYPL. Webb was Susan Gray's assistant and one of the women invited by Gray to become an associate manager.

71. Alonzo Josselyn "to the New England Woman's Auxiliary Association," December 24, 1861; Employees in the Iron Foundry of Alonzo Josselyn to the New England Woman's Auxiliary Association, December 24, 1861, USSC, NYPL.

72. Mary A. Hedrick, to Miss [Annette P.] Rogers, September 29, 1864, USSC, NEWAA, NYPL.

73. M. L. Newhall to Miss [Annette P.] Rogers, May 12, 1864, USSC, NEWAA, NYPL.

74. Mrs. J. Sumner to Miss [Annette P.] Rogers, March 9, 1864, USSC, NEWAA, NYPL.

75. Lucy M. Reynolds to Miss [Annette P.] Rogers, May 9, [1864], USSC, NEWAA, NYPL.

76. P. G. Bowman to Mrs. [A. L.] Endicott, June 25, 1864, USSC, NEWAA, NYPL.

77. Mrs. J. Sumner to Miss [Annette P.] Rogers, March 9, 1864, USSC, NEWAA, NYPL.

78. E. H. Dickerson to Miss [Isa] Gray, November 5, 1863, USSC, NEWAA, NYPL.

79. E. H. Dickerson to Miss [Isa] Gray, November 5, 1863, USSC, NEWAA, NYPL.

80. Eleanor Gardiner (Gardiner, Me), to Mrs. [A. L.] Endicott, June 16, 1864, USSC, NEWAA, NYPL. McPherson, *Battle Cry of Freedom*, 494, 592. On copperheads, see also Etcheson, *A Generation at War*, 99–102.

81. Emeline E. Coolidge to Mrs. [A. L.] Endicott, July 3, 1864, USSC, NEWAA, NYPL.

82. P. G. Bowman to Mrs. [A. L.] Endicott, June 25, 1864, USSC, NEWAA, NYPL.

83. Ursula M. Penniman to Mrs. [A. L.] Endicott, June 15, 1864, USSC, NEWAA, NYPL.

84. M. L. Newhall to Miss [Isa] Gray, January 23, 1863, USSC, NEWAA, NYPL.

85. M. L. Newhall to Miss [Isa] Gray, June 19, 1863, USSC, NEWAA, NYPL. Despite

these problems, Lynn, Massachusetts, had a very active chapter of 550 members, though only 60 regularly attended meetings. Members paid an assessment of fifty cents. Some churches also preferred to continue a focus on foreign missions.

86. P. G. Bowman to Mrs. [A. L.] Endicott, June 25, 1864, USSC, NEWAA, NYPL.

87. [Miss] H. B. Chickering to Miss [Isa] Gray, June 3, 1863, USSC, NEWAA, NYPL.

88. [Miss] H. B. Chickering to Miss Gray, June 3, 1863, USSC, NEWAA, NYPL. In 1864, Chickering resigned both her position as associate manager of the USSC for Dedham (despite being asked by Gray to reconsider) and as secretary of the Dedham Society. H. B. Chickering to Miss [Annette P.] Rogers, Dedham, April 5, 1864, USSC, NEWAA, NYPL.

89. S. T. Phelps to Mrs. Endicott, July 15, 1864, USSC, NEWAA, NYPL.

90. D. L. Stevens to Mrs. [A. L.] Endicott, July 11, 1864, USSC, NEWAA, NYPL.

91. A. H. W. [Abby Howland Woolsey] to G. [Georgiana Woolsey] and E. [Eliza Newton Woolsey], July 22, 1861, 127; C. C. W. [Caroline Carson Woolsey] to G. & E. [Georgeanna and Eliza Woolsey], January 13, [1862], in Bacon and Howland, *Letters of a Family*, vol. 1, 248–49; U.S. Census, 1850 and 1860.

92. Mary W. Bean (Athens, Me.) to My dear Mrs. [A. L.] Endicott, June 13, 1864, USSC, NEWAA, NYPL.

93. Marvel, *Lincoln's Mercenaries*, 78–79.

94. On the racism in aid societies, see Silber, *Daughters of the Union*, 166–67.

95. Wilder, *Ebony and Ivy*, 50–53, quote at 280.

96. Bacon and Howland, *Letters of a Family*, vol. 1,1.

97. Bacon and Howland, *Letters of a Family*, vol. 1, viii.

98. Bacon and Howland, *Letters of a Family*, vol. 1, 1–2.

99. A. H. W. [Abby Howland Woolsey] to E. W. H. [Eliza Woolsey Howland], April 14, 1861; G.'s Journal [Georgeanna Woolsey], March 20, 1862; A. H. W. [Abby Howland Woolsey] to E. [Eliza Woolsey], Friday, May 17, 1861, in Bacon and Howland, *Letters of a Family*, vol. 1, 1–2, 38, 285–87, 284. For a print edition of the letters of the Woolsey family, see Howland and Bacon, *My Heart toward Home*.

100. *Sheldon & Co.'s Business or Advertising Directory*, 155.

101. Howland, *Family Records*, vol. 1, 233–36.

102. Howland, *Family Records*, vol. 1, 234, 235; Chambers, *No God but Gain*, 134. Francis Adams moved his family to the plantation at the conclusion of his appointment on August 8, 1823 as U.S. consular commercial agent in Matanzas by President Monroe. Adams subsequently held the position of U.S. Consular Commercial Agent at Matanzas, Cuba. New York merchant John Latting had previously held the position of U.S. vice consul to Matanzas.

103. DeWolf, *Inheriting the Trade*; "War Reminiscences of Alicia Hopton Middleton," 1865, SCHS, https://www.middletonplace.org.

104. Wilder, *Ebony and Ivy*, 280; Howland, *Family Records*, 230.

105. The story remained a part of the heritage passed down in the Howland, Woolsey, and Adams branches of the family. See Howland, *Family Records*, 234–36. James Truslow Adams, a descendant of Francis and Mary R. Adams, recalled

virtually the same story of the slave revolt and the rescue of his great-great-grandmother by the leader of the revolt that we find in *Family Records*. See Nevins, *James Truslow Adams*, 7–8. The revolt began on June 15, 1828, on a small plantation near the village of Guamacaro, east of the port of Matanzas. The story the descendants told about the slave who saved the lives of the women in the family is similar to others. At the second plantation the rebels attacked, a slave woman is said to have saved the life of one of the planter's three children. The other two were killed along with the parents. On the 1825 revolt, see Barcia, *The Great African Slave Revolt of 1825*; Chambers, *No God but Gain*, 134–37, 141–57, 162.

106. Howland, *Family Records*, 237.

107. Wilder, *Ebony and Ivy*, quote at 283. See also Pérez, *Cuba and the United States*, 18; Chambers, *No God but Gain*, 140–42.

108. Latting, Adams, and Stewart to E. [Edward Spalding], Matanzas, February 25, 1825, Edward Spalding Papers, University of Miami Libraries, Cuban Heritage Collection, http://merrick.librray.miami.edu/digital projects/copyright.html. On the continued problems of American investors in Cuba, see Drake & Hoit to Moses Taylor, Esq., Matanzas, 19 July, 1838, and Wright Books and Co. to Moses Taylor, Esq., Santiago De Cuba, April 9, 1842, via Charleston, Moses Taylor Collection, NYPL; Chambers, *No God but Gain*, 134–37. Albert O. Newton reported the death of his brother-in-law, whom he sought to replace as commercial agent at Matanzas. He did not receive the appointment. Hopkins, *The Papers of Henry Clay*, 4:236. On the possible suicide, see Chambers, *No God but Gain*, 134–37.

109. Ely, "The Old Cuba Trade," 470. The sugar trade has received far less scrutiny than the cotton trade.

110. Chambers, *No God but Gain*, 167–68.

111. For a fuller discussion of this point, see chapter 5.

112. See Chambers, *No God but Gain*. Nell Painter shows how Harriet Beecher Stowe also profited from slavery. Beecher had no direct ties to plantations but was financially invested in its tropes for the maintenance of her lifestyle which, Painter argues, increasingly depended on trafficking in racist notions. See Painter, *Sojourner Truth*, 151–57.

113. Many Americans who invested in the China trade first grew wealthy in Cuba. Howland & Aspinwall traded in South America, Cuba, and the Mediterranean and was particularly famous for its China trade in porcelain, silk, and tea.

114. G. [Georgeanna Woolsey] to E. [Eliza Woolsey], May 15, 1861, in Bacon and Howland, *Letters of a Family*, vol. 1, 86.

115. Mother [Jane Eliza Woolsey] to E. [Eliza Woolsey], New York, April 13, [1865], in Bacon and Howland, *Letters of a Family*, vol. 2, 656.

116. Will of Jane Stuart Woolsey, December 21, 1883, Ancestry.com, New York, Wills and Probate Records, 1659–1999, database online. In 2018 dollars, $53,000 translates to an income value of $14.5 million and wealth value of $1,370,000; http://www.measuringworth.com/uscompare/relativevalue.php.

117. The equivalent of $11,176,112 in 2014 dollars is $48,800,000,000 as measured

in economic power value and $316,000,000 in standard of living value. In the Matter of the Final Accounting of William H. Aspinwall, John L. Aspinwall, & Charles H. Russell of Samuel S. Howland, deceased, filed January 29, 1855, Fold3 Database. Howland's investments included the following: New Orleans Gas Company; the Panama Railroad, Pacific Mail Steamship Company bonds; shares in the Metropolitan Fire Insurance Company; the New York Life and Trust Insurance Company; the New Orleans Canal Company; Mechanics Bank, Alabama; Manhattan Bank; railroads; New York real estate; Illinois state bonds; Manhattan Insurance Company; Manhattan Gas Company; New York Fire and Marine Insurance Company; and Woolsey and Woolsey. Howland was also a founder of the Society for the Prevention of Cruelty to Animals and helped found the Metropolitan Museum of Art.

118. Gardiner Howland Will, January 3, 1852, Fold3 Database. Gardiner Howland died in 1851.

119. In the Matter of the Final Accounting of William H. Aspinwall, John L. Aspinwall, & Charles H. Russell of Samuel S. Howland, deceased, filed January 29, 1855, Fold3 Database.

120. Davidoff and Hall, *Family Fortunes*, 18; Ryan, *Women in Public*; Ryan, *Civic Wars*.

121. A. H. W. [Abby Woolsey] to E. [Eliza Woolsey], 8 Brevoort Place, Saturday, July 5, 1862; JSW [Jane Stewart Woolsey] to a friend in Paris, August 8, 1861, Bacon and Howland, *Letters of a Family*, vol. 2, 442; vol. 1, 168.

122. A. H. W. [Abby Woolsey] to E. [Eliza Woolsey], 8 Brevoort Place, July 11, 1862, Friday Morning, Bacon and Howland, *Letters of a Family*, vol. 2, 457.

123. A. H. W. [Abby Woolsey] to E. [Eliza Woolsey] 8 Brevoort Place, July 11, 1862, Friday Morning, Bacon and Howland, *Letters of a Family*, vol. 2, 457. Alexander Turney Stewart, an Irish immigrant, founded Stewart's Department Store in 1823.

124. See chapter 5.

125. Harris, *In the Shadow of Slavery*; Giesberg, *Army at Home*, 129–30.

126. Bacon and Howland, *Letters of a Family*, vol. 2, 539.

127. On the debate over the question of Northern motivations, see, for example, Gallagher, *The Union War*; Oaks, *Freedom National*.

128. Francis Leland, M.D., U.S. Surgeon Second Reg., Mass. Vol., Charleston, Va., March 20, 1862, in Metcalf, *The Irrepressible Conflict*, 9.

129. Julia A. Wilbur to Anna M. C. Barnes, Washington, D.C., October 24, [1862], RASP, Clements Library, University of Michigan.

130. Julia A. Wilbur to Mrs. B. [Anna M. C. Barnes] October 2, 1863, RASP, Clements Library.

131. G. [Georgeanna Woolsey] to Mother [Jane Eliza Woolsey], Steamer *Knickerbocker*, n.d., in Bacon and Howland, *Letters of a Family*, vol. 1, 358.

132. J. S. W. [Jane Stuart Woolsey] to a friend in Paris, 8 Brevoort Place, Friday, May 10, 1861, in Bacon and Howland, *Letters of a Family*, vol. 1, 67.

133. Bacon and Howland, *Letters of a Family*, vol. 1, 14–15. At the time of the

meeting with Sherman and Stanton, Cox was fifty-eight years old. Born in Savannah, he had been in the ministry for fifteen years. Second African Baptist Church supported a congregation of 1,222. For a copy of the minutes from the meeting reprinted from the *New York Daily Tribune*, see Berlin et al., *The Wartime Genesis of Free Labor: The Lower South*, 332.

134. Satirra Ford Douglass was married to H. Ford Douglas, who enlisted in the Ninety-Fifth Regiment, Illinois Infantry, a white regiment organized at Rockford, Ill., on July 26, 1862, and mustered in with the regiment on September 4, 1862. Harris, "H. Ford Douglas," 228–29.

135. Jeffrey, *The Great Silent Army of Abolitionism*, 217–18.

136. On the question of confluence of class, gender, and race in the North, see Giesberg, *Army at Home*; and Ball, *To Live an Antislavery Life*.

137. A. S. Hartwell, Col. Com'd'g Regt., Headquarters, Fifty-Fifth Mass. Vols., to My dear Kinsley, April 7, 1864, Edward W. Kinsley Papers, David M. Rubenstein Rare Book and Manuscript Library, DU.

138. James M. Trotter to Edward Kinsley, Folly Island, November 21, 1864, Kinsley Papers, Rubenstein Library, DU.

139. As quoted in Esther MacCarthy, "The Home for Aged Colored Women," 62.

140. Swint, *Dear Ones at Home*, 154; MacCarthy, "The Home for Aged Colored Women," 55–73, quotes at 55–56, 57, 61, and 66.

141. U.S. Sanitary Commission, Department of NC for the Year 1864 [January 1–July 2], entries for February 3 and February 18, Monthly Record, USSC Dept. of NC Archives, NYPL.

142. Schultz, *Women at the Front*, 99–100.

CHAPTER FIVE

1. Holland, *Letters and Diary of Laura M. Towne*, 172.

2. The views of many Northern women in this regard were similar to the maternalist ideas that supported colonial empires and the removal of children from Native American and aboriginal Australian mothers in the late nineteenth and early twentieth centuries. See Jacobs, *White Mother to a Dark Race*, 87–148; Hall, *Civilising Subjects*. As a large body of literature has noted, Northern missionaries were also deployed to help convince black people that it was more in their interest to grow cotton for the government than to grow corn to sustain their bodies. See, for example, Rose, *Rehearsal for Reconstruction*; Saville, *The Work of Reconstruction*; and Silber, "A Compound of Wonderful Potency." See also Stoler, *Race and the Education of Desire*; and Stoler, *Carnal Knowledge and Imperial Power*. See, among the many excellent books on slavery, portraiture, and the representation of race, Willis and Krauthamer, *Envisioning Emancipation*; Rosenheim, *Photography and the American Civil War*; Fox-Amato, *Exposing Slavery*; Wood, *The Horrible Gift of Freedom*.

3. Holland, *Letters and Diary of Laura M. Towne*, 172.

4. U.S. Census, 1870 and 1880, St. Helena Island, Beaufort, S.C. Maria Wyne died in 1925 at the age of sixty-nine of malarial fever. Her death certificate lists her mother as Celia Wyne (sometimes spelled Caely Wyne in census records) and her father as Jack Wyne. State of South Carolina Bureau of Vital Statistics, State Bureau of Health, Certificate of Death, St. Helena, Beaufort County, April 20, 1925. Available at Ancestry.com. Maria Wyne would have been around nine years old when she was posed in the photograph with Towne.

5. Stowe, *Uncle Tom's Cabin*, 170.

6. Emerson as quoted in Simpson, *Mind and the American Civil War*, 35, 55, 73; Fields, "Lost Causes," 65–71.

7. Silber, *Daughters of the Union*, 224; Fields, "Lost Causes," 67.

8. [Laura Severence Fiske] to Dear son [Asa Fiske], Shelburne Falls, February 1863, Asa Severance Fiske Correspondence, Stephenson Papers, LOC.

9. Jeffrey, *The Great Silent Army of Abolitionism*, 223.

10. Brown, *Foul Bodies*, 262–66, 344–48, quotes at 344 and 346; Glymph, *Out of the House of Bondage*, 63–96.

11. Holland, *Letters and Diary of Laura M. Towne*, xiii.

12. Haley, *No Mercy Here*, 7.

13. Brinton, *Personal Memoirs*, 43–44; T. J. Goldby to Col. Ned Stokes, Selma, September 8, 1863, Confederate States of America File, box 3, folder 3, AAS.

14. Sarah Chase to Father [Anthony Chase], April 20, 1861, Chase Family Papers, AAS; Asa [Fiske] to "My child" [Elizabeth Fiske], Memphis, Jan'y Office of Sup't of Contrabands, Asa Severance Fiske Correspondence, Stephenson Papers, LOC. It was his wife, Elizabeth, that Asa Fiske addressed as "My child."

15. Swint, *Dear Ones at Home*, 13–14, 16, quotes at 16 and 14, respectively.

16. G. [Georgeanna Woolsey] to E. [Eliza Woolsey], May 15, 1861, and A. H. W. [Abby Woolsey] to E. [Eliza Woolsey], Friday, May 17, 1861, in Bacon and Howland, *Letters of a Family*, vol. 1, 77–78, 86.

17. E. [Ellen Noyes] to [Catherine Noyes], Campton Village, July 8, [1863], Noyes-Balch Family Papers, 1854–1957, Rubenstein Library, DU. Campton Village, New Hampshire, was where Ellen Notes was vacationing at the time.

18. A. Conant to Kate [Conant], February 7 and 9, 1863, Kate Conant Linsley Papers, Rubenstein Library, DU.

19. Holland, *Letters and Diary of Laura M. Towne*, St. Helenaville, S.C., Saturday, January 21, 1865; St. Helenaville, Thursday, January 26, 1865, 150, 154, quote at 154.

20. Holland, *Letters and Diary of Laura M. Towne*, Pope's Plantation, St. Helena Island, April 21, 1862, 11; Jacoway, *Yankee Missionaries in the South*, 29, 147–48, quote at 29.

21. Brown, *Foul Bodies*, 354, 255.

22. Litwack, *Been in the Storm So Long*, 455–66.

23. Julia A. Wilbur to Anna M. C. Barnes, November 12, 1862, RASP.

24. Hawks, *A Woman Doctor's Civil War*, [October 1863], 56.

25. Hawks, *A Woman Doctor's Civil War*, February 24, 1865, 116.

26. Faulkner, *Women's Radical Reconstruction*, 7.

27. Lucy Chase to Dear home folks, Craney Island, January 29 [1863]. https://www.americanantiquarian.org/Freedmen/Manuscripts/Chase/09-30-1863.html.

28. Pearson, *Letters from Port Royal Written at the Time of the Civil War*, 126.

29. As quoted in Faulkner, *Women's Radical Reconstruction*, 13.

30. Quote from "Report of D. O. McCord, Surg. 63 USCI, Med. Director and Inspector Freedmen, Depts. of Miss. and Ark. Makes Final Report, Vicksburg, Miss.," to Col. John Eaton, Jr. Superintendent of Freedmen, August 3, 1865, M1914, Misc. Reports from Subordinate Offices, RG 105, NARA.

31. Samuel [Fiske] to My Dear Bro. & Sis. [Asa and Lizzie Fiske], Camp near Elkton, Va., August 8, 1863, Asa Severance Fiske Correspondence, Stephenson Papers, LOC.

32. Samuel Sawyer, Superintendent of Contrabands, "To Any Whom It May Concern," July 24, 1863, Mary Tyler Peabody Mann Papers [Mrs. Horace Mann], Manuscript Division, LOC [hereafter Mann Papers, LOC]. James Yeatman, president of the Western Sanitary Commission Board, appointed Mann to her position.

33. Maria [R. Mann] to Aunt Mary [Mary Tyler Peabody Mann], [1863], Mann Papers, LOC.

34. Maria [R. Mann] to Aunt Mary, [Mary Tyler Peabody Mann], [1863]; [Maria R. Mann] to Eliza [Eliza S. Mann Wilbur], February 10, 1863, Mann Papers, LOC.

35. Holland, *Letters and Diary of Laura M. Towne*, May 1, 1862, 32. Rose, *Rehearsal for Reconstruction*, 21–31, 43–62. By 1862, when Pierce, a graduate of Brown University and Harvard Law, was tapped to lead the U.S. Treasury Department's plantation system in the South Carolina Sea Islands, he had already gained experience working with former slave men at Hampton, Va.

36. Rose, *Rehearsal for Reconstruction*, 32–62; Berlin et al., *The Wartime Genesis of Free Labor: The Lower South*, 17, 99.

37. Holland, *Letters and Diary of Laura M. Towne*, April 21, 1862, Pope's Plantation, St. Helena Island, April 24, 1862, 11–13, 16.

38. Lucy [Chase] to Dear home folks, February 7, 1863, AAS. https://www.american antiquarian.org/Freedmen/Manuscripts/Chase/02-07-1863.html.

39. Holland, *Letters and Diary of Laura M. Towne*, April 21, 1862, Pope's Plantation, St. Helena Island, 13.

40. Holland, *Letters and Diary of Laura M. Towne*, April 21, 1862, Pope's Plantation, St. Helena Island, 13.

41. Holland, *Letters and Diary of Laura M. Towne*, May 13, 1863, St. Helena Island, 47, Diary, August 23, [1862], 86.

42. Holland, *Letters and Diary of Laura M. Towne*, April 24, 1862, April 27, 1862, May 11, 1862, 16, 17, 40.

43. Holland, *Letters and Diary of Laura M. Towne*, April 28, 1862, 30.

44. Holland, *Letters and Diary of Laura M. Towne*, April 18, 1862, January 21, 1865, 30, 149.

45. Holland, *Letters and Diary of Laura M. Towne*, April 27, 1862, April 28, 1862,

20, 22. Lucy Chase described the religious services of black people as "wild, dancing-dervish flourishes." As quoted in Litwack, *Been in the Storm So Long*, 460. Some black Northerners, like Henry M. Turner and Thomas W. Cardozo, who observed black religious practice in the South during and after the war, shared this view. Litwack, *Been in the Storm So Long*.

46. Hawks, *A Woman Doctor's Civil War*, October 16, 1862, 38–39, quote at 38. Hawks joined her husband, Dr. John Milton Hawks, who was already in South Carolina as part of the Port Royal Expedition.

47. E. B. Sewell to Kate [D. Conant], October 8, 1863, Linsley Papers, DU.

48. [Charles] C. Leigh to Miss Kate D. Conant, New York, December 22, 1864, Linsley Papers, DU.

49. See, for example, Holland, *Letters and Diary of Laura M. Towne*, April 21, 1862, 14.

50. Holland, *Letters and Diary of Laura M. Towne*, April 21, 1862, 14; Hawks, *A Woman Doctor's Civil War*, May 13, 1865, 141–42.

51. Holland, *Letters and Diary of Laura M. Towne*, April 21, 1862, Pope's Plantation, St. Helena Island, 13.

52. Holland, *Letters and Diary of Laura M. Towne*, April 21, 1862, Pope's Plantation, St. Helena Island, 13–15.

53. Berlin et al., *The Wartime Genesis of Free Labor: The Lower South*, 160–61. For his part, Pierce sought several hundred dollars in reimbursement of his expense traveling to South Carolina, including $100 for clothing (161).

54. Holland, *Letters and Diary of Laura M. Towne*, Sunday, April 27, 1862, St. Helena Island, 17.

55. Holland, *Letters and Diary of Laura M. Towne*, April 21, 1862, Pope's Plantation, St. Helena Island, 14.

56. Holland, *Letters and Diary of Laura M. Towne*, Sunday, April 27, 1862, St. Helena Island, 17.

57. Berlin et al., *The Wartime Genesis of Free Labor: The Lower South*, 177.

58. Berlin et al., *The Wartime Genesis of Free Labor: The Lower South*, 160.

59. Holland, *Letters and Diary of Laura M. Towne*, February 7, 1804, St. Helena Island, 127.

60. Faulkner, *Women's Radical Reconstruction*, 12–13.

61. M. [Maria] R. Mann to Rev. Wm. L. Ropes, April 13, 1863, Mann Papers, LOC.

62. Holland, *Letters and Diary of Laura M. Towne*, April 28, 1862; May 12, 1862, May 23 [1862], August 23, 1862, 28–29, 57–58, 86, 230, quote at 29; Forten, *Journal*, November 18, 1862, 151–52.

63. Holland, *Letters and Diary of Laura M. Towne*, March 8, [1863], 104–5.

64. Holland, *Letters and Diary of Laura M. Towne*, January 21, 1865, 151; Forten, *Journal*, November 23, 1862, 154; Silber, "A Compound of Wonderful Potency," 43–44.

65. Holland, *Letters and Diary of Laura M. Towne*, April 27, 1862, 21.

66. Sterling, *We Are Your Sisters*, 253.

67. Painter, *Sojourner Truth*, 215. As Painter writes, "Truth flattered herself that differences in status explained differences in her reception. She said, for instance, that she had received only the 'kindest attention' from people in power, including the President." Of course, as Painter and other scholars point out, this was not true.

68. Sterling, *We Are Your Sisters*, 258, 260. For quote, see Forten, *Journal*, January 31, 1863, 180. Tubman also modeled a feminist black womanhood by adopting bloomers as better suited for the military expeditions she participated in.

69. Painter, *Sojourner Truth*, 202–3, 215.

70. Holland, *Letters and Diary of Laura M. Towne*, March, 3, 1867, 179.

71. Taylor, *Reminiscences of My Life in Camp*, 40–41.

72. Holland, *Letters and Diary of Laura M. Towne*, August 25, [1862], 87.

73. Hawks, *A Woman Doctor's Civil War*, October 16, 1862, 38–39.

74. Holland, *Letters and Diary of Laura M. Towne*, September 1865, 166.

75. Will of Laura M. Towne, March 6, 1901, Pennsylvania, Wills and Probates, Ancestry.com. Towne requested that ownership of the Peoples Graveyard be turned over to the island inhabitants "as a burial ground forever." Edward Pierce made it clear that the government would provide transportation and subsistence but not salaries, which, if any, would be the responsibility of the Boston, Philadelphia, and New York sponsoring committees. The original plan called for providing rations to a few individuals who had means of their own to receive. A couple of people would have their expenses paid and the rest twenty-five to fifty dollars per month by sponsors. Berlin et al., *The Wartime Genesis of Free Labor: The Lower South*, 157–58. Even at the top rate, with a salary beginning only in September 1865, Towne would not have amassed enough to leave an estate of the size she did. It is possible that some of her wealth came from an inheritance; she came from a wealthy merchant family.

76. Julia Wilbur to Anna M. C. Barnes, October 24, [1862], RASP; Wilbur to Barnes, November 12, 1862, RASP. The Rochester Ladies' Anti-slavery Society was founded in 1851.

77. Julia Wilbur to Anna M. C. Barnes, December 15, 1862, Wilbur to Barnes, November 12, 1862, RASP. For Jacobs's account of her work at Alexandria, see Yellin, *The Harriet Jacobs Family Papers*, 2:429, 2:485–87. Jacobs was sponsored by the Committee of Representatives of the New York Monthly Meeting of the Religious Society of Friends. See Yellen, *The Harriet Jacobs Family Papers*, 2:429–30.

78. Faulkner, *Women's Radical Reconstruction*, 24.

79. On cooperation between the two women, see, for example, Yellin, *The Harriet Jacobs Family Papers*, 2:420, 473–76. Faulkner notes that Jacobs and Wilbur later made amends and worked together constructively. Faulkner, *Women's Radical Reconstruction*, 24–25.

80. For quote, see Faulkner, *Women's Radical Reconstruction*, 23.

81. Faulkner, *Women's Radical Reconstruction*, 24; Yellin, *The Harriet Jacobs Family Papers*, 2:447–48.

82. Sterling, *We Are Your Sisters*, quotes at 245, 246, 247, and 248.

83. Julia Wilbur to Anna M. C. Barnes, November 13, [1862], RASP.

84. Brown, *Foul Bodies*, 252, Forten, *Journal*, September 25, 1854, May 1, 1855, September 12, 1855, October 19, 1855, October 26, 1855, January 18, 1866, December 16, 1857, July 5, 1858, April 23, 1859, 58, 72, 74, 75, 85, 90, 104, 112, 122, 128.

85. Fields and Fields, *Racecraft*.

86. Fannie Green Diary, Saturday, July 12, 1862; Monday, [July] 7, [1862], EU.

87. Fannie Green Diary, [November] 10, [1862]; [November] 22, [1862]; September 23, [1862], EU.

88. Fannie Green Diary, Wednesday, October 1, 1862; Saturday, December 6, 1862; Tuesday, [December] 31, [1862]; Wednesday April 1, 1863; Thursday April 2, [1863], EU.

89. Fannie Green Diary, Monday, [May] 4, [1863]; Saturday, [May] 23, 1863. In May 1863, Fannie also "hired a sewing girl." (Monday, [May] 11 [1863]), EU.

90. Telegraph, L. Thomas to Mrs. S. W. Dade, American Telegraph Company, Received at Metropolitan Hotel, [NY] Oct 15th 1862, giving Dade permission to travel to Beaufort S.C. [Mrs. S. W. Dade] to My dear Sisters, Beaufort, LC Sunday Nov 2nd, 1862; Tuesday morning, Jany 27th [1863] to dear sisters, Mrs. Irving H. McJesson Collection No. 1542, Henderson Section, Henderson Letters, 1851–1917; Asa [Fiske] to Lizzie [Elizabeth Fiske], January 20, 1863, Memphis, Office Sup't Contrabands, Asa Severence Fiske Correspondence, John Aldrich Stephenson Collection, LOC. It was not the first time Elizabeth Fiske had lived in the South. Before her marriage, she followed the path of many Northern educated women who went to the South as teachers in private homes and girls' academies before the war. Hers was a brief and unhappy experience at a free school in Shepherdstown, Virginia. Fiske entered military service during the Civil War as the chaplain of the Fourth Minnesota Volunteer Infantry in the fall of 1861 where he served for a year and a half before being transferred by special order of General Grant in January 1863 to the position of superintendent of contrabands in the military district of Memphis.

91. Asa [Fiske] to Lizzie [Elizabeth Fiske], January 20, 1863, Asa Fiske Papers, Stephenson Collection, LOC.

92. Lizzie [Elizabeth Fiske] to My Dear Mother [Mrs. C. [Catherine] H. Hand, Madison, Conn.], February 22, 1863, Memphis, Tenn., Asa Fiske Correspondence, Stephenson Papers, LOC. Like other occupation cities, Memphis attracted a host of reputable and not so reputable people from merchants and lawyers to prostitutes, making housing scarce and expensive.

93. Lizzie [Elizabeth] H. Fiske to Mother [Mrs. C. [Catherine] W. Hand], Memphis, July 25, 1863, Asa Fiske Papers, Stephenson Papers, LOC.

94. Sister Rebecca to My Dear Lizzie, Philadelphia, April 13, 1863, Stephenson Papers, LOC.

95. Elizabeth Hand Journal, October 7, 1849; October 28, 1849; Tuesday, November 27, 1849, Stephenson Papers, LOC. *The Greek Slave*, now in the permanent collection of the Corcoran School of the Arts and Design, toured the United States in

1847 and 1848 and is currently the subject of a major exhibition at the Smithsonian Institution, Stephenson Papers, LOC.

96. Yellin, *Women and Sisters*, 99–124, quotes at 124. Most white Americans who viewed Powers's *The Greek Slave* during its tour of American cities from New England to New York and Philadelphia and south to Baltimore, Washington, Louisville, St. Louis, and New Orleans would not have found it difficult to disassociate the statue from American slavery and enslaved women. As Charmaine A. Nelson argues, Powers's decision to represent slavery through the body of a Greek woman enslaved during the Greek War of Independence "effectively disavowed the specificity and immediacy of American slavery and the black female slaves on which it depended." Hand could thus be touched by the statue but not see it as a way to think about the enslavement of women in her world, in her own country. When she encountered human beings who were actually enslaved, she did not see dignity, sorrow, or disdain in their faces. In a similar way, Nell Irvin Painter writes, William Story's *Libyan Sibyl* (1860) avoided "a look associated with the enslaved American working classes." See Nelson, "Hiram Powers's America," 173. See also Nelson, *The Color of Stone*, 75–140; Kasson, *Marble Queens and Captives*; and Painter, *Sojourner Truth*, 158.

97. Elizabeth Hand Journal, September 1, 1849, Stephenson Papers, LOC.

98. Elizabeth Hand Journal, May 28, 1857; Friday, June 19, 1857; July 30, 1857, Stephenson Papers, LOC.

99. Elizabeth Hand Journal, June 7, 1857, Stephenson Papers, LOC.

100. A. Conant to Kate Conant, Thetford, February 7, 1863, A. Conant to Kate Conant, Monday Eve, February 9, 1863, Linsley Papers, DU; Jeffrey, *The Great Silent Army of Abolitionism*, 266.

101. French, *Slavery in South Carolina*; Forten, *Journal*, November 10, 1862, December 19, 1862, 151, 167.

102. Silber, *Daughters of the Union*, 231.

103. Geo. A. Nourse to [Asa] Fiske, St. Paul, Minn., February 14, 1863, Fiske Papers, Stephenson Collection, LOC. For Nourse's reputation as an antislavery Democratic-Republican, see Foner, *Free Soil, Free Labor, Free Men*, 185.

104. Geo. A. Nourse to [Asa] Fiske, April 21, 1863, Fiske Papers, Stephenson Collection, LOC.

105. [Catherine Noyes] to My dear Nelly, from Capt. John Fripp's St. Helena, January 3, 1864, Catherine P. Noyes Correspondence, Noyes-Balch Family Papers, DU; Forten, *Journal*, November 5, 1862, 148.

106. Sterling, *We Are Your Sisters*, 255–56. The PAS was founded as the Society for the Relief of Free Negroes Unlawfully Held in Bondage. It established a Committee on Employment in 1862 to aid refugees fleeing to the city. Bacon, "The Pennsylvania Abolition Society's Mission for Black Education," 24.

107. Sterling, *We Are Your Sisters*, 255.

108. Holland, *Letters and Diary of Laura M. Towne*, April 27, 1867, 182.

109. Holland, *Letters and Diary of Laura M. Towne*, July, 17, 1862, 78.

110. Silber, *Daughters of the Union*, 230–31.

111. MacCarthy, "The Home for Aged Colored Women," 69–70.

112. Sterling, *We Are Your Sisters*, 255–56, quote at 256.

113. Saturday, [June] 29; Sunday, [June] 30; Monday, July 1; Thursday, [October 11], Monday, [October 15], Tuesday, October 16, 1855, Ravella Balch Diaries, Noyes-Balch Family Papers, Rubenstein Library, DU.

114. Bacon and Howland, *Letters of a Family*, vol. 2, GMW [Georgeanna M. Woolsey] to Mother [Jane S. Woolsey], June 28, [1862], 433.

115. H. A. Adams to My Dear Miss Gaylord, Western Sanitary Com., Huntsville, Ala., March 28, 1864, Civil War Soldiers' Letters, box 76, Ladies Soldiers' Aid Society Papers, folder 2, Clements Library, University of Michigan; Fannie Green Diary, March 30, 1862, EU.

116. Fannie Green Diary, Sunday, [July] 6, [1862], EU.

117. Sunday, [January 17], Catherine P. Noyes Correspondence, Noyes-Balch Family Papers, Rubenstein Library, DU.

118. Eleanor J. W. Baker to Dear Friend, [Anna Gurney], Richmond, Va., January 25, 1848, Mrs. Eleanor J. W. Baker Journal, 1848, Rubenstein Library, DU. Weir's painting was commissioned by the U.S. government in 1836 and completed in 1843. Americans around the country turned out to view *Embarkation of the Pilgrims* before it was placed in the Capitol Rotunda. The painting was first exhibited at the U.S. Military Academy at West Point and traveled to Boston and New York. It was later exhibited at the Philadelphia Centennial Exhibition of 1876.

119. Mrs. Eleanor J. W. Baker Journal, 1848, undated entry, DU.

120. Berlin et al., *The Wartime Genesis of Free Labor: The Lower South*, 156.

121. Holland, *Letters and Diary of Laura M. Towne*, June 13, 1865, 164; Fields, "Lost Causes," 67.

CHAPTER SIX

1. Zillah Haynie Brandon Diary, August 19, 1864, vo. 4, 381, ADAH; Hardin, *The Private War of Lizzie Hardin*, 266.

2. Edmondston, *"Journal of a Secesh Lady,"* May 8, 1865, 710.

3. Kate [Catherine Crosland] to Nellie, Walnut Hill, S.C., December 28, 1864, Thomas M. McIntosh Papers, Rubenstein Library, DU. Crossland was a teacher before the war and lived at home. Her family owned nineteen slaves in 1860. U.S. Census, 1860.

4. Sherman, *Memoirs*, 2:575.

5. Brandon Diary, December 9, 1864, vol. 4, 369, ADAH. See also Rubin, *A Shattered Nation*, 86–87.

6. Rable, *Civil Wars*, 154. The turn to what is described as "hard war" is attributed to several factors, from the use of guerrilla warfare and technological and industrial innovations like the long-range rifle musket that fueled the number of

battlefield casualties to the collapse of the line dividing the battlefield from the home front.

7. Rable, *Civil Wars*, 155.

8. Grimsley, *The Hard Hand of War*.

9. Neely, *The Civil War and the Limits of Destruction*, 199.

10. Rubin, *A Shattered Nation*, 87–89.

11. Brandon Diary, July 6, 1876, vol. 4, ADAH; Eleanora Willauer Diary, October 3, 1862, Special Collections Online, University Libraries, UT.

12. Willauer Diary, February 4, 1863, and Sunday, March 19, 1865, Special Collections Online, University Libraries, UT; East, *Sarah Morgan*, May 31 [1862], 96.

13. Kate D. Foster Diary, July 13, [1863], near Natchez, Miss., Rubenstein Library, DU.

14. William Sherman to Maria Boyle Ewing Sherman, Memphis, Tenn., August 6, 1862, in Simpson and Berlin, *Sherman's Civil War*, 262.

15. Williams, "Letters of General Thomas Williams," 320. Such views were also captured in "she-devil" moniker.

16. Myers, *The Children of Pride*, 1229; Huckaby and Simpson, *Tulip Evermore*, 28.

17. Furry, *The Preacher's Tale*, 93.

18. Glatthaar, *The March to the Sea and Beyond*, quotes at 136, 116, and 133.

19. F. B. [Francis Bacon] to G. M. W. [Georgeanna M. Woolsey], July 6, 1863, in Bacon and Howland, *Letters of a Family*, vol. 2, 522.

20. Royster, *The Destructive War*, 87.

21. William T. Sherman to Hon. S. P. Chase, Memphis, Tenn., August 11, 1862; to Ellen Sherman, August 29, 1862, in Simpson and Berlin, *Sherman's Civil War*, 271, 281.

22. Sherman to Chase, Memphis, Tenn., August 11, 1862, in Simpson and Berlin, *Sherman's Civil War*, 271. The letter was in response to Chase's letter of August 2. See *OR*, 3:2, p. 349.

23. *OR*, 1:17, pt. 2, p. 98–99. General Orders No. 15, which modified General Orders No. 14, allowed some white residents to remain but ordered the majority to leave or be escorted ten miles out of the city. Royster, *The Destructive War*, 86.

24. Royster, *The Destructive War*, 79–143, quotes at 79, 80, and 81.

25. Edmondston, *"Journal of a Secesh Lady,"* February 15, 1862, 117–18.

26. Maj. Gen. Wm. T. Sherman, Commanding, Headquarters Fifteenth Army Corps, Camp on Big Black to H. W. Hill, Esq., Chairman of Meeting of Citizens of Warren County, Miss., September, 7, 1863, in "Maj.-Gen. W. T. Sherman on the War: His Views on the Negro Question," *New York Times*, January 17, 1864.

27. As quoted in Walters, "General William T. Sherman and Total War," 473.

28. Meriwether, *Recollections of 92 Years*, 64.

29. *OR*, 1:17, pt. 2, p. 98.

30. *OR*, 1:17, pt. 2, p. 98.

31. Meriwether, *Recollections of 92 Years*, 80–81.

32. Sherman to Maj. J. [John] A. Rawlins, Asst. Adj. Gen. Corinth, Head Quarters Fifth Division, Army of the Tennessee, Memphis, August 14, 1862, in Simpson and Berlin, *Sherman's Civil War*, 277. Fisher, "Prepare Them for My Coming"; Walters, "General William T. Sherman and Total War"; Meriwether, *Recollections of 92 Years*, 82–83. In 1867, Meriwether and her husband hosted one of the first meetings of the Ku Klux Klan in their Memphis home, currently the site of the Peabody Hotel. Meriwether, *Recollections of 92 Years*, v. She later became a prominent advocate of women's suffrage.

33. Sherman to Dr. E. S. Plummer & others, physicians in Memphis, signing to a petition, Head Quarters, Fifth Division, Army of Tennessee, Memphis, July 23, 1862, in Simpson and Berlin, *Sherman's Civil War*, 256–57. For the full response to the physicians, see *OR*, I, 17: pt. 2, p. 114.

34. *OR*, I, 17: pt. 2, p. 114.

35. *ORN*, ser. 1, vol. 19, p. 140. A committee of men from the town protested the destruction of property, arguing that such attacks contributed to "the demoralizing of our servile population" (142).

36. *ORN*, ser. 1, vol. 19, pp. 143, 141. The first occupation was brief, lasting only two days (*ORN*, ser. 1, vol. 19, p. 215). Despite these measures, Confederate guerrilla activity continued in the area. Donaldsonville was twice reoccupied by Union forces, in September and October 1862 (*ORN*, ser. 1, vol. 19, p. 776). Donaldsonville continued to be a problem into 1863 (*ORN*, ser. 1, vol. 19, p. 487); Extract of Journal of the U.S.S. *Richmond*, Commander Alden, U.S. Navy, commanding, July 15, 1862–March 15, 1863, entry for January 16, 1863, 1:19, pp. 763–64; Extract from diary of Lieutenant [F. A.] Roe, [Executive Officer], U.S. Navy, U.S.S. *Pensacola*, *ORN*, ser. 1, vol. 19, pp. 773–76, July 22–30, 1862).

37. *ORN*, ser. 1, vol. 19, p. 251.

38. *ORN*, ser. 1, vol. 24, p. 361.

39. *OR*, ser. 1, vol. 24, pt. 3, p. 158.

40. See chapter 7.

41. *ORN*, ser. 1, vol. 19, pp. 191, 192.

42. Mitchell, *The Vacant Chair*, 89–103.

43. General Orders No. 100, "Instructions for the Government of Armies of the United States in the Field."

44. Witt, *Lincoln's Code*, 182.

45. General Orders No. 100, "Instructions for the Government of Armies of the United States in the Field."

46. *ORN*, ser. 1, vol. 24, pp. 365–67, quotes at 367, 365.

47. *ORN*, ser. 1, vol. 24, p. 493.

48. *ORN*, ser. 1, vol. 19, p. 215.

49. *ORN*, ser. 1, vol. 19, p. 215; *ORN*, ser. 1, vol. 19, pp. 251, 776. Sarah Morgan of nearby Baton Rouge saw the Union response as excessive. She dismissed the attacks as the work of "some fool [who] fired at a gunboat." East, *Sarah Morgan*, 257.

50. Whites, "Forty Shirts and a Wagonload of Wheat," 61, 62, 66. The problem

led General Ewing to banish the guerrilla women from a three-and-a-half county area under General Order No. 11.

51. Memorandum of C. W. W. (Charley) [Charles W. Woolsey], in camp before Fredericksburg [Spring 1863], in Bacon and Howland, *Letters of a Family*, vol. 2, 506–7. Charles Woolsey was the Union soldier sent to deliver the warning to Seddon, whose house was protected by a Union guard.

52. *ORN*, ser. 1, vol. 24, p. 362.

53. *ORN*, ser. 1, vol. 24, p. 362; Sherman to Ellen [Sherman], Memphis, August 10, 1862, in Simpson and Berlin, *Sherman's Civil War*, 266.

54. Sherman to Ellen Sherman, July 31, 1862, in Simpson and Berlin, *Sherman's Civil War*, 260.

55. Sherman to Ellen [Sherman], Memphis, August 10, 1862, in Simpson and Berlin, *Sherman's Civil War*, 267, 266.

56. Haviland, *A Woman's Life Work*, 266.

57. Sherman to Hill, September 7, 1863, in "Maj.-Gen. W. T. Sherman on the War: His Views on the Negro Question," *New York Times*, January 17, 1864.

58. *OR*, ser. 1, vol. 17, pt. 2, pp. 113, 158–60. He also made it clear that the refugees were free to return to slavery if they so desired.

59. William T. Sherman to Thomas Ewing, August 10, 1862; Sherman to John Sherman, Memphis, August 13, 1862, in Simpson and Berlin, *Sherman's Civil War*, 262–64, 272–73.

60. Simpson and Berlin, *Sherman's Civil War*, 264. Ewing was also a former U.S. senator and served for brief periods as secretary of treasury and secretary of the interior. Ewing's son and Sherman's brother-in-law and foster brother, Gen. Thomas Ewing Jr., would famously issue General Order No. 11 on August 25, 1863, exiling the population of several counties on the Missouri side of the Missouri-Kansas border (the counties of Jackson, Cass, Bates, and northern Vernon County that directly adjoined in a line beginning with Jackson, the northernmost of the four, down to Vernon) in response to guerrilla activity. Ewing's order inspired the protest painting by George Caleb Bingham currently displayed at Central Branch of the Kansas City Public Library.

61. On such acknowledgements and mistresses' ambivalence toward them, see, for example, Rable, *Civil Wars*, 164–67.

62. Rowland and Croxall, *The Journal of Julia Le Grand*, 62–63.

63. Rowland and Croxall, *The Journal of Julia Le Grand*, 62–63.

64. Mrs. Mary Rhodes, "War Times in Alabama," in *Our Women in the War*, 274.

65. Mrs. Mary Rhodes, "War Times in Alabama," in *Our Women in the War*, 274.

66. Charles Francis Adams Jr., to his Father, Camp of the First Massachusetts Cavalry, Warrenton, Va., September 5, 1863, in Worthington, *A Cycle of Adams Letters*, 77–78.

67. Brandon Diary, Transcription of Excerpts and Partial Index, 350, ADAH; Simpson and Berlin, *Sherman's Civil War*, 266.

68. George E. Butler to My ever dear Sister Emma [Emma Butler] in Tulip, camp

near Knoxville, Tenn., December 2, 1863, in Huckaby and Simpson, *Tulip Evermore*, 38. Butler served with the Third Arkansas Regiment.

69. Brandon Diary, [1855], June 14, 1865, vol. 4, ADAH.

70. Wood, *Masterful Women*, 21.

71. Dubose, "Reminiscences of St. Stephen's Parish," quotes at 70 and 74, respectively.

72. Dubose, "Address Delivered at the Seventeenth Anniversary of the Black Oak Society," 11.

73. Porcher, "Historical and Social Sketch of Craven County," 112.

74. Allen, *Tories*, 248.

75. Jasanoff, *Liberty's Exiles*, 11.

76. Frey, *Water from the Rock*, 82–85, 91–92, 99–102, 116–18, 133–34; Norton, *Liberty's Daughters*, 208; Wood, *Masterful Women*, 20–23.

77. Frey, *Water from the Rock*, 85.

78. As quoted on Frey, *Water from the Rock*, 83.

79. As quoted in Allen, *Tories*, 118. On April 16, 1861, three regiments from Marblehead were the first in Massachusetts to report for duty in the Civil War.

80. While my focus here is on the question of the collapse of the home front, the historiography linking women's experience in the American Revolution and the Civil War has focused largely on how the Revolution provided a source of inspiration for sacrifice and political identity. See, for example, Silber, *Gender and the Sectional Conflict*, 37–39; and Kerber, *Women of the Republic*.

81. Chorley, *History of St. Philips's Church*, quotes at 132 and 133; Jasanoff, *Liberty's Exiles*, 34–35, quotes at 42 and 35. Robinson remained loyal to the king. His personal property was seized by the Commissioners of Sequestration and sold on April 21, 1777. He would suffer additional losses, including his entire landed estate of 60,000 acres. Chorley, *History of St. Philips's Church*, 133, 134–35.

82. Mrs. Mary Rhodes, "War Times in Alabama," in *Our Women in the War*, 273.

83. For a brief discussion of this point, see Silber, *Gender and Sectional Conflict*, 38–39.

84. Exceptions include Whites, "Forty Shirts and a Wagonload of Wheat," 64: Clinton, *Tara Revisited*; Clinton, *Stepdaughters of History*; Faust, *Mothers of Invention*; Giesberg, *Army at Home*; McCurry, *Confederate Reckoning*; Silber, *Gender and Sectional Conflict*.

85. Maj. W. T. Sherman to M. Tomeny, Esq., "A Letter to the Union League in Memphis, Headquarters, Fifteenth Army Corps, Walnut Hills, Memphis, May 25, 1863," *New York Times*, June 21, 1863.

86. Sherman to Ewing, August 10, 1862; Sherman to John Sherman, Memphis, August 13, 1862, in Simpson and Berlin, *Sherman's Civil War*, 262–64, 272–73.

87. Moss, *Annals of the United States Christian Commission*, 505; Sherman, *Memoirs*, vol. 2, 653.

88. *OR*, ser. 1, vol. 44, p. 799.

89. Over the past two decades, studies that feature the home front prominently have proliferated in Civil War studies. See, for example, Vinovskis, *Toward a Social History of the Civil War*; Rable, *Civil Wars*; Mitchell, *The Vacant Chair*; Clinton and Silber, *Divided Houses*; Leonard, *Yankee Women*; Faust, *Mothers of Invention*; McPherson, *For Cause and Comrades*; Bleser and Gordon, *Intimate Strategies of the Civil War*; Cashin, *The War Was You and Me*; Campbell, *When Sherman Marched North from the Sea*; Silber, *Daughters of the Union*; McCurry, *Confederate Reckoning*; and Whites and Long, *Occupied Women*.

90. Campbell and Jensen, "Gendering Two Wars," 101.

91. Ella to Grandfather and Mother, March 1865, Woodside, Sams Family Papers, SCL.

92. Taylor, Matthews, and Power, *The Leverett Letters*, November 26, 1864, December 8, 1864, February 24, [1865], 376–87, quotes at 380, 376, 386, 384.

93. As quoted in Kerber, *Women of the Republic*, 35.

94. For quote, see McCurry, *Confederate Reckoning*.

95. The most cited figures estimate the number of slaves who entered Union lines at 500,000 and the number of white Southerners who became refugees at 200,000. Wagner, Gallagher, and Finkelman, *The Library of Congress Civil War Desk Reference*, 721; Berlin et al., *The Wartime Genesis of Free Labor: The Lower South*, 77–81.

96. Charles Francis Adams to his Father [John Quincy Adams], Camp of the First Massachusetts Cavalry, September 5, 1863, in Worthington, *A Cycle of Adams Letters*, 79.

CHAPTER SEVEN

1. [Maria R. Mann] to Eliza [Eliza S. Mann Wilbur], February 10, 1863, Helena, Ark. (Freedman's Camps), February–April 1863. The Papers of Mary Tyler Peabody Mann [Mrs. Horace Mann], Manuscript Division, LOC (hereafter Letters from Helena, Ark.).

2. See West, *Family or Freedom*, for a compelling account of reenslavement petitions during slavery.

3. Chaplain Samuel Sawyer to Major General Curtis, January 26, 1863, enclosing Samuel Sawyer et al. to Major General Curtis, December 29, 1862, RG 108, in Berlin et al., *The Wartime Genesis of Free Labor: The Lower South*, 675.

4. Maria [R. Mann] to Aunt Mary [Mary Tyler Peabody Mann], May 18, 1863, Mann, Letters from Helena, Ark, LOC.

5. *ORN*, ser. 1, vol. 24, p. 494.

6. Louisa Alexander to Archer Alexander, November 16, 1863, William Greenleaf Papers, Missouri History Museum, St. Louis. Louisa Alexander's husband, Archer, arranged for a German farmer to rescue her and a daughter. Eliot, *The Story of Archer Alexander*, 80–83. Archer Alexander was the model for the kneeling slave

on the Emancipation Statue in Freedom Park on Capitol Hill dedicated in 1876. See also Glymph, "Invisible Disabilities." On slavery's destruction in Missouri, see Burke, *On Slavery's Border*, 268–307.

7. Eliot, *The Story of Archer Alexander*. See also Burke, *On Slavery's Border*, 223–24.

8. Lincoln used the phrase "actual freedom" in his December 1, 1862, address to Congress and the Preliminary Emancipation Proclamation. For an extended discussion, see Glymph, "Rose's War"; and Glymph, "Du Bois's *Black Reconstruction*."

9. Yeatman, *Report to the Western Sanitary Commission*, 8.

10. Foner, "The Civil War and Slavery," 93; Hahn, *A Nation under Our Feet*; Downs, *Sick from Freedom*; Oakes, "The Political Significance of Slave Resistance"; Oakes, *Freedom National*, 192–255. For new and forthcoming work on slave flight during the war, see Manning, *Troubled Refuge*; and Taylor, *Embattled Freedom*.

11. Du Bois, *Black Reconstruction in America*; Berlin, *Many Thousands Gone*; Franklin and Schweninger, *Runaway Slaves*; Hahn, *A Nation under Our Feet*; Hahn, *Political Worlds*; Litwack, *Been in the Storm So Long*; Schwalm, *Emancipation's Diaspora*. On the question of slave community and family dynamics, see, for example, Camp, *Closer to Freedom*, 123–27; Frankel, *Freedom's Women*, 160–71; Penningroth, *The Claims of Kinfolk*, 164–76; Regosin, *Freedom's Promise*; Stevenson, *Life in Black and White*; and White, *Ar'n't I a Woman?* More broadly on Civil War women refugees, see Cashin, "Into the Trackless Wilderness"; Faust, *Mothers of Invention*; and Sternhell, *Routes of War*. My analysis of community formation is also informed by Deutsch, *No Separate Refuge*.

12. Rations Reports, Reports of Freedmen in Different Camps and Quarters, August 15, 1864, Miss., Freedmen's Dept., Box 36, Misc. Records, 1863–65, RG 105; A. S. [Asa Severance] Fiske, Assistant Superintendent of Contrabands, to [John Eaton]. January 29, 1863; [Asa Fiske] to Chaplain [John] Eaton, April 23, 1863, Asa Severence Fiske Dairies, LOC. Fiske wrote that burials averaged fifteen per day. Infant mortality was extremely high. On one day alone, three babies died; Berlin et al., *The Wartime Genesis of Free Labor: The Lower South*, 686.

13. Deposition of Charles Washington, Co. E, Forty-Seventh Civil War Pension File of Charles Washington, RG 15, NA. James Berry owned eighty-four slaves in 1860. U.S. Census, 1860; Slave Schedules, 1860.

14. Deposition E, Cynthia Hobson, March 23, 1901, Vicksburg, Mississippi, in Lutitia Taylor, Widow of Henry Taylor, Widow's Certificate, No, 115149, NARA..

15. Deposition E, Cynthia Hobson, Lutitia Taylor Pension File. The *Hannibal*, made famous through the work of Mark Twain, sank in September 1863. Report of the Secretary of the Treasury. Buchanan, *Black Life on the Mississippi*, 10, 13, 65–66, 82–102, 153–54; Johnson, *River of Dark Dreams*, 141–50, quote at 146. See also Hines, "Geographies of Freedom."

16. *ORN*, ser. 1, vol. 24, p. 494.

17. *OR*, series 1, vol. 24, p. 701; *ORN*, ser. 1, vol. 24, p. 361.

18. Louisa Smith Widow's Pension Certificate, 121431; Hunter, *Bound in Wedlock*;

Gutman, *The Black Family in Slavery and Freedom*; Williams, *Help Me to Find My People*.

19. The arrival of Adj. Gen. Lorenzo Thomas in March 1863 on orders from Secretary of War Edwin Stanton energized black enlistment in the valley. Depositions of Louisa Smith, Malinda Johnson, and Thomas Payne, Louisa Smith Pension File No. 121431, RG 15, NA.

20. A. Lincoln, to Hon. James C. Conkling, August 26, 1863, abrahamlincolnonline.org.

21. Berlin et al., *The Wartime Genesis of Free Labor: The Lower South*, 682.

22. Graham and Hartwell, *Report by the Committee of the Contrabands' Relief Commission*, 8.

23. Berlin et al., *The Wartime Genesis of Free Labor in the Lower South*, 632.

24. *OR*, series 1, vol. 24, pt. 3, pp. 158, 177, 631, 105, 158; *ORN*, ser. 1, vol. 24, pp. 492–99, 474–78.

25. *OR*, ser. 1, vol. 24, pt. 1, p. 105; *OR*, ser. 1, vol. 24, pt. 3, p. 476.

26. "An Act to Suppress Insurrection," U.S. Statutes at Large, vol. 12, 589–92.

27. See Quiner, *The Military History of Wisconsin*, 213–14.

28. Special Field Orders No. 18, December 9, 1862, *OR*, ser. 1, vol. 17, pt. 2, p. 396; Du Bois, *Black Reconstruction*, 68–70. Special Field Orders No. 18 also called for the removal of white women and children "from the army in the field" to Holly Springs, the supply base of Grant's advancing army or to some place north of that point.

29. Eaton, *Grant, Lincoln, and the Freedmen*, 2–3, 20–21; 26; Du Bois, *Black Reconstruction*, 70.

30. Rogers, *War Pictures*, 110, 117, 122–23.

31. *Report by the Committee of the Contrabands' Relief Commission*, 8; Berlin et al., *The Wartime Genesis of Free Labor: The Lower South*, 680, 686.

32. Berlin et al., *The Wartime Genesis of Free Labor: The Lower South*, 680.

33. Stevenson, *Life in Black and White*, 221, 254–55.

34. Penningroth, *The Claims of Kinfolk*, 170.

35. We still know comparatively little about household formations of this sort during slavery.

36. As Leslie Schwalm has shown, ties of kin and community were also vital to black women's survival in the South Carolina lowcountry. See Schwalm, *A Hard Fight for We*, 103.

37. Affidavit of Louisa Smith, Case of Louisa Smith, Warren County, Mississippi, Widow of Israel Smith, Pension No. 161625; Affidavits of Malinda Johnson (Johnston), September 16, 1874, Vicksburg, Mississippi; Louisa Johnston (Johnson), February 17, 1875, [Vicksburg]; Thomas Payne, September 16, 1874, Vicksburg; and Sam Christmas, March 23, 1902, Vicksburg, in Louisa Smith Pension File No. 121431, RG 15, NARA. Robinson was among those who came forward to testify in support of Louisa's application for a widow's pension years later, along with Thomas Payne

who had also witnessed the marriage. Deposition of Lutitia Taylor, Lutitia Taylor Pension File No. 115149. Israel Smith and the other men of the Forty-Seventh Regiment, United States Colored Infantry, initially joined the Eighth Regiment Infantry, organized at Lake Providence, La., in May 1863, a predecessor unit to the Forty-Seventh Regiment. Malinda and Louisa Johnson's last name is sometimes spelled Johnston in the records.

38. *OR*, ser., 1, vol. 24, pt. 3, p. 158; Berlin et al., *The Wartime Genesis of Free Labor: The Lower South*, 637.

39. Affidavit of Malinda Johnson, September 16, 1874, in Louisa Smith Pension File. Like many new recruits, Israel died (on July 27, 1863) of dysentery, one of the three principal contributors to the high mortality rate of Civil War soldiers, before he could ever see a battle or fire a gun. Dora Costa and Matthew Kahn estimate a 23 percent mortality rate for black soldiers, more than 90 percent of which is attributable to disease. See Costa and Kahn, "Forging a New Identity," 11. On disease, see Steiner, *Disease in the Civil War*, 10–11; and Humphreys, *Marrow of Tradition*.

40. Affidavit of Sallie Kiger, September 15, 1874, in Louisa Smith Pension File.

41. Exhibit 11, [Affidavit of] Charles Anderson, December 15, 1874, Vicksburg, Mississippi; Affidavit of Sallie Kiger, September 15, 1874, [Vicksburg]; Affidavit of Malinda Johnson, all in Louisa Smith Pension File. When Company D mustered out at Vicksburg in March 1866, Sallie Kiger and Louisa Smith rekindled their friendship and remained close over the coming years. In 1867, Louisa returned to the plantation where she had been enslaved and her mother remained, once again earning a living as a laundress. In 1868, she moved back to Vicksburg and supported herself on the proceeds of her garden, the chickens she raised, and money earned picking cotton as a day laborer. For a discussion of the expanded "social landscape" women experienced during the war, the importance of friendships made before and during the war, and the resilience of these relationships after the war, see Frankel, *Freedom's Women*, 164–65.

42. Affidavit of Thomas Payne, September 16, 1874; Deposition C, Emeline Anderson, Vicksburg, in Taylor Pension File. The mobility of black women would become even more difficult in 1864 with the establishment of a pass system to regulate their passing "from one place to another" under General Orders No. 9. Berlin et al., *The Wartime Genesis of Free Labor: The Lower South*, 803. General Orders No. 9 also established new regulations on the employment of laborers on the plantations.

43. Deposition C, Emeline Anderson in Taylor Pension File. Taylor also eventually moved to Vicksburg. Enslaved women came to refugee camps by various routes. Some would remain in the camps for the duration of the war. Others would be transferred to labor camps. A small minority secured work at military posts as cooks and laundresses.

44. Deposition C, Emeline Anderson; Deposition D, Clarissa Anderson, March 23, 1901, Vicksburg; Deposition C, Alberta Lovings, November 28, 1901, Shelby, Bolivar County; Deposition E, Cynthia Hobson; Deposition F, Leonard Owens, April 23,

1901, Brunswick, Warren County, Mississippi; Deposition G, Deposition of Lutitia Taylor Deposition, all in Lutitia Taylor Pension File. Owens and Hill enlisted on the same day and place as Israel Smith, May 1, 1863, at Lake Providence. Born in Richmond, Va., Henry was one of the million slaves moved to the Deep South in the decades before the war. In 1855, he had ended up in the slave market at Vicksburg, where he was purchased by Lutitia's master and taken to the Deer Creek, Washington County, Miss., plantation where he met and married Lutitia.

45. Berlin et al., *The Wartime Genesis of Free Labor: The Lower South*, 680.

46. Berlin et al., *The Wartime Genesis of Free Labor: The Lower South*, 650–55.

47. Deposition E, Cynthia Hobson; Sam Christmas, March 23, 1902, Vicksburg, Deposition D, Clarissa Christmas, March 23, 1902, Vicksburg, all in Taylor Pension File.

48. Hahn, *A Nation under Our Feet*, 79–82; Berlin and Rowland, *Families and Freedom*, 36, 100; Moss, *Annals of the United States Christian Commission*, 402–3.

49. Deposition E, Cynthia Hobson, March 23, 1901, Taylor Pension File.

50. Costa and Kahn, "Forging a New Identity," 12–13. On the importance of social factors that promote survival in war, see Costa and Kahn, *Heroes and Cowards*.

51. Berlin et al., *The Wartime Genesis of Free Labor: The Lower South*, 637.

52. Bond and Sherman, *Memphis in Black and White*, 54–56.

53. [Maria R. Mann] to Eliza [Eliza S. Mann Wilbur], February 10, 1863, Letters from Helena, Ark., Mann Papers, LOC; Glymph, "Refugee Camp at Helena."

54. [Maria R. Mann], to Eliza [Eliza S. Mann Wilbur], February 10, 1863; Mann to Aunt Mary [Mary Tyler Peabody Mann], [July 1863], Letters from Helena, Ark.

55. Berlin et al., *The Wartime Genesis of Free Labor: The Lower South*, 711.

56. Samuel Sawyer, Pearl P. Ingall, and J. G. Gorman to Major General Curtis, December 29, 1862, enclosed in Chaplain Samuel Sawyer to Maj. Gen. Curtis, January 26, 1863, LR, ser. 22, RG 108, in Berlin et al., *The Wartime Genesis of Free Labor: The Lower South*, 675–76. Sawyer took over as superintendent of contrabands at Helena in January 1863.

57. Bussey, *Civil War Reminiscences* (1864), 26, 29, Iowa State University Library Special Collections and University Archives.

58. Chaplain Samuel Sawyer to Major General [Samuel] Curtis, January 26, 1863, Berlin et al., *The Wartime Genesis of Free Labor: The Lower South*, 674–75.

59. Rogers, *War Pictures*, 122–23.

60. [Maria R. Mann] to Eliza [Eliza S. Mann Wilbur], February 10, 1863, Letters from Helena, Ark., Mann Papers, LOC.

61. Shinault, "Camp Life of Contrabands and Freedmen."

62. [Maria R. Mann] to Eliza [Eliza S. Mann Wilbur], February 10, 1863, Letters from Helena, Ark., Mann Papers, LOC. See also Glymph, "Refugee Camp at Helena, Arkansas."

63. [Maria R. Mann] to Eliza [Eliza S. Mann Wilbur], February 10, 1863, Letters from Helena, Ark., Mann Papers, LOC; Sawyer to Curtin, *The Wartime Genesis of Free Labor: The Lower South*, 675.

64. Confederate general Earl Van Dorn's victory at Holly Springs was the highlight of a military career diminished by losses at Pea Ridge, Ark., and Corinth, Miss., and a well-gossiped-about reputation for drunkenness and general "licentiousness," including relations with prostitutes. Five months after the battle at Holly Springs, Van Dorn was shot and killed by a Tennessee doctor and slave trader, George B. Peters, allegedly for having conducted an adulterous affair with the doctor's wife. Hartje, *Van Dorn*, 307–20.

65. *OR*, ser. 1, vol. 17, pt. 2, p. 99.

66. Sherman to Ellen Sherman, Memphis, August 20, 1862, in Simpson and Berlin, *Sherman's Civil War*, 281.

67. Sherman to Thomas Ewing, Memphis, August 10, 1862, in Simpson and Berlin, *Sherman's Civil War*, 263–64.

68. Berlin et al., *The Wartime Genesis of Free Labor: The Lower South*, 652–53.

69. John Eaton, Office of Gen. Supt. Contrabands, to Captain Lyman, AQM, in charge of Transportation, Memphis, March 31, 1863, Freedmen's Department, RG 105, NA; Rogers, *War Pictures*, 211; Daniel and Bock, *Island No. 10*.

70. Gen. U. S. Grant, Special Field Orders No. 2, February 12, 1863, *OR* ser. 1, vol. 24, pt. 3, 46, 47, quote at 46; *OR*, ser. 1, vol. 24, pt. 3, p. 144. Fisk would later become assistant commissioner of the Freedmen's Bureau for Texas and Kentucky. Fisk University is named for him.

71. Affidavit of Willis Smith, September 14, 1874, 3 miles outside Vicksburg, Louisa Smith Pension File.

72. Col. H. [Hermann] Lieb to Lieut. Col. H. C. Rodgers, September 13, 1864, Letters Received, 1864, RG 393. Lieb was the commander of Union forces at Milliken's Bend when it was attacked on June 7, 1863.

73. Camp, *Closer to Freedom*, 129. A manuscript in progress explores the question of refugee camps as sites of containment more systematically.

74. I borrow the term *labor camps* from Wood, "Slave Labor Camps in Early America."

75. Bryan to Stanton, July 27, 1863, ser. 360, box 3, B-108 (1863), [B-612].

76. See Glymph, "I'm a Radical Girl."

77. Endorsement by T. W. Sherman, Col. Henry Rust Jr. to Capt. H. Hoffman, March 26, 1863, So. Div., La., LR box 1, Ft. Jackson, La., NARA [C-1004].

78. Maj. Gen. John A. McClernand to Maj. Gen. U. S. Grant, April 1, 1863, Military Commands, Thirteenth AC, LS, pt. 2, No 352, NARA.

79. Eaton, *Grant, Lincoln, and the Freedmen*, 70.

80. Howard, *Autobiography*, 2:264–65. After the war, the bulk of the funds remaining was distributed to the following educational institutions, with Howard University receiving by far the largest share: Howard University, Fisk University, Florida Institute, St. Augustine Normal School and Collegiate Institute, Marysville College, Atlanta University, Storer College, East Tennessee Wesleyan College, Berea College, Richmond Educational Association, St. Martin's School for Loyal Refugees and Freedmen, and the National Theological Institute and University.

See U.S. House of Representatives, Committee on Education and Labor, *Charges against General Howard*.

81. "Report of D. O. McCord, Surg. 63 USCI, Med. Director and Inspector Freedmen, Depts. of Miss. and Ark. Makes Final Report, Vicksburg, Miss.," to Col. John Eaton, Jr. Superintendent of Freedmen, August 3, 1865, M1914, Misc. Reports from Subordinate Offices, RG 105, NARA.

82. "Report of D. O. McCord, Surg. 63 USCI, Med. Director and Inspector Freedmen, Depts. of Miss. and Ark. Makes Final Report, Vicksburg, Miss.," to Col. John Eaton, Jr. Superintendent of Freedmen, August 3, 1865, M1914, Misc. Reports from Subordinate Offices, RG 105, NARA.

83. *Report of the Commissioners of Investigation of Colored Refugees*, 12–16, quote at 14. Complaints of lessee abuse and refusal to pay were common. See Berlin et al., *The Wartime Genesis of Free Labor: The Lower South*, 634–65.

84. Berlin and Rowland, *Families and Freedom*, 100.

85. Asst. Adj. Gen. C. W. Foster to Brig. Gen. L. Thomas, July 28, 1864, LR, Colored Troops Division, RG 94, NARA. See also Berlin, Reidy, and Rowland, *The Black Military Experience*, 262–63.

86. Kate D. Foster Diary, July 4, 1863, Rubenstein Library, DU.

87. Kate D. Foster Diary, July 16, [1863] near Natchez, Miss., Rubenstein Library, DU.

88. Kate D. Foster Diary, July 28, July 30, and Sunday, November 15, 1863, Rubenstein Library, DU.

89. Correspondent, "Natchez."

90. Louisa Smith Deposition, NARA.

91. William D. Butler to Rev. William G. Eliot, September 2, 1863, William D. Butler Papers, Missouri History Museum Archives, St. Louis, Missouri.

92. William D. Butler to Rev. William G. Eliot, September 2, 1863, William D. Butler Papers, Missouri History Museum Archives, St. Louis, Missouri.

93. *ORN*, ser. 1, vol. 24, p. 366; *OR*, ser. 1, vol. 32, pt. 2, pp. 568–69. Life for black refugees on leased plantations was a sordid affair before the raids.

94. *OR*, ser. 1, vol. 32, pt. 2, pp. 568–71; McPherson, *Battle Cry of Freedom*, 784–85. To augment regiment strength, local commanders regularly used detached units in the Mississippi valley. See, for example, *OR*, ser. 1, vol. 24, pt. 2, p. 458. In January 1864, the Confederate Congress ordered these units disbanded and merged into regular forces. But, as McPherson points out, it was "a paper change only."

95. C. W. Montross to William P. Mellen, June 28, 1864, Records of the General Agent, Letters Received [Q-117].

96. *OR*, 1:32, pt. 2, pp. 571, 568–70; Col. Henry Moore to Capt. L. H. Pelouze, March 11, 1862, NARA [C1642.]

97. [Maria R. Mann] to Aunt Mary [Mary Tyler Peabody Mann], Helena, May 18, 1863, Mann Papers, LOC.

98. James Bryan to E. M. Stanton, July 27, 1863, ser. 360, box 3, B-108 (1863), [B-612]; Berlin et al., *The Wartime Genesis of Free Labor: The Lower South*, 715.

322 Notes to Pages 243–44

99. Society of Survivors, *History of the Ram Fleet*, 311.

100. *OR*, ser. 1, vol. 25, pp. 212–16, quotes at 215–16; *OR*, ser. 1, vol. 24, pt. 2, p. 450. Glymph, "This Species of Property," 68. Marine brigades were designed to operate as quick-strike forces against Confederate guerrillas but arrived too late to help in this case.

101. *OR*, ser. 1, vol. 24, pt. 2, pp. 516–17, quote at 517. Society of Survivors, *History of the Ram Fleet*; McPherson, *War on the Waters*, 154–55; Wish, "Slave Disloyalty," 444. For one assessment of the ongoing debate over what exactly happened at Goodrich Landing and Milliken's Bend, see Barnickel, *Milliken's Bend*, 122–38.

102. *OR*, ser. 1, vol. 24, pt. 1, p. 105.

103. *OR*, ser. 1, vol. 25, pp. 213–14, 215; "The War in the Southwest"; McPherson, *Battle Cry of Freedom*, 634. The arrival of two Union gunboats forced a Confederate retreat. The capture of the black soldiers, wrote a Confederate commander on the scene, was an "unfortunate" development, as the preferred policy was to kill them even if they surrendered. Brown, *The Negro in the American Rebellion*, 137–41. Deserters from the Confederate army reported that black and white Federal prisoners captured at Milliken's Bend in June had been hanged in Delhi, La., "in the presence of General Taylor and his forces." *OR*, ser. 1, vol. 24, pt. 1, p. 105. A Union sergeant taken from the Perkins plantation was also reportedly hanged.

104. *OR*, ser. 1, vol. 24, pt. 2, p. 457.

105. Reports of T. C. Calliot, Asst. Special Agent of the Treasury Department, Monthly Reports of the Special Agent, box 2, RG 366; Alsen Mygott's Certificate of Abandonment of Donnell Plantation; J. C. Groshong's Certificate of Abandonment of "Stone" Plantation, RG 366. Nevins, *The War for Union*, 3:417; Berlin et al., *The Wartime Genesis of Free Labor: The Lower South*, 434–36.

106. Trudeau, *Like Men of War*, 100–102. Lieut. Geo. H. Hanks to Maj. Gen. N. P. Banks, July 12, 1863, in Berlin et al., *The Wartime Genesis of Free Labor: The Lower South*, 459. In his capacity as Superintendent of Negro Labor, Hanks was responsible for thirty-three plantations and 12,189 refugees in two Louisiana parishes.

107. *OR*, ser. 1, vol. 24, pt. 2, p. 466.

108. Kate D. Foster Diary, July 7, [1863], near Natchez, Rubenstein Library, DU.

109. J. Coles, Jeremy Porter, and T. M. Stephenson, "Report of the Numbers and Wants of the Contrabands in the Department of the Tennessee, by Committee Appointed by the Chaplains' Association, Vicksburgh [*sic*], Miss., October 19, 1863, published in the *New York Times*, November 12, 1863." On the health and mortality of black people during the Civil War, see Downs, *Sick from Freedom*, 3–41; and Long, *Doctoring Freedom*, 44–69. For a focused discussion of the health of black soldiers, see Humphreys, *Intensely Human*.

110. A. S. [Asa Severance] Fiske to [John Eaton], January 29, 1863; [Asa Severance Fiske] to Chaplain [John] Eaton, April 23, 1863, Asa Severence Fiske Dairies, LOC.

111. Berlin et al., *The Wartime Genesis of Free Labor: The Lower South*, 642–43; Nevins, *The War for Union*, 3:441.

112. *OR*, ser. 1, vol. 32, pt. 2, p. 826. On the Meridian campaign, see *OR*, ser. 1, vol. 32, pt. 2, pp. 146–47; *OR*, ser., 1, vol. 32, pt. 1, pp. 195, 338.

113. *OR*, ser. 1, vol. 34, pp. 714–15. See also Faust, *This Republic of Suffering*, 45; Urwin, "We *Cannot* Treat Negroes . . . as Prisoners of War," 142–43; *OR*, ser. 1, vol. 34, pt. 1, p. 715.

114. As quoted in Burkhardt, *Confederate Rage, Yankee Wrath*, 129–30.

115. "Raid on a Plantation."

116. Marten, *The Children's War*, 129–32.

117. Yeatman, *Report to the Western Sanitary Commission*, 6.

118. Eaton, *Grant, Lincoln, and the Freedmen*, 157–58.

119. Col. R. Owen to Col. [W. B.] Scates, Perkins Plantation, La., May 9, 1863, CN, Thirteenth Army Corps, LR, vol. 3/3. 12 AC, LR, NARA [C-8812].

120. For quote, see Litwack, *Been in the Storm So Long*, 52; Berlin, Reidy, and Rowland, *The Black Military Experience*, 269–71.

121. Asst. Spl. Agt. Tho. Heater, Treasury Department, to Hon. Wm. P. Mellen, May 10, 1864, [Q-19]; Asst. Spl. Agt. C. A. Montross, to W. P. Mellen, April 28, 1864, NARA [Q-169]; Yeatman, *Report to the Western Sanitary Commission*, 6–7.

122. *OR*, ser. 1, vol. 24, pt. 2, pp. 455–56, quote at 456. For the Confederate report of the attacks, see *OR*, ser. 1, vol. 24, pt. 2, pp. 457–61.

123. "Statement of Claims of Lessees Relating to Guerrilla Raids," 405, box 10.

124. *Report by the Committee of the Contrabands' Relief Commission*, 6, 12.

125. Col. N. Niles to Lieut. Col. W. B. Scates, Milliken's Bend, La., April 8, 1863, CN 352, LR, vol. 2/2, 13AC [C-8805]; Col. D. Shunk to Col. W. B. Scates, Milliken's Bend, April 9, 1863, CN 352, LR, vol. 2/2, 13AC, NARA [C-8805].

126. Acting Rear Adm. David Dixon Porter to Hon. Gideon Welles, July 2, 1863; [Brig. Gen.] Alfred W. Ellet to Adm. David Dixon Porter, July 30, 1863, ser. 30, Squadron Letters, MS Squadron, July–August, vol. 4, pp. 54–59, encl. in Acting Rear Adm. David D. Porter to Honorable Gideon Welles, NARA [T-516].

127. *OR*, ser. 1, vol. 24, pt. 2, pp. 460, 466.

128. *OR*, ser. 1, vol. 32, pt. 2, pp. 571, 568–70; Col. Henry Moore to Capt. L. H. Pelouze, March 11, 1862 [C-1642].

129. "The War in the Southwest." These silences continue into the present. The National Park Service's Civil War Battle Summaries page on Goodrich's Landing, for example, notes that despite the destruction of property and capture of Union guns, "the raid was a minor setback for the Union." http://www.cr/nps.gov.hps /abpp/battles/la014.htm.

130. "The Experiment of Free Labor in Plantations"; Adj. Gen. L. Thomas to Edwin M. Stanton, October 15, 1863 [K-60].

131. "The Contrabands at Helena."

132. Eaton, *Grant, Lincoln, and the Freedmen*, 105.

133. [Maria R. Mann] to Eliza [Eliza S. Mann Wilbur], February 10, 1863, Letters from Helena, Ark., Mann Papers, LOC.

134. "The Experiment of Free Labor in Plantations"; Adj. Gen. L. Thomas to Edwin M. Stanton, October 15, 1863 [K-60].

135. Berlin et al., *The Wartime Genesis of Free Labor: The Lower South*, 813.

136. Yeatman, *Report to the Western Sanitary Commission*, 6. See also Powell, *New Masters*.

137. Berlin et al., *The Wartime Genesis of Free Labor: The Lower South*, 627.

138. Fiske to [Eaton], January 29, 1863; [Fiske] to Eaton, April 23. 1863, Fiske Diaries, LOC.

139. Berlin et al., *The Wartime Genesis of Free Labor: The Lower South*, 835.

140. Hahn, *A Nation under Our Feet*, 73.

141. Berlin et al., *The Wartime Genesis of Free Labor: The Lower South*, 650–55.

142. Hobson Deposition, Taylor Pension File.

143. V. Warren, Commissioner to Mrs. Lutitia Taylor, Shelby, Bolivar County, Taylor Pension File.

144. General Affidavits of Ann Dunbar, Susan Taylor, and John Hampton all in Lutitia Taylor Pension File.

145. By entirely new, I mean revolutionary change in the sense Marx defined as "creating something perfectly new." Marx, *The Eighteenth Brumaire of Louis Bonaparte*, 23. The translation has also been rendered as "creating something that did not exist before."

CONCLUSION

1. Hawks, *A Woman Doctor's Civil War*, 31.

2. As quoted in Fox-Genovese and Genovese, *The Mind of the Master Class*, 389. During the congressional debates in 1850 over the passage of a new fugitive slave act, the admission of California, and a decision over how the question of slavery would be settled in the territories, the presence of women in the galleries bothered Outlaw. While he was perfectly comfortable sharing news of the debates in great detail with his wife as well as discussions that came before Congress on a wide variety of matters, from foreign policy to the arrival of Hungarian refugees, he apparently believed women's modesty was threatened by the "violent" speeches of his fellow Southerners and the "mob" atmosphere that he worried would turn into "a scene of bloodshed." David Outlaw to Mrs. Emily B. Outlaw, January 14, 1850; D. Outlaw to Mrs. Emily B. Outlaw, January 17, 1850, David Outlaw Papers, 1847–1855, 1866, SHC.

3. "Roll of Freedmen Employed by William Ashby & Wash West on Jacob Sartorius Plantation up to October 30th 1864"; Parish of Plaquemine Right Bank, Provost Marshal Census Return, Point Celeste Plantation, Freedmen's Bureau, Miss.: Freedmen's Department, 1863–65, Misc. records, Box 36, RG 105; Agreements of Planters & Lessees, Filed under "Ashley," Mississippi Box #5, ser. 2387, Reports of Examination of Rolls of Freedmen, Mississippi Asst. Comr., Pre-Bureau Records Freedmen's Department, ser. 2020, Records of Renting & Leasing of Abandoned Property, RG 105; U.S. Census, 1870; U.S. Census, 1880.

4. "Partial List of Supplies Sent from No. 8 Brevoort Place to the Army Hospitals; Most of them through G. and E. and Jane," Howland, *Letters of a Family*, vol. 2, 665–66; Zallen, *American Lucifers*.

5. Taylor et al., *South Carolina Women in the Confederacy*, 4.

6. Taylor et al., *South Carolina Women in the Confederacy*, 3, 4.

7. Sarah R. Espy Private Journal, 1859–1868, entry for December 2, 1859, ADAH. U.S. Census, 1850, 1860, and 1870; U.S. Census, Slave Schedules, 1850 and 1860. http://digital.archives.alabama.gov/cdm/ref/collection/voices/id/3607.

8. Faust, *Mothers of Invention*, 41.

9. Espy Journal, entries for December 2, 1859, December 6, 1859, December 18, 1863, January 10, 1860, and January 28, 1864, ADAH Faust, *Mothers of Invention*, 57.

10. Espy Journal, entry for July 29, 1864, ADAH.

11. Espy Journal, entries for December 18, 1863, January 10, 1860, December 2, 1859, July 1861, and February 3, 1864, ADAH. Espy and her husband reported a personal estate of $1,700 in 1860 (U.S. Census, 1860).

12. Espy Journal, entries for February 3, 1864, and May 4, 1864, ADAH.

13. Espy Journal, entry for July 29, 1864, ADAH.

14. Espy Journal, entries for June 11, 1865, and July 3, 1865, ADAH.

15. *Daily Constitutionalist* (Augusta, Ga.), January 1, 1861.

16. Emilie Quiner's Diary, entry for Monday, April 14, 1861, Wisconsin State Historical Society Online; Livermore, *My Story of the War*, 109.

17. Marvel, *Lincoln's Mercenaries*; Livermore, *My Story of the War*, 111.

18. Livermore, *My Story of the War*, 458–59, 345.

19. Buchanan, *Black Life on the Mississippi*, 92. Stokes enlisted as a nurse on the U.S.S. *Red Rover* at Memphis on June 1, 1863. Rendezvous Report, Ann Stokes, Fourth Aud., no. 6363–90, Records of the Bureau of Naval Personnel, RG 24, NA, M1953. [MR281, pt. 3]; "Widow's Declaration for Pension or Increase of Pension," January 26, 1899, Stokes Widows Pension File, No. 5457; King, "In Search of Women of African Descent." While the records indicate that Gilbert and Ann married in December 1864, the Rendezvous Report and other documents suggest that the marriage occurred prior to her enlistment. It is also possible that she began using Stokes's name before they were legally married. Bradford's position as a formally enlisted nurse was a rarity for black women. The *Red Rover* was a floating hospital and ambulance transport that carried wounded soldiers between Memphis and Mound City. Their service on the *Red Rover* meant that Ann and Gilbert Stokes were familiar with the town and its diasporic population. Located six miles north of Cairo near the strategic junction of the Mississippi, Ohio, and Cumberland Rivers, Mound City was an important shipbuilding town and the site of a key Union naval repair facility for the Union Mississippi Squadron and home to a major Union military hospital complex. The Union ironclad gunboats U.S.S. *Cairo*, U.S.S. *Cincinnati*, and U.S.S. *Mound City* were all built there.

20. Livermore, *My Story of the War*, 588.

21. On the question of citizenship, see Jones, *"Hughes v. Jackson"*; and Jones, *Birthright Citizens*.

22. "Resolution by Boston Negroes," *The Liberator*, May 31, 1861, reprinted in Fishel and Quarles, *The Negro American*, 222.

23. *OR*, ser. 1, vol. 9, pp. 352–53; OR, ser. 1, vol. 5, pp. 431–32; Glymph, "This Species of Property," 57.

24. As quoted in Grimsley, *Hard Hand of War*, 126.

25. Brig. Gen. John P. Hawkins to Col. Samuel Thomas, January 31, 1865, M1914, roll 5, NARA.

26. [Charles Iverson Graves] to Chichi [Margaret Iverson], Thursday, July 15, 1875; Chichi [Margaret Iverson] to [Charles Iverson], January 7, 1878; January 21, 1878, Charles Iverson Papers, SHC.

27. Massey, *Refugee Life in the Confederacy*, 9.

28. Ellen Cook Whitehurst to William White Griffin, [December 11, 1930], Ellen Whitehurst Papers, SHC. I am indebted to Camilla Herlevich for bringing this document to my attention. Herlevich and her sister Ann Brennan are descendants of Ellen Cook Whitehurst's mistress, Emily Cook, and donated the letter to the Wilson Library. They also kindly supplied other information on the family. Email correspondence, May 29–30, 2016.

29. Du Bois, *Black Reconstruction in America*, 125. Walt Whitman referred to African Americans as "so many baboons." Whitman as quoted in Aaron, *The Unwritten War*, 61.

BIBLIOGRAPHY

MANUSCRIPT COLLECTIONS

Alabama Department of Archives and History, Montgomery, Ala.
  Zillah Haynie Brandon Diaries, 4 vols. 1858–71
  Sarah R. Espy Private Journal, 1859–68
American Antiquarian Society, Worcester, Mass.
  Chase Family Papers, 1787–1915
  Confederate States of America Papers
  Hammond, James Henry. Speech of Hon. James H. Hammond, of South
    Carolina on the Admission of Kansas, under the LeCompton Constitu-
    tion: Delivered in the Senate of the United States, March 14, 1858.
  Metcalf, John G., MD. *The Irrepressible Conflict: A Scrap Book of the Great
    Rebellion of 1861.* Northeast Historical and General Society, Janu-
    ary 1, 1870.
  Partial Diary of an unidentified Union soldier stationed at Ft. Pile,
    Louisiana, 1863, Civil War Collection, 1861–68
Duke University, David M. Rubenstein Rare Book and Manuscript Library,
  Durham, N.C.
  Mrs. Eleanor J. W. Baker Journal, 1848, Eleanor Jameson Williams Baker
    Papers, 1848–95
  Ravella Balch Diaries, Noyes-Balch Family Papers, 1854–1957 and undated
  Harriette H. Branham Diary, 1861–63
  Kate D. Foster Diary, 1863–72
  Robert W. Hooke Papers, 1861–77
  John F. Housser Papers, 1863–1879
  Edward W. Kinsley Correspondence, 1862–89
  Kate D. (Conant) Linsley Papers, 1853–1928
  Thomas McIntosh Papers, 1822–95
  Minutes of Greenville Ladies' Association
  Catherine P. Noyes Correspondence, Noyes-Balch Family Papers, 1854–
    1957 and undated
  Augustin Louis Taveau Papers, 1741–1931
  Gertrude Gertrude Clanton Thomas Papers, 1848–1978 and undated
  Manchester Ward Weld Papers, 1847–[7–]

Emory University, Stuart A. Rose Manuscript, Archives, and Rare Book Library,
    Atlanta, Ga.
    Graves Family Papers, 1818–1949
    Fannie Green Diary, Green Family, Civil War Papers, 1861–63
    Lockmiller Family Papers, 1862–1863, 1881–1927
    Diary of Miss Sue Richardson, October 1, 1863–May 23, 1865
Historic New Orleans Collection, Williams Research Center, New Orleans, La.
    Clerk of the Civil District Court for the Parish of Orleans
    Notarial Archives
Historical Society of Pennsylvania, Philadelphia, Pa.
    Mrs. Irving H. McJesson Collection, Henderson Section, Henderson Letters,
        1851–1917
Iowa State University Library Special Collections and University Archives, Ames,
    Iowa
    Civil War Reminiscences of Cyrus Bussey, 1864
Library of Congress, Manuscript Division, Washington, D.C.
    George S. Denison Papers, 1851–84
    Mary Tyler Peabody Mann Papers, 1863–76
    John S. Mosby Papers, 1861–66
    Benjamin F. and Catherine Oliphant Papers, Miscellaneous Manuscript
        Collection
    John Aldrich Stephenson Collection of the Hand, Fiske, and Aldrich
        Families
Missouri History Museum Archives, St. Louis, Mo.
    William D. Butler Papers, 1863–1923
    William Greenleaf Elliot Papers, 1832–1961
National Archives and Records Administration, Washington, D.C.
    RG 15. Civil War Widows' Pension Claims, Records of the Veteran's
        Administration
    RG 24. Records of the Bureau of Naval Personnel
    RG 56. Records of the Division of Captured Property, Claims, and Lands,
        1855–1900
    RG 92. Records of the Office of the Quartermaster General
    RG 94. Records of the Adjutant General, 1780s–1917
    RG 105. Records of the Bureau of Refugees, Freedmen, and Abandoned
        Lands (BRFAL)
    RG 109. Confederate Papers Relating to Citizens or Business Firms
    RG 366. Records of the Civil War Special Agencies of the Treasury
        Department
    RG 393. Records of United States Army Continental Commands, 1821–1920
    Case Files of Approved Pension Applications of Widows and Other Veterans,
        1861–1934
New York Public Library, Manuscripts and Archives Collection, New York, N.Y.
    H. Landsdale Boardman Civil War Letters, 1862

New England Women's Auxiliary Association Archives, United States
  Sanitary Commission Records, 1861–1879. Army and Navy Claim Agency
  Archives, 1861–70.
Sophia Amelia and Mary Tyler Peabody Papers, 1775–1949
Moses Taylor Collection, 1793–1906.
United States Sanitary Commission Records, 1861–1879, Department of
  North Carolina Archives
North Carolina Department of Natural and Cultural Resources, Office of
  Archives and History Raleigh, N.C.
South Carolina Historical Society, Charleston, S.C.
  Journal of Meta M. Grimball (Née Morris), December 1860–February 1866.
    Typescript.
  Harriott Middleton Family Papers, 1848–1917
  Middleton Family Papers, 1820–1937
  War Reminiscences of Alicia Hopton Middleton, 1865, Middleton Family
    Papers, 1820–1937
  Miller-Furman-Dabbs Family Papers, 1751–1865
  Octavius Theodore Porcher Papers, 1829–73
  Thomas Ravenel Journals
  Thomas Porcher Ravenel Diaries, 1845–1903, 3 vols.; vol. 1, 1845–54; vol. 2.
    1855–65; vol. 3, 1866–1903, Thomas Porcher Ravenel Papers, 1810–
    1904
  Ravenel Family Papers, 1695–1925
University of Maryland, College Park, Manuscripts Collection and University
  Libraries Digital Collections
University of Massachusetts, Special Collections and University Archives,
  Amherst, Mass.
  Edward W. Kinsley Papers, 1863–91
University of Miami Libraries, Cuban Heritage Collection, Coral Gables, Fla.
  Edward Spalding Papers
University of Michigan, William L. Clements Library, Ann Arbor, Mich.
  Civil War Soldiers' Letters, Ladies Soldiers' Aid Society Papers
  Juliette F. Gaylord Collection, 1861–65
  The Rochester Ladies' Anti-Slavery Society Papers, 1851–68
  Simmons Civil War Sketchbook
  N. S. [Norton Strange] Townshend Papers
University of North Carolina, Southern Historical Collection, Louis Round
  Wilson Special Collections Library, Chapel Hill, N.C.
  Cameron Family Papers, 1757–1978
  Recollections of Katherine Polk Gale, undated
  Gale and Polk Family Papers, 1815–1940
  Elliott and Gonzales Family Papers, 1701–1898
  Charles Iverson Graves Papers, 1831–1962
  Margaret Ann Meta Morris Grimball Diary, 1860–66

David Outlaw Papers, 1847–55, 1866
Ravenel Family Papers, 1790–1918
University of South Carolina, South Caroliniana Library, Columbia, S.C.
    Thomas P. Ravenel Journal
    The Private Journal of William Henry Ravenel
    Sams Family Papers
University of Tennessee, Special Collections, University Libraries, Knoxville,
    Tenn.
    Eleanora Willauer Diary, October 1, 1862–November 9, 1869, Special Collec-
        tions Online
U.S. National Library of Medicine, Bethesda, Md.
    Mississippi Valley Sanitary Fair, Freedmen and Union Refugees Department
        of the Mississippi Valley Sanitary Fair, St. Louis, Mo., March 17, 1864.
        Digital Collections.
Western Reserve Historical Society, Cleveland, Ohio
    William L. Gross Papers, 1856–67
Wisconsin Historical Society, Madison, Wisc.
    Emilie Quiner's Diary, April 14, 1861–September 27, 1863

GOVERNMENT DOCUMENTS

Congressional Globe. 37th Cong., 1st Sess. Washington, D.C., 1861.
The Public Statutes at Large of the United States of America. 125 vols. Washing-
    ton, D.C.: Government Printing Office, 1845–.
Report of the Secretary of the Treasury on the State of the Finances. 38th Cong.,
    11th Sess. Washington, D.C.: Government Printing Office, 1864.
Senate Executive Documents for the Second Session of the Thirty-Eighth Con-
    gress of the United States of America, 1864–'65. Washington, D.C.: Government
    Printing Office, 1865.
U.S. Naval Records Office. *Official Records of the Union and Confederate Navies
    in the War of the Rebellion.* Washington, D.C.: Government Printing Office,
    1894–1922.
U.S. Statutes at Large, Treaties, and Proclamations. Vol. 12. Boston, 1863.
U.S. War Department. *The War of the Rebellion: A Compilation of the Official
    Records of the Union and Confederate Armies.* 128 vols. Washington, D.C.:
    Government Printing Office, 1880–1901.

CENSUSES

New York Census, 1855.
U.S. Census, 1840, 1850, 1860, 1870, 1880.
U.S. Census, Slave Schedules, 1850, 1860.

NEWSPAPERS

The Crisis
Daily Constitutionalist (Augusta, Ga.)
Daily Journal (Wilmington, N.C.)
Daily Morning Chronicle (Washington, D.C.)
New York Times

PRINTED PRIMARY SOURCES

"An Act to Suppress Insurrection, to Punish Treason and Rebellion, to Seize and Confiscate the Property of Rebels, and for Other Purposes" (July 17, 1862). In *Statutes at Large, Treaties, and Proclamations of the United States of America*, 12:589–92. Boston, 1863.

Alcott, Louisa May. *Civil War Hospital Sketches*. New York: James Redpath, 1863.

Bacon, Georgeanna Woolsey, and Eliza Woolsey Howland, eds. *Letters of a Family during the War for the Union, 1861–1865*. 2 vols. Printed for private distribution. New Haven, Conn.: Tuttle, Morehouse & Taylor, 1899.

Bell, Malcolm, Jr. *Major Butler's Legacy; Five Generations of a Slaveholding Family*. Athens: University of Georgia Press, 1987.

Berlin, Ira, and Leslie S. Rowland, eds. *Families and Freedom: A Documentary History of African American Kinship in the Civil War Era*. New York: New Press, 1997.

Berlin, Ira, Joseph P. Reidy, and Leslie S. Rowland, eds. *Freedom: A Documentary History of Emancipation, 1861–1867*, ser. 2, *The Black Military Experience*. Cambridge: Cambridge University Press, 1982.

Berlin, Ira, Barbara J. Fields, Thavolia Glymph, Joseph P. Reidy, and Leslie S. Rowland, eds. *Freedom: A Documentary History of Emancipation, 1861–1867*, ser. 1, vol. 1, *The Destruction of Slavery*. Cambridge: Cambridge University Press, 1985.

Berlin, Ira, Thavolia Glymph, Steven F. Miller, Joseph P. Reidy, Leslie S. Rowland, and Julie Saville, eds. *Freedom: A Documentary History of Emancipation, 1861–1867*, ser. 1, vol. 3, *The Wartime Genesis of Free Labor: The Lower South*. Cambridge: Cambridge University Press, 1990.

Billington, Ray Allen, Jr. *The Journal of Charlotte L. Forten: A Free Negro in the Slave Era*. New York: W. W. Norton & Co., 1953.

Blackford, Susan Leigh, comp. *Letters from Lee's Army or Memoirs of Life in and out of the Army in Virginia during the War between the States*. New York: Charles Scribner's Sons, 1947.

Bostwick, S. W., and Thomas Hood. "Report of the Commissioners of Investigation of Colored Refugees in Kentucky, Tennessee, and Alabama." Washington, D.C., December 28, 1864. pp. 1–23. *Letter of the Secretary of War*

Communicating, In compliance with a resolution of the Senate of the 11th instant, a copy of the report of Hon. Thomas Hood and Hon. S. W. Bostwick, special commissioners upon the condition and treatment of colored refugees in Kentucky, Tennessee and Alabama, February 27, 1865.—Read, ordered to lie on the table and be printed. 38th Cong., 2nd Sess., Exec. Doc. 28, February 27, 1865. In Senate Executive Documents for the Second Session of the Thirty-Eighth Congress of the United States of America, 1864–'65. Washington, D.C.: Government Printing Office, 1865.

Bremer, Fredrika. *The Homes in the New World: Impressions of America*. New York: Harper & Brothers, 1853.

Brinton, John H. *Personal Memoirs of John H. Brinton, Major and Surgeon, U.S.V., 1861–1868*. New York: Neale, 1914.

Bruce, H. C. *The New Man: Twenty-Nine Years a Slave, Twenty-Nine Years a Free Man*. Anstadt and Sons, 1895. Reprint. New York: Negro Universities Press, 1969.

Burkhead, Rev. L. S. *History of the Difficulties of the Pastorate of the Front Street Methodist Church, Wilmington, N. C., for the Year 1865*. Annual Publication of Historical Papers, vol. 8. Durham, N.C.: Historical Society of Trinity College, 1808–1909.

Child, David Lee. *Rights and Duties of the United States Relative to Slavery under the Laws of War*. Republished with notes from *The Liberator*. Boston: R. F. Wallcut, 1861.

Coles, J., Chaplain, Jeremiah Porter, and T. M. Stephenson. "Report of the Numbers and Wants of the Contrabands in the Department of the Tennessee, by Committee Appointed by the Chaplain's Association, Vicksburg, Miss., October 19, 1863." *New York Times*, November 12, 1863.

"The Contrabands at Helena, Ark.: An Appeal for Aid." *New York Times*, November 8, 1862.

Correspondent. "Natchez: The First Town on the River Gen. Grant on a Visit Runaway Negroes in the Contraband Camp Secesh in Despair, &c." *New York Times*, September 6, 1863. https://www.nytimes.com/1863/09/06/archives/natchez-the-first-town-on-the-river-gen-grant-on-a-visit-runaway.html.

Crist, Lynda Lasswell, Kenneth H. Williams, and Peggy L. Dillard, eds. *The Papers of Jefferson Davis*. 14 vols. Baton Rouge: Louisiana State University Press, 1999.

Cumming, Kate. *Journal of Hospital Life in the Confederate Army of Tennessee from the Battle of Shiloh to the End of the War*. Louisville, Ky.: John P. Morton, 1866.

Cuthbert, Robert B., ed. *Flat Rock of the Old Time: Letters from the Mountains to the Lowcountry, 1837–1939*. Columbia: University of South Carolina Press, 2016.

Cutrer, Thomas, and T. Michael Parrish, *Brothers in Gray: The Civil War Letters of the Pierson Family*. Baton Rouge: Louisiana State University Press, 1997.

Douglass, Frederick. *Life and Times of Frederick Douglass*. Reprint. New York: Collier Books, 1962.

———. "The Mission of the War." *New York Times*, January 13, 1864.

Dubose, Samuel. "Address Delivered at the Seventeenth Anniversary of the Black Oak Society, April 27, 1858." In Samuel Dubose, Esq., and Prof. Frederick A. Porcher, A *Contribution to the History of South Carolina Consisting of Pamphlets by Samuel Dubose, Esq. and Prof. Frederick A. Porcher*, 1–34. Republished for private circulation by T. Gaillard Thomas. New York: Knickerbocker Press, 1887. Press of G. P. Putnam's Sons, 1887.

———. "Reminiscences of St. Stephen's Parish, Craven County, and Notices of the Old Homestead." In Samuel Dubose, Esq., and Prof. Frederick A. Porcher, A *Contribution to the History of the Huguenots of South Carolina Consisting of Pamphlets by Samuel Dubose, Esq. and Prof. Frederick A. Porcher*, 35–85. Republished for private circulation by T. Gaillard Thomas. New York: Knickerbocker, 1887, Press of G. P. Putnam's Sons, 1887.

East, Charles, ed. *Sarah Morgan: The Civil War Diary of a Southern Woman*. New York: Simon and Schuster, 1991.

Eaton, John. *Grant, Lincoln, and the Freedmen: Reminiscences of the Civil War*. Originally published 1907. New York: Negro Universities Press, 1969.

Edmondston, Catherine Anne Deveareaux. *"Journal of a Secesh Lady": The Diary of Catherine Anne Deveareaux Edmondston, 1860–1866*. Edited by Beth Gilbert Crabtree and James Patton. Raleigh: North Carolina Division of Archives and History, 1979.

"The Experiment of Free Labor in Plantations: Adjutant-General Thomas Reports It a Success." *New York Times*, November 13, 1863.

Forten, Charlotte. *The Journal of Charlotte L. Forten: A Free Negro in the Slave Era*. Edited by Ray Allen Billington. New York: Norton and Company, 1981.

French, A. M., Mrs. *Slavery in South Carolina and the Ex-slaves, or, the Port Royal Mission*. New York: Winchell M. French, 1862.

Furry, William, ed. *The Preacher's Tale: The Civil War Journal of Rev. Francis Springer, Chaplain, U.S. Army of the Frontier*. Fayetteville: University of Arkansas Press, 2001.

Giesberg, Judith, ed. *Emilie Davis's Civil War: The Diaries of a Free Black Woman in Philadelphia, 1863–1865*. University Park: Pennsylvania State University Press, 2014.

Grant, U. S. *Personal Memoirs of U. S. Grant*. New York: Grosset & Dunlap, 1952.

Hagy, James William. *Charleston, South Carolina City Directories for the Years 1830–31, 1835–36, 1836, 1837–38, and 1840–41*. Baltimore: Clearfield, 1997, 2002.

Hancock, Cornelia. *Letters of a Civil War Nurse: Cornelia Hancock, 1863–1865*. Edited by Henrietta Stratton Jaquette. Lincoln: University of Nebraska Press, 1998.

Hardin, Elizabeth Pendleton. *The Private War of Lizzie Hardin: A Kentucky Confederate Girl's Diary of the War in Kentucky, Tennessee, Alabama, and Georgia*. Edited by G. Glenn Clift. Frankfort: Kentucky Historical Society, 1963.

Haviland, Laura S. *A Woman's Life Work: Including Thirty Years' Service on the Underground Railroad and in the War*. Memorial ed. Chicago: S. B. Shaw, 1881.

Hawks, Esther Hill. *A Woman Doctor's Civil War: Esther Hill Hawkes' Diary.* Edited by Gerald Schwartz. Columbia: University of South Carolina Press, 1984.

Hodge, Robert A. *The Civil War Diary of Betty Herndon Maury (June 3, 1861–February 18, 1863).* Fredericksburg, Va.: privately published, 1985.

Holland, Rupert Sargent, ed. *Letters and Diary of Laura M. Towne: Written from the Sea Islands of South Carolina, 1862–1864.* Cambridge, U.K.: Wilberforce Press, 1912.

Holston Salt & Plaster Co. v. Campbell et al. Supreme Court of Appeals of Virginia, November 17, 1892. In *The Southeastern Reporter,* vol. 16, *Containing All the Decisions of the Supreme Court of Appeals of Virginia, and Supreme Courts of North Carolina, South Carolina, Georgia,* November 22, 1892–March 18, 1893. St. Paul, Minn.: West, 1893.

Hopkins, James F., ed. *The Papers of Henry Clay.* Vol. 4, *Secretary of State.* Lexington: University of Kentucky Press, 1972.

Howard, O. O. *Autobiography of Oliver O. Howard.* Vol. 2. New York: Baker & Taylor, 1908.

Howland, Eliza Newton, with Charles William Woolsey. *Family Records: Being Some Account of the Ancestry of My Father and Mother.* New Haven, Conn.: Tuttle, Morehouse, & Taylor, 1900.

Howland, Eliza Woolsey, and Georgeanna Woolsey Bacon. *My Heart toward Home: Letters of a Family during the Civil War.* Edited by Daniel John Hoisington. Rossville, Minn.: Edinborough, 2001.

Huckaby, Elizabeth Paisley, and Ethel C. Simpson, eds. *Tulip Evermore: Emma Butler and William Paisley, Their Lives in Letters, 1857–1887.* Fayetteville: University of Arkansas Press, 1986.

Jackson, Mattie J. *The Story of Mattie J. Jackson; Her Parentage, Experience of Eighteen Years in Slavery, Incidents during the War, Her Escape from Slavery: A True Story.* Lawrence, Mass.: Sentinel Office, 1866.

Johnston, Frontis W., ed. *The Papers of Zebulon Baird Vance.* 3 vols. Raleigh: North Carolina Department of Archives and History, 1963.

Keckley, Elizabeth. *Behind the Scenes; or, Thirty Years a Slave and Four Years in the White House.* New York: G. W. Carleton, 1868.

Knox, Thomas W. *Camp-Fire and Cotton-Field: Southern Adventure in Time of War: Life with the Union Armies, and Residence on a Louisiana Plantation.* Philadelphia: Jones Bros., 1865.

LeConte, Emma. *When the World Ended: The Diary of Emma LeConte.* Edited by Earl Schenck Miers. Originally published 1957. Lincoln: University of Nebraska Press, 1987.

Lee, Capt. Robert E. *Recollections and Letters of Robert E. Lee.* New York: Casimo Classics, 1904.

Lincoln, Abraham. "A Letter from President Lincoln: Reply to Hon. Horace Greeley." *New York Times,* August 24, 1862.

Livermore, Mary A. *My Story of the War: The Civil War Memoirs of the Famous*

Nurse, Relief Organizer and Suffragette. Originally published 1887. New York: Da Capo, 1995.

Manigault, Arthur Middleton. *A Carolinian Goes to War: The Civil War Narrative of Arthur Middleton Manigault.* Edited by R. Lockwood Tower. Columbia: Published for the Charleston Library Society by the University of South Carolina Press, 1983.

McGuire, Judith W. *Diary of a Southern Refugee during the War by a Lady of Virginia.* Edited by Jean Berlin. Originally published 1867. Lincoln: University of Nebraska Press, 1995.

Meriwether, Elizabeth Avery. *Recollections of 92 Years, 1824–1916.* Nashville: Tennessee Historical Commission, 1958.

Mobley, Joe A., ed. *The Papers of Zebulon Baird Vance.* Vol. 2. Raleigh, N.C.: Office of Archives and History, North Carolina Department of Natural and Cultural Resources, 1995.

Moore, James Hammond, ed. *The Diary of Keziah Goodwyn Hopkins Brevard: A Plantation Mistress on the Eve of the Civil War.* Columbia: University of South Carolina Press, 1993.

Moss, Lemuel. *Annals of the United States Christian Commission.* Philadelphia: J. B. Lippincott, 1868.

Myers, Robert Manson, ed. *The Children of Pride: A True Story of Georgia and the Civil War.* New Haven, Conn.: Yale University Press, 1972.

Nevins, Allan, ed. *James Truslow Adams: Select Correspondence.* 4 vols. Urbana: University of Illinois Press, 1968.

Northup, Solomon. *Twelve Years a Slave: Narrative of Solomon Northup.* New York: Derby and Miller, 1853.

Oldham, William S., C.S.A. *The Rise and Fall of the Confederacy: The Memoir of Senator William S. Oldham, CSA.* Edited by Clayton E. Jewett. Columbia: University of Missouri Press, 2006.

Olmsted, Frederick Law. *The Cotton Kingdom: A Traveller's Observations on Cotton and Slavery in the American Slave States in Two Volumes.* New York: Mason Brothers, 1861.

Our Women in the War: The Lives They Lived, the Deaths They Died. Charleston, S.C.: News and Courier Book Press, 1885.

Pearson, Elizabeth Ware, ed. *Letters from Port Royal Written at the Time of the Civil War.* Boston: W. B. Clarke, 1906.

Phillips, Ulrich B. *Plantation and Frontier Documents: 1649–1863, Illustrative of Industrial History in the Colonial & Ante-bellum South.* 2 vols. Cleveland: Arthur H. Clark, 1909.

Phillips, Wendell. "Toussaint L'Ouverture: Lecture by Mr. Wendell Phillips." *New York Times*, February 1, 1860.

———. "The War for the Union." Lecture delivered in New York and Boston, December 1861. Reported by Andrew J. Graham. New York: E. D. Barker, 1862.

Puritan, A [George Bourne]. *The Abrogation of the Seventh Commandment, by the American Churches*. New York: David Ruggles, 1835.

Quiner, E. B. *The Military History of Wisconsin: A Record of The Civil and Military Patriotism of the State, in the War for the Union, with a History of the Campaigns in Which Wisconsin Soldiers Have Been Conspicuous, Regimental Histories, Sketches of Distinguished Officers, the Roll of the Illustrious Dead, Movements of the Legislature and State Officers, etc.* Vol. 10. Chicago: Clarke, 1866.

Racine, Philip N., ed. *Piedmont Farmer: The Journals of David Golightly Harris, 1855–1870.* Knoxville: University of Tennessee Press, 1900.

"Raid on a Plantation." *New York Times*, September 12, 1864.

Ravenel, Henry William. *The Private Journal of Henry William Ravenel, 1859–1887.* Edited by Arney R. Childs. Columbia: University of South Carolina Press, 1947.

Rawick, George P., et al., eds. *The American Slave: A Composite Autobiography*. 41 vols. Westport, Conn.: Greenwood, 1972–1979.

Redkey, Edwin S., ed. *A Grand Army of Black Men: Letters from African-American Soldiers in the Union Army, 1861–1865.* Reprint. Cambridge: Cambridge University Press, 1992.

Reed, Emmala. *A Faithful Heart: The Journals of Emmala Reed, 1865 and 1866.* Edited by Robert T. Oliver. Columbia: University of South Carolina Press, 2004.

Report by the Committee of the Contrabands' Relief Commission of Cincinnati, Ohio: Proposing a Plan for the Occupation and Government of Vacated Territory in the Seceded States. Cincinnati: Gazette Steam Printing House, 1863.

Report of the Commissioners of Investigation of Colored Refugees in Kentucky, Tennessee, and Alabama. Washington, D.C., December 28, 1864.

Report of the Maine Soldiers Relief Association. Washington, D.C., October 1866.

Rogers, James B. *War Pictures: Experiences and Observations of a Chaplain in the U.S. Army, in the War of the Southern Rebellion.* Chicago: Church & Goodman, 1863.

Rowland, Kate Mason, and (Mrs.) Morris L. Croxall, eds. *The Journal of Julia Le Grand, New Orleans, 1862–1863.* Richmond, Va.: Everett Wadley, 1911.

Russell, Miss May. "Sketch of Old Confederate Treasury." In *Dixie Chapter, Daughters of the Confederacy, of Anderson, S.C., Dixie*, 11–13. Anderson, S.C.: Anderson Printing and Stationery, 1903. Reprinted in *Confederate Veteran* 40, no. 2 (February 1903): 71.

Scarborough, William Kaufman, ed. *The Diary of Edmund Ruffin.* Vol. 2, *The Years of Hope, April, 1861–June, 1863.* Baton Rouge: Louisiana State University Press, 1976.

Sheldon & Co.'s Business or Advertising Directory: Containing the Cards, Circulars, and Advertisements of the Principal Firms of the Cities of New York, Philadelphia, Boston, etc., etc. New York: John F. Trow, 1845.

Sherman, William Tecumseh. *Memoirs of W. T. Sherman.* 2 vols. Edited by Charles Royster. Originally published 1875. New York: Library of America, 1990.

Simpson, Brooks D., and Jean V. Berlin, eds. *Sherman's Civil War: Selected*

Correspondence of William T. Sherman, 1860–1865. Chapel Hill: University of North Carolina Press, 1999.

Society of Survivors. *History of the Ram Fleet and the Mississippi Marine Brigade in the War for the Union on the Mississippi and Its Tributaries.* St. Louis: Society of Survivors, 1907.

Sterling, Dorothy, ed. *We Are Your Sisters: Black Women in the Nineteenth Century.* New York: W. W. Norton, 1984.

Stevenson, Brenda, ed. *The Journals of Charlotte Forten Grimké.* New York: Oxford University Press, 1988.

Stone, Kate. *Brokenburn: The Journal of Kate Stone, 1861–1868.* Edited by John Q. Anderson. Baton Rouge: Louisiana State University Press, 1972.

Stowe, Harriet Beecher. *Uncle Tom's Cabin.* Originally published 1852. New York: Harper & Row, 1965.

Strong, Robert Hale. *A Yankee Private's Civil War.* Edited by Ashley Halsey. Chicago: Henry Regnery Co., 1961.

Swint, Henry L. *Dear Ones at Home: Letters from Contraband Camps.* Nashville: Vanderbilt University Press, 1966.

Taylor, Frances Wallace, Catherine Taylor Matthews, and J. Tracy Power, eds. *The Leverett Letters: Correspondence of a South Carolina Family, 1852–1868.* Columbia: University of South Carolina Press, 2000.

Taylor, Susie King. *Reminiscences of My Life in Camp with the 33rd U.S. Colored Troops, Late 1st South Carolina Volunteers: A Black Woman's Civil War.* Edited by Patricia W. Romero and Willie Lee Rose. Originally published 1902. New York: Marcus Weiner, 1988.

Taylor, Mrs. Thomas, et al. *South Carolina Women in the Confederacy.* Columbia, S.C.: The State Company, 1903.

Thomson, Mortimer Neal. "A Great Slave Auction: 400 Men, Women and Children Sold." *New York Tribune,* March 9, 1859.

Toussaint Louverture. *Memoir of Pierre Toussaint, Born a Slave in St. Domingo.* Boston: Crosby, Nichols, 1854.

Towles, Louis P., ed. *A World Turned Upside Down: The Palmers of South Santee, 1818–1881.* Columbia: University of South Carolina Press, 1996.

U.S. House of Representatives, Committee on Education and Labor. *Charges against General Howard* (Howard Investigation). 41st Cong., 2nd Sess. Report no. 121. In *Index to the Reports of the Committees for the Second Session of the Forty-First Congress, 1869–70,* 1–521. Washington, D.C.: Government Printing Office, 1870.

U.S. Sanitary Commission. *Hospital Transports: A Memoir of the Embarkation of the Sick and Wounded from the Peninsula of Virginia in the Summer of 1862.* Boston: Ticknor and Fields, 1863.

"The War in the Southwest: Reports from Vicksburg." *New York Times,* July 22, 1863.

Williams, Thomas. "Letters of General Thomas Williams, 1862." *American Historical Review* 14, no. 2 (January 1909): 304–28.

Woodward, C. Vann, ed. *Mary Chesnut's Civil War*. New Haven, Conn.: Yale University Press, 1981.

Woodward, C. Vann, and Elisabeth Muhlenfeld, eds. *The Private Mary Chesnut: The Unpublished Civil War Diaries*. New York: Oxford University Press, 1984.

Worthington, Chauncey Ford, ed. *A Cycle of Adams Letters, 1861–1865*. Boston: Houghton Mifflin, 1920.

Yacovone, Donald, ed. *A Voice of Thunder: The Civil War Letters of George E. Stephens*. Urbana: University of Illinois Press, 1997.

Yeatman, James E. *Report to the Western Sanitary Commission in Regard to Leasing Abandoned Plantations with Rules and Regulations Governing the Same*. St. Louis: Western Sanitary Commission, 1864.

Yellin, Jean Fagan, ed. *The Harriet Jacobs Family Papers*. 2 vols. Chapel Hill: University of North Carolina Press, 2008.

Younce, W. H. *The Adventures of a Conscript*. Cincinnati: Edition Publishing, 1901.

SECONDARY SOURCES

Aaron, Daniel. *The Unwritten War: American Writers and the Civil War*. New York: Knopf, 1973.

Allen, Thomas B. *Tories: Fighting for the King in America's First Civil War*. New York: Harper, 2011.

Ash, Steven V. *When the Yankees Came: Conflict and Class in the Occupied South*. Chapel Hill: University of North Carolina Press, 1995.

Attie, Jeanie. *Patriotic Toil: Northern Women and the American Civil War*. Ithaca, N.Y.: Cornell University Press, 1998.

Ayers, Edward L. *In the Presence of Mine Enemies: The Civil War in the Heart of America, 1859–1863*. New York: Norton, 2003.

———. *Thin Light of Freedom: The Civil War and Emancipation in the Heart of America*. New York: Norton, 2017.

Bacon, Margaret Hope. "The Pennsylvania Abolition Society's Mission for Black Education." *Pennsylvania Legacies*, November 2005.

Bailey, Anne C. *The Weeping Time: Memory and the Largest Slave Auction in American History*. Cambridge: Cambridge University Press, 2017.

Ball, Erica L. *To Live an Antislavery Life: Personal Politics and the Antebellum Black Middle Class*. Athens: University of Georgia Press, 2012.

Baptist, Edward E. *Creating an Old South: Middle Florida's Plantation Frontier before the Civil War*. Chapel Hill: University of North Carolina Press, 2002.

Barber, E. Susan, and Charles F. Ritter. "Dangerous Liaisons: Working Women and Sexual Justice in the American Civil War." *European Journal of American Studies*, October 1, 2015, 1–28. https://journals.openedition.org/ejas/10695.

Barcia, Manuel. *The Great African Slave Revolt of 1825: Cuba and the Fight for Freedom in Matanzas*. Baton Rouge: Louisiana State University Press, 2012.

Barnickel, Linda. *Milliken's Bend: A Civil War Battle in History and Memory*. Baton Rouge: Louisiana State University Press, 2013.

Barrett, John G. *The Civil War in North Carolina*. Chapel Hill: University of North Carolina Press, 1963.

Beard, John R. *The Life of Toussaint L'Ouverture, the Negro Patriot of Hayti*. London: Ingram, Cook, 1853.

———. *Toussaint L'Ouverture: Biography and Autobiography*. Boston: James Redpath, 1863.

Bell, Madison Smartt. *Toussaint Louverture: A Biography*. New York: Vintage, 2007.

Bercaw, Nancy D. *Gendered Freedoms: Race, Rights, and the Politics of Household in the Delta, 1861–1875*. Gainesville: University Press of Florida, 2003.

Berlin, Ira. *Many Thousands Gone: The First Two Centuries of Slavery in North America*. Cambridge, Mass.: Belknap, 1998.

Berry, Daina Ramey. *The Price for Their Pound of Flesh: The Value of the Enslaved, from Womb to Grave, in the Building of a Nation*. Boston: Beacon, 2017.

Blackett, R. J. M. *The Captive's Quest for Freedom: Fugitive Slaves, the 1850 Fugitive Slave Law, and the Politics of Slavery*. Cambridge: Cambridge University Press, 2018.

———. *Making Freedom: The Underground Railroad and the Politics of Slavery*. Chapel Hill: University of North Carolina Press, 2013.

Blackmun, Ora. *Western North Carolina: Its Mountains and Its People*. Boone, N.C.: Appalachian State University Press, 1977.

Blair, William A. *Virginia's Private War: Feeding Body and Soul in the Confederacy, 1861–1865*. New York: Oxford University Press, 1998.

———. *With Malice toward Some: Treason and Loyalty in the Civil War Era*. Chapel Hill: University of North Carolina Press, 2014.

Blanton, DeAnne, and Lauren M. Cook. *They Fought Like Demons: Women Soldiers in the American Civil War*. Baton Rouge: Louisiana State University Press, 2002.

Bleser, Carol, ed. *In Joy and in Sorrow: Women, Family, and Marriage in the Victorian South*. New York: Oxford University Press, 1991.

Bleser, Carol K., and Lesley J. Gordon. *Intimate Strategies of the Civil War: Military Commanders and Their Wives*. New York: Oxford University Press, 2001.

Blight, David W. *American Oracle*. Cambridge, Mass.: Harvard University Press, 2011.

———. *Frederick Douglass: Prophet of Freedom*. New York: Simon & Shuster, 2018.

———. *Race and Reunion: The Civil War in American Memory*. Cambridge, Mass.: Harvard University Press, 2001.

Boddie, William Willis. *History of Williamsburg: Something about the People of Williamsburg County, South Carolina, from the First Settlement by Europeans about 1705 until 1923*. Columbia, S.C.: The State Company, 1923.

Bond, Beverly G., and Janann Sherman. *Memphis in Black and White*. Charleston, S.C.: Arcadia, 2003.

Bonner, Robert E. *Mastering America: Southern Slaveholders and the Crisis of American Nationhood*. Cambridge: Cambridge University Press, 2009.

Brown, Elsa Barkley. "Negotiating and Transforming the Public Sphere: African American Political Life in the Transition from Slavery to Freedom." *Public Culture* 7 (1994): 107–46.

Brown, Kathleen M. *Foul Bodies: Cleanliness in Early America*. New Haven, Conn.: Yale University Press, 2009.

Brown, Wendy. *States of Injury: Power and Freedom in Late Modernity*. Princeton, N.J.: Princeton University Press, 1995.

Brown, William Wells. *The Negro in the American Rebellion: His Heroism and His Fidelity*. Boston: A. G. Brown, 1880.

Brundage, W. Fitzhugh. *The Southern Past: A Clash of Race and Memory*. Cambridge, Mass.: Belknap, 2008.

Brundage, W. Fitzhugh, ed. *Where These Memories Grow: History, Memory, and Southern Identity*. Chapel Hill: University of North Carolina Press, 2000.

Buchanan, Thomas C. *Black Life on the Mississippi: Slaves, Free Blacks, and the Western Steamboat World*. Chapel Hill: University of North Carolina Press, 2004.

Burke, Diane Mutti. *On Slavery's Border: Missouri's Small Slaveholding Households, 1815–1865*. Athens: University of Georgia Press, 2010.

Burkhardt, George S. *Confederate Rage, Yankee Wrath: No Quarter in the Civil War*. Carbondale: Southern Illinois University Press, 2007.

Burton, Orville Vernon, and Robert C. McMath, eds. *Class, Conflict, and Consensus: Antebellum Southern Community Studies*. Westport, Conn.: Greenwood, 1982.

Butler, Judith. "Is Kinship Always Already Heterosexual?" *differences: A Journal of Feminist Cultural Studies* 13, no.1 (Spring 2002): 14–44.

Bynum, Victoria. *Unruly Women: The Politics of Social and Sexual Control in the Old South*. Chapel Hill: University of North Carolina Press, 1992.

Camp, Stephanie M. H. *Closer to Freedom: Enslaved Women and Everyday Resistance in the Plantation South*. Chapel Hill: University of North Carolina Press, 2004.

Campbell, D'Ann, and Richard Jensen. "Gendering Two Wars." In *War Comes Again: Comparative Vistas on the Civil War and World War II*, edited by Gabor Boritt, 101–24. New York: Oxford University Press, 1995.

Campbell, Jacqueline Glass. *When Sherman Marched North from the Sea: Resistance on the Confederate Home Front*. Chapel Hill: University of North Carolina Press, 2003.

Cashin, Joan E. *A Family Venture: Men and Women on the Southern Frontier.* New York: Oxford University Press, 1991.

———. "Into the Trackless Wilderness: The Refugee Experience in the Civil War." In *A Woman's War: Southern Women, Civil War, and the Confederate Legacy,* edited by Edward D. C. Campbell and Kym Rice, 29–53. Charlottesville: University Press of Virginia, 1996.

———, ed. *The War Was You and Me: Civilians in the American Civil War.* Princeton, N.J.: Princeton University Press, 2002.

Cecelski, David S. *The Fire of Freedom: Abraham Galloway and the Slave's Civil War.* Chapel Hill: University of North Carolina Press, 2012.

Chambers, Stephen. *No God but Gain: The Untold Story of Cuban Slavery, the Monroe Doctrine, and the Making of the United States.* New York: Verso, 2015.

Chaplin, Joyce E. *An Anxious Pursuit: Agricultural Innovation and Modernity in the Lower South, 1730–1815.* Published for the Omohundro Institute of Early American History and Culture, Williamsburg, Virginia. Chapel Hill: University of North Carolina Press, 1993.

Chorley, E. Clowes. *History of St. Philips's Church in the Highlands.* New York: Edwin S. Gorham, 1912.

Clark, James C. *Last Train South: The Flight of the Confederate Government from Richmond.* New York: McFarland, 1984.

Clavin, Matthew J. *Toussaint Louverture and the American Civil War: The Promise and Peril of a Second Haitian Revolution.* Philadelphia: University of Pennsylvania Press, 2011.

Clinton, Catherine. "Southern Dishonor: Flesh, Blood, Race, and Bondage." In *In Joy and Sorrow: Women, Family, and Marriage in the Victorian South, 1830–1900,* edited by Carol Bleser. New York: Oxford University Press, 1992.

———. *Stepdaughters of History: Southern Women and the American Civil War.* Baton Rouge: Louisiana State University Press, 2016.

———. *Tara Revisited: Women, War, and the Plantation Legend.* New York: Abbeville, 1995.

Clinton, Catherine, and Nina Silber, eds. *Divided Houses: Gender and the Civil War.* New York: Oxford University Press, 1992.

Costa, Dora L., and Matthew E. Kahn. "Forging a New Identity: The Costs and Benefits of Diversity in Civil War Combat Units for Black Slaves and Freemen." NBER Working Paper no. 11013 (December 2004). https://www.nber.org/papers/w11013.

———. *Heroes and Cowards: The Social Face of War.* Princeton, N.J.: Princeton University Press, 2008.

Côté, Richard N. *Mary's World: Love, War, and Family Ties in Nineteenth-Century Charleston.* Mount Pleasant, S.C.: Corinthian, 2001.

Cox, Karen L. *Dixie's Daughters: The United Daughters of the Confederacy and the Preservation of Confederate Culture.* Gainesville: University Press of Florida, 2003.

Crandall, Warren Daniel, and Newell Isaac Denison. *History of the Ram Fleet and the Mississippi Marine Brigade in the War for the Union on the Mississippi and Its Tributaries.* St. Louis: Buschart Brothers, 1907.

Creighton, Margaret. *The Colors of Courage; Gettysburg's Hidden History: Immigrants, Women, and African Americans in the Civil War's Defining Battle.* New York: Basic Books, 2007.

Daniel, Larry J., and Lynn N. Bock. *Island No. 10: Struggle for the Mississippi Valley.* Tuscaloosa: University of Alabama Press, 1996.

Davidoff, Leonore, and Catherine Hall. *Family Fortunes: Men and Women of the English Middle Class, 1780–1850.* New York: Routledge, 2003.

Deiler, J. Hanno. *The Settlement of the German Coast of Louisiana and the Creoles of German Descent.* Philadelphia: American Germanica Press, 1909.

Deutsch, Sarah. *No Separate Refuge: Culture, Class, and Gender on an Anglo-Hispanic Frontier in the American Southwest, 1880–1940.* New York: Oxford University Press, 1989.

Dew, Charles B. *Apostles of Disunion: Southern Secession Commissioners and the Causes of the Civil War.* Charlottesville: University Press of Virginia, 2001.

DeWolf, Thomas Norman. *Inheriting the Trade: A Northern Family Confronts Its Legacy as the Largest Slave-Trading Dynasty in U.S. History.* Boston: Beacon, 2008.

Downs, Jim. *Sick from Freedom: African American Illness and Suffering during the Civil War and Reconstruction.* New York: Oxford, 2012.

Duane, Anna Mae. *Suffering Childhood in Early America: Violence, Race, and the Making of the Child Victim.* Athens: University of Georgia Press, 2010.

Dubois, Laurent. *Avengers of the New World.* Cambridge, Mass.: Belknap, 2004.

———. *A Colony of Citizens: Revolution and Slave Emancipation in the French Caribbean, 1787–1804.* Published for the Omohundro Institute of Early American History and Culture, Williamsburg, Virginia. Chapel Hill: University of North Carolina Press, 2004.

Du Bois, W. E. B. *Black Reconstruction in America: An Essay toward a History of the Part Which Black Folk Played in the Attempt to Reconstruct Democracy in America, 1860–1880.* New York: Harcourt, 1935.

Dusinberre, William. *Them Dark Days: Slavery in the American Rice Swamps.* Athens: University of Georgia Press, 2000.

Duyckinck, Evert A. *National History of the War for the Union, Civil, Military and Naval.* 3 vols. New York: Johnson, Fry, 1861.

Edgar, Walter. *South Carolina: A History.* Columbia: University of South Carolina Press, 1998.

Edwards, Laura F. *Gendered Strife and Confusion: The Political Culture of Reconstruction.* Urbana: University of Illinois Press, 1997.

———. *Scarlett Doesn't Live Here Anymore: Southern Women in the Civil War Era.* Urbana: University of Illinois Press, 2000.

Eliot, William Greenleaf. *The Story of Archer Alexander from Slavery to Freedom.* Boston: Cupples, Upham, 1885.

Ely, Roland T. "The Old Cuba Trade: Highlights and Case Studies of Cuban-American Interdependence during the Nineteenth Century." *Business History Review* 38, no. 4 (Winter 1964): 470.

Etcheson, Nicole. *A Generation at War: The Civil War Era in a Northern Community.* Lawrence: University Press of Kansas, 2011.

Evans, David. *Sherman's Horsemen: Union Cavalry Operations in the Atlanta Campaign.* Bloomington: Indiana University Press, 1996.

Fahs, Alice. *The Imagined Civil War: Popular Literature of the North and South, 1861–1865.* Chapel Hill: University of North Carolina Press, 2001.

Faulkner, Carol. *Women's Radical Reconstruction: The Freedmen's Aid Movement.* Philadelphia: University of Pennsylvania Press, 2007.

Faust, Drew Gilpin. *The Creation of Confederate Nationalism: Ideology and Identity in the Civil War South.* Baton Rouge: Louisiana State University Press, 1988.

———. Epilogue to *In Joy and in Sorrow: Women, Family, and Marriage in the Victorian South*, edited by Carol Bleser. New York: Oxford University Press, 1991.

———. *Mothers of Invention: Women of the Slaveholding South in the American Civil War.* Chapel Hill: University of North Carolina Press, 1996.

———. *This Republic of Suffering: Death and the American Civil War.* New York: Vintage Books, 2008.

Feimster, Crystal N. "General Benjamin Butler and the Threat of Sexual Violence during the American Civil War." *Daedalus* 138, no. 2 (Spring 2009): 126–34.

———. "Rape and Justice in the Civil War." *New York Times*, April 25, 2013.

———. *Southern Horrors: Women and the Politics of Rape and Lynching.* Cambridge, Mass.: Harvard University Press, 2009.

Fellman, Michael. *Inside War: The Guerrilla Conflict in Missouri during the American Civil War.* New York: Oxford University Press, 1989.

Fett, Sharla. *Working Cures: Healing, Health, and Power on Southern Plantations.* Chapel Hill: University of North Carolina Press, 2002.

Fields, Barbara Jeanne. "Lost Causes, North and South." *Reviews in American History* 20, no. 1 (March 1992): 65–71.

———. *Slavery and Freedom on the Middle Ground: Maryland during the Nineteenth Century.* New Haven, Conn.: Yale University Press, 1985.

———. "Slavery, Race and Ideology in the United States of America." *New Left Review* 181 (May 1990): 95–118.

Fields, Karen E., and Barbara Jeanne Fields. *Racecraft: The Soul of Inequality in American Life.* New York: Verso, 2014.

Fishel, Leslie H., Jr., and Benjamin Quarles. *The Negro American: A Documentary History.* New York: Scott, Foresman and William Morrow, 1967.

Fisher, Noel C. "'Prepare Them for My Coming': General William T. Sherman,

Total War, and Pacification in West Tennessee." *Tennessee Historical Quarterly* 51, no. 2 (Summer 1992): 75–86.

Foner, Eric. "The Civil War and Slavery: A Response." *Historical Materialism* 19, no. 4 (2011): 92–98.

———. *Free Soil, Free Labor, Free Men: The Ideology of the Republican Party before the Civil War.* New York: Oxford University Press, 1995.

———. *Nothing but Freedom: Emancipation and Its Legacy.* Baton Rouge: Louisiana State University Press, 1983.

Forbes, Ella. *African American Women during the Civil War.* New York: Garland, 1998.

Ford, Lacy K., Jr. *Origins of Southern Radicalism: The South Carolina Upcountry, 1800–1860.* New York: Oxford University Press, 1988.

Foret, Jeff. *Slave against Slave: Plantation Violence in the Old South.* Baton Rouge: Louisiana State University Press, 2015.

Forsyth, Alice D. *German "Pest Ships," 1720–21.* New Orleans: Genealogical Research Society, 1969.

Foster, Gaines. *Ghosts of the Confederacy: Defeat, the Lost Cause, and the Emergence of the New South, 1865 to 1913.* New York: Oxford University Press, 1987.

Fox-Amato, Matthew. *Exposing Slavery: Photography, Human Bondage, and the Birth of Modern Visual Politics in America.* New York: Oxford University Press, 2019.

Fox-Genovese, Elizabeth. *Within the Plantation Household: Black and White Women of the Old South.* Chapel Hill: University of North Carolina Press, 1988.

Fox-Genovese, Elizabeth, and Eugene Genovese. *The Mind of the Master Class: History and Faith in the Southern Slaveholders' Worldview.* New York: Cambridge University Press, 2005.

Frank, Lisa Tendrich. *The Civilian War: Confederate Women and Union Soldiers during Sherman's March.* Baton Rouge: Louisiana State University Press, 2015.

Frankel, Noralee. *Freedom's Women: Black Women and Families in Civil War Era Mississippi.* Bloomington: Indiana University Press, 1999.

Franklin, John Hope, and Loren Schweninger. *Runaway Slaves: Rebels on the Plantation.* New York: Oxford University Press, 1999.

Frey, Sylvia R. *Water from the Rock: Black Resistance in a Revolutionary Age.* Princeton, N.J.: Princeton University Press, 1991.

Funk, Arville L. "A Hoosier Regiment in Alabama." *Alabama Historical Quarterly* 27 (Spring and Summer 1965): 92–94.

Gallagher, Gary W. *Becoming Confederates: Paths to a New National Loyalty.* Athens: University of Georgia Press, 2013.

———. *The Confederate War: How Popular Will, Nationalism, and Military Strategy Could Not Stave Off Defeat.* Cambridge, Mass.: Harvard University Press, 1997.

———. *The Union War.* Cambridge, Mass.: Harvard University Press, 2011.

Gallagher, Gary W., and Alan T. Nolan, eds. *The Myth of the Lost Cause and Civil War.* Bloomington: Indiana University Press, 2000.

Genovese, Eugene D. *Roll, Jordan, Roll: The World the Slaves Made.* New York: Vintage, 1974.

———, ed. *The Slave Economy of the Old South: Selected Essays in Economic and Social History.* Baton Rouge: Louisiana State University Press, 1968.

Genovese, Eugene D., and Elizabeth Fox-Genovese. *Fatal Self-Deception: Slave-holding Paternalism in the Old South.* Cambridge: Cambridge University Press, 2011.

Giesberg, Judith. *Army at Home: Women and the Civil War on the Northern Home Front.* Chapel Hill: University of North Carolina Press, 2009.

Giesberg, Judith Ann. *Civil War Sisterhood: The U.S. Sanitary Commission and Women's Politics in Transition.* Boston: Northeastern University Press, 2000.

Ginzberg, Lori D. *Untidy Origins: A Story of Woman's Rights in Antebellum New York.* Chapel Hill: University of North Carolina Press, 2005.

Girard, Philippe. *Toussaint Louverture: A Revolutionary Life.* New York: Basic Books, 2016.

Glatthaar, Joseph T. *The March to the Sea and Beyond: Sherman's Troops in the Savannah and Carolinas Campaigns.* New York: New York University Press, 1985.

Glymph, Thavolia. "Black Women and Children in the Civil War: Archive Notes." In *Beyond Freedom: Disrupting the History of Emancipation*, edited by David Blight and Jim Downs, 121–35. Athens: University of Georgia Press, 2017.

———. "The Civil War Era." In *A Companion to American Women's History*, edited by Nancy A. Hewitt, 166–92. Oxford, U.K.: Blackwell, 2002.

———. "Du Bois's *Black Reconstruction* and Slave Women's War for Freedom." *South Atlantic Quarterly* 112, no. 3 (Summer 2013): 489–505.

———. "'I'm a Radical Girl': Black Women Unionists and the Politics of Civil War History." *Journal of the Civil War Era* 8, no. 3 (September 2018): 359–87.

———. "'Invisible Disabilities': Black Women in War and in Freedom." *Proceedings of the American Philosophical Society* 160 (September 2016): 237–53.

———. *Out of the House of Bondage: The Destruction of the Plantation Household.* Cambridge: Cambridge University Press, 2008.

———. "Refugee Camp at Helena, Arkansas, 1863." In *The Lens of War: Historians Reflect on Their Favorite Civil War Photographs*, edited by Gary Gallagher and Matthew Gallman, 133–40. Athens: University of Georgia Press, 2015.

———. "Rose's War and the Gendered Politics of a Slave Insurgency in the Civil War." *Journal of the Civil War Era* 3, no. 4 (December 2013): 501–32.

———. "'This Species of Property': Female Slave Contrabands in the Civil War." In *A Woman's War: Southern Women, Civil War, and the Confederate Legacy*, edited by Edward D. C. Campbell Jr. and Kym S. Rice, 54–71. Charlottesville: University Press of Virginia, 1996.

Goldfield, David. *Still Fighting the Civil War: The American South and Southern History*. Baton Rouge: Louisiana Press, 2013.

Grimsley, Mark. *The Hard Hand of War: Union Military Policy toward Southern Civilians, 1861–1865*. Cambridge: Cambridge University Press, 1995.

Grimsley, Mark, and Brooks D. Simpson, eds. *The Collapse of the Confederacy*. Lincoln: University of Nebraska Press, 2001.

Gutman, Herbert. *The Black Family in Slavery and Freedom, 1750–1925*. New York: Vintage, 1977.

Hahn, Steven. *A Nation under Our Feet: Black Political Struggles in the Rural South from Slavery to the Great Migration*. Cambridge, Mass.: Belknap, 2005.

———. *The Political Worlds of Slavery and Freedom*. Cambridge, Mass.: Harvard University Press, 2009.

———. *The Roots of Southern Populism: Yeoman Farmers and the Transformation of the Georgia Upcountry, 1850–1890*. New York: Oxford University Press, 1983.

———. "The 'Unmaking' of the Southern Yeomanry: The Transformation of the Georgia Upcountry, 1860–1890." In *The Countryside in the Age of Capitalist Formation: Essays in the Social History of Rural America*, edited by Steven Hahn and Jonathan Prude, 179–203. Chapel Hill: University of North Carolina Press, 1985.

Haley, Sarah. *No Mercy Here: Gender, Punishment, and the Making of Jim Crow Modernity*. Chapel Hill: University of North Carolina Press, 2016.

Hall, Catherine. *Civilising Subjects: Metropole and Colony in the English Imagination, 1830–1867*. Chicago: University of Chicago Press, 2002.

———. "The Sweet Delights of Home." In *A History of Private Life*, vol. 4, *From the Fires of Revolution to the Great War*, edited by Michelle Perrot, 47–94. Cambridge, Mass.: Harvard University Press, 1990.

Hall, Randal L. *Mountains on the Market: Industry, the Environment, and the South*. Lexington: University Press of Kentucky, 2012.

Harris, Leslie M. *In the Shadow of Slavery: African Americans in New York City, 1626–1863*. Chicago: University of Chicago Press, 2003.

Harris, Robert L. "H. Ford Douglas: Afro-American Antislavery Emigrationist." *Journal of Negro History* 62 (July 1977).

Hartje, Robert G. *Van Dorn: The Life and Times of a Confederate General*. Nashville: Vanderbilt University Press, 1967.

Hartman, Saidiya V. *Scenes of Subjection: Terror, Slavery, and Self-Making in Nineteenth-Century America*. New York: Oxford University Press, 1997.

Higginson, John. "A Tale of Two Counties: Power, Property and Collective Violence in Edgefield County, South Carolina and Caddo Parish, Louisiana, 1865–1900." In author's possession and used with permission.

———. "Upending the Century of Wrong: Agrarian Elites, Collective Violence, and the Transformation of State Power in the American South and South Africa." *Social Identities* 4, no. 3 (October 1998): 399–415.

Hine, Darlene Clark. "Rape and the Inner Lives of Black Women: Thoughts on the Culture of Dissemblance." In *Hinesight: Black Women and the Re-Construction of American History*. New York: Carlson Publishing, 1994.

———. "Rape and the Inner Lives of Black Women in the Middle West: Thoughts on the Culture of Dissemblance." *Signs: Journal of Women in Culture and Society* (Summer 1989): 912–20.

Hines, Alisha. "Geographies of Freedom: Black Women's Mobility and the Making of the Western River World, 1814–1865." PhD diss., Duke University, 2018.

Hodes, Martha. *Mourning Lincoln*. New Haven, Conn.: Yale University Press, 2015.

———. *White Women, Black Men: Illicit Sex in the Nineteenth-Century South*. New Haven, Conn.: Yale University Press, 1997.

Holt, Thomas. *Children of Fire: A History of African Americans*. New York: Hill & Wang, 2011.

Horn, Stanley F. "Nashville during the Civil War." *Tennessee Historical Quarterly* 4, no. 1 (March 1945): 3–22.

Horwitz, Tony. *Spying on the South: An Odyssey Across the American Divide*. New York: Penguin Press, 2019.

Hsieh, Wayne Wei-Shiang. "Total War and the American Civil War Reconsidered: The End of an Outdated Master Narrative." *Journal of the Civil War Era* 1, no. 3 (September 2011): 398.

Humphreys, Margaret. *Intensely Human: The Health of the Black Soldier in the Civil War*. Baltimore: Johns Hopkins University Press, 2008.

———. *Marrow of Tradition: The Health Crisis of the American Civil War*. Baltimore: Johns Hopkins University Press, 2013.

Hundley, D. R. *Social Relations in Our Southern States*. New York: Henry P. Price, 1860.

Hunter, Tera W. *Bound in Wedlock: Slave and Free Black Marriage in the Nineteenth Century*. Cambridge, Mass.: Harvard University Press, 2017.

Inscoe, John C. *Mountain Masters: Slavery and the Sectional Crisis in Western North Carolina*. Knoxville: University of Tennessee Press, 1989.

Inscoe, John C., and Gordon B. McKinney. *The Heart of Confederate Appalachia: Western North Carolina in the Civil War*. Chapel Hill: University of North Carolina Press, 2000.

Isenberg, Nancy. *Sex and Citizenship in Antebellum America*. Chapel Hill: University of North Carolina Press, 1998.

Jacobs, Margaret D. *White Mother to a Dark Race: Settler Colonialism and the Removal of Indigenous Children in the American West and Australia, 1880–1840*. Lincoln: University of Nebraska Press, 2009.

Jacoway, Elizabeth. *Yankee Missionaries in the South: The Penn School Experiment*. Baton Rouge: Louisiana State University Press, 1980.

Jasanoff, Maya. *Liberty's Exiles: American Loyalists in the Revolutionary World*. New York: Knopf, 2011.

Jeffrey, Julie Roy. *The Great Silent Army of Abolitionism: Ordinary Women in the Antislavery Movement*. Chapel Hill: University of North Carolina Press, 1998.

Johnson, Michael P. *Toward a Patriarchal Republic: The Secession of Georgia*. Baton Rouge: Louisiana State University Press, 1977.

Johnson, Walter. *River of Dark Dreams: Slavery and Empire in the Cotton Kingdom*. Cambridge, Mass.: Belknap, 2013.

———. *Soul by Soul: Life inside the Antebellum Slave Market*. Cambridge, Mass.: Harvard University Press, 1999.

Jones, Martha S. *Birthright Citizens: A History of Race and Rights in Antebellum America*. Cambridge: Cambridge University Press, 2018.

———. "*Hughes v. Jackson*: Race and Rights beyond *Dred Scott*." *North Carolina Law Review* 91, no. 5 (June 2013): 1757–83.

Jones-Rogers, Stephanie E. "'Nobody Couldn't Sell 'Em but Her': Slaveowning Women, Mastery, and the Gendered Politics of the Antebellum Slave Market." PhD diss., Rutgers University, 2012.

———. *They Were Her Property: White Women as Slave Owners in the American South*. New Haven: Yale University Press, 2019.

Jordan, Ervin L., Jr. *Black Confederates and Afro-Yankees in Civil War Virginia*. Charlottesville: University Press of Virginia, 1995.

———. "Sleeping with the Enemy: Sex, Black Women, and the Civil War." *Western Journal of Black Studies* 18, no. 2 (Summer 1994): 55–63.

Jordan, Winthrop D. *Tumult and Silence at Second Creek: An Inquiry into a Civil War Slave Conspiracy*. Baton Rouge: Louisiana State University Press, 1993.

Karp, Matthew. *This Vast Southern Empire: Slaveholders at the Helm of American Foreign Policy*. Cambridge, Mass.: Harvard University Press, 2016.

Kasson, Joy S. *Marble Queens and Captives: Women in Nineteenth-Century American Sculpture*. New Haven, Conn.: Yale University Press, 1990.

Kerber, Linda K. *Women of the Republic: Intellect and Ideology in Revolutionary America*. Chapel Hill: University of North Carolina Press, 1997.

Kimball, William J. "The Bread Riot in Richmond, 1863." *Civil War History* 7 (June 1961): 149–54.

King, Lisa Y. "In Search of Women of African Descent Who Served in the Civil War Union Navy." *Journal of Negro History* 83, no. 4 (Autumn 1998): 302–9.

Kurlansky, Mark. *Salt: A World History*. New York: Penguin, 2002.

Lebsock, Suzanne. *The Free Women of Petersburg: Status and Culture Southern Town, 1784–1860*. New York: W. W. Norton & Company, 1984.

Leonard, Elizabeth. *Yankee Women: Gender Battles in the Civil War*. New York: Norton, 1994.

Leonard, Elizabeth D. *Lincoln's Forgotten Ally: Judge Advocate General Joseph Holt*. Chapel Hill: University of North Carolina Press, 2011.

Levine, Bruce. *The Fall of the House of Dixie: The Civil War and the Social Revolution that Transformed the South*. New York: Random House, 2013.

Litwack, Leon F. *Been in the Storm So Long: The Aftermath of Slavery*. New York: Vintage, 1979.

Lockley, Tim. "The Forming and Fracturing of Families on a South Carolina
   Rice Plantation, 1812–1865." *History of the Family* (June 2017): 1–15.
Long, E. B., with Barbara Long. *The Civil War Day by Day: An Almanac, 1861–1865.*
   New York: Da Capo, 1971.
Long, Gretchen. *Doctoring Freedom: The Politics of African American Medical Care
   in Slavery and Emancipation.* Chapel Hill: University of North Carolina Press,
   2012.
MacCarthy, Esther. "The Home for Aged Colored Women, 1861–1944." *Historical
   Journal of Massachusetts* 21, no. 1 (Winter 1993): 55–73.
Manning, Chandra. *Troubled Refuge: Struggling for Freedom in the Civil War.* New
   York: Vintage, 2017.
Marszalek, John F. *Sherman: A Soldier's Passion for Order.* New York: Free Press,
   1993.
Marten, James. *The Children's War.* Chapel Hill: University of North Carolina
   Press, 2000.
Marvel, William. *Lincoln's Mercenaries: Economic Motivation among Union
   Soldiers during the Civil War.* Baton Rouge: Louisiana State University Press,
   2018.
Marx, Karl. *The Eighteenth Brumaire of Louis Bonaparte.* Translated by Eden Paul
   and Cedar Paul. New York: International, 1926.
Massey, Mary Elizabeth. *Bonnet Brigades: American Women in the Civil War.* New
   York: Alfred A. Knopf, 1966.
———. *Ersatz in the Confederacy: Shortages and Substitutes on the Homefront.*
   Originally published 1952. Columbia: University of South Carolina Press, 1993.
———. "The Free Market of New Orleans, 1861–1862." *Louisiana History* 3 (Sum-
   mer 1962): 202–20.
———. *Refugee Life in the Confederacy.* Originally published 1964. Baton Rouge:
   Louisiana State University Press, 2001.
———. *Women in the Civil War.* Originally published (as *Bonnet Brigades*) 1966.
   Lincoln: University of Nebraska Press, 1994.
McCurry, Stephanie. *Confederate Reckoning: Power and Politics in the Civil War
   South.* Cambridge, Mass.: Harvard University Press, 2010.
———. *Masters of Small Worlds: Yeoman Households, Gender Relations, and the
   Political Culture of the Antebellum South Carolina Low Country.* New York:
   Oxford University Press, 1995.
McPherson, James. *Battle Cry of Freedom: The Civil War Era.* New York: Oxford
   University Press, 1988.
———. *For Cause and Comrades: Why Men Fought in the Civil War.* New York:
   Oxford University Press, 1997.
———. *Ordeal by Fire: The Civil War and Reconstruction.* New York: Knopf, 1982.
———. *War on the Waters: The Union and Confederate Navies, 1861–1865.* Chapel
   Hill: University of North Carolina Press, 2012.

Mitchell, Reid. *The Vacant Chair: The Northern Soldier Leaves Home*. New York: Oxford University Press, 1993.

Mohr, Clarence. *On the Threshold of Freedom: Masters and Slaves in Civil War Georgia*. Athens: University of Georgia Press, 1986.

Moore, Albert B. *Conscription and Conflict in the Confederacy*. New York: Macmillan, 1924.

Mulderink, Earl F. *New Bedford's Civil War*. New York: Fordham University Press, 2012.

Murphy, Kim. *I Had Rather Die: Rape in the Civil War*. New York: Coachlight, 2014.

Myers, Barton A. *Rebels against the Confederacy: North Carolina Unionists*. Cambridge: Cambridge University Press, 2014.

Neely, Mark E., Jr. *The Civil War and the Limits of Destruction*. Cambridge, Mass.: Harvard University Press, 2007.

Nelson, Charmaine. *The Color of Stone: Sculpting the Black Female Subject in Nineteenth-Century America*. Minneapolis: University of Minnesota Press, 2007.

———. "Hiram Powers's America: Shackles, Slaves, and the Racial Limits of Nineteenth Century Identity." *Canadian Review of American Studies* 34, no. 2 (2004): 167–83.

Nepveau, Ethel Trenholm Seabrook. *George Alfred Trenholm: The Company That Went to War, 1861–1865*. Charleston, S.C.: E. T. S. Nepveau, 1994.

———. *George A. Trenholm, Financial Genius of the Confederacy: His Associates and His Ships that Ran the Blockade*. Charleston, S.C.: E. T. S. Nepveau, 1999.

Nevins, Allan. *The War for Union*. 4 vols. New York: Charles Scribner's Sons, 1971.

Nichols, George Ward. *The Story of the Great March, from the Diary of a Staff Officer*. New York: Harper and Brothers, 1866.

Nolan, Jacqueline V., and Edward J. Redmond. "Civil War Cartography Then and Now." *Library of Congress Magazine* 1, no. 2 (November–December 2012): 12–13.

Norton, Mary Beth. *Liberty's Daughters: The Revolutionary Experience of American Women, 1750–1800*. Boston: Little, Brown, 1980.

Oakes, James. *Freedom National: The Destruction of Slavery in the United States, 1861–1865*. New York: Norton, 2013.

———. "The Political Significance of Slave Resistance." *History Workshop Journal* 22, no. 1 (Autumn 1986): 89–107.

Oates, Stephen B. *A Woman of Valor: Clara Barton and the Civil War*. New York: Free Press, 1994.

O'Donovan, Susan Eva. *Becoming Free in the Cotton South*. Cambridge, Mass.: Harvard University Press, 2007.

O'Leary, Cecilia Elizabeth. *To Die For: The Paradox of American Patriotism*. Princeton, N.J.: Princeton University Press, 1999.

Ortiz, Paul. *Emancipation Betrayed: The Hidden History of Black Organizing and*

White Violence in Florida from Reconstruction to the Bloody Election of 1920. Berkeley: University of California Press, 2005.

Owens, Deirdre Cooper. *Medical Bondage: Race, Gender, and the Origins of American Gynecology*. Athens: University of Georgia Press, 2017.

Painter, Nell. *Sojourner Truth: A Life, a Symbol*. New York: W. W. Norton, 1996.

Paludan, Phillip Shaw. *A People's Contest: The Union and Civil War, 1861–1865*. Lawrence, Kan.: University Press of Kansas, 1988.

Parish, Peter J. Parish. *Slavery: History and Historians*. Boulder, Colo.: Westview, 1989.

Penningroth, Dylan C. *The Claims of Kinfolk: African American Property and Community in the Nineteenth-Century South*. Chapel Hill: University of North Carolina Press, 2004.

Pepper, George W. *Personal Recollections of Sherman's Campaigns in Georgia and the Carolinas*. Zanesville, Ohio: Hughes Dunne, 1866.

Pérez, Louis A. *Cuba and the United States: Ties of Singular Intimacy*. 3rd ed. Athens: University of Georgia Press, 2003.

Pérez, Louis A., Jr. *Slaves, Sugar, and Colonial Society: Travel Accounts of Cuba, 1801–1899*. Wilmington, Del.: Scholarly Resources, 1992.

Peterson, Merrill D. *Lincoln in American Memory*. New York: Oxford University Press, 1994.

Porcher, Frederick A. "Historical and Social Sketch of Craven County, South Carolina." In *A Contribution to the History of the Huguenots of South Carolina Consisting of Pamphlets*, by Samuel Dubose, Esq., and Prof. Frederick A. Porcher, 87–168. New York: Knickerbocker, 1887.

Porcher, Richard Dwight, and Sarah Fick. *The Story of Sea Island Cotton*. Layton, Utah: Gibbs Smith, 2005.

Porter, Dorothy B. "Sarah Parker Remond, Abolitionist and Physician." *Journal of Negro History* 20, no. 3 (July 1935): 287–93.

Powell, Lawrence N. *New Masters: Northern Planters during the Civil War and Reconstruction*. New Haven, Conn.: Yale University Press, 1980.

Quarles, Benjamin. *Black Abolitionists*. New York: Oxford University Press, 1970.

Rable, George C. *Civil Wars: Women and the Crisis of Southern Nationalism*. Urbana: University of Illinois Press, 1989.

———. "Despair, Hope, and Delusion: The Collapse of Confederate Morale Reexamined." In *The Collapse of the Confederacy*, edited by Mark Grimsley and Brooks D. Simpson, 129–67. Lincoln: University of Nebraska Press, 2001.

Ramsdell, Charles W. *Behind the Lines in the Southern Confederacy*. Baton Rouge: Louisiana State University Press, 1944.

Regosin, Elizabeth. *Freedom's Promise: Ex-Slave Families and Citizenship in the Age of Emancipation*. Charlottesville: University of Virginia Press, 2002.

Robinson, Armstead L. *Bitter Fruits of Bondage: The Demise of Slavery and the Collapse of the Confederacy, 1861–1865*. Charlottesville: University of Virginia Press, 2005.

Roediger, David. *Seizing Freedom: Slave Emancipation and Liberty for All*. New York: Verso 2014.

Rogers, George, Jr. *Charleston in the Age of the Pinckneys*. Originally published 1969. Columbia: University of South Carolina Press, 1980.

Rose, Willie Lee. *Rehearsal for Reconstruction: The Port Royal Experiment*. London: Oxford University Press, 1964.

Rosen, Hannah. *Terror in the Heart of Freedom: Citizenship, Sexual Violence, and the Meaning of Race in the Postemancipation South*. Chapel Hill: University of North Carolina Press, 2009.

Rosengarten, Theodore, ed. *Tombee: Portrait of a Cotton Planter: With the Plantation Journal of Thomas B. Chaplin, 1822–1890*. New York: Morrow, 1986.

Rosenheim, Jeff L. *Photography and the American Civil War*. New York: Metropolitan Museum of Art, 2013.

Royster, Charles. *The Destructive War: William Tecumseh Sherman, Stonewall Jackson, and the Americans*. New York: Knopf, 1991.

Rubin, Anne Sarah. *A Shattered Nation: The Rise and Fall of the Confederacy, 1861–1868*. Chapel Hill: University of North Carolina Press, 2005.

Ryan, Mary P. *Civic Wars: Democracy and Public Life in the American City during the Nineteenth Century*. Berkeley: University of California Press, 1998.

———. *Women in Public: Between Banners and Ballots, 1825–1880*. Baltimore: Johns Hopkins University Press, 1992.

Saville, Julie. *The Work of Reconstruction: From Slave to Wage Labor in South Carolina, 1860–1870*. Cambridge: Cambridge University Press, 1996.

Savitt, Todd L. *Medicine and Slavery: The Diseases and Health Care of Blacks in Ante-bellum Virginia*. Urbana: University of Illinois Press, 1878.

Schultz, Jane E. *Women at the Front: Hospital Workers in Civil War America*. Chapel Hill: University of North Carolina Press, 2004.

Schwalm, Leslie A. *Emancipation's Diaspora: Race and Reconstruction in the Upper Midwest*. Chapel Hill: University of North Carolina Press, 2009.

———. *A Hard Fight for We: Women's Transition to Freedom in South Carolina*. Urbana: University of Illinois Press, 1997.

Schwartz, Marie Jenkins. *Birthing a Slave: Motherhood and Medicine in the Antebellum South*. Cambridge, Mass.: Harvard University Press, 2006.

Scott, Rebecca J. "Social Facts, Legal Fictions, and the Attribution of Slave Status: The Puzzle of Prescription." *Law and History Review* 35, no. 1 (February 2017): 9–30.

Sheehan-Dean, Aaron. *Why Confederates Fought: Family and Nation in Civil War Virginia*. Chapel Hill: University of North Carolina Press, 2007.

Shinault, Joel W. "Camp Life of Contrabands and Freedmen, 1861–1865." Master's thesis, Atlanta University, 1979.

Silber, Nina. "A Compound of Wonderful Potency: Women Teachers of the North in the Civil War South." In *The War Was You and Me: Civilians in the American*

Civil War, edited by Joan E. Cashin, 35–59. Princeton, N.J.: Princeton University Press, 2002.

———. *Daughters of the Union: Northern Women Fight the Civil War.* Cambridge, Mass.: Harvard University Press, 2005.

———. *Gender and the Sectional Conflict.* Chapel Hill: University of North Carolina Press, 2008.

Simkins, Francis Butler, and Charles Pierce Roland. *A History of the South.* 4th ed. Originally published 1947. New York: Knopf, 1972.

Simms, William Gillmore. *Sack and Destruction of Columbia, South Carolina.* Columbia, S.C., 1865.

Simpson, Lewis P. *Mind and the American Civil War: A Meditation on Lost Causes.* Baton Rouge: Louisiana State University Press, 1989.

Sinha, Manisha. *The Slave's Cause: A History of Abolition.* New Haven, Conn.: Yale University Press, 2016.

Sizer, Lyde Cullen. *The Political Work of Northern Women Writers and the Civil War, 1850–1872.* Chapel Hill: University of North Carolina Press, 2000.

Stanley, Amy Dru. *From Bondage to Contract: Wage Labor, Marriage, and the Market in the Age of Slave Emancipation.* Cambridge: Cambridge University Press, 1998.

———. "Instead of Waiting for the Thirteenth Amendment: The War Power, Slave Marriage, and Inviolate Human Rights." *American Historical Review* 115, no. 3 (June 2010): 732–65.

Steiner, Paul E. *Disease in the Civil War: Natural Biological Warfare in 1861–1865.* Springfield, Ill.: Thomas, 1968.

Sterkx, H. E. *Partners in Rebellion: Alabama Women in the Civil War.* Rutherford, N.J.: Fairleigh Dickinson University Press.

Sternhell, Yael. "Papers, Please!" Disunion Series. *New York Times*, August 8, 2014.

———. *Routes of War: The World of Movement in the Confederate South.* Cambridge, Mass.: Harvard University Press, 2012.

Stevenson, Brenda E. *Life in Black and White: Family and Community in the Slave South.* New York: Oxford University Press, 1996.

Stoler, Ann Laura. *Carnal Knowledge and Imperial Power: Race and the Intimate in Colonial Rule.* Berkeley: University of California Press, 2002.

———. *Race and the Education of Desire: Foucault's "History of Sexuality" and the Colonial Order of Things.* Durham, N.C.: Duke University Press, 1995.

Stowe, Steven M. *Keep the Days: Reading the Civil War Diaries of Southern Women.* Chapel Hill: University of North Carolina Press, 2018.

Sullivan, Walter, ed. *The War the Women Lived: Female Voices from the Confederate South.* Nashville: J. S. Sanders, 1995.

Sutherland, Daniel E. *A Savage Conflict: The Decisive Role of Guerrillas in the American Civil War.* Chapel Hill: University of North Carolina Press, 2009.

———, ed. *Guerrillas, Unionists, and Violence on the Confederate Home Front.*
  Fayetteville: University of Arkansas Press, 1999.
Tatum, Georgia Lee. *Disloyalty in the Confederacy.* Chapel Hill: University of
  North Carolina Press, 1934.
Taylor, Alan. *The Internal Enemy: Slavery and War in Virginia, 1772–1832.* New
  York: W. W. Norton, 2013.
Taylor, Amy Murrell. *The Divided Family in Civil War America.* Chapel Hill:
  University of North Carolina Press, 2005.
———. *Embattled Freedom: Journeys through the Civil War's Slave Refugee Camps.*
  Chapel Hill: University of North Carolina Press, 2018.
Thomas, Frances Taliaferro. *A Portrait of Historical Athens and Clark County.*
  Athens: University of Georgia Press, 2009.
Thornton, J. Mills, III. *Politics and Power in a Slave Society: Alabama, 1800–1860.*
  Baton Rouge: Louisiana State University Press, 1978.
Trudeau, Noah Andrew. *Like Men of War: Black Troops in the Civil War, 1862–1865.*
  Boston: Little, Brown, 1998.
Tyler, Mrs. Julia Gardner. "To the Duchess of Sutherland and Ladies of England."
  Southern Literary Messenger 19, no. 2 (February 1853): 120–26.
Urwin, Gregory J. W. "'We *Cannot* Treat Negroes . . . as Prisoners of War': Racial
  Atrocities and Reprisals in Civil War Arkansas." In *Black Flag over Dixie: Racial
  Atrocities and Reprisals in the Civil War,* edited by Gregory J. W. Urwin, 132–52.
  Carbondale: Southern Illinois Press, 2004.
Varon, Elizabeth R. *Disunion! The Coming of the American Civil War, 1789–1859.*
  Chapel Hill: University of North Carolina Press, 2008.
Venet, Wendy Hamand. *Neither Ballots nor Bullets: Women Abolitionists and the
  Civil War.* Charlottesville: University Press of Virginia, 1991.
Verner, Elizabeth O'Neill. *Mellowed by Time.* Columbia, S.C.: Bostick and Thorn-
  ley, 1953.
Vinovskis, Maris, ed. *Toward a Social History of the Civil War.* Cambridge:
  Cambridge University Press, 1990.
Wagner, Margaret E., Gary W. Gallagher, and Paul Finkelman, eds. *The Library
  of Congress Civil War Desk Reference.* New York: Simon and Schuster, 2002.
Walters, John Bennett. "General William T. Sherman and Total War." *Journal
  of Southern History* 14, no. 4 (November 1948): 447–80.
Weiner, Marli F. *Mistresses and Slaves: Plantation Women in South Carolina,
  1830–80.* Urbana: University of Illinois Press, 1998.
Wesley, Charles H. *Collapse of the Confederacy.* Washington, D.C.: Associated
  Publishers, 1937.
West, Emily. *Family or Freedom: People of Color in the Antebellum South.*
  Lexington: University of Kentucky Press, 2012.
White, Deborah Gray. *Ar'n't I a Woman? Female Slaves in the Plantation South.*
  New York: Norton, 1985.

Whitehead, Karsonya Wise. *Notes from a Colored Girl: The Civil War Pocket Diaries of Emilie Frances Davis*. Columbia: University of South Carolina, 2014.

Whites, LeeAnn. *The Civil War as a Crisis in Gender: Augusta, Georgia, 1860–1890*. Athens: University of Georgia Press, 1995.

———. "Forty Shirts and a Wagonload of Wheat: Women, the Domestic Supply Line, and the Civil War on the Western Border." *Journal of the Civil War Era* 1, no. 1 (March 2011): 56–78.

Whites, LeeAnn, and Alecia P. Long. *Occupied Women: Gender, Military Occupation, and the American Civil War*. Baton Rouge: Louisiana State University Press, 2009.

Wilder, Craig Steven. *Ebony and Ivy: Race, Slavery, and the Troubled History of America's Universities*. New York: Bloomsbury, 2013.

Wiley, Bell I. *The Life of Billy Yank: The Common Soldier of the Union*. Indianapolis: Bobbs-Merrill, 1952.

Wilkerson, Warren. *Mother May You Never See the Sights I've Seen: The Fifty-Seventh Massachusetts Veteran Volunteers in the Army of the Potomac, 1864–1865*. New York: Harper and Row, 1990.

Williams, Heather Andrea. *Help Me to Find My People: The African American Search for Family Lost in Slavery*. Chapel Hill: University of North Carolina Press, 2012.

Willis, Deborah, and Barbara Krauthamer. *Envisioning Emancipation: Black Americans and the End of the Civil War*. Philadelphia: University of Pennsylvania Press, 2013.

Wilson, Charles Reagan. *Baptized in Blood: The Religion of the Lost Cause, 1865–1920*. Athens: University of Georgia Press, 1980.

Wish, Harvey. "Slave Disloyalty under the Confederacy." *Journal of Negro History* 23, no. 4 (October 1938): 435–50.

Witt, John Fabian. *Lincoln's Code: The Laws of War in American History*. New York: Free Press, 2012.

Wood, Kirsten E. *Masterful Women: Slaveholding Widows from the American Revolution through the Civil War*. Chapel Hill: University of North Carolina Press, 2004.

Wood, Marcus. *The Horrible Gift of Freedom: Atlantic Slavery and the Representation of Emancipation*. Athens: University of Georgia Press, 2010.

Wood, Peter H. "Slave Labor Camps in Early America: Overcoming Denial and Discovering the Gulag." In *Inequality in Early America*, edited by Carla Gardina Pestana and Sharon V. Salinger, 222–38. Hanover, N.H.: University Press of New England, 1999.

Woodman, Harold D. *King Cotton and His Retainers*. Lexington: University of Kentucky Press, 1968.

———. "The Profitability of Slavery: A Historical Perennial." *Journal of Southern History* 29, no. 3 (August 1963): 303–25.

Woodruff, Nan Elizabeth. *American Congo: The African American Freedom Struggle in the Delta*. Cambridge, Mass: Harvard University Press, 2003.

Woods, Clyde. *Development Arrested: Race, Power, and the Blues in the Mississippi Delta*. New York: Verso, 1999.

Yellin, Jean Fagan. *Women and Sisters: The Antislavery Feminists in American Culture*. New Haven: Yale University Press, 1989.

Zallen, Jeremy. *American Lucifers: The Dark History of Artificial Light, 1750–1865*. Chapel Hill: University of North Carolina Press, 2019.

INDEX OF NAMES

Page numbers in italics refer to illustrations.

INDEX OF SUBJECTS

Page numbers in italics refer to illustrations.

black; refugees, black women; refugees, white women
refugees, black, 6, 26, 114, 173, 269n16;
destitution, 238; families of black
soldiers, 115; fear of camps, 223; forced
labor, 10, 232, 228, 233, 237–38, 240,
242–48, 269n16, 322n106; gendered
dynamics, 223; hostility of Northern
white women toward, 183–86, 257; lack
of news coverage, 246–48; Northern
black abolitionist support, 160, 171,
309n106; orphans, 120, 170, 229–20,
238, 244; starvation, 114; strain of
new arrivals on established camps,
114–15; U.S. Army, field orders related
to, 228, 236; U.S. Army interactions
with, 97–98, 104–8, 112–14, 228, 233–34,
236–38, 240–41, 247–48, 292n107, 313n58;
violence against, 119, 241–48. *See
also* reenlavement of refugees; black
women
refugees, black, camps for, 10, 97, 120,
178, 182, 185, 223, 228, 229–41; broken
up by federal army, 228, 236, 246; Cairo,
228, 236; Camp Fiske, 232; conditions
in, 115, 233–36, 239, 245, 321n93; Confederate attacks, 222, 224, 235, 241–49;
Corinth, 228; as cultural and political
meeting grounds, 248–49; as feed-
ers for plantation labor camps, 237,
247; Goodrich's Landing, 225, 231–32,
241–43; Helena, Arkansas, 221–22,
229, 233–34; housing, 230, 234–37, 242;
Island No. 10, 236; Lake Providence
area, 225, 231–32, 237–38, 242–44, 248,
319n44; Mason's Island, 181; Natchez,
241; rations, 10, 115, 177–78, 181, 211,
223, 237–39, 247, 307n75; reconstitution
of community, 229–30; Shiloh, 233, 236;
Springfield, 250
refugees, black women, 6, 108, 172–73,
56, 97, 221–50, 256; abortion, 120; black
communities created by, 223, 230, 239–
40; Confederate raids on, 182, 241–44;
gendered path to freedom, 225; health,
119, 120, 185, 233, 241, 244–46; intellectual work of, 249; laborers' widows

denied wages of husbands, 239; labor
on abandoned plantations, 253–54;
labor in homes of Northern women in
the South, 187–88; labor taxed, 239; as
military laundresses (Confederate),
99; as military laundresses (Union), 9,
114–15, 181, 231, 237, 244, 318n41, 318n4;
numbers of, 223, 231–32; opportunities
to build free lives and homes, 32, 37,
52, 224; politics and political identities
of, 89, 90, 96–101, 116–18, 122, 222; and
Sojourner Truth, 180–81; soldiers' widows, 230–32, 249–50; soldiers' wives,
245; trauma, 119; and Union army, 222,
228, 237–38; Unionist, 259; Union lines,
106–17; Union policy and, 108; Union
soldiers' ill treatment, 221, 233, 228,
258; viewed as a nuisance by Union
officers, 106, 247; wartime flight, 101–3,
224, 252; work demanded of, 10, 232,
233, 237–38, 240, 242–48, 250, 254
refugees, white women, 6, 12–13, 19, 20,
22, 23–24, 26, 27–28, 31–32, 38, 43, 49–50,
52, 55–56, 57, 161, 209, 215, 219, 255,
259, 317n28; Atlanta exiles, 43; camps,
52; crowded condition in upcountry,
39–40; deserving and undeserving
categories, 44; ideological problem,
23–24, 28, 42; life among, 44, 46–47; as
new social class, 23–24; resemblance
to enslaved women, 29–31; resentment
of among local people, 40, 42, 44, 56,
60–69, 82–83; Revolutionary War, 21,
215–17; sale of belongings to support
families, 46–47
refugees, white Union, 84–85, 161, 202,
259
"Report of the Commissioners of Colored Refugees in Kentucky, Tennessee, and Alabama," 115–16
Republican Party, 17, 86–87, 225, 287n129
Retreat (plantation), 35
Revolutionary War, 11, 21, 52, 213–17; as
civil war, 65, 216
Rhode Island, 118, 131, 151–54
Richmond Daily Examiner, 70
Richmond food riot (1863), 70